PC Disaster
and Recovery

PC Disaster and Recovery

Kate J. Chase

SYBEX®

San Francisco   London

Associate Publisher: Joel Fugazzotto
Acquisitions Editor: Ellen L. Dendy
Developmental Editor: Brianne Hope Agatep
Editor: Sarah Lemaire
Production Editor: Dennis Fitzgerald
Technical Editor: Don Fuller
Electronic Publishing Specialist: Franz Baumhackl
Proofreaders: Amey Garber, Emily Hsuan, Laurie O'Connell, Nancy Riddiough
Indexer: Ted Laux
Photographer: Emily Sherrill Weadock
Cover Designer and Illustrator: Richard Miller, Calyx Design

Library of Congress Card Number: 2002113567

ISBN: 0-7821-4182-X

*This book is dedicated to
Tim Barwick, Arnold Brackman,
Robert Pratt, and Richard H. Slone,
all teachers of one type or another
who showed me how to hone my craft
and find my voice in helping others.*

Acknowledgments

Few books are ever the product of one person, and this book is no exception. The first thoughts for this book were written down the morning after the attacks on New York and Washington, D.C. on September 11, 2001, when brave people at both sites were already talking about how they could get back to work.

Yet this project was just a bundle of notes until Ellen Dendy, an acquisitions editor at Sybex, came to me and asked if I was interested in doing a book on PC disaster and recovery for real people. We both agreed it was time for a book of this type.

As the manuscript progressed, Brianne Agatep, the developmental editor, and Dennis Fitzgerald, the production editor, plus Don Fuller, the technical editor, and Sarah Lemaire, the copyeditor, brought their gifted and efficient diligence to making certain all the necessary material was covered, checked and double-checked, and clear in its presentation.

Thanks, too, to Emily Sherrill Weadock, who shared her photographs for this book, and to John Bedell, who offered many great tips and ideas.

In addition, I must acknowledge the thousands of work associates, friends, and users who have shared their experiences and their suggestions during my many years of providing online help for Windows, hardware, and applications through online services like America Online and The Microsoft Network, and through Internet newsgroups.

And finally, let me say farewell to the Pentium II 350MHz system that gave up its life for this project so that other PCs might process onward. I certainly got my money's worth, considering it saw me through four years, almost a dozen books and guides, hundreds of articles and columns, thousands of newsgroup postings, two dozen beta tests, four operating systems, three disasters, and one major move. And, interestingly, it survived two years longer than the manufacturer who made it.

Contents at a Glance

Contents

Introduction

Congratulations! Just arriving at this first page indicates that you are a person who chooses to act intelligently before a problem occurs rather than react to trouble after the fact. And you're someone who realizes how critical your PC and data are and recognizes the need to protect them.

First, it's important to note that not all disasters come from natural catastrophes or terrorism and vandalism. In fact, most PC disasters are created by the person using the PC. These disasters may be caused by operating the PC unsafely, without proper maintenance or safeguards, or by adding lots of new software and hardware to a system without checking first for incompatibilities that may arise.

However, even when you do exercise proper care, defective hardware or software can wreak terrible havoc. You need to know how to recognize such problems when they occur, prevent them from causing too much damage, and resolve them with a minimal loss of data.

Yet you are also living, working, and playing in a world that has become tougher and more complex in many respects. New technology, some tested better than others, comes at you all the time. Trying to incorporate it into your PCs can create unforeseen disasters.

Global warming is creating increasingly extreme weather conditions, resulting in more hurricanes, floods, and power-draining heat waves. We've experienced a few years where electrical shortages and rolling brownouts have made big news. The instability of the international political climate has brought horrifically destructive acts of terrorism to some American places of business, as it already has to many other parts of the world.

All of these factors have many smart people, you included, thinking about how to reduce their risks, both at home and on the job. This is why I wrote this book.

It can be tough to analyze problems once a disaster has struck, so this book is designed to help you check the same details a good technician would check. You'll also learn how to think like a skilled repair person, picking up valuable tips and tricks without having to study thick tomes on PC hardware and operation. In fact, you'll finish this book understanding what I mean when I say that solid knowledge and preparedness can really reduce the stress and downtime when disaster strikes.

The best way to protect your PC and the data on your PC's hard drives is to couple a better understanding of your PC and how it works with smart planning about how to keep your PC running—or at least cut your losses—in the event of a disaster. And today, that's a wise approach for just about everyone.

Just like that famed Boy Scout motto, the message throughout this book is, "Be prepared!" After all, you just never know when the unthinkable may happen to you and your precious PC data.

In the first chapter, you'll get an understanding of the types of disasters you can encounter, You'll also get a preview of the software, services, and support open to you as you try to grapple with a PC that no longer works properly. After that, you'll learn ways to troubleshoot your problems and you'll learn how to prevent them altogether. By the time you finish the last chapter, you'll feel a great deal more in control of your PC and data's destiny.

With so much to cover, let's jump in!

CHAPTER 1

PC Disasters and
Recovery Overview

A disaster, like beauty, is often defined by the beholder.

While you might claim that losing an e-mail letter you're writing to a friend or colleague is a disaster, others might reserve the term "disaster" for losing all their financial information stored in a product such as Intuit's Quicken. On the other hand, I define a disaster as anything I can't resolve quickly and effectively given my years of experience.

Even most dictionaries give widely varying definitions for the term "disaster," ranging from "an unfortunate event" to "a catastrophic situation with widespread negative ramifications." Most of us, however, call just about any major PC inconvenience a disaster.

None of us likes to think about it, but disasters can happen anytime, anywhere.

Like it or not, the most common cause of a PC disaster is users—the way they use and abuse their systems. If users are struggling to find time to get all of their work done, they often don't feel they have enough time to learn enough about their systems to make them work faster and more effectively. PC users improperly connect, misconfigure, and misuse their systems all the time.

But even if they use their PCs correctly, users can still face hardware and software malfunctions due to badly written programs and drivers (special software for communicating with hardware), poorly tested hardware, and instability that can arise in Windows itself. And that's not all. Fire, flood, hurricanes, tornadoes, earthquakes, lightning, horrific accidents, and today, even acts of terrorism may strike at any time, with or without advance notice, mindless of whether or not a user is prepared and whether or not there's a deadline for work, school, or a community project. They can disrupt and even obliterate the ways in which users work, create, and live.

But disasters aren't limited to the type of eye-catching, headline-producing event you see on the evening news. A sudden summer thunderstorm—or power surges, blackouts, and brownouts created by too much demand on the power grid during a summer heat wave—can total any unprotected electronics device, such as a computer.

You can't make disasters stop happening. What you can affect is how easily you can get your life back in order after the fact. The focus of this book is how to recover your functional PC operation and data after various types of disasters.

Let's get going!

Types of Disasters

When information professionals (the folks charged with protecting major companies' data) develop plans for dealing with catastrophes, they usually classify potential disasters into several categories. These include:

Hardware Failure   Hardware failures occur when a critical piece of hardware, through some flaw or because of serious wear, ceases to do its job.

Human Error   Human errors occur when a user unintentionally causes the damage or creates conditions that cause it.

Natural   Natural disasters include hurricanes, storms, floods, and earthquakes.

Man-Made   Man-made disasters can be any situation that doesn't fall into the other categories. These can include a worker or family member simply taking out his or her frustrations on a PC or network in a way that may render the system inoperable.

Political/Situational   These types of disasters are usually defined as acts of terrorism or sabotage or as the result of riot-induced vandalism.

Thankfully, most of us are far more apt to see natural, human error, and hardware failure disasters than the other types.

But before you start to relax, understand that even the most common disasters can have expensive and incapacitating effects. You'll read more about this in the next section.

Profile of a Disaster Risk: The Intrepid Upgrader

My friend Kevin is the epitome of someone with more enthusiasm about what his PC can do than willingness to learn how to handle things well and keep them running that way. Although he needs his computer for the business he's setting up, he tends to take a number of unnecessary risks that frequently leave him either unable to use some part of his system (usually the modem) or stuck with a system that won't always boot up.

While Kevin keeps his physical system immaculate (you'll never find dust, for example), his tendency to download and install everything he sees often confuses his Windows configuration and leads to problems running applications. Add to this the fact that whenever Kevin hits a snag, he reinstalls his operating system (losing the updated drivers for his hardware), and you can understand why my head starts to pound whenever he calls to say, "I've got this little problem."

He likes to buy seriously older PC hardware on sale, and this leads to issues of compatibility, especially since he's not familiar with hardware concepts such as jumpers and COM ports and drivers.

"Why can't they make this stuff easier to understand?" he frequently bemoans in my ear after he drives his PC a considerable distance to have me get it operational again.

The last two times this happened, I made him promise to run a full backup or create a drive image (an actual image of the contents and structure of a hard drive) as soon as he returned home. Each time, he told me later, "I would have done it, but it seemed too complicated. But I've got this new little problem I was thinking you could help me with…"

Profile of a Disaster Risk: Lightning

It may be hard for you to picture the type of conflagrations often talked about in disaster recovery scenarios. After all, it's hard to imagine your home or business obliterated in the immediate aftermath of a nuclear attack, bombing, or jumbo jet impact.

So let's look instead at something that may occur hundreds of times a day around the planet and that can be responsible for a fair amount of damage even though it is so commonplace: a thunderstorm.

As your grandmother always told you, it isn't the thunder that poses a problem but the electrical atmospheric changes and discharges that occur with lightning. Traditionally, the most violent storms occur when much cooler air moves into a region that has been oppressively hot. A turbulent clash develops, the energy of which must be dissipated somehow, and lightning is the result.

Have you ever seen ball lightning? While this is a rare occurrence, anyone who ever observes this arcing, fiery plasma ball of light and power begins to respect the kind of force that any type of lightning can carry.

Ordinary lightning can hurt your home, office, and electronics both directly and indirectly. Even with some of the limited grounding built into both newer and older homes, energy from lightning can travel inside your home or office, travel along your wiring, and damage the equipment directly, sometimes resulting in fire.

For those who remember or still use an outdoor antenna, you know that lightning can hit the antenna and travel in along the wiring into the back of the TV or radio and blow it out. Likewise, lightning hitting the phone line can send the charge shooting along the phone line into your home or office. In rare instances, it can kill a person talking on the phone when it does. If that phone line is connected to a modem that is in turn connected to your PC (the typical setup for a regular dialup Internet connection), the charge can enter the PC, frying the modem and sometimes frying the motherboard the modem is connected to. Since everything else in a PC is connected either directly or indirectly to the motherboard, the result can be a smoking heap.

Even if the lightning strike doesn't occur immediately near your home or office, you're still at risk because you're connected to a string of other potential strike sites. For example, if your power substation takes a powerful strike from lightning, it can cause surges or at least create electrical ripples throughout the neighborhood the substation serves. The same is true when a car accidentally plows into a utility pole carrying above-ground power lines.

Other Potential Disasters

Also bear in mind that violent storms can bring about flash flooding, which may endanger basement and ground level areas where electronics may be located. Heavy rains can also send rain cascading into open windows and through poor roofing.

Not a lot of PCs—or TVs, stereos, kitchen appliances, and so on—survive being immersed, even when they are turned off and disconnected from power at the time the water reaches them. If they are plugged in and in use at the time the water hits, they short out and may likely become a total loss. Unfortunately, that's the good news, because as long as the power connection is in place, the electronics pose a serious danger for electrical shock if you touch them or touch anything that touches them (for example, the corner of a metal desk on which a wet PC sits).

Believe it or not, much damage can also occur well after a storm is finished. Many people, especially since the Year 2000 scare when everyone was afraid the power grids might shut down, have installed backup generators for their homes and offices to keep at least minimal services available when the main power supply is out. But an improperly installed generator can send a powerful surge out along the power lines once power is restored, sometimes resulting in a second blackout or at least spotty power all along the line. Likewise, damaged electronics and appliances that weren't fully killed before the power winked out may roar to life again once the power is restored, causing further problems or fire risk.

Where I live in a very rural area of northern New England, we often see "rocking" power, where a storm hits along the electrical chain and sends the power switching on and off several times a minute. Over time, even with protective measures employed, I've still lost some equipment to this kind of electrical misbehavior.

The message I'm trying to convey is don't be scared of the potential damage but understand that it doesn't take a terrorist attack or other horrific event to put you at risk. Mother Nature supplies more than enough phenomena to make emergency planning a necessity for everyone.

NOTE *Learn more about protecting your PC and its power in Chapter 11, "Avoiding Power and Overheating Problems."*

A Few Statistics on PC Disaster

Statistically speaking, users lose far more data and productive time with their PCs than they have to simply because of their own actions—or inactions. According to information from a 2001 Bruskin Research survey posted on Iomega's web site (Iomega is a manufacturer of removable data storage solutions), nearly one in every four PC users has lost data due to blackouts, viruses, and hacker attacks. And that statistic represents only the reported cases, which of course represent only a small portion of the risks involved since you can meet with disaster in many more ways.

What is worse, given the fact that the survey reports almost half of Americans polled fear losing data from power failures alone, is how almost half of PC users don't back up their data at all. Those who do back up tend to do so only once a month or less often even though they create and work with new data each and every day.

Statistics on the aftermath of a disaster aren't too promising. For enterprise types of businesses (*enterprise* usually describes any large business organization whose operation is largely tied to computers and data), as many as two out of five companies go out of business within a year or two after experiencing a disaster, according to the Gartner Group.

For much smaller companies and businesses, as well as for individuals, some estimates say that between 50 and 70 percent will lose all their data and records in a disaster, with most of them having to start over again completely from scratch. Without necessarily knowing what to do next, they either replace the PC entirely (even if less than $100 in repairs is needed), or they just struggle through without a PC.

These figures are devastating even before you factor in the time, heartache, and massive inconvenience associated with the event as you struggle to re-create the forms, the addresses, the work, and other critical documents that may be lost. Whether you're a business or simply an individual who gets a lot of use out of your PC, finding yourself in this situation hurts, and usually in more ways than one.

Recovering from a Disaster

Not very long ago, disaster recovery was almost the exclusive domain of big business, which stood to lose millions if not billions of dollars in customers, lost work, and accounting chaos if they didn't protect their data.

With gigabyte upon gigabyte of precious data, businesses were advised to protect their data or risk spending months or years trying to recoup their losses—both data and financial. So businesses developed ideas for contingency plans—usually called Business Continuity or Disaster Recovery Procedures—that involve careful details for:

- Different types of backups of data performed at different times of the day.

- Storing all data both offsite as well as onsite. (Many New York and California companies, for example, store their records with huge data repository firms in Colorado.)

- Keeping copies of all forms, documents, and financial instruments (such as checks) in at least one other location.

- Having a backup physical site that can double as an interim business site if the main site is made unavailable; there are online sites that allow you to store data by uploading it, too.

- Performing regular dry runs of a disaster plan to make sure everyone knows what to do to keep the business running in an emergency.

But today, almost everyone—including the most casual PC user—has many gigabytes of data. And the more room you have for data, the greater the likelihood that some of this data is precious or cannot be easily duplicated.

Thus, you need to have a disaster recovery plan as well, but one tailored toward your smaller budget and less complicated operation.

Not completely convinced? Keep reading.

Why You Need a Recovery Plan

Who needs a disaster recovery plan?

Ask yourself these questions:

- Are you a proprietor of a small business that depends on your PC(s) to operate?

- Does your job often require you to bring work home to do on the PC?

- Does your job require that you communicate with the company network from home?

- Are you a student who depends on your PC to research and compile information and to produce papers for school programs?

- Do you sell materials either through your own web site or by participating with online venues such as eBay to conduct online auctions?

- Are you a hobbyist who stores important files and information on your hard disk?

- Do you have a fair amount of money invested in your home or office computer setup?

- Have you set up your home or office finances and bill paying using your PC?

- Does the job of keeping your home or office's PCs running always fall to you?

- Are you concerned about losing material on your PC in the event of a problem?

If you answered yes to any of these questions, you need to have a game plan in place to be able to get the system up and running again if a problem keeps you from using your PC. Many of you will say yes more than once, making it all the more important that you have a way to take control of a bad situation rather than having a bad situation control you.

The Bigger the Drive, the Greater the Loss

Most of the material you work with on your PCs is written as a series of 0s and 1s (the binary language of computers) to specially coated platters that spin within the metal housings of your hard drives. Hard drives are usually mounted inside the PC, under the cover.

Today, PC hard drives have never been cheaper or more capacious. The average minimum hard disk is now 20GB, which can store many thousands of different types of files. You need the disk space, too, because you download huge files from the Internet (including 50MB sound files and 100MB videos) and install mammoth applications such as Microsoft Office.

But the larger your hard drive, and the more important and irreplaceable the data is stored to it, the greater the risk you run if the hard drive fails. You'll read more about this in the section "About Recovery Software and Services" in a moment.

The Myth of the Paperless Office

Remember the old wives' tale that computers were going to make your office paperless? You would be freed from cluttered desks, ink-stained hands, and bulky filing cabinets, they said.

Unfortunately, those old wives were so-called computer visionaries, and they were patently wrong. It was as misguided as the Internal Revenue Service's Reduction of Paperwork Act that seems to demand more paperwork to fulfill. In fact, most offices report they actually consume more paper than they did before the major advent of PCs in the 1980s. Even at home, you're swimming in papers you're forced to keep.

For this reason, it's not surprising that many users—myself included—are turning to cheaper, more reliable disk space (hard disks as well as recordable CD and DVD discs) to store the thousands of documents that need to be kept in archived records over long periods of time.

Disk storage has some serious advantages over "all paper." For one, it consumes a great deal less space. You can fit hundreds of documents and many dozens of graphics on a single CD (and both recordable DVDs as well as hard drives are far more capacious). For another, if your file drawer of folders and papers gets wet, you're out of luck. Get a CD wet, and all you need to do is wipe it dry and you're ready to load your documents and print fresh—and dry—copies.

For this to work, you need to regularly copy the data to more than one location so that if one location gets hit by a problem, you can still grab the stored data from another. You see, once you try to centralize your records into digital format, it's better protected than paper, but only if you keep the data safe.

Imagine, too, that you have a natural disaster such as a flood or fire. Let's say you've had the smarts to combine all your most important papers and photos into four large cartons. Now, would you rather—in the face of disaster—lug out four huge boxes or a CD or two that contain the digitized contents of all four boxes?

A Cautionary Tale: When the IRS Comes Knocking

Let me give you an example of why your PC and its attached hardware can be a disaster recovery tool all in itself.

A few years ago, I took the unheard-of route of shopping and getting a mortgage for a new home online. If you've been through the mortgage process, you know it's an endless series of forms, tax returns, and other documents. But because I was doing it online, I had to turn all this paper into a digital format the computer could handle, which I accomplished by using a flat-bed scanner (one that cost under $100) to scan in all the paperwork I needed to send to the mortgage broker. This process was so easy, it made me wonder how else I could use it.

Continued on next page

A Cautionary Tale: When the IRS Comes Knocking *(Continued)*

You see, I had already experienced a non-PC office disaster. A year or two before my mortgage process, a record snowfall led to record snowmelt and flooded part of my old home/home office. This completely ruined several boxes of old, must-keep papers, including tax returns, old receipts, newspaper and magazine clippings of my work, and such. It was a nightmare trying to replace all the papers and forms that I could, while worrying I would later desperately need some record I no longer had. Reconstructing one's life is not easy.

When I was scanning those mortgage forms into my PC, that unpleasant memory was still fresh in my mind. So while I was scanning the mortgage papers, I scanned dozens more of my other records into my PC *just in case* disaster should revisit me. Later, in the process of moving, I lost a carton of essential business papers, including tax returns. The carton simply disappeared, never to be found again. More angst.

This year, I had to call the tax folks about one matter and learned they could find no record of my actual tax return for a specific year. They had my tax payment and my filing-extension form, but said they simply saw no return filed for that year.

Can you say, "panic?" See, I was fairly certain that 1997 return was either in the lost carton or among the papers destroyed by a flood. Sure enough, it was nowhere to be found, and the prospect of trying to re-create a document I produced almost five years earlier loomed large before me. Since my records from that time period were already rendered incomplete—extinct really—by the flood, I figured I was in trouble.

Then I remembered all those records I had scanned into the computer. These records had long ago been copied onto CD (making a few copies, to be safe). I found a CD copy within an hour of looking through hundreds of documents, brought up my scanned copy of my old tax return, printed it off, and sent it to the tax folks.

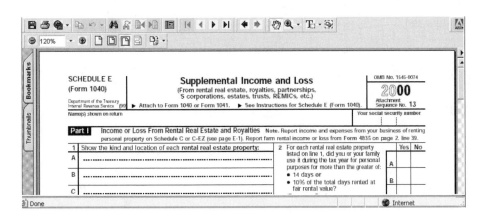

It was one of those moments that remind you that technology can—and often does—help you even more than it can confound you.

About Recovery Software and Services

One of the reasons this book was developed was because so many users lose data—or the use of their PCs—unnecessarily because they lack the information needed to fully troubleshoot, diagnose, and repair a problem. PCs are filled with electricity and seemingly mystical parts that make some people feel they need a degree from MIT (Massachusetts Institute of Technology) to work with them.

Many users panic when a problem hits, and they try the reformat-and-reinstall route, where you basically wipe the hard drive clean of all data (not good if your files only exist on that hard drive) and then reinstall the operating system (usually one of the many versions of Microsoft Windows). This solves some types of PC problems, but won't correct 70–80 percent of what can go wrong. What this does is erase your data and make you start over from scratch.

Such a situation can leave other users looking for services and software that can—for a cost—tell them what's wrong with their computer and perform any necessary repairs.

Software, however, has some serious limitations in what it can do. One critical factor is that PCs can vary greatly in the hardware and software installed on them and in the ways they can break. Also, many PC problems, particularly problems based on a hardware failure, cannot be solved with software.

Another issue, of course, is that it can be tough—although not impossible—to load and run fix-it software on a PC that appears to be dead. After all, if you could get the PC to boot at all, you might not need the software, right?

Of course, if your PC dies—and "dead PC" can mean anything from a damaged motherboard to a blown central processor unit (CPU) and beyond—you have two major options:

- Get the PC repaired.

- Remove the hard drive and install it into another PC.

Let's look at these two options in more detail.

Get the PC Repaired

Unfortunately, getting a PC repaired can be something of a crapshoot. As you will learn the further into this book you go, literally anyone can call themselves a PC technician.

In my years of managing PC technical support communities, I've heard some real horror stories—people going in for a new video card and coming back with a broken motherboard (which can happen if you apply too much weight to the motherboard or try to force a new video adapter into a motherboard slot). A broken motherboard can cause far more problems than most video adapters, which meant this user's upgrade turned into a dead-grade.

My eyes have witnessed people with advanced training doing truly lame things like trying to install a regular hard drive while the PC is up and running (a great way to ruin the drive because it will short out the components at the very least). Sorry to say, I've known several repair technicians who appeared to have no better technical skills or knowledge than the average computer user they're in business to serve.

However, there are many, many excellent technicians out there. You can find them working in all kinds of venues. In fact, I just heard that one of the most knowledgeable PC technicians I know does repairs during the day and mans a psychic hotline at night. But it can be very difficult to tell a good technician from a bad technician when you walk in off the street.

NOTE *Chapter 18, "Knowing When to Call the Professionals," provides you with solid suggestions for how to choose the right professional and describes your various options.*

Repair vs. Replacement

Another issue you have to consider, whether you do a PC repair or have it done by a professional, is cost. The price difference between the two can be significant because when you do the repair yourself, you're paying only for the replacement parts, while a professional repair typically involves an hourly labor charge.

Of course, if you approach a repair blindly, with little knowledge of your PC, the do-it-yourself route can become quite expensive, both in terms of time and possibly replacing other parts you might damage in the process.

If you have a slightly older PC, it may be easier and cheaper to replace the whole PC than to replace a few components, such as a motherboard and onboard memory damaged due to storm-related electrical activity. The closer a repair gets to $300 and above, the more it may be worth considering getting a new PC. With Dell and Gateway—two brands where you often pay a premium for the name—offering PCs for under $1,000 (and well under if you don't need a monitor because you're using your old monitor), a big repair bill could easily pay for half of the new PC.

Should you opt to buy a new PC, one option is to take a working hard drive from the dead system and place it in the new computer. And there's the rub—the hard drive has to be working in order to accomplish that.

What do you do if it's the hard drive, rather than the PC, that is dead? Read on to find out.

TIP *One thing you should avoid doing is replacing a PC with a new one immediately without good reason (example: you were planning to do so anyway) or until you have some idea of what's wrong with the old one. It's very possible that the problem could cost simply between $5 and $100 to resolve—or nothing, if it's something you can fix without replacement hardware.*

Hard Drive Recovery

Hard drives pose a thorny problem when they malfunction because your PCs typically use them to boot the full system. If the drive isn't working, the PC may not boot unless you use a specially formatted floppy disk (called a *boot disk*) or a CD to start the PC from.

If you've ever seen a hard drive (see Figure 1.1), you'll find that while you can change the way you hook them into the PC (and other drives) as well as change their location in the drive bays of your PC, there really isn't anything inside the hard drive's cover that you can take apart and repair.

Photo courtesy of Emily Sherrill Weadock

Figure 1.1 A PC hard drive

NOTE In the 1980s, when hard drives were still new and a tiny 20MB hard drive could cost hundreds of dollars, people would take them apart to try to fix them. But their efforts weren't usually successful, and the drive technology has changed; typically, they're smaller, making them virtually impossible for most technicians to repair at all.

This leaves you to check the physical connections of the hardware and how it's recognized (or not) by your PC's onboard hardware auditor, the BIOS, or using some type of boot disk to get the machine up and running so you can run disk-checking software.

Again, software, including old favorites such as Norton Utilities/System Works, can only go so far because they only solve certain types of hard drive issues. For example, software can be used to repair the physical organization of files stored to the hard drive or to reformat the disk. Software can't fix an actual defect or unusual physical wear within the hard disk.

You might be asking yourself, "Can't I just send the hard drive back to the manufacturer and have them recover the data and send it back to me on a new drive?"

Only part of that is true. A hard drive manufacturer will often replace a problem drive (with limitations; see Chapter 17, "Resurrecting a Dead Hard Drive"). But they won't take responsibility for the data stored on it. So if you want the material saved from the dead drive before you return it, it's up to you to try to accomplish that.

Aren't there professional data recovery services? Absolutely—there are quite a few. But affording them is another matter unless you are a company or corporation with reasonably deep pockets. That 40GB drive you bought at a great sale price of about $100 could cost you anywhere between $500 and $5,000 (or more) to have a drive recovery service try to extract data once you hit a problem. The emphasis here is on "try" because there is no guarantee the service will be able to harvest much of any usable data from the dead drive.

Many require the same fee whether or not they are successful (fair, considering they expended the labor). Others offer a lower flat fee if they can't pull your data from the drive. As you'll learn in Chapter 17, it's important to identify the fees for the service upfront to avoid nasty and pricy surprises.

Since you never know when disaster will strike, it's important that you get some background understanding of how your PC works when it operates properly. This information can be invaluable when you're trying to figure out what's wrong.

Meet me in Chapter 2, and we'll review some facts about how your PC, its operating system, and all the applications play together to produce the desktop work environment you want and need.

CHAPTER 2

How Your Hardware, Operating System, and Applications Work Together

Ever construct one of those great domino structures where you use dozens of pieces to make an elaborate design? If you have, then you know how difficult it can be to create it, only to have to pull one piece out without sending a rippling effect through everything in the chain.

A friend of mine likens the whole PC setup to such a game of dominoes, especially today when computing design has evolved into such an integrated system. He says that if you break or damage one piece of the PC puzzle, you'll feel it throughout your PC. I think there's something to be said for this analogy, and I bet you do, too.

I'm telling you this because you're likely to encounter this issue with PC work—either in run-of-the-mill problems or when recovering from a major disaster. PC integration makes it easy to set things up initially. For example, plug in a piece of hardware and Windows usually detects that something new has been installed and prompts you to install its driver. But the Windows infrastructure that creates such convenience can sometimes make it tougher to diagnose and fix problems in an emergency.

Unless you can appreciate the inter-connections of almost everything on and in a PC, it'll be harder for you to do the work necessary to get a disaster-ed system back up. You'll hear the old refrain about "taking things one step at a time" often in this book because following that old adage helps you avoid the pitfalls of integration.

Toward that end, this chapter focuses on helping you understand the role of the three major components of any working computer:

- the PC hardware itself (the box, the monitor, and anything attached to the box)

- the operating system

- the applications installed to the operating system

Take a deep breath and jump into the first section.

The Role of Hardware

If you find PC hardware more confusing than the under-the-hood components in your car or reprogramming your VCR after a major power failure, don't feel alone. Many people using PCs after even several years often confuse their hard drives with installed memory or think a poor display is the result of a bad monitor when it's likely the video card that's installed or integrated into your PC's motherboard.

For this reason, I'm going to devote some time to a major overview of the main hardware used in your PC configuration. I'll describe the types of disaster-related damage or symptoms you might see with each major component. This single chapter, of course, can't serve as an everything-you-need-to-know-about-working-with-PC-hardware guide. There are many books on this subject, and they often run more than 1,000 pages focusing just on hardware. A great example of this is Mark Minasi's *The Complete PC Upgrade and Maintenance Guide* (Sybex). There are also some great web-based resources for understanding all the details and connections both inside and outside your PC. I'll take you through those in Chapter 15, "Finding Help Online."

As you read about the basic PC components, I'll alert you to the types of damage you might encounter in each category of hardware.

About the Easy PC Initiative

You may have heard of something called the *Easy PC* or the *Easy PC Initiative* and wonder why PC hardware seems to be such a technically dense subject considering that PCs were supposed to become easier to use as time progressed.

Today's PC standards are attempting—by fits and starts—to make hardware that is simple to both install and uninstall without great knowledge or skill needed by the person doing so. One example of this is Plug-and-Play (PNP) technology. PNP is just what it sounds like—you can plug in the peripheral (printer, camera, speakers, etc.) and the component immediately works or works after rebooting. Technically speaking, PNP, in part, helps something like a newly installed printer be recognized when Windows first starts up (true with standard parallel port printers) or when the printer is plugged into a port with Windows up and running. (This latter situation is possible for printers only with Universal Serial Bus (USB) technology, where you plug a USB device into an external USB port.)

Both USB and IEEE 1394 (known as FireWire for Apple/Macintosh) are hot plug-hot swap types of PNP technology, meaning that you can connect them and disconnect them with the system running. Just think, no more procrastinating for three months before installing that printer you bought on sale! FireWire also makes it a cinch to swap out damaged equipment, as you might have to do after a flood.

The Easy PC Initiative also means that a PC is always on unless it has been specifically turned off. This is great because you aren't left sitting waiting for the PC to start up again from a complete off state. However, an always-on PC is at more risk from power-related problems such as lightning and power fluctuations.

Unfortunately, convenience usually has a cost. In this case, the cost is often seen in the form of you not being able to clearly see a problem (or understand that there is a problem) when you're troubleshooting a system that will no longer start or operate properly, as you might see after some type of disaster.

I'll describe some examples of how convenience and integration can make your post-disaster analysis tougher in the last section of this chapter. Right now, let's go over an important concept: PNP vs. non-PNP hardware.

PNP vs. Non-PNP Hardware

Even though PNP hardware has been around for more than a decade, we haven't reached a point where all hardware is PNP-ready, although the most recent PCs and their operating systems are ready for PNP hardware. As a result, hardware is divided into two major types:

- PNP hardware

- Non-PNP hardware (often referred to as *legacy hardware*)

The difference between the two types of hardware is significant, both for how your PC and operating system detect the hardware installed to it and for your ease of installation. After all, a PNP device should be much easier to install—and reinstall, as you might do after a disaster—because a PNP device is designed to install and configure pretty much automatically. Of course, you still have to physically install the device itself, and you need to have the device driver (discussed soon) when Windows Add New Hardware Wizard prompts you for it.

Let's talk for a second about the Add New Hardware Wizard, available by pressing the Add Hardware icon in Windows Control Panel; here's where you see one of the differences between PNP and non-PNP hardware. With non-PNP hardware, as you often find when using older devices such as older modems and sound cards, your newly installed or reinstalled device may not be detected when Windows first loads after the device installation. You may need to start the Add New Hardware wizard manually. With PNP devices, the wizard should load automatically as soon as Windows loads and detects the new or reinstalled piece of hardware.

But below the surface, you and your PC will handle PNP and non-PNP hardware quite differently. For example, non-PNP devices may require that you change settings on the hardware to configure it for use (for example, setting the physical port or the software IRQ you want a modem to use). This is usually accomplished by moving a tiny rocker switch or by a process known as *jumpering*, where you move a plastic shunt over the same number pin in two parallel rows that turns on a specific feature (like setting the port).

On the PC side, during the early stages of the PC bootup (discussed in the next section), your PC decides which devices are PNP and which aren't. Because PNP is designed to work better with the operating system, your PC passes the PNP devices on to Windows to set up for operation. PNP devices are automatically assigned the hardware resources (see the sidebar "About Hardware Resources") that they need around the needs of other devices that require specific settings.

WARNING *Hardware studies tend to report that up to 50% of the PCs and PC hardware returned as defective each year (accounting for up to 30% of sales) are simply misconfigured.*

But your PC still needs to accept that non-PNP hardware is connected, too. So based on the way your non-PNP device is configured to work (those jumpers or switches), the PC assigns hardware resources, which include an address in memory used as a point of communications and a hardware interrupt request (IRQ) for getting the system's attention when the hardware needs it. These resources are critical because without them, a device cannot operate properly. Older devices in particular cannot share the same hardware resources used by another device, or something called a *hardware conflict* may result. A hardware conflict occurs when two or more devices sharing the same resources either don't work properly or work intermittently when the other devices sharing the same resources aren't being used.

TIP *How do you tell PNP from non-PNP devices? PNP hardware is usually very clearly marked, while non-PNP hardware is not. Instead it may read "ISA" or gives you an indirect clue by failing to mention PNP at all.*

While we're on the subject, familiarize yourself with the hardware resources being used by the devices installed to your PC. You can find these in Device Manager by taking these steps:

1. From the Windows Start menu, click Control Panel. (For earlier versions of Windows, click Settings and then Control Panel, or choose Control Panel after double-clicking on the My Computer icon on the Windows desktop.)

2. Double-click the System icon.

3. Click the Hardware tab and then click the Device Manager button. (Windows 95/98/Me users should choose the Device Manager tab.)

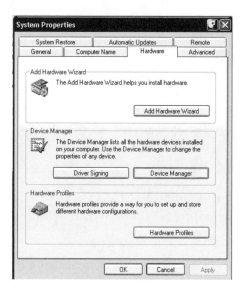

4. From Device Manager, open the View menu and select Resources by Type. (For Windows 95/98/Me users, choose View Devices by Type and then double-click the computer name.)

5. Click to select from Direct Memory Access (DMA), Input/Output (I/O), Interrupt Request (IRQ), and Memory.

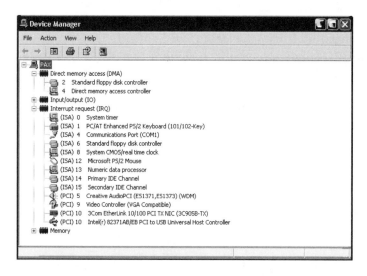

If you've never looked at this information before, don't worry if it looks confusing. Think of these resources, which I break out for you in the following sidebar, as people you know. To let people know about something, you need to be able to communicate with them and they need to be able to communicate with you.

Let's say you need to contact Joe Smith. You could send him a letter; for that, Joe has a mailing address. You could call him because Joe has a phone with his own unique phone number. You could also go visit him to talk to him personally because Joe has a home at a specific street address (which may differ a bit from his mailing address), or you can send him e-mail because Joe has his own unique e-mail address.

The hardware resources discussed in the "About Hardware Resources" sidebar function very much like these avenues of communication, except that instead of communication between two people, it's communication between a specific device and the rest of the PC (including the motherboard, CPU, and the operating system).

About Hardware Resources

The hardware resources discussed here are four means of communication between the hardware and the PC:

Hardware interrupt requests (IRQs)   IRQs are actual hardware wires along which interrupt signals are sent to and from the CPU. There is a maximum number of 16 IRQs available on any PC, only some of which can be used for adding hardware.

Direct memory address (DMA)   DMA is the use of one of up to eight channels on the PC that communicate directly with certain types of hardware such as some sound and network adapters.

Input/output (I/O) address   The I/O address is a specific address range where I/O communication occurs between hardware and the PC; the I/O address appears in hexadecimal (for example, 00000072–0000007F).

Memory   Memory in this context specifically refers to a physical memory address, also represented in hexadecimal (for example, 0000004C–0000006F).

What Happens When a PC Boots Up

You're accustomed to flipping a switch or pressing a button and then waiting for the Windows desktop to load. You might notice some text scrolling on and off the screen between turning the PC on and the system becoming available for work, and you might have noticed a beep or two.

But what goes on inside your PC is a symphony of events as devices and connections are tested, assigned resources to communicate properly with the PC and operating system, and made available to applications so you can open and save files, access hardware like your printer or scanner, and connect to the Internet.

Since most of this goes on beyond your vision, it's hard to appreciate not just how much goes on, but how much can go wrong. There are many steps in a bootup and each step needs to complete flawlessly so that everything functions correctly when your Windows desktop loads. I'm going to break this process down to help you understand it.

This step-by-step process assumes that the PC is being started by a *cold boot* (sometimes called a *hard boot*), meaning that the PC is cold or hasn't been running immediately prior to the power being applied. A *warm boot* (often referred to as a *soft boot*) is one performed on a system that has already been started and initialized. A warm boot does not repeat the first seven steps listed here:

1. When you press the power button, the power supply engages power and initializes. There is a time delay while the power supply begins to feed electricity to other components of the system. Take note of the sounds you hear well before a display appears.

2. Everything is on hold (in *reset signal mode*) until the system's chipsets get a signal that the power supply's initialization is complete so that the bootup process may proceed.

3. The CPU awakes and looks in the BIOS memory to launch the BIOS startup routine (known as Power-On Self Test or POST).

NOTE *BIOS (Basic Input/Output System) is a type of software recorded right onto a chip on the motherboard that stores information about the hardware connected to your PC. Often, this BIOS information can be updated or at least reinitialized by applying software referred to as flashing the BIOS. The section "The Role of BIOS" in this chapter contains more information.*

4. POST executes. If POST is successful, the bootup continues. If POST is not successful, a series of beeps may sound to alert you to a problem. Those beeps vary in number and signal, depending on what is wrong (such as a RAM failure or RAM not found, etc.) and on which company developed the BIOS (see Chapter 7, "Restarting a Problem PC").

NOTE *POST is actually a series of tests your PC performs on itself during the first phase of bootup to make sure that essential hardware devices (keyboard, memory, CPU, and drives) are detected and everything is found to be OK to proceed with the full start. If you look at the keyboard closely, you'll see a scan of the keyboard (the Num Lock, Caps Lock, and Scroll Lock LEDs flash). If this scan does not occur, the processor or motherboard is not working. If the scan occurs and there is no video, the video board is the probable culprit.*

5. The BIOS checks the video adapter to instigate getting a display in place for user confirmation, meaning you can see text on the screen. If found, the video adapter is initialized and a display appears on the monitor.

6. Next, the BIOS looks for any other devices that have read-only memory (ROM) that needs to be checked and initialized, including that of the hard disk. If a problem is detected, an error message displays on the monitor because video was engaged in the previous step.

7. The BIOS then begins a virtual inventory of all hardware attached so that it understands what the system must acknowledge and work with in the course of preparing the operating system to load.

8. Then the BIOS looks for and configures all Plug-and-Play devices for use, trying to fit resource demands (such as hardware interrupt requests or IRQs) around non-PNP elements.

9. BIOS information displays on the monitor, giving you a picture of what hardware it has found and what resources are being used. Depending on the speed of your system, you'll need to read very fast or press the Pause button.

10. BIOS looks for a boot drive to initialize the final major stage of the boot process—the loading of the operating system. If set to do so, BIOS may look at the floppy drive or even the CD or DVD drive first to determine if a system boot disk is present. If not, it proceeds to look at the primary hard drive, searching for the Master Boot Record (MBR) to start the drive. (Note that newer BIOSes let you select a boot drive from a roster of hard drives available—check your BIOS for details.) If no boot drive or disk is found, BIOS reports an error to the monitor display.

11. Once the MBR is successfully found, BIOS commands the hard disk to boot and begin loading the installed operating system. If you're using multiple operating systems, the BIOS presents you with a menu from your boot management tool that lets you select the operating system to run during that session.

NOTE *The MBR is actually a tiny piece of software, usually stored on the first sector of the booting hard drive in your PC, that is executed as the first step of the bootup process after POST. If the MBR is missing or damaged, the PC won't boot off the hard drive.*

12. The operating system then works with the hardware information that the BIOS has already gathered to make these devices available—including loading device drivers and any necessary ancillary support for devices—as the desktop loads or when you reach a command-line interface.

13. If you're part of a network or you have a password set to access your system, you're prompted to log in.

14. You're ready to work!

The Major Hardware Components of a PC

With advances in PC hardware and changes that make it easier to install, along with the convergence of consumer electronics such as still and moving image cameras and video editing with your PC, there is relatively little you can't add to your PC. On any given day, depending on the work or play I'm engaged in, I may have a few cameras, a drawing pad, a digital voice recorder, and a microscope attached to my computer in addition to the regular hardware (monitor, printer, scanner, keyboard, mouse, et. al.).

However, this section describes the most typical hardware components of a modern PC, from the motherboard and its main processor to the external connections for hardware that operates outside the PC case.

Checking Against Your Own PC

You may find this all easier to follow if you check the hardware components listed here against those found in your own PC.

Going inside your system, however, requires a few steps and some precautions. Don't worry—these steps become second nature once you've gone inside your case a few times.

Before you start, you'll need the following:

- Screwdriver (see the section "Hardware Tools" in Chapter 4, "Assembling Your PC Recovery Resource Kit")

- A container for removed screws

- A grounding strap (also called an *anti-static strap*)

- Your PC manual or documentation

Continued on next page

Checking Against Your Own PC *(Continued)*

Next, take these steps to check your PC against the component list in this section so you can identify the parts of your system:

1. From the Windows Start menu, choose Shut Down or Turn Off Computer and then Shut Down or Turn Off.

2. If the PC doesn't fully shut down at the end of this process, turn it off using the power button.

3. Disconnect the power from the back of the PC.

4. Locate the screws holding the PC case cover in place and remove them. Place the screws in a container so that you can retrieve them easily. Set this container aside temporarily.

5. Slide or pull the cover off (consult your documentation for detailed instructions).

6. Attach your anti-static strap following directions for your strap. *Do not touch anything inside the PC* until you are properly grounded because you can damage components.

7. Follow along in this section, and then, if appropriate (meaning you don't have something to repair or replace), replace the cover, screw it back into place, reconnect power, and turn your PC back on.

The Motherboard

If you look inside most PCs, you'll often find that there isn't one printed circuit board inside but many of them, of various shapes, sizes, and configurations. There is just one main board, however, called the *motherboard*. It is to this motherboard that almost everything else in your PC—memory, drives, audio and video, and so on—is either directly or indirectly connected.

Motherboards vary a great deal, depending on

- When they were manufactured

- What type of CPU they were designed to work with (motherboards and CPUs must be matched together)

- Whether they came with a lower cost system or whether you upgraded a system to get one with more features

- What type of BIOS is used by the motherboard

The layout of motherboards can vary quite a bit, so don't be surprised if the motherboard pictured in Figure 2.1 doesn't look exactly like yours.

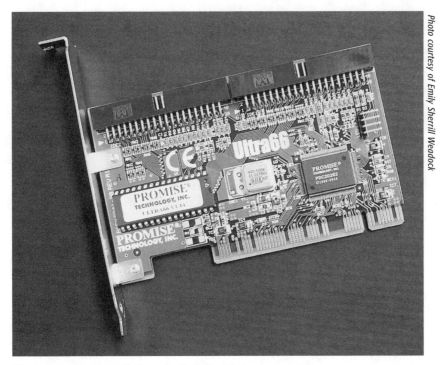

Photo courtesy of Emily Sherrill Weadock

Figure 2.1 *An installed motherboard with its connections.*

A motherboard is mounted to the chassis or frame of the PC case (the bottom of the motherboard does not touch the case—this would cause a short), and then connections and components are installed to it.

The major connections and components found on a motherboard include:

System chipset   The system chipset is a complex set of integrated circuits that provide the core functionality of the motherboard. The system chipset may be one or more integrated circuits, typically more than one.

CPU   The CPU is a microprocessor installed in a cartridge that plugs into either a CPU socket or slot, depending on the type of motherboard. Inside this cartridge (on recent systems) are up to three types of high-speed memory caches.

Memory   PC memory is installed to memory slot(s) located near the CPU on the motherboard.

Electrical   The power supply connects into the motherboard to provide power for components; additional connector(s) from the power supply may be used for internal fans such as the CPU fan.

CMOS battery   A CMOS battery is a replaceable electronics battery used to store system settings such as the current time, when the PC is turned off, etc.

IDE/ATA Channel Connections   Usually two IDE controller connections allow up to four IDE/ATA drives to be installed, two—a master and a slave—to each controller connection.

Accelerated Graphics Port (AGP)   An AGP is a video-dedicated port for installing an AGP-type video adapter; the AGP is located close to the CPU for faster graphics handling than video adapters installed to the Peripheral Component Interconnect (PCI) bus (see the description of expansion bus slots).

Expansion bus slots   These are slot-shaped connectors in the motherboard (often between three and six connectors) for the addition of peripheral device adapters such as video adapters, sound adapters, network cards, or Small Computer Serial Interface (SCSI) host adapters (for installing SCSI drives and devices). Peripheral device adapters are typically installed in the short, white, horizontal slots (PCI slots), although older systems may still have longer, black Industry Standard Architecture (ISA) slots (see the section "BIOS and How Hardware Connects to the PC").

Integrated components   Integrated components are any components, normally available as adapters installed into the expansion bus, that have been integrated into the motherboard. Types of integrated components include modems, networks, and video and sound adapters.

External connections   External connections include anything that can be connected to the PC through a jack, a port, or other plug at the back or front of the PC.

Motherboard-Related Disasters

One of the commonly seen motherboard-related disasters is man-made and is caused by improper handling. The motherboard usually cannot tolerate any pressure or flexing when installing it into a case, when moving it into a new case, or when installing other components into it. In these situations, you may be able to spot a hairline or larger fracture to the motherboard. Some motherboards can continue to function even with such stress fractures, but they may be unreliable and may potentially cause a small fire within the unit or damage other components attached to it.

Improper installation of a motherboard into the PC chassis can cause a disaster of sorts because the motherboard circuitry may short itself against the chassis. This could completely and permanently disable the motherboard or cause strange, intermittent symptoms such as the PC seeming to turn itself off on its own, faltering on bootup, or producing system lockups that defy resolution. (Chapter 12, "PC Performance: Diagnosing, Monitoring, and Troubleshooting" contains many tips for overcoming these types of problems.)

If any device attached to a motherboard takes a direct hit from a power surge or lightning discharge, the motherboard may be damaged because virtually all hardware connects into the motherboard. The only solution is to replace the motherboard. A knowledgeable PC repair shop can test a motherboard for you.

Should the PC become doused or submerged by water, especially if it was connected to power and turned on at the time, the motherboard and many other components are probably damaged beyond repair.

You don't need to toss your PC if the motherboard alone is damaged. All working components and connections can be carefully removed from a damaged motherboard. Then the bad motherboard itself can be replaced with a working one, with the components and connections reinstalled.

CPU

The CPU (see Figure 2.2) is frequently referred to as the PC's brain. The job of any processor is to handle and run instructions and calculations that are sent to it. The CPU is the master processor in a PC that may contain several different types of processors (your sound adapter and video adapter, for example, probably both have on-board processors). Almost everything attached either inside or outside your PC case vies for the attention of the CPU.

> **NOTE** *Why have more than one processor in your PC? Because by giving some heavier duty devices such as video adapters their own processors, you reduce the workload of the main CPU. This reduces the time it takes for the central CPU to accomplish other tasks.*

The CPU is often identified in two different ways:

- By platform type, such as Intel Pentium I, II, III or IV, Intel Celeron or AMD Athlon XP, AMD Thunderbird or AMD Duron

- By processor speed in megahertz (MHz) or gigahertz (GHz), represented by figures such as 700MHz, 1.5GHz, or 2.5GHz

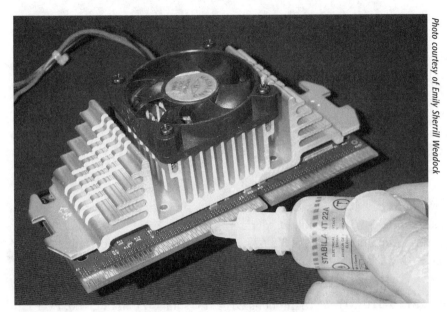

Photo courtesy of Emily Sherrill Weadock

Figure 2.2 *A CPU package and its fan installed to a motherboard.*

CPU-Related Disasters

A CPU usually works or does not work.

The CPU on most machines today is installed in a package mount that plugs directly into the motherboard. Immediately next to the CPU, usually clipped to its housing, is a fan assembly. That fan is necessary because fast processors run hot. It's also mandatory because a CPU has a specific operating temperature range (often 95–115 degrees Fahrenheit) beyond which it can malfunction or become damaged.

If the fan that is part of the CPU installation fails, heat radiated from the CPU begins to build. If the motherboard has a heat monitor installed and enabled, it may shut down the system when a critical temperature is reached. If the PC continues operating with the CPU fan not running, the PC begins to behave erratically, stops functioning altogether, and potentially damages both the CPU and the motherboard.

TIP *The CPU fan assembly can be removed—with the PC turned off and disconnected from power—from the CPU for cleaning and/or replacement.*

If the motherboard becomes damaged, the CPU may or may not be ruined, too. If you believe the CPU is damaged, first make sure that it is firmly installed into the motherboard and that its fan appears to work. If it's properly installed, you can either remove it and test the CPU in another PC or directly replace it.

PC Memory and Caches

This section gives you a quick appreciation of two PC workhorses: PC memory (also called *main memory*) and the processor caches.

Memory

PC memory refers to random access memory (RAM) and provides a working environment in which to run programs and process data on the PC desktop.

Memory is sold in various quantities (8, 16, 32, 64, 128, 256MB, and beyond), and in three major types of dynamic RAM (DRAM). Dynamic memory simply means that its data needs to be refreshed constantly in order to maintain it. There are three major types of DRAM:

Synchronous DRAM (SDRAM)   Synchronous DRAM is sold as PC66, PC100, PC133, and PC150 in dual inline memory modules (DIMMs) mostly used in Pentium III and earlier systems.

Rambus DRAM (RDRAM)   RDRAM is an expensive form of DRAM promoted through a joint venture between Intel (the CPU manufacturer) and Rambus Corp, with speeds of up to 800MHz and sold in RIMMs that look similar to SDRAM DIMMs but fit into a different type of memory slot.

Double Data Rate RAM (DDR RAM)   DDR RAM is a faster form of DRAM than SDRAM and is promoted by Intel's rival CPU manufacturer, Advanced Micro Devices (AMD). DDR RAM is now used in some Intel-based PCs.

A unit of memory (see Figure 2.3) is frequently called a *stick* of memory, and each memory slot on the motherboard takes one stick. Each filled memory slot is called a *bank* of memory, and these banks are usually numbered 0–2 or 0–3. Filling your motherboard's memory slots is called *populating*.

Don't confuse PC memory with the hard disk. It's a common mistake, but it can muddy troubleshooting. The memory acts as short-term storage for open or recently opened files and programs. The hard disk acts as your permanent storage for files and programs, meaning longer than just your current desktop session.

Photo courtesy of Emily Sherrill Weadock

Figure 2.3 *Installed PC memory (SDRAM).*

A small amount of hard disk space in Windows is set aside as *virtual memory*. It's called virtual because it's not memory in the sense of physically installed memory chips. Virtual memory is a chunk of disk space (50–200MB on a standard PC) temporarily used as a holding area for data being moved on and off your desktop. For example, this afternoon you've had six Word documents open on your desktop but you're only actively working in one; the other five are still semi-open and sitting in virtual memory. Establishing this virtual memory area (which Windows does automatically) means the data and programs open much faster than they would if you had to open them from the hard drive through Windows. This is still much slower than executing programs from RAM, which is why high-performance PCs contain a great deal of RAM.

You'll learn more about how your PC works with memory to open and work with files in the "Caches" section.

Memory-Related Disasters

Problems with memory can be among the toughest problems to analyze because bad or damaged memory can manifest itself in so many different ways, including but not limited to the following:

- A change in the amount of memory reported at bootup

- A PC that fails to boot

- A PC that boots but fails to load Windows (with or without an error message)

- Sudden appearance or increase in video display problems while working in graphically changing programs like a web browser

- Unexpected "low on memory" errors, even with large amounts of memory installed

- A CPU monitoring utility that shows a CPU usage jump that stays close to 100% because memory isn't available to help the CPU juggle its many duties

- Declining or sharply poorer overall performance in using the system

- Intermittent or constant "blue screen of death" Windows fatal or protection errors

- Formerly well-behaved games and applications that run without stability or lock up randomly, usually forcing you to power your PC off and back on again to return to a working Windows desktop

Without any working memory in a PC, there is very little you can do. Windows demands that a certain amount of memory be actively available just to start to load; if it does not see it, Windows typically fails with an insufficient memory warning.

More frequently, you'll see memory either fail to start or die on its own rather than see it devastated from a motherboard-related disaster. Frequent installing and removal of memory—as well as a rough installation—can damage memory as well. It's also possible to see these types of memory problems when you purchase the wrong type of memory for your system; some motherboards have memory sockets for more than one type of memory while others do not.

However, memory prices have remained quite low overall, and replacement isn't cost-prohibitive.

TIP *It's often better to keep the amount of memory you have concentrated in the least number of memory sticks possible. For example, it's easier and safer to install one 256MB memory stick than two 128MB sticks for a PC that requires 256MB of memory. With fewer installed sticks, there's less chance of a faulty installation. Consult your PC or motherboard manual for the maximum memory figures for your particular setup. With PC memory so cheap, you may want to pick up an extra stick and set it aside. Chapter 4 explains this in more detail.*

Caches

Typically, when you hear the term *cache* or *caches*, it refers to special caches of high-speed memory (much faster than the installed memory making up your PC's main memory) that are located close to the processor within the CPU package. Depending on the type of PC and CPU you have, you may have either two or three of these caches, numbered L1, L2, and sometimes, L3. Caches help speed up the bootup process, but they also serve an important role in normal PC work because they act as a bridge between the CPU and the main memory installed in your PC.

You need this bridge because the speed at which the CPU operates (referred to as its *clock speed*) is much faster than the speed at which your PC main memory operates. Without that bridge, you force your CPU into a situation where it has to sit and wait on the slower hard drive, reducing the PC's efficiency *and* yours.

Where you really see the file-loading process slow down is when you need to retrieve data from your much slower hard drive rather than from memory. For peak performance with your system, it's best to look at the hard drive last when looking for data. So PC design manufacturers came up with a reasonably effective way of handling this: caches.

The caches, which are slower than the CPU but faster than your main memory, act as intercessors. When the CPU makes a request for data, it begins drilling down through the list of storage devices, from the most temporary but fastest storage (the caches) to the next slowest (main memory) to the slowest but permanent storage (your hard drive). If your CPU finds what it needs in the L1 or L2 cache, it stops there and the data is quickly loaded into the processor's instruction register. If the data isn't found there, it looks through main memory. Only if it can't find the data there does the CPU search the hard drive.

Cache-Related Disasters   Rarely does a cache fail, outside of a catastrophe occurring to the rest of the CPU or motherboard, so what applies to both motherboard and CPU disasters applies here.

Typically, you'll replace the entire CPU package (or motherboard with CPU package), including caches, at one time. In the unlikely event that a specific cache fails when the rest of the CPU package is working, you may still find it both cheaper and easier to replace the entire CPU package. This is because the individual amounts of memory making up these caches can be cost-prohibitive when purchased separately and can be hard to match later. (You may be able to obtain it through your PC manufacturer if you bought a name brand PC clone.)

NOTE *If this cache memory is so fast, why not use it for PC main memory? Cost is a major factor; your PC would cost far more.*

Power

Your PC depends on a power supply within the case to provide power to the motherboard and its connections, as well as to the drives installed to the bays within your PC. Often ranging between 150 watts (lower end) and 400 watts (for a PC with lots of heavy-duty drives), the power supply doesn't just channel power. It must convert the house/office electrical current into a form that can be used by the PC, and it must supply power to PC components in the right doses of regulated voltage.

As you'll read later in Chapter 11, "Avoiding Power and Overheating Problems," your PC power supply is often all that stands between the delicate electronics within your PC and those nasty power fluctuations you see in your home as large appliances such as refrigerators and air conditioners cycle up and down. Your refrigerator, however, is built to withstand those ups and downs, while your CPU and your PC memory are not.

Notably, the power supply, illustrated in Figure 2.4, has a fan that vents to the outside of the PC and many bundles of multi-colored wires, each ending in a usually white power connector. These power connectors plug into the motherboard and to the drives, thus connecting them to the feed of power from the power supply.

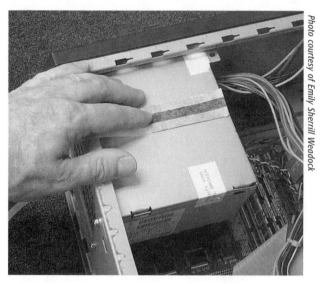

Photo courtesy of Emily Sherrill Weadock

Figure 2.4 *PC power supply with connectors.*

Power-Related Disasters

The greatest risk to the power system of a computer comes from outside the PC, from any major jolt of electricity sent through the house or office wiring into the PC through the power supply. This supply is meant to convert and empower, but by itself it does not have strong protection qualities to stand between the jolt and the motherboard and other connections. For this, you need the type of disaster planning described in Chapter 4 and the type of power protection discussed in Chapter 11.

Be aware, however, that man-made disasters caused by improper installation and connections and failing to keep interior PC fans clean of dust and debris (and working) probably account for the majority of damage.

Communications

Very few PCs sold in the United States—or anywhere—these days are meant to be stand-alone PCs without connections either to another PC or to a huge network such as the Internet. Even small homes and offices often have more than one PC, and setting up just a simple network lets you share files and programs and share a high-speed Internet connection.

The communications hardware inside a PC typically consists of one or both of the following:

A modem   An analog modem is used for dial-up phone connections. Digital modems are cable modems used for high-speed Internet access (also called *broadband*), digital subscriber line (DSL) modems, and satellite modems. Both types of modems may be present.

Network interface card (NIC)   The NIC, also known as the network adapter, is used for communicating between two or more PCs.

These devices are typically installed as adapters into the expansion bus slots, although external versions allow modems to connect via the serial ports or USB ports and allow networks to connect through the USB ports.

There are also integrated versions of both dial-up modems and network adapters that incorporate the functions and features of these devices right into the motherboard itself, with no additional hardware device needed.

Communications-Related Disasters

Because communications hardware such as modems and network adapters are designed to connect to other equipment by attaching a phone line or network cable to them, they operate at slightly more risk.

A normal phone line is especially susceptible. A car hitting a utility pole carrying overhead telephone and power lines and lightning can produce powerful ripple effects. These effects can be carried back along the phone line into a modem installed within the PC, which in turn can damage the motherboard and anything connected to it.

But even on a small, two-computer network, power-induced damage to one computer can travel across the network cable to the other computer. Usually, the damage is limited to the network cable itself or to the network adapter of the second computer. Sometimes, only the software configuration of the network rather than the hardware is affected. You'll learn more about protecting your PC and small network in other chapters, starting with Chapter 3, "Prevention: Limiting Your Risks."

Video System

What you see on your monitor depends on four different components, only two of which are hardware:

Video adapter (a/k/a video card)   A video adapter is the physical chipset that processes images and translates them from the digital form used by the system into an analog signal that the monitor understands. In many of today's systems, there may be no installed video adapter because the video chipset has been integrated into the motherboard itself.

Monitor   A monitor is the actual TV-style box where you watch the output of the video adapter. Monitors are rated in diagonal viewing area and dots per inch (DPI). The higher the number of DPI, the greater the clarity and cost. The monitor plugs into both a power source (electrical outlet) and, via cable, into the back of the PC where it meets the connector edge of the video adapter, as shown in Figure 2.5.

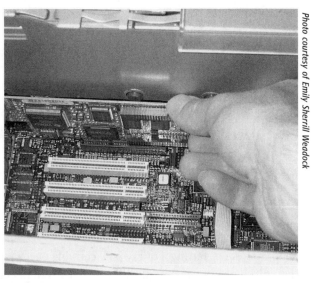

Photo courtesy of Emily Sherrill Weadock

Figure 2.5 *Connecting a monitor to a video adapter.*

Video (card) driver   The video driver is a piece of software that allows the video adapter to work well with the PC and its operating system.

Windows graphics subsystem   The graphics subsystem is the part of the Windows operating system that works with video hardware to produce a decent display. The video adapter is installed either to a PCI expansion bus slot or to the AGP port on the motherboard (see Figure 2.6), depending on the type of video adapter you have. (AGP adapters run faster than

PCI adapters.) There are also motherboards with the features of a separate video adapter integrated into them.

Photo courtesy of Emily Sherrill Weadlock

Figure 2.6 *AGP video port with a video adapter.*

Video-Related Disasters

A monitor is often the most vulnerable piece of your display setup because it plugs directly into your household or office power, which may be quite dirty even under the best circumstances. The monitor is also at risk because the internal hardware required for displaying the desktop representation isn't tolerant of getting bumped, struck, exposed to extremes of temperature, or doused by flood waters or sprinklers as you might have in a disaster situation.

I've seen permanent negative effects on brand-new, unprotected monitors that have been in use during periods when power rocked on and off, when used on the same circuit with a heavy-duty appliance like a dishwasher or refrigerator, and when heartily slapped in frustration.

These negative effects, besides causing the monitor to fail altogether, include:

- The display remains tinted toward a specific color (often green or blue).

- The display becomes fuzzy or no longer fills the entire screen.

- All colors become muted.

- Permanent distortion is left in a particular field of the display.

- Loud humming or faint vibration is observed when in use.

You might think to yourself, "Well, the monitor is very much like my TV, and my TV isn't that sensitive." But there are important differences between your TV and your monitor. The most important difference is that you don't look at your TV close up and you don't usually try to read your TV for long periods at a time. Even small changes and distortions will be much more noticeable with a monitor than they will be on the living room TV, although it can be subject to the same types of damage as a monitor.

Actual damage to a video adapter itself is usually limited to the same types of power and overheating issues as the motherboard and other components. However, a power surge experienced by a monitor can be carried across the video cable into the video adapter.

Some people install TV tuner adapters, either in addition to or as a feature of their video adapters, allowing them to pick up TV channels on their PC. This usually requires the user to attach an antenna of some type (a lead from an aerial antenna or cable or satellite TV line) directly into the TV tuner that is installed into the motherboard. Any power spiking carried into a home or office on this line can potentially damage the adapter—and the rest of the PC it's connected to.

Audio System

The audio system on a typical PC consists of the following hardware:

- Sound adapter (also called the *sound card*) or a sound chipset mounted directly on the PC motherboard

- External speakers

Like communications and video adapters, sound adapters are typically installed as a card into an available expansion bus slot on the motherboard, although many motherboards today (especially budget ones and laptops) incorporate audio into the motherboard itself rather than installing a separate adapter.

The speakers—along with other audio-related hardware such as a microphone, headphones, and accessory patch lines to other audio devices—plug into jacks located on the connector edge of the sound adapter at the back of the PC (see Figure 2.7).

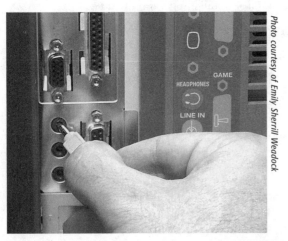

Figure 2.7 *Sound adapter connections at the back of the PC.*

Audio-Related Disasters

Audio-related disasters are rare unless you plug other devices—such as a receiver—into them that can be damaged by water or a power surge and carry that impact back into the PC through the jack where the sound adapter meets the back of the PC. However, because sound adapters are installed into the motherboard, any disaster that befalls an entire PC or its motherboard can damage the sound adapter as well.

One advantage, however, is that while a sound adapter is usually highly desirable, your PC will function without one installed or working.

Drives

Not so long ago, you typically had just two types of drives attached to your PCs:

- a floppy drive so that you could write to a floppy disk

- a hard drive that collected everything else you installed to your operating system or saved through your programs

These drives were usually mounted internally, meaning they were installed into drive bays inside the PC case at the front of the PC and connected either directly to the motherboard or to another drive that was so connected.

Many drives today (see Figure 2.8) can be installed to either a USB or a IEEE 1394 port outside the PC, although these external drives usually supplement the existing internal drives.

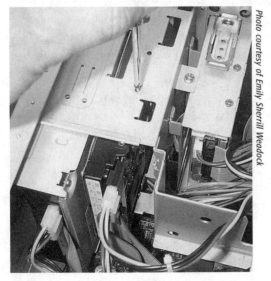

Photo courtesy of Emily Sherill Weadock

Figure 2.8 *Drives installed inside the PC.*

There are several major types of drives common in today's PCs:

Compact disc (CD) drives   CD-ROM drives are read-only, CD-R drives allow for both recording and reading, and CD-RW drives play, record, and re-record (writing over a previous recording). These connect to the IDE/ATA channel connector (or to another drive that is so connected), to a SCSI adapter installed into the expansion bus slots in the motherboard (or to another drive that is), or externally through the parallel, USB, or IEEE 1394 ports.

Digital versatile disc (DVD) drives   Like CD drives, these drives can be for DVD (and CD) playing only, for DVD recording, or for DVD re-recording. DVD drives connect either to the IDE/ATA channel connector (or to another drive that is so connected), to a SCSI adapter installed to the expansion bus slots in the motherboard (or to another drive that is), or externally through the USB or IEEE 1394 ports.

Floppy drives   Floppy drives are an older form of removable media drive where files can be copied to a 3½" hard plastic-covered magnetic media disk. However, floppy disks are limited to about 1.44MB of data.

Hard drives   Hard drives are the main permanent storage area of your PC where the operating system, its applications, related files, and data are stored by default. These drives connect to the IDE/ATA channel connector (or to another drive that is so connected), to a SCSI adapter installed to the expansion bus slots in the motherboard (or to another drive that is), or externally through the USB or IEEE 1394 ports.

Tape drives   Tape drives are used for data backup onto tape cartridges. Tape drives are typically installed to a drive bay inside the PC and connect to the IDE/ATA channel connector (or to another drive that is so connected), to a SCSI adapter installed into the expansion bus slots in the motherboard (or to another drive that is), or externally through the parallel, USB, or IEEE 1394 ports.

Zip drives and others   These are special-format drives, meaning they can be used to copy or back up files to a special type of disk that can typically be read only by other drives of the same type. Examples of these types of drives are Iomega's Zip and Jazz drives, the Castlewood Orb, and the Imation SuperDisk. These drives can attach through the IDE/ATA channel on the motherboard (or to another drive so connected), to a SCSI adapter (or another connected SCSI drive), or externally to the parallel, USB, and IEEE 1394 ports.

Drive-Related Disasters

Overheating and severe power surges (as may happen during a disaster or a closely centered electrical storm) represent some of the main potential for drive-related errors and failures.

Hard drives pose the most concern, because it's on those disks that the greatest amount of original data may be lost. Other types of drives (CD, DVD, floppy, Zip, and so on) are often read-only or are only engaged in recording data to these drives for relatively short periods of time.

You also see errors, damage, and excessive wear caused by poor treatment. An example of this occurs when you turn off your PC during an active Windows session without shutting down the PC, especially when the PC is reading from or writing to these drives. Doing so can crosslink files (where data from two or more files can become jumbled together), create bad clusters where no data can be written (and which the rest of your data must be written around), or cause premature drive death.

Another situation happens with overheating or when the PC case is so full of components and cables that hot air cannot be drawn away from hot-operating components and out through the PC vents. Short-term overheating can lead to strange errors when you try to open, save, or work with data because the system can behave as if it's very confused. Long-term overheating can push delicate components, including drives, past the point of no return, thus placing all the data stored permanently on a hard disk into jeopardy.

User-Input Devices

User-input devices include anything you touch that provides input to a PC:

- Keyboard
- Pointing device (mouse, trackball, other)
- Joystick
- Graphics tablet

Of these, only the keyboard and pointing device are standard equipment. Both devices are most in jeopardy from user carelessness in keeping food and liquids away from them.

User-input devices can attach to the PC in different ways. Traditional keyboards and pointing devices are usually connected to the PS/2 or USB ports positioned at the back of the PC (see Figure 2.9). Traditional joysticks connect through the game port often found on the sound adapter and graphics tablets by way of the serial port at the back of the PC.

However, virtually all user-input devices are now available in USB versions that allow for easy plug-in and removal from the USB ports typically located at the rear (or sometimes at the front) of your PC.

Photo courtesy of Emily Sherrill Weadock

Figure 2.9 *Keyboard and mouse ports.*

User-Input Device-Related Disasters

Any of these user-input devices when immersed in water will likely never work again and must be replaced. A greater concern, since most of these devices can be replaced inexpensively, is whether the damage transfers somehow into the PC.

For example, if you accidentally spill a cup of coffee into your PC keyboard, it's likely that only the keyboard will be affected. Sometimes, you can simply power down your PC, disconnect the keyboard, and turn it upside down so that the liquid drains from the keyboard onto a towel or into a pan. Then you clean the keyboard, let it dry, and return it to service.

In rare cases, however, you might see the keyboard short out, and in turn damage the keyboard controller that's located near where the keyboard plugs into the back of the PC on the motherboard. You can replace the keyboard itself for between $10 and $100, but the keyboard controller usually requires a complete motherboard replacement unless it is socketed.

But most situations you run into with user-input devices are easy to repair: remove the device and replace it with another similar device if it's the only device affected.

TIP *Remember the discussion of USB versions of input devices earlier? One advantage with a USB device is that you can unplug it at any time. I recently toppled an extra-large container of coffee into my keyboard in the middle of writing an e-mail. Normally, I would have to shut down the PC as quickly as possible and then manually remove the keyboard from the back of the PC. But because it was a USB keyboard, I was able to swiftly pull it from the port, flip the keyboard over to drain, and plug in a backup USB keyboard without losing any time or equipment or shutting down.*

External Connections

As mentioned in the section on motherboards, external connections (see Figure 2.10) are anything that can connect to the PC externally.

Photo courtesy of Emily Sherrill Weadock

Figure 2.10 *External ports and connectors.*

External connections include

Serial ports   Serial ports are used for attaching serial devices such as external modems, some pointing devices (mouse, trackball), and digital cameras.

Parallel port(s)   Parallel ports are used for attaching parallel devices such as printers, scanners, and external drives. Parallel ports are also called *printer ports*.

PS/2 connectors   PS/2 connectors are used for attaching standard keyboards and mice.

Universal Serial Bus (USB) ports   USB ports are used for attaching USB devices such as keyboards, cameras, printers, graphics tablets, and external drives and modems.

IEEE 1394 ports   IEEE 1394 ports are used for attaching IEEE 1394 devices such as high-speed external drives, backup equipment, and digital video cameras.

Adapter-based connections   Adapter-based connections are used for adding devices by plugging them into the back of the PC into a specific adapter, for example,

- a network cable into the back of a network adapter
- a phone line into the back of an internal modem
- speaker jacks
- microphones
- Musical Instrument Digital Interface (MIDI) keyboards
- game joysticks into the back of a sound adapter
- the monitor into the connector at the back of a video adapter

External Connection-Related Disasters

Any time you have a device connected to the PC either internally or externally, you run the risk that a problem with that device—through its connection to the PC—could cause a problem with the PC itself. The resulting damage may not always be immediately obvious; in fact, symptoms may occur long enough after the damage that make you believe the two problems (the original damage and the new issue) are completely unrelated.

Here's an example of a perplexing situation that you can be faced with regarding external connections and how they can affect internal components: In October 1989, during the big Loma Prieta earthquake in California's Bay Area, a friend was in the middle of a complicated color brochure printing job as the quake began. Power began to fluctuate and before she could respond by getting her system shut down, the commercial-grade printer she was working with caught fire (probably because of an electrical overload). While the power surge initially only hurt the printer, the problem traveled through the printer cable to the computer where she was managing the print job and completely fried the connection but left the motherboard working. The motherboard worked for a period of time after the power surge.

Within a few weeks, she began to see a sharp rise in crashes, varying error messages, and other problems that made it difficult to perform her work. When she spoke with a PC repair person, she was told that if the motherboard was damaged at all during the power surge, it would have stopped working altogether at the time of the incident. But my friend learned this isn't always true.

After attempting numerous "fixes" such as reformatting her drives and reinstalling everything that did nothing to stabilize her system, I suggested she give serious thought to replacing the motherboard after having it tested for proper electrical activity at a decent repair shop. Sure enough, the testing showed that parts of the motherboard would drop power (as if something was intermittently blocking power), particularly in the area of the original printer connection, which was very close to the area of the motherboard where the CPU and memory are located. Once the motherboard was replaced, all problems ceased.

The Role of BIOS

You may think that your PC really doesn't roar to life until Windows loads. Actually, the PC has a lot of work to do to get to that moment, as you already learned in the section "What Happens When a PC Boots Up." Then, as you'll learn in a moment when reading about the role of the operating system, you'll see that Windows takes over control of your PC once it does load.

So what controls the PC from that first push of the power button to the instant the hourglass on the desktop disappears? Something, after all, has to shepherd all those devices like your keyboard, display, and hard drive into service.

That something is the BIOS, located on a chip on the motherboard, that awakens when power is first supplied to the motherboard after the PC is switched on. Once awake, the BIOS performs an initial inventory of all hardware connected to the PC and manages routines that help bring the hardware online so that the PC bootup process runs smoothly and Windows can indeed load.

In the process of Windows loading, Windows looks to the BIOS for information about that hardware and divides it between the PNP vs. non-PNP hardware explained earlier in this chapter.

BIOS and How Hardware Connects to the PC

When you first install—or reinstall—a troubled device to a PC, the device first communicates with the BIOS, which has the job of fitting it into its master schedule of the other hardware resources.

If the BIOS for some reason—the BIOS has been corrupted, the motherboard is damaged, or the hardware is defective, for example—cannot see the device you've installed or doesn't recognize the connection type the device is connected to, the device will *not* work. In this respect, the BIOS is the first hurdle you have to pass in working with your hardware.

However, BIOSes can be updated and repaired to help a device be recognized and properly installed. BIOS updating is often done through software specifically written for your motherboard and current BIOS type (more about this in Chapter 8, "When Upgrades Go Wrong").

Becoming Familiar with Your BIOS

Make sure you become familiar with your BIOS, especially the settings you can enable/disable or alter within it, before you get too deeply into a situation that requires you to understand the BIOS.

The BIOS can only be accessed by you when the PC is first started. The initial bootup display includes a message stating something like

```
Press <this key> to enter Setup.
```

The exact key or combination of keys you need to press depends on the make and model of your PC. Often, this is the Delete key.

Once pressed, the system should bring up the BIOS configuration window, sometimes called *CMOS Setup*. Your available options depend on the make and age of your BIOS, but you should see a menu of categories like these:

Standard Settings   This category includes date and time settings, drives connected, and basic hardware found.

Advanced Settings   Advanced settings include whether to look at the floppy drive to see if a boot disk is present before booting off the hard drive, cache options, and memory tests.

Bus Settings   This category provides configurable options for tweaking performance regarding the hardware installed into the expansion bus slots.

Integrated Peripherals   This section contains information on whether certain hardware devices and connectors are enabled or disabled, including the USB controller, drive controllers, and the serial and parallel ports.

Power Management   This section contains options for setting or disabling power management features to reduce the power supplied to certain hardware components (monitor, drives, and so on) when the PC is not in active use.

You can use PC information sites such as PC Guide (`www.pcguide.com`) and PCMechanic (`www.pcmechanic.com`) to learn more about these BIOS options.

WARNING *Don't change any of these settings until you become more familiar with what they are and what they do. When prompted, exit the BIOS without making any changes, and the PC will proceed with its usual startup.*

Other Needed BIOS Information

Three important pieces of BIOS information are

- your BIOS type

- its unique identifier (known as the *BIOS identifier string*)

- its version or date of release

This information is crucial for determining whether a BIOS update will help you overcome a particular problem you might encounter.

The easiest way to determine your BIOS information is to look in your PC documentation (where it may or may not be listed). If you bought your PC from a major PC manufacturer such as Dell, you can visit the manufacturer's web site and look up this information by PC model. Calling the manufacturer's support line is another way to get your BIOS information.

A third way is to look at the BIOS information as it's displayed on your monitor right after the PC starts to boot and before Windows loads. The BIOS type (such as AMI, Award, or Phoenix), its date of release, and the very long BIOS identifier string are usually found there. But you may have to press the Pause key to slow down the display.

Once you have that information, you can visit an online resource site such as Motherboard.org (`www.motherboard.org`), plug that number into a manufacturer database, and retrieve more details about your BIOS and your motherboard. You can then go through your PC or motherboard manufacturer or through a specialty site like eSupport.com (`www.mrbios.com`) to determine whether a BIOS upgrade or fix is available for you, along with instructions for how to obtain and install it.

The Changing Role of BIOS

BIOS has always been a major determining factor in how well—or how poorly—a device works with a PC. However, this relationship is changing with the advent of Windows XP because Windows XP can perform some of the actual hardware configuration and setup itself. Let me explain with an example.

You may have noticed that Windows XP allows you to physically install a hard drive to a system and then Windows XP configures it and prepares it for use. This is a rather cool advancement because it saves some clunky interim steps. Earlier versions of Windows required you to do all these other steps between installing a new hard drive and first using it for Windows:

1. Boot the system with a boot disk.

2. Make sure the new drive is detected in BIOS.

3. *Format* the new drive using the commands **FORMAT <drive letter>:** or **FORMAT <drive letter>: /s** to format a drive onto which an operating system would then be installed.

4. *Partition* the new drive using the command **FDISK <drive letter>:** to create a primary partition for the operating system (if needed on the new drive) as well as additional partitions as needed.

5. Install the operating system if this to be the primary hard drive or if you run more than one operating system on your PC.

As you can see, that's a fair number of steps just to get a new drive ready. But Windows XP jumps in to wipe out the need for a boot disk since the XP CD is a boot disk (and its Recovery Console feature, discussed in Chapter 7, can help you post-install) and takes care of the obligatory BIOS detection (XP can work through or around this). Run Setup from the CD, and you have the option of installing XP directly to the new drive, while XP expedites the formatting and partitioning of the drive for you based on information you supply (for example, the size and number of partitions).

In this respect, Windows almost seems to be cutting out the middle man—the BIOS and old hardware prep methods—to make it faster and easier to install new components without great hardware expertise.

The Role of Device Drivers

Think of device drivers as the bridge between the hardware you have and the operating system you're running on your PC.

As the term is used here, device drivers are a special type of software designed to communicate with and manipulate the features of a particular device through the PC's operating system. It's for this reason that having a device known to support your version of Windows (or another operating system) should reduce problems you might otherwise encounter without that support.

Device drivers come in several types; the most common examples are generic device drivers and device-specific device drivers. A generic device driver is one that can be used by almost any piece of hardware meeting some designated standard for that class of hardware. A device-specific driver is one that has been designed for a particular make and model of a device.

By default, Windows comes with a number of device drivers for a wide range of hardware types, manufacturers, and models. When working with a piece of hardware that does not have a default driver available in Windows, it's usually possible to obtain an updated one by visiting the device manufacturer's web site and checking under either Support or Downloads.

> **TIP** *A damaged or outdated device driver is one of the top five reasons a hardware device is either not detected or refuses to operate as it should. It's also one of the most easily solved—by updating the driver.*

The Role of the Operating System

This section explains what an operating system is, what it does, and what its relationship is to your hardware and to the applications installed in it.

> **NOTE** *This book focuses mostly on systems running the Windows operating system for one simple reason: 85–90% of PCs run Windows in one or more versions.*

What an Operating System Is

An operating system is a sophisticated piece of software designed to create and control the environment in which you and your PC work. An operating system serves three major functions:

- The operating system understands the needs of the various components of the PC and communicates with them, the PC's BIOS services, and the hardware controls.

- The operating system provides a way for you, as a user, to enter input to the system by typing commands or clicking on an icon to perform a specific function.

- The operating system communicates information to you in the form of error messages, on-screen prompts (for example, Press *<this button>* to Perform this Function), and other important information.

Operating systems tend to fall into two major categories:

Command-line   A command-line operating system is where commands are typed at a command prompt as you see with the Windows Recovery Console discussed in Chapter 7 and with Windows' predecessor, the DOS operating system.

Graphical user interface (GUI)   In a GUI-based operating system, a pointing device such as a mouse is used to select options by pointing to and clicking icons, filenames, or other objects.

Windows is a GUI.

What an Operating System Does

Only one piece of software is needed universally by almost every computing device in the world: an operating system. It is so named because its job is to control and operate your PC as a total system, from taking information about your PC from BIOS to managing the PC's hardware operations and the other software installed on it to starting up and shutting down your PC.

Since the birth of the first IBM PC in 1981, when the operating system was limited to a few commands typed at a black screen containing only a prompt and could easily fit on a floppy disk (and had to, since hard drives hit the scene much later), the operating system has been growing in power, complexity, and size.

To appreciate how things have changed, let's look at an example. In the early days of the PC, printing was a much tougher job to accomplish for a number of reasons. For one, the PC processor was very slow (under 25MHz). There was no way to print in the background, so once you decided to print, everything on your desktop froze until the slow, clunky process of printing the page or document was done.

But more importantly, printing support wasn't integrated into the operating system as it is today when you go to Windows Control Panel and see the Printers icon sitting there waiting for you. If you had five applications installed on your system and you needed to print from each one, you had to install your printer to each different application rather than just install your printer to Windows, as you do now, and have it automatically available from each Windows application that allows printing.

TIP *The operating system produces some logs—some by default, some that you can turn on—to help diagnose problems during the bootup process or with the initialization of hardware. You'll learn more about these in Chapter 7.*

How the Operating System Works in Connection with Hardware and Applications

From the moment you begin to load an operating system on a PC, it becomes heavily involved in understanding and working with everything already attached or installed to a PC. For example, there are three major phases to a Windows Setup, regardless of the version of consumer Windows being used. These phases are:

1. Collection of data about the system on which it is to install (including detailed information about the attached hardware).

2. Physical copying of the new Windows files to the designated hard drive.

3. PC restarts and the configuration of the new operating system is complete from an installation perspective.

Windows—and its subsystems such as the Windows graphics subsystem described in the section "Video System"—takes its initial information about your hardware from the BIOS and then configures the hardware resources needed for the PNP hardware from those left after the BIOS makes assignments for the non-PNP hardware.

Once a device is properly installed, Windows and its subsystems work through the device drivers for the various pieces of hardware attached to your system to help control the hardware's behavior and its communication with the other PC components.

The Role of the Windows Registry

A core component of the Windows operating system is something called the Windows Registry. This serves as a central index file or database of all the specifics of your system, storing information such as:

- What hardware is attached

- What settings are enabled/disabled for that hardware

- User-configured settings for how the operating system looks and feels to each user authorized to use the PC

- Product ID and software registration numbers

- What applications are installed

- What kinds of files the operating system and its applications can open and work with

Notice that the Registry is keeping track of far more than basic Windows information because it also includes details about hardware and applications. If Windows is operating properly, there is not much you can install, remove, or change about your system that won't be reflected in your Windows Registry.

Did you ever delete a file you thought you didn't need, only to find Windows giving you a warning about the file being missing next time you loaded Windows? It's another example of the integration and interconnectedness of everything on your PC and a reminder that Windows effectively monitors all that you do. You must be aware that each action you take can have effects throughout the system.

You'll learn more about the Registry as you go through this book. This is necessary because you'll see situations in which a piece of hardware or application that you have removed may remain listed in the Registry and potentially interfere with your ability to install other hardware or applications.

The Role of Applications

Regardless of how you use your computer, applications are the meat and potatoes of your PC. Just as an operating system helps your PCs work, your applications help you work, providing an interface to create your documents and files, manipulate images you capture from a digital camera or scanner, write a piece of music, or even play a game (yes, even games are applications).

In the computer industry, applications are called *end-user software* because they are typically designed to be (relatively) easy to use by someone regardless of his or her level of knowledge of the PC.

Let's dig a bit deeper.

What an Application Is

An application can be either a single program (for example, Microsoft Word) or a suite of related programs tied together into one package (for example, Microsoft Office) that is designed to let you learn, produce, look up information, or have fun.

What an application can't do is run entirely on its own; it needs an operating system to run. Applications are written for specific platforms, meaning types of computer setups. Examples of two different platforms are Windows Consumer (Windows 95/98/Me/XP Home Edition) and Windows Professional (Windows NT/2000/XP Professional). The majority of people today use the Windows Consumer platform, so it's not surprising that most applications are written to run under Windows Consumer.

These programs usually focus on a particular area and include these major types of products:

- Word processors
- Databases
- Spreadsheets
- Almost anything else that isn't a system tool

NOTE *Is an operating system an application? No. Most software is divided into two main categories: system software and application software. System software is any type of software or utility that acts to specifically control or manage the PC itself. This includes operating systems and PC utility packages, as well as essential programming tools for software developers. An application, by contrast, cannot run on its own without an operating system.*

How an Application Installs

It's easy to take for granted the process of installing a new application to your Windows PC because—as with other elements discussed in this book—so much happens that you won't normally see. You'll learn more about these hidden tasks in the next section on integration. Right now, let's look at the typical steps when installing an application. These are:

1. Run the application's Setup.

2. Setup launches an installation wizard that helps you configure the way you want the application to reside on your system (for example, in what folder it should install itself).

3. Setup checks to make sure your system meets the minimum requirements for its installation, that you have enough hard drive space and memory available, that your CPU is powerful enough, and that you're running a compatible operating system.

4. Setup looks to see if another version of this program is already on your system. If it finds one, it asks if you want to install this new version as an upgrade, completely updating your current application.

5. Setup may also check to make sure that core Windows files are present in case they need to be installed or reinstalled (see the next section, "How an Application Integrates").

6. Setup begins preparing your system to accept the application and begins copying files from the disk or CD.

7. The application is registered with one or more entries into your Windows Registry.

8. Once everything is copied, Setup asks you whether you want to add this application to a specific group (for example, Games), and whether you want it to come up on startup, meaning that each time Windows reloads, the application will automatically load on the desktop.

9. Setup notifies you that the installation is successful and that it is now ready to use.

How an Application Integrates

Many if not most Windows applications are developed using certain program development standards that take into account the common files, features, and functions of the Windows operating system. The developers try to match the keystrokes and overall characteristics of major functions (such as printing) throughout all the applications you can install and run. In this way, you can press Ctrl+P in many different applications to initiate printing or Ctrl+O to open files.

Remember how you're always warned to close all other programs before you install a new piece of software? Many people ignore this advice, but the need to close other applications is apparent once you understand the complexity of an application installation.

As I said, these applications are based on something called the Windows *Application Programming Interface (API)* that try to take advantage of what is already in Windows to help them install and work. The applications may be looking to access or even modify certain core files installed and used as part of Windows—as well as by other applications—as the application installs. If other applications have these core files open, the files may be locked so that the new application can't use them and then can't install properly. If the new application isn't locked out of these files, some confusion can result because two applications are trying to use or modify the same files at the same time. For this reason, you and your PC are better off if you close all other applications before installing a new one.

You should also know that applications don't always install in a tidy fashion. By this, I mean that an application doesn't just install itself to its own program folder, although it does that, too. Many applications copy files to a number of different locations, including to main folders under Windows. This can make it very difficult for even an experienced technician to hunt down every file associated with a particular application.

Another example of integration is seen in the Windows Registry, because information about the application, the types of files the application works with, and the way you've configured the application to work is stored to entries in the Registry. It's for this reason that you don't just delete applications you no longer want; you must uninstall them using the Add/Remove Programs icon in Control Panel, and follow the wizard to select the application components you want to remove.

Of course, there's a significant benefit from the application's integration into the Registry. For one, other applications may be able to work in correlation with your new application. For example, Word 2000, when I need to add a document to it that I have digitized using my flatbed scanner, automatically knows to load my scanner interface application to help me accomplish this task. Also, when you go to open a file used by the new application, you'll find that Windows has registered—in the Registry—the types of file formats the new application will work with. Thus, you simply click the file to open it and Windows knows to automatically load the application registered to work with that file format.

The message to take from all of this is (again) that your PC as a whole—from hardware to software to operating system—is a composite of everything you've installed to it. Take care not to take actions that seem like they solve one problem when they may create other problems. After all, you don't want to create a disaster or compound an existing one.

The Pride and Pitfalls of Today's Integrated PC

Now that you have an idea of the interconnectedness of hardware, software, and the operating system within your PC, you should be able to appreciate two main points.

First, integration throughout the PC makes your keyboard-based lives easier because you don't have to know as much about installing hardware, or applications, or configuring your systems:

- You can install a printer once and have it available immediately to dozens of applications you have installed that allow you to print.

- You can plug in a digital camera and immediately use your photos in a document you're creating in Microsoft Word, a web page you're designing in FrontPage or DreamWeaver, or in an Internet chat program where you can share your pictures with others.

- You can upgrade your web browser and find that every time you click a link to automatically load your web browser, the new link loads and picks up the preferences and favorite sites listing from your old one.

- As you learned in the BIOS section, you can even take a new hard drive right out of the box and physically install it to your PC, and Windows XP will take care of the rest, saving you many steps of normal drive preparation.

But the second major point is that these interrelationships and conveniences may make it more difficult when you have to analyze and troubleshoot your system to turn a disaster into a recovery.

Think back for a moment about the video system discussed earlier. You don't have just one component responsible for providing your display but four. If your system takes some type of hit that results in serious display problems, how do you know which of these four components is the guilty party? Did lightning zap the monitor or somehow affect the video adapter installed within the PC? Did the fact that you used System Restore (the feature in Windows Millennium and later that allows you to return your system back to a "safe" point before a problem developed) after the incident mean that your video device driver was changed back to an older version that causes problems with your display? Or is there something amiss with Windows itself that also affects your PC picture?

A good troubleshooter, as you'll learn in Chapter 7, isn't someone who necessarily knows everything. Instead, it's someone who takes into account all these possibilities and then examines them systematically starting with the most likely suspect and working down the list of possibilities until he or she finds the problem and its solution.

This will be your challenge as you read through this book and beyond when you encounter a situation that requires serious troubleshooting and recovery. If you're lucky enough to avoid all disasters (and the next few chapters should help you toward that end), you'll at least come away with a lot of new information and great new sleuthing skills.

But before we jump ahead, let me offer one more example of how integration can raise the level of complication.

Today's Integrated Motherboards

All motherboards are integrated, meaning they have more than one chipset and component directly installed in them, working together. In this case, however, an *integrated motherboard* is one that incorporates into its design the features and functions of one or more other components such as a video adapter, sound adapter, modem, or network card, usually available as separate cards installed to ports or connectors on the motherboard.

This kind of integration isn't new. It was done before, as recently as the early 1990s, to try to make PCs more affordable for the masses at a time when a very good desktop system started at near $3,000. Mobile computers such as laptops often use integrated motherboards, then and now. But as the 1990s progressed, integrated motherboards were largely abandoned for "good" desktop PCs because integrated components such as video and audio were not always of the same quality as those components that required a separate, installed adapter. Now, the more comfortable users become with their PCs and the more demands they place on their PCs, the more likely it is that they'll want to customize their PC components.

However, the concept of integration has been embraced again as a means of lowering the total cost of ownership (TCO), a figure used by businesses to describe the actual cost of owning a computer over time. PC manufacturers and resellers, most working with razor-thin profit margins, pay less to buy these integrated boards. Now, you're seeing them on all types of systems rather than just on budget PCs.

On the one hand, such integration certainly lowers the price of installing separate adapters (and at least in theory, frees up some bus slots for installing other adapter-style devices). But it's a situation where you put many of your PC hardware eggs into one basket. An electrical surge to the motherboard, for example, wipes out not just the motherboard but everything directly mounted in it such as integrated video or networking adapters. This happens with adapters installed to non-integrated motherboards, too, but it's statistically less likely to fry everything else outside of a catastrophic motherboard event.

Also, if one of the integrated components on an integrated motherboard fails or is damaged, you may have to replace the motherboard, even if other integrated components work fine. Finally, some integrated motherboards allow you to install a physical adapter and disable the onboard (meaning integrated into the motherboard) component, while others do not. Using video as an example, if your video chipset integrated into the motherboard dies or seriously distorts your display, you may not be able to install a separate video card adapter to get past this. You're stuck with replacing the motherboard.

Replacing the motherboard isn't the end of the world. But in the best scenario, even with good electronics or computer shops nearby, the likelihood is slim that you can replace the motherboard in less than a day or two. A colleague who does this type of work tells me that even with overnight delivery of parts, a PC stays at his shop for an average of four days for a motherboard replacement. That's something to think about as you move into preparing a disaster plan in Chapter 5, "Drafting Your Disaster Recovery Plan," especially if you depend on your PC for your livelihood.

When you reach Chapter 6, "Transforming Yourself into a Smart Troubleshooter: Detecting, Analyzing, and Diagnosing," you'll get into the real meat of smart troubleshooting, using this chapter as your primer on the parts of a PC.

However, I would be remiss if I didn't describe the many ways you can protect your PC from the types of damage that can befall it from man-made and human errors and from the external influences you and your PC may work under. Move on to Chapter 3 to learn more.

CHAPTER 3

Prevention: Limiting Your Risks

Common sense—not a computer degree—tells you that there is one best way to deal with a disaster.

Don't get yourself into one in the first place.

Unfortunately, you can't always avoid all the potential hazards, but you can certainly take measures designed to reduce

- conditions that might contribute to a disaster

- the degree of your losses should you experience one.

Toward that end, I've devoted this chapter to what could best be described as PC health and the steps you can take to keep it out of harm's way. That harm can be a disaster, but it's actually more likely to be misuse. Users are, after all, sometimes their PC's worst enemy, and they're far more likely to strike than a tsunami, a tornado, or a terrorist.

I don't use the word "health" glibly either because you need a system that is both protected and in good operating order or you risk one of the most common kinds of disaster: hardware that fails prematurely from abuse. You can't afford a dead CPU or a dying hard drive any more when you're on a big deadline for school, work, or a community project than you can when rains penetrate your roof or your part of the power grid goes down.

Pair the recommendations in this chapter with the disaster recovery plan you design and implement in the next chapter, and you should substantially trim your concerns about your PC and its files and applications.

The Best Practices for Operating Your PC

Operating your PC means more than sitting at the keyboard or clicking the mouse. It also means following good usage procedures and creating the right conditions to allow your PC to run well while also protecting it from unnecessary harm.

This section tackles two of the most common areas where bad habits can result in human-created problems that could lead to disasters: startup/shutdown and making changes to your system.

NOTE *"Every five minutes you invest keeping your system in good shape and preventing the loss of files can save you as many as five hours in troubleshooting and recovery," a wise old tech once told me. In my experience, he was right.*

Avoiding Unnecessary Restarts

Some of the greatest effort your total PC system undergoes happens when you hit the power button to turn it on. A close second occurs again when you shut the system down.

Motors, fans, chips, drives, and so on must initiate, and they begin to warm as they do so because electricity is flowing to them after being converted by the power supply. As a result, there's a fair amount of stress on the equipment—stress that is only exacerbated if you don't operate the system as it was designed to be operated.

Some hardware specialists will tell you that every time you boot or reboot your system, you're reducing its life expectancy (although the same could be said about celebrating birthdays). But whether that is completely accurate or not, you're certainly putting your computer chips and other components through unnecessary stress if you create situations where you have to reboot frequently.

In Chapter 8, "When Upgrades Go Wrong," Chapter 9, "Stabilizing Your Operating System," and Chapter 12, "PC Performance: Diagnosing, Monitoring, and Troubleshooting," you'll get some experience in situations that can cause a PC to run badly enough to require extra restarts, as well as recommendations for resolving them.

How Often You Need to Restart

If you're someone who usually leaves your PC running all the time, you may be wondering how often you need to restart Windows.

Clearly, you need to restart it when the system is frozen or hung, or when a situation presents itself (such as installing a new application) that requires or could benefit from a refreshed desktop.

As a user of consumer Windows, you may find that you can go no more than a few days or a week without restarting Windows. This depends on the version you're using (Windows XP gives me more time between needed restarts than earlier versions), your computer setup (how much memory and virtual memory you have, for example), and how you use your system. Users who rarely use their PCs for more than e-mail and light web browsing may go weeks before they notice the common warning signs of a system needing a restart, which include the following:

- A growing sluggishness (windows and files opening more slowly) is noticeable throughout the system.

- The display becomes slow to refresh and/or you notice an increasing distortion as you work, where pages appear to keep the "garbage" from previous screens.

- You begin receiving error messages and warnings that Windows is low on virtual memory or there is not enough memory.

Be aware that as Windows runs over the course of many hours and many days and as files and programs are opened and closed, you can end up with waning desktop resources. There are many reasons for this, including the fact that just because you close a program or a file does not mean that Windows automatically frees up the working overhead space used by that file or program.

Shutting Down and Starting Up Properly

You've all done it: accidentally disconnected the PC in the middle of a session, turned off the machine by mistake, or pressed the Reset button rather than wait the few moments it takes to go through proper shutdown in Windows. You already learned this can be tough on the hardware, but it can be tough on the rest of your system as well.

The Windows shutdown procedure isn't just what you see on the screen. As with other processes, a number of functions occur both at and below the surface: windows open and applications close, you're prompted to save unsaved files, open caches are shut, and any modifications made to the system since your last startup are verified so they can be applied when you next start the system.

In this respect, the shutdown process is intimately tied to the startup process because it paves the way for a successful next session that recognizes any changes you may have made to Windows, to hardware, and/or to applications.

By forcing the system into a premature shutdown, you play something akin to roulette because you never know what important function Windows won't get to complete or what problems this may create for you later on. Thus, you want to shut down Windows using the correct procedure rather than going the faster, unprescribed route.

> **TIP** *Are you experiencing problems with shutdown on your system? Microsoft Knowledgebase has a number of good articles to help. Visit them at* http:// support.microsoft.com/default.aspx, *specify your version of Windows, and search on "shutdown". I find article Q308029 very helpful for pointing out resources in overcoming shutdown issues in Windows XP, for example.*

Turn It Off or Leave It On?

One of the five most common questions about good PC use is whether you should leave your PC on all the time or turn it off when it's not in use. I believe the answer depends on your individual circumstances. I know many people, for example, who do a great deal of work on a computer—but only for two days or evenings each week. These folks concentrate their time spent at the keyboard, and I can't see leaving the PC running for three or four days with no one using it at all.

Also, I would not leave an unprotected PC on and unattended for many hours every day or night if you tend to experience a high number of power problems. Even with protection, you run some risk. Here at my office, with decent-quality surge protection devices, I've run into situations where I wished I had simply turned off and disconnected the PC. One involved a fire caused when a surge suppressor took the wallop of a surge sent by the explosion of a transformer at the local power substation. Another involved an older office space where ancient wiring killed several different devices before I called an electrician.

However, it's usually pretty safe to leave your PC on most of the time if

- You use your PC frequently (every day, especially if you tend to get on and off the system throughout the day).

- Your equipment is well-protected.

- Your area doesn't tend to suffer from heavy storms or frequent power problems such as blackouts and brownouts.

Before moving on, let me tell you a little bit about Advanced Power Management (APM) and power-saving hardware features that can make it more attractive to keep your PC turned on rather than switched off.

Advanced Power Management and Power-Saving Features

In the last chapter, I told you that there is a movement within the computer industry for an "always on" PC that simply goes to sleep whenever you aren't actively using it. The initial stages of this technology have been with us for a few years, although—for reasons I'll explain in a moment—it seems to be a masterpiece still in the making.

In Windows, the control feature for this is called Advanced Power Management (the Power Options in Control Panel—or Power Management in Windows 98), but this is an offshoot of a PC industry standard specification called the Advanced Configuration and Power Interface (ACPI). The idea behind ACPI is that the power and level of activity for certain types of hardware devices can be monitored and managed through the operating system rather than having the user turn devices on and off or having the BIOS and Windows fight for control.

ACPI support is usually part of the motherboard's BIOS, and this feature can be turned on and off by going into BIOS setup (as discussed in the previous chapter), selecting the power management menu, and following on-screen directions for changing it from disabled to enabled, and vice versa.

Windows XP, when it first installs, looks to see whether ACPI is enabled on the PC. If it's not, XP automatically installs support for APM so you can use some of these power management features anyway.

It's likely that you see this feature each time you shut down your PC because it's APM/ACPI that allows you to make a selection from your keyboard that physically turns off the hardware. If you don't have APM enabled (out of choice, because you're using a much older PC that doesn't support it or due to a problem with your system), your PC is left on at the "It is now safe to turn off your computer" message after you choose Shut Down. You also see it when you go to shut down your Windows PC and see the Standby option listed as one of the options.

All this does is put some of your PC into a lower power state, which can shave a little off the electrical bills and computer wear.

If you want to try APM, read the next section first. Then you can turn this feature on (if it's not turned on already) by following these steps:

1. From Control Panel, click Power Options.

2. Click to Enable Power Management. (For those readers using earlier versions of Windows, choose the APM tab and then perform this.) Click OK.

You can then use the Power Schemes tab illustrated in Figure 3.1 to choose your options, some of which apply more to mobile computers running on batteries than to desktop systems.

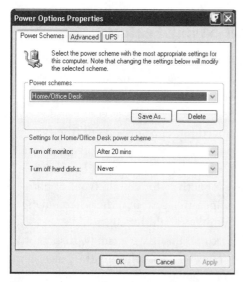

Figure 3.1 *Windows power management options*

The Perils of Power Management

Earlier, I referred to ACPI and power management as a masterpiece in the making. By this, I mean that not every piece of hardware, every hardware driver, and every PC setup plays nicely together with Windows when you actively use APM or ACPI. This is particularly true if the hardware involved is more than a few years old, because it predates some of the standards being used now.

The result is too often a situation that locks up the PC or fails to bring the display back when trying to come back from a reduced power state. These reduced power states are the Standby option under Windows shutdown or hibernation, which is used mostly for mobile computers such as laptops. Typically, you have to reboot the PC (another improper shutdown) to get control of your PC back from power management; this rather defeats one of the purposes of sending it to lower power mode in the first place.

NOTE *Power problems occur even in new devices. My recently issued laptop hangs on Standby power mode, and it won't power off or on until I remove the laptop battery. From what I've read, this isn't an isolated incident.*

But there are two pieces of good news here.

First, power management problems usually show themselves soon after ACPI or APM is enabled. If your PC purrs along perfectly, you're among the majority for whom power management works decently.

Second, if you're in the slight minority (and informally, my own support experience says it's about 40–60 percent) for whom power management doesn't play well, you can turn it off again. And you should disable it again if you find yourself forced into rebooting the system each time it goes into low power mode.

TIP *If you have a recent vintage PC that doesn't work well with APM/ACPI enabled, contact your PC manufacturer for ideas. A BIOS update or a patch is sometimes available that will reduce or eliminate the problems.*

Making Acceptable Changes

What seems like a small, insignificant change you make to your system can often blow up into a disaster all on its own. Nor will you always know that a modification you made is responsible for a problem because time may elapse before the issue makes itself known to you. By the time it does, you may not remember that you changed something, let alone the specific changes you made.

Although Chapter 6, "Transforming Yourself into a Smart Troubleshooter: Detecting, Analyzing, and Diagnosing," covers this concept and more, let me share some good advice for handling system changes the way a seasoned tech who wants to avoid problems would. These recommendations are

- Make a backup of whatever you're changing before you change it.

- Never make changes or perform installations or removals when you're very tired or otherwise "under the weather." It will be harder to remember what you did.

- Think about the change before you do it. Can you think of any problems it might create?

- Never add more than one piece of hardware or software or make more than one major change at a time.

- Test the installation or change immediately. If you can't get it to work properly, undo the change you made before you do anything else.

WARNING *You may not always be aware that changes are being made to your system because they may be made automatically. For example, many software packages, when installed, automatically modify your configuration to make that package run more efficiently.*

- Make certain the previous installation is working well before you install the next.

- It doesn't hurt to jot down a few notes about each thing you do in a notebook or even in a word processing document you can treat as a PC log. This way, you can refer back to it later. It can refresh your memory about where you had both successes and obstacles.

TIP *One way to get around automatic changes made during software installation is to always choose the Custom installation method when adding new software to your PC. The Custom option usually steps you through all the possible options, allowing you to monitor what it intends to do as well as (often) reject a particular change the package wants to make.*

Maintenance: An Ounce of Prevention

In my experience, folks tend to fall into two types of categories with regard to PC maintenance: those who maintain their PCs perfectly with never a file out of place or a hint of dust in the keyboard spaces and those—like myself—who operate on the chaos principle that leaves them having to clean up after their slovenly ways.

Maintaining Software

Walk into the utility section of any large software or computer store and you'll likely find at least a half dozen choices for programs that promise to make your system easier to manage or otherwise take care of some important function you may not know how to do. Likewise, many online download sites offer both free software as well as demos and shareware versions of some utilities.

Some of the functions these packages perform include:

- Finding and removing duplicate files

- Removing unused software and device drivers

- Executing performance tests on various parts of your system, including memory, video, and hard drive tests

- Disk cleanup and optimization (where the drive's file storage gets rebuilt for better organization)

- Scanning for and removing viruses or other contaminants

WARNING *Make sure that any utilities you use specifically state that they work with your version of Windows. Utilities written for earlier versions of Windows may not load at all; if they do, they can sometimes have catastrophic effects because of incompatibilities with the operating system.*

Exactly which packages you want to have for your maintenance collection depends on your needs.

Certainly, the most important needs here are removing unused software (which you can do yourself through Add/Remove Programs in Control Panel), disk cleanup and optimization, and virus scanning. Of the two functions you need software to handle, disk cleanup and optimization is available in Windows itself, as you'll learn in the next section. This leaves you with the need for anti-virus software, which I'll discuss later in this chapter.

NOTE *While today's hard drives make it possible to store an incredible amount of material, be careful about clogging your system up with thousands of temporary files created as interim working files while you're working in applications and utilities, as well as when you're browsing the Internet.*

Disk Maintenance Utilities that Come with Windows

Let's take a moment to look at some of the software that comes with Windows to help you maintain the file structure health of your hard drive, one of the hardest working pieces of hardware on your system.

The three major tools—most of them scaled-down versions of other products—included in Windows XP (and most other versions of Windows) are

- CHKDSK (for Check Disk) in Windows XP and ScanDisk for Windows Millennium and earlier

- Disk Cleanup

- Disk Defragmenter (disk optimizer)

ScanDisk

As its name implies, the job of ScanDisk is to look carefully at the overall structure and working of your hard drive and analyze it for problems. ScanDisk runs automatically on the next start whenever your system hasn't shut down properly. An improper shutdown is one of the culprits in creating file and disk confusion since not all open files may get saved and closed before the system is turned off or restarted. You should always let ScanDisk run to completion when this occurs because it may save you from experiencing problems with files or the drive itself.

In earlier versions of Windows, ScanDisk is available as an option under the System Tools menu (from Windows Start ➤ Programs ➤ Accessories). In Windows XP, ScanDisk isn't directly supported, having been replaced by an updated version of an older tool called CHKDSK (for Check Disk), which I'll tell you about in later chapters when we talk about more serious drive issues.

TIP *If you're eager to check out CHKDSK before we get to it, go to Windows Start, choose Help & Support, and search for "CHKDSK" to get a list of switches and options available to you when using it.*

Disk Cleanup

Are you one of the roughly 20–40 percent of users who opt to use special disk cleanup software such as Clean Sweep or the cleanup tools in Norton System Works to remove temporary, duplicate, and no-longer-needed files? It's understandable why these packages seem attractive because your system works with hundreds of more files than you create yourself. It makes it impossible to know all the files that install with each program, let alone know for sure which ones you still need and which ones you can safely toss.

Yet my experience in working with people who've watched these programs remove vital files and cause incapacitating system problems keeps me from recommending them. It's not that these utilities themselves are bad or necessarily work improperly. It is, however, tough for any software to be able to get this delicate process of sorting out the needed files from the not-perfect files each time it's run. After all, almost every PC is different in its hardware, its software, how you've configured them for use, and so on. This type of software often has to make an edu-cated guess on what you should dump, and sometimes it guesses wrong.

You can opt instead to use the simpler Disk Cleanup included in Windows Start ➤ Programs ➤ Accessories ➤ System Tools ➤ Disk Cleanup, which cleans up temporary Internet files, other temporary files on your disk created while using applications, and any unneeded/unused compo-nents. You can also empty the files in your Recycle Bin (the repository of files deleted in Win-dows) from Disk Cleanup.

NOTE *If the temporary Internet files grow to represent a large number of files, they can interfere with your disk operation but more likely, they'll interfere with your ability to move about easily in your Web browser.*

Let's say you want to remove all your temporary Internet files from your C drive. You take the following steps:

1. From Windows Start, select Programs ➤ Accessories ➤ System Tools ➤ Disk Cleanup.

2. From Disk Cleanup, select the drive you want to clean (choose C:) and click OK.

3. From the Disk Cleanup tab, click to check Temporary Internet Files in the list of avail-able cleanup options (any other files checked will also be processed). You can click View Files to see what's included in your temporary Internet files, too. Then click OK.

4. When asked to confirm your choice, click OK.

Disk Defragmenter

Often called Defrag, the Disk Defragmenter is a disk-optimization utility that attempts to organize your hard drive's contents and eliminate unused space that's trapped between files written to that drive.

To use Disk Defragmenter, take the following steps:

1. Quit all open programs and files. Any open files or programs can cause Disk Defragmenter to repeatedly stop and restart its processing.

2. From Windows Start, choose Programs ➤ Accessories ➤ System Tools ➤ Disk Defragmenter.

3. From the Disk Defragmenter window, select the drive you want to check, and then click one of the following options:

   Analyze   Look at the hard drive without moving files.

   Defragment   Analyze and begin moving files for optimization.

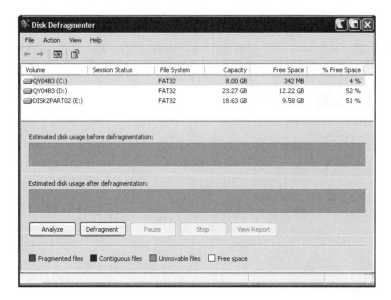

Task Scheduler

You don't have to work at remembering to perform certain tasks as part of basic maintenance. You can use Scheduled Tasks in Windows to automate these jobs and many other functions.

Let's walk through an example of the steps you need to take to automate your disk cleanup so that it happens once a week:

1. From Windows Control Panel, choose Scheduled Tasks.

2. From Scheduled Tasks, click Add Scheduled Task, which initiates the wizard to help step you through. Click Next.

3. Select the program you want to run (Disk Cleanup) from the list of applications provided. Click Next.

4. Provide a custom name for the task (if desired) and click the desired frequency at which you want to run Disk Cleanup (weekly). Click Next.

5. Select your start time and the day of the week you want this task to run.

6. Click Finish.

Maintaining Hardware

Believe it or not, one of the best things you can do to maintain your hardware is to keep your PC work area physically clean. The less dust, debris, smoke, and food in the area, the better.

TIP *Always keep hardware not currently in use stored in its anti-static bag or case to prevent dust, dirt, and moisture from collecting on it. Never install a dusty or dirty part into the PC.*

On a regular basis you should clean around the PC, performing at least these basic chores:

-   Promptly remove any food, dishes, or liquids.

-   Overturn the keyboard to let dust and debris shake out into a wastebasket.

-   Wipe the monitor screen down with a soft, *dry*, dust-free cloth. You can buy screen wipes but you may need to shop around to find a type you like and that doesn't produce streaks.

-   Make sure nothing is blocking the PC vents (including the vents on the monitor and any peripherals). If the vents appear dusty, remove the dust with the PC off so the loose dust isn't sucked into the case.

-   Again with the PC off, remove dust and debris from the vicinity of the desk/workstation area.

-   Store loose disks away in their proper locations; you should wipe dusty CDs and DVDs down with a soft, *dry* cloth.

- Wipe down the mouse pad and check the bottom of the mouse for dust or debris.

- Keep cables and cords organized and out of the way; use twine or non-metal ties to secure them, if desired.

NOTE *Chapter 11, "Avoiding Power and Overheating Problems," describes how to clean inside your PC to make sure dust isn't heating up your adapters and your fans aren't blocked by debris. This should be done at least once a year, and more often if you operate the PC in an environment with a lot of smoke, grease, dirt, or particulate matter.*

Cleaning Up the Environment

You already know that your work environment plays a major role in the quality of your life and work. Your work environment also affects your PC setup, and it can impact your productivity as well as the life span of your equipment. This section looks at some of the major environmental factors and asks you to look at your PC setup area with a new, analytical eye.

Finding the Best Location

For too many users, the "best location" for a PC is wherever there's an available outlet and enough free surface space. In other words, users often don't give the subject a great deal of thought. After they get the system set up and working, they often don't give the space much thought at all.

But they should, because location of the PC can matter, especially in a physical disaster. The location of your PC also help ward off some disasters-in-the-making created by the workspace.

The best way to approach this is for you to leave your PC setup (if you're sitting right there), and enter the room again, asking yourself the following questions:

What kind of platform does your PC rest upon?   PCs are sometimes set up on flimsy card tables, frail antique writing desks, and even heavy-duty boxes. However, you drop your risk potential significantly by setting up your PC on a stable surface large enough to accommodate the equipment without any parts overhanging the surface, putting them in danger of being knocked off.

Is your PC located near a window?   The problem here is two-fold: a computer visible from a window is more likely to become the target of thieves (another type of disaster), and it makes the PC more vulnerable if a storm or other factor breaks the window. But simply leaving a window open, whether it rains directly onto the PC or not, can increase the ambient humidity to the point where some parts of the computer will not work properly, including the monitor and PC power supply. A PC in a sunny window runs a greater risk of being affected by overheating from direct sunlight.

Is your PC directly beneath—or within the path—of weighty objects?   Heavily laden shelves, filing cabinets, and other weighty objects can topple onto your PC if the wind blows in a window, an earthquake strikes, or even a big dog or teenager rumbles through the room. Try to situate the PC where it runs little—or at least less—risk of being the victim of toppling furniture and shelves.

Is there a heat source near your PC?   This isn't a good idea, even in a cold room in winter. A heat source can cause the PC to overheat at some times, and in that cold room, this causes too much temperature variation. The dry heat that often blasts from a radiator or furnace vent may also reduce the life of components and cause cables to dry and crack.

Is your PC sandwiched into a tiny space, with peripherals or parts stacked atop one another?   Most PC equipment isn't designed to stack well. Consider adding a tier shelf where you can store speakers and other devices you don't need right next to you on the desk. Also be sure there is decent airflow around the PC case vents to prevent overheating.

Is your PC set up in a high traffic area?   You increase your chances of man-made disasters, not to mention idle fingers playing at the keyboard, when a PC is so readily accessible.

Is your PC located in a room where less cautious types—such as very small children and pets—have free, unattended access?   Even a small cat (mine, for example) can topple a PC tower case, and toddlers with juice cups and melting ice pops can cause more than a little chaos.

Is there a quick, efficient way to kill power to your PC if needed?   As you'll learn a bit more in this chapter and in depth in Chapter 11, there are situations in which you may need to kill power very quickly (such as with a brownout or rocking power that goes on-off-on-off). It behooves you to have the PC connected to a power source that allows you to shut everything down speedily.

How is your PC plugged in?   A PC is a sensitive—and expensive—compilation of chips and circuitry. Don't defeat its grounding (the third prong on the plug end) by plugging it into a two-prong extension cord or into an overloaded outlet. Calling an electrician may be cheaper than a problem caused by overloaded wiring.

If your PC is in an office setting, where are the sprinklers?   Countless offices have PCs set up directly beneath sprinklers mounted in the ceiling. In a fire, this would be bad enough, but sprinklers often get set off accidentally.

NOTE *Location is a concern for laptops and handheld computers, too. While commercials and ads love to show someone using their expensive mobile computer while sitting on a sandy beach as the tide is starting to come in, these are people who may not be able to use their mobiles the next day. One good breeze begins to deposit particles of sand and beads of moisture into the keypad and onto the display screen that can work their way into the PC as you swap out floppy disks and CDs. Be smart about where you use your mobile computing devices.*

Is your PC being exposed to anything harsh like smoke, ash, and grease?   Because you set up your PCs virtually anywhere, many systems get positioned in or near a kitchen in the trail taken by greasy smoke from the stove, and likewise for other types of work areas. If you do this, you'll open your PC one day to find some of that grease is now layered atop some of your components such as installed adapters. If you have very bad karma, you'll also discover tiny flying insects met their final resting place on top of that greasy dust coating your components.

Likewise, a PC positioned near a woodstove or fireplace or used by a heavy smoker can increase the amount of unwelcome particles that end up being pulled in by the PC vents and deposited within your system. While a dear friend of mine loves to joke that the grease and ash inside his PC case helps his system run at peak efficiency, it really doesn't.

WARNING *In a fire situation, kill power to the PC ASAP because continued electricity can feed the fire. Never throw water on a fire arising from or next to your PC. Use a fire extinguisher designed for electrical fires.*

Is the room equipped with standard safety devices?

It's wise to have at least the following located near the PC in the room where it is used:

- smoke detector (A carbon monoxide detector is good, too, but for your needs rather than the PC's.)

- fire extinguisher rated for electrical fires

- flashlight

TIP *Worried about fire? Keep combustible materials away from your immediate PC work area, and avoid placing lots of paper right around the PC. Many people thoughtlessly place paper on top of their monitors or other hardware blocking vents, and are surprised to find how hot their hardware becomes.*

TIP *Want more ideas for trying to keep your PC area safe? Many home improvement centers and hardware stores, along with your local home/office insurance agent and your electric company, have brochures that can help you design a safer work area.*

Getting the Temperature Right

A little more than a decade ago, more than one popular name brand model of PC would experience serious—and often bizarre—problems once the ambient room temperature started edging up over 75 degrees Fahrenheit. On some systems, the keyboard would appear to become confused because you would type one key and a different character—often one of the so-called garbage characters because they weren't letters or numbers but symbols—appeared on the screen. Or you would try to open a file and receive a seek error from the operating system, as if the hard drive was confused, too.

WARNING *Most electronics are meant to be operated at a normal room temperature (65–78 degrees Fahrenheit).*

Some things have changed since then. More homes and offices have air conditioning to keep high temperatures more moderate, for one. PC architecture and hardware design tends to be a bit more cognizant of the potential for overheating. One evolution is that PCs tend to be more energy efficient than they were 10 years ago. Also, current PCs typically feature more internal fans than they once did in order to push hot air away from components such as the CPU and your video adapter's graphics processor.

However, that said, users are also installing more devices within their PCs that can seriously heat up the interior of a PC case. Many of the hottest video adapters in terms of popularity have traditionally produced the most heat. Not all video adapters ship with an onboard fan (although many do), and even with their own fan, they can still raise internal temperatures.

In Chapter 11, you'll learn more about reducing the internal temperature, so let's focus on room temperature here because environmental temperature affects the PC. A PC operating in a particularly warm room will draw very warm air in through its vents to mix with the already hot air within the PC, so you increase the chance that you will start to see symptoms of your PC overheating.

The initial effects of this overheating are apt to be temporary, such as garbage on the screen or drive errors or hardware not being properly detected. The symptoms should disappear after the PC has been turned off and allowed to cool for a period of time. Cumulatively, however, this overheating stands a high probability of permanently affecting chip life and drive reliability.

For this reason, if you don't have air conditioning available in your PC area during a period of extreme heat, you may want to relocate the PC to a cooler spot in your home or office. You can also avoid using the PC during the hottest times of the day

But overheating is just one of the issues surrounding environmental temperature. Operating a PC in a particularly cold spot is also not good for the system. For years, my mechanic kept his office PC in a completely unheated corner of his garage, and for years, he experienced some type of PC equipment failure each winter.

However, the real killer of electronics, especially those involved in a PC, is a situation in which temperatures can widely vary. For this reason, unless you happen to live in a climate where temperatures and conditions almost always remain very moderate, it usually isn't wise to place a PC in a room without some type of climate control (heating and cooling).

At very low temperatures, you can get such chilling of the metal and other parts that you'll see condensation (moisture beads) form as the unit begins to warm up either because it has been turned on or because the ambient room temperature is rising. Moisture and electricity are a bad combination and can kill your PC either very quickly or very slowly.

In the Not So Distant Past

In the days when companies needed huge room-sized or warehouse-sized computer setups costing millions of dollars to accomplish just some of what can be done today on leaner, meaner, even desktop-sized systems, businesses went to extreme measures to keep their computer environments optimal.

Many built refrigeration/cooling units into the walls, ceilings, and floors of computer centers to be sure that these massive systems could continue to operate. And these systems liked it cold, too. I worked as an IBM computer operator in college, and on the hottest summer nights I would be huddled over my terminal rubbing my ice-blue–tinged hands together for warmth.

Small variations from the proper operating temperature range could degrade the quality of data being recorded on huge magnetic disks or tapes or even punch cards, so it became critically important to keep the computers much colder than the rest of the building. Humidity and dust levels were carefully monitored, too.

Computer facilities were also equipped with a nasty agent called halon–a type of halocarbon combining halogen with carbon–that would disperse in the facility if a fire was detected. Halon is very effective at putting out fires with minimal equipment damage because it removes all oxygen (needed to fuel a fire) from the immediate vicinity. You just had to hope that the human occupants of the room had decamped first because neither fires nor people usually survive exposure to halon.

Thankfully, our needs today are a bit more modest. Still, we need to think about temperature, humidity, and dirt.

WARNING *Never bring your PC—or any other electronics—in from a cold situation (such as the interior of your vehicle during the winter months) and immediately plug it in. Allow the unit to sit and gradually warm to room temperature over the course of a few hours, depending on the severity of the cold to which it was exposed.*

Reducing Moisture, Static, and Other Factors

Let's discuss some of the major no-nos of your physical environment. For long-term best results, you'll want to reduce these factors as much as possible, since all can eventually affect PC operation in one way or another.

Moisture

Needless to say, water or any liquid combined with electronics is a poor mix.

Moisture doesn't have to cause major damage to make itself a real pain. On humid days or whenever moisture levels in a room rise, you're likely to notice that your mouse or pointing device won't move as fluidly and keyboard keys are more apt to hesitate or stick.

The best way to prevent problems is to keep any windows directly next to a PC shut (to keep out rain) and keep any beverages or fluid containers (including flower vases with water or potted plants) away from the PC or its parts.

If you're concerned about overall humidity levels and feel you need to purchase a dehumidifier to remove moisture from the air, don't place it near your PC.

Static Electricity

Static electricity is more than an annoyance; it can pose a serious danger to components.

While this is especially true when working inside the case where you may be touching memory, the CPU, and other parts that should not receive the shock, it's wise as a general rule to reduce static as much as possible all the time.

For this reason, you may want to avoid placing the PC in an area where carpeting is being used. This is particularly true of carpeting or rugs with a heavy acrylic composition. Combine those with a bit of acrylic in our sweaters or casual clothing and movement across the rug, and you can build up a fair amount of charge.

If you have no other choice for placement, consider purchasing an anti-static mat. Even a large under-rolling-office-chair rubber mat can help significantly.

Also make sure to obtain and use an anti-static grounding wrist-strap or similar device to keep static electricity away from PC parts when working inside the case.

Dust and Other Factors

The less dust, ash, grease, or particulate matter you have in the general vicinity of your system, the better. This material often ends up being drawn into the vents of the PC and coating the internal components. It can also get into the floppy drive gate, CD tray, and keyboard.

Use the tips for keeping your area clean described in the section "Maintenance: An Ounce of Prevention," and avoid engaging in any activity that creates a lot of dust or fine matter.

> **NOTE** *Can you dust the inside of the PC? Not the usual way, for sure. You can use the instructions in Chapter 2, "How Your Hardware, Operating System, and Applications Work Together," for going inside the case with the PC powered off and yourself grounded. Don't blow dust off parts because your breath is moist. Use a can of compressed air, sometimes sold in office supply and PC stores as "compressed gas duster," to remove dust. It's best if you remove a part such as an adapter (video, sound, etc.), dust it outside the case (where the dust won't simply blow onto another component), and then replace it. Blowing it directly into the PC can sometimes send dust and debris flying into other components, causing whole new issues as my friend, Terri Stratton, a Microsoft MVPer, discovered when she cleaned dust from one area only to have it end up in her drive connections, making a large drive "disappear".*

That Age-Old Debate: PC Cover On or Off?

Another one of the most commonly asked PC questions of all time is, "Is it OK to run my PC all the time with the cover off?"

Most PCs and their cases were designed with the assumption that the cover would be in place. The cover reduces the amount of dust, debris, and moisture that can enter the PC. It also blocks fingers—and pet paws—from reaching in to touch moving, electrified parts. For many systems, too, running the PC without the cover can invalidate the warranty because doing so is outside of normal operation (although it might be hard for a manufacturer to prove you treated your PC like a Mustang convertible.)

I think this issue depends on individual circumstances, because there are a few situations in which running the PC for extended periods of time without the cover is useful. I have one system in my office that is constantly undergoing changes because I use it to test products and PC procedures, so that system spends little time with its cover on.

Continued on next page

That Age-Old Debate: PC Cover On or Off? *(Continued)*

But I should also tell you that this machine's components get pretty caked with unwanted material such as dust, even with the frequent activity. On one summer night not so long ago, a moth—attracted by the desk light next to the open system—flew into an accessory fan on my motherboard and I spent the next morning cleaning a hundred moth bits off my video adapter. On another occasion, my cat experienced a decent shock as she chased a bug up onto my desk and into my open tower case.

Most people, however, aren't constantly installing and removing hardware. You normally only need to remove the cover for the time it takes to check something inside the case or to install, remove, or change something within it.

Yet there are acceptable reasons for leaving the cover off for longer than the time it takes you to perform a specific in-case chore. For example, you may want to leave a PC cover off until you're comfortable that a newly installed device is causing no conflicts and is properly configured. You can take the PC cover off to monitor whether your fans are working and to better tell where a strange sound may be originating from. And you can hasten cooldown of an overheated PC by removing the cover for about an hour. But do it when there is no danger that children, pets, or someone devoid of common sense can access the open case.

The rest of the time, keep the cover on.

Securing Your System

So many of the disasters that can befall your system won't be because a terrorist or a tornado struck, but because you—or someone with ready access to your system—does something dumb. Join the club.

I'm going to assume for purposes of expediency that *you* can control your behavior. Now you need to be able to control the behavior of anyone who gets near your PC.

Of course, controlling someone else isn't always easy. You might find it easier to control the overall security and protectedness of your PC from them.

Password and Other Basic Controls

Security controls in Windows consumer products aren't exactly tough to defeat. You see this whenever you're presented with the need for a password when you either first log into Windows or first connect to the network—just entering your username and clicking OK will get you where you want to go.

That said—and even without adding additional security measures—turning on passwords will prevent some people at your keyboard from being able to get into the system and do things you would rather they did not. For this reason, it's wise to use passwords and, when prompted to do so, don't check "provide password automatically" in programs that allow you to do so. Anything that makes it easy for you to get into a file, a game, or an online service also makes it much easier for someone else to access it.

An example of this is the Welcome screen in Windows XP (something earlier versions of Windows don't have). If you're using the Welcome screen, you'll see the user accounts presented on this screen. All someone needs to do is click one of them to enter Windows without any hassle.

Establish user accounts for anyone you want to be able to use your system and then password-protect each user account. To do this, take the following steps:

1. From Windows Control Panel, click Users or User Accounts.

2. From the User Accounts window, choose Create a New Account.

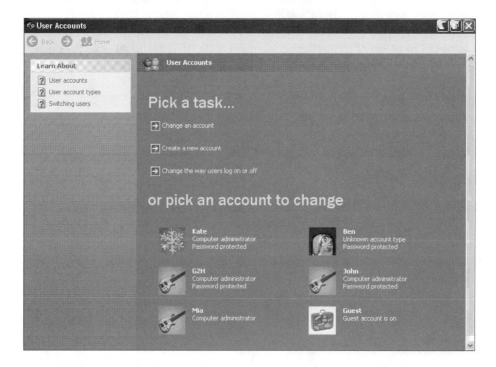

3. When prompted, type the username you want to use. Click Next.

4. From Pick an Account Type, select Computer Administrator or Limited. (Computer Administrator gives someone full access to make changes; use Limited unless you're very sure.)

5. Click Create Account.

If you already have accounts set up, simply add passwords to them from the User Account window as follows:

1. Click Change an Account.

2. Click to select the account you want to change.

3. Click Create a Password.

4. From the Create a Password for Your Account screen, type the password you want to use for the account, retype it to verify it, and then provide a password hint.

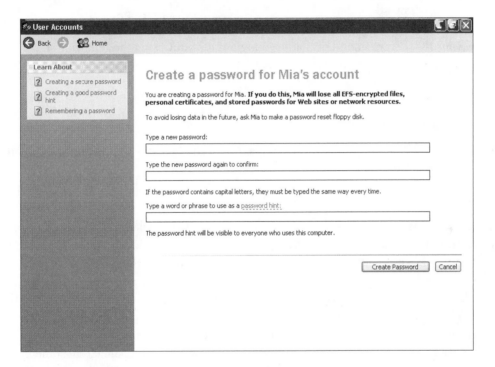

NOTE *Sadly, from a security standpoint, the most commonly used computer password is the word "password."*

5. Click Create Password.

Once you have done this, you can choose Log Off from the Windows Start Menu to log your user account off the system. This prevents someone else from using the system when you step away from the keyboard.

WARNING *Don't make passwords so easy even someone who barely knows you could guess it. The best passwords are combinations of alphanumerics combined with symbols, such as "Cap66istrano7?" or "swod516niw!." But make it something you can remember.*

Disabling Guest Accounts

A guest account on a PC or network refers to a special type of limited account available to anyone who sits down at the keyboard and wants to use the computer, but doesn't have a regular user account or password.

If you want to keep your system more secure and you don't have a strong need to allow others to use your PC, I recommend disabling your guest account using the following steps:

1. From Control Panel, click Users or User Accounts.

2. Select the Or Pick an Account to Change option.

3. Choose the Guest account.

4. From the What Do You Want to Change About the Guest Account window, click the check box Turn Off the Guest Account.

Physical Locks

Many PCs come with a lock mechanism that requires you to unlock the PC before you can physically turn it on. These locks used to be a defacto standard back in the days when even cheap PCs could cost $3,000 or more, although people rarely used them.

If you have such a locking mechanism—and you're one of the three people who didn't toss the key along with the PC box—you can use it with the understanding that one, many of the keys are so flimsy that it isn't altogether uncommon to see them snap off in the lock and two, a common hairpin can often get around the need for a key.

While passwords and other control mechanisms can reduce the chance that someone will stroll past your keyboard and opt to pull up all your private financial data, and a PC lock itself can keep many people from turning on your system, it doesn't really address the issue of other types of damage that can be caused to the physical PC setup itself.

Towers can topple over, including the one housing your PC components. Your dog can get caught in the spaghetti wires hanging off the back of your PC desk. Your neighbor's five-year-old can wander in and begin playing that little game of on-off with the power switch. And, sadly, more than one argument has escalated because one party to a fight decided to vent his or her frustrations on the PC of another party (at least, according to stories I've heard and tales told on those TV court shows).

For example, a colleague of mine bought one of the large, flat-panel monitors back when they were brand new and cost even more than they do today. He no sooner set it up in his home office and went out to put the carton from it in the garage when his sons happened to take their shoving match into his office and around the area of the desk. Later that evening, this colleague forked over hundreds of dollars more to replace the monitor his sons toppled off the desk.

You may find it more useful to simply put the PC behind a door with a lock so you can keep unwanted guests from entering when you can't be there.

TIP *If you're worried about your PC being physically stolen, you'll find that some office supply stores offer various types of devices meant to secure a PC to a desk, much as some hotels and motels bolt down lamps and televisions.*

Checking for Viruses

A computer virus can do many miserable things:

- It can keep your PC from booting up properly or loading Windows.

- It can make it impossible to run or open any files on your system.

- It can prevent your PC from recognizing certain types of hardware, including your hard drive.

- It can make Swiss cheese of your BIOS configuration, and it can surreptitiously send out infection-spreading e-mail to people in your address book.

- It can even disable your virus protection software, and in fact, many viruses are smart enough to do just that.

New viruses are being released out to the Internet each and every day. On a regular basis, you see viruses appear that exploit software and hardware flaws almost as soon as they hit the market. Corporate and school networks can grind to a halt under the sheer volume of viruses being proliferated in their systems.

With that said, computer viruses are usually more hype than horror, meaning that while they certainly have the potential to do damage, many of them simply annoy or inconvenience you.

Yet people blame viruses for almost everything that goes wrong with a PC.

What is most frustrating about all of this is that it doesn't take a great amount of knowledge or skill to keep your system virus-free, regardless of how much you use the Internet. Anti-virus software is one piece of that protection plan.

I've designed this section to help you eliminate viruses as a possible cause of problems you may encounter. More importantly, my goal is to keep you from most risks altogether.

"It's a Virus, I Tell You!"

In my experience working with sometimes thousands of users each week, I have to say that for every 100 people who come to me worried about a virus, less than 5% actually have one.

I'm reminded of a fellow who wrote me e-mail recently telling me that he had just weathered a serious home office fire that produced tremendous heat. The PC didn't melt, he told me, but it was acting a little strangely now. He asked, "Do you think it could be a virus?"

"Gosh, no," I told him. "I suspect it was heat damage to interior components from the fire. Don't you?"

Sure enough, his interior PC fans were clogged with debris, some of the plastic and wiring had slightly melted, and his CPU was failing.

Yet right up until the last moment before he installed the replacement CPU and all became wonderful again, he was sure it was a virus. He just didn't want to shell out $50 on anti-virus software to check it.

You: The First Line of Defense

The biggest defensive shield between your PC and a virus is you. Exercise smart file handling, and you'll reduce your risks considerably. If you use poor judgment in file handling, the best anti-virus software ever written may not keep you safe.

For example, I've downloaded, tested, reviewed, and created tens of thousands of files over the last dozen years, and I've worked for some of the largest online services where you often hear that computer viruses run rampant. Yet I've never caught a virus through any of these means.

Here's what I do:

- Keep my anti-virus software updated.

- Perform a complete virus scan once a day.

- Never open e-mail with attachments from anyone I don't know.

- Scan the attachments I do accept before I open them.

- Only download files from trusted web sites and always check those files for viruses.

- Discourage others from bringing disks to load in my office because I can't be sure they're as careful as I am.

- If they insist on loading a disk anyway, it has to be scanned first.

NOTE *To be honest, one of my PCs did catch a virus once. A friend—a computer expert, too, who should have known better—brought a floppy disk to my office to print a document. He decided to reboot the PC and accidentally left the floppy disk in the drive when he did so. The floppy disk was infected with something called a boot sector virus, transmitted by floppy disks and "caught" when you leave a floppy in the drive to restart a system. It in turn infected my PC.*

Major Virus-Scanning Utilities

Two of the best known and most widely purchased commercial virus scanners are Norton AntiVirus (NAV) and McAfee VirusScan, and both offer versions that install as any other application. You then configure each utility the way you want it to work: all the time running in the background or run it yourself to do a scan.

But you'll find many others, both in stores and for download via the Internet. For examples, sites such as `www.Download.com` let you download trial versions of both commercial and shareware ("try before you register and buy" software).

Web-Based Virus Scanning

While many service-oriented web sites have come and gone, you can still find a few that offer free web-based virus scanning. One of the most popular sites is PC Pitstop, available at `www.pcpitstop.com`. This site features a wide range of utilities you can run from your web browser, including Internet connection speed, overall disk health, and PC performance tests.

With PC Pitstop's site, you simply

1. Visit the site and click the AntiVirus option.

2. Accept the required download.

3. Choose from Quick Scan (a fast scan of essential files and directories), Full Scan (a more exhaustive virus check), or Custom Scan (you choose the drive(s), directories, or subdirectories to check). Click OK to confirm.

4. Check the web page as it reports results during and after the scan.

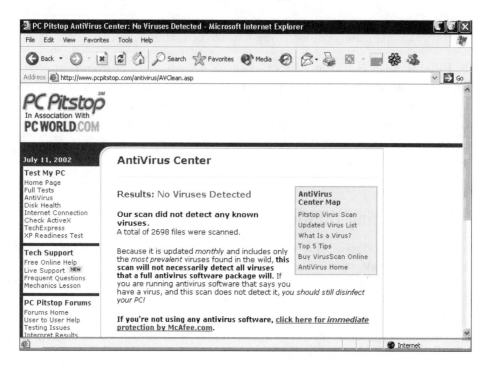

NOTE *McAfee also offers an online version of their software, called VirusScan Online, but it's not free ($29.95 for a one-year subscription).*

How Viruses Work

Many computer viruses usually strike in certain types of files (executable files ending in **.exe** or **.com**, Word macro files, and so on), and they often target specific directories such as Windows itself and even any anti-virus software you have installed.

Anti-virus software checks those types of files and directories, as well as monitors your system for changes and "fingerprints" that indicate a virus may be present. If the software thinks it has something, it checks the features of that problem against its roster of known viruses and known symptoms. If it feels the match is strong, the software reports the suspected virus and usually makes an attempt to clean your system of the virus or at least isolate the affected file(s) so you can delete them.

Most anti-virus software can be operated a number of different ways, including

- Looking only at a particular file or file type

- Working in the background, whenever Windows is loaded, to monitor for changes

- Not run in the background but executed on a regular basis to make a complete scan of the files on the desired drives

Anti-virus software is only as good as its ability to be updated to add *signatures*. Signatures contain fingerprints of any new viruses detected. These signatures detect new viruses released since the software's last update.

As a result, many anti-virus software packages feature a "live update" feature that uses your Internet connection to regularly check for and automatically download updates to your software's virus-control list. Most virus software purchases include free signature updates for a period of one year.

What to Expect When Running a Virus Scan

Anti-virus software usually does a pretty good job of identifying suspected viruses and eliminating them from your system. What they aren't, however, is a magic pill that can let you skate through without personal vigilance in keeping your system safe.

In order to achieve the best results, you must still be careful what you download and open in e-mail and files, and you must keep your anti-virus software updated and performing regular scans.

However, even if you do all that, it's always possible you may encounter a new type of virus that the software hasn't yet been updated to work against. The good news is that developers of such software are constantly monitoring global news about new computer viruses, so a fix to handle the situation is rarely more than a few days away.

There is also a secondary issue with anti-virus software, and this concerns the rather typical way most of them monitor your system continuously in the background. On the one hand, constant monitoring can be very useful and gives you the best chance of being able to spot something before it affects your files or the operating system. On the other hand, this background scanning can interfere with other programs, produce many false positive reports (meaning it reports there is a virus when there really isn't one) simply because they perceive changes in files you are legitimately modifying and make a mess of installing other software as well as some hardware devices.

On my systems, I prefer to perform a complete scan at least once a day rather than monitoring for viruses continuously. It's too easy to forget that the virus scanner is running (although all of these programs place an icon in the System Tray at the bottom right-hand corner of your screen), and I've messed up a few too many installations by leaving the virus scanner running.

PC Protection Devices

While this is another issue that will be dealt with in greater detail in Chapter 11, it's important for you, as you consider your PC environment, to be aware of what type of protection you have against negative external influences, such as power surges or serious fluctuations.

At the very least, evaluate the following issues as part of analyzing your workspace:

- Determine whether your home or office has proper grounding, which can discourage lightning from traveling into your home and hitting sensitive devices like your PC.

- Determine whether your PC setup can have everything related to the PC plugged into outlets or devices working off a master switch that you can use to kill power to the system quickly. Doing this can help a PC and its peripherals from going on-off repeatedly.

- Determine whether your PC is plugged into any kind of power protection device, such as a good-quality surge suppressor.

- Determine whether your PC is plugged into any auxiliary backup power device, such as an uninterruptible power supply (UPS), that uses a battery between your power and PC to give you a period of time (usually a few minutes) to properly save your files and shut down your PC during a power outage.

How Backups and Drive Imaging Can Save You from Big Problems

The best way to prevent the loss of data is to have more than one copy of that data and to have that copy stored just about anywhere but where the original data is stored.

One way to do that, of course, is to simply copy your files to another medium besides your main hard drive because the hard drive can be vulnerable to the kinds of disaster you've been reading about. But if you're serious enough to be reading this book, it's likely that you need a more organized solution than simply copying individual files to another medium such as a floppy, Zip disk, or CD.

This is where backup and drive-imaging software comes in. Understand that these are two different types of software, although you may find some of their different features packaged together.

The term *backup* refers to a process by which you back up usually a complete volume of data, such as an entire hard drive or specific folders on that drive into an archive or master file, which is then stored on some other type of medium, such as tape cartridge, floppy, Zip disk, CD, and so on. MS Backup, included with Windows XP (although you'll need to install it specifically since it doesn't install to your desktop automatically) and earlier versions, is an example of backup software, but there are dozens available commercially as shareware, and even a few public domain or freeware types.

Installing Backup for Windows XP

Locate your Windows XP install CD and slide it into the drive. Using Windows Explorer or My Computer, look at the contents of the install CD to locate the file `\ValueAdd\MSFT\NTBACKUP\ntbackup.msi`. Just click the file, and it will launch a wizard to help you install Backup.

The idea here is that if you suffer a data loss or other problem with your system, you can use a process known as restore to copy back the data you stored in the backup archive.

Drive imaging is a different animal from backing up because this process actually makes a virtual copy of your hard drive as it exists at the time you make the image. Where drive imaging is most useful is when you want to replace one hard drive with another: you can make an image of your current drive (assuming it's in good shape) and restore that drive image on the new drive once it's prepared for use. It also makes the job of setting up more than one PC much faster because you can create a master drive image that you then install on each additional PC.

But you can also restore individual files from a drive image (at least, with recent versions of imaging software); you don't have to restore the entire drive image at once.

Some of the most widely used drive-imaging software packages include PowerQuest's Drive Image, Norton/Symantec's Ghost, and Nero's Drive Imager.

When you devise your disaster recovery plan in the next chapter, you'll learn more about using backups and drive images as part of your prevention/restoration game plan.

Doing Prep Work:
What You Should Do Before an Installation

Another effective way to limit or prevent problems with your PC has to do with making certain the hardware and software you install is fully compatible and that you have followed all the directions.

Let's touch on a few points that may seem incredibly obvious, but these steps are often overlooked until sometime after a conflict, failure, or frustration strikes.

Reading the Manual/Documentation

This is also known in the computer business as RTFM or "Read the (Fine) Manual."

Before buying any hardware or software, always read the product information stated on the box or in the product description. While this is often written by marketing people, it often provides details such as

- Minimum requirements for operating it (example: what type of CPU, how much memory, and which version of Windows is needed)

- Other programs and/or hardware the product will work with

- Where to get more information

Once you've read the product description, be sure to go through both the printed as well as the online documentation. In particular, pay attention to the sections on installation and troubleshooting so you can get an idea of the types of problems you may encounter.

For example, when I upgraded some graphics-editing software last week, I saw that there were special instructions listed for installing this to work with a second package I use. The documentation also offered suggestions on ways to get around a problem that might occur while installing the package.

Doing Some Online Research

Use manufacturer web sites, online technical information sites, and web-based message boards focusing on hardware and software to research information about these products before and after you buy them.

For example, I typically check price and availability against a computer sales reference site called PriceWatch available at `www.pricewatch.com`, then check its compatibility against the Windows Hardware Compatibility List (HCL) as illustrated in Figure 3.2 if it's a device (see the following Warning). Then I jump over to see what folks in the Microsoft.com, ExtremeTech.com, and AnandTech technical sites are saying about it.

You'll pick up some excellent online resources in Chapter 15, "Finding Help Online."

WARNING *Before you buy any PC hardware device, make sure it's fully compatible with your version of Windows. One of the single best resources to check is the Windows Hardware Compatibility List, available on Microsoft at* `www.microsoft.com/hcl`*. Search by type of device or manufacturer, and you'll see results divided by the Windows version the device supports.*

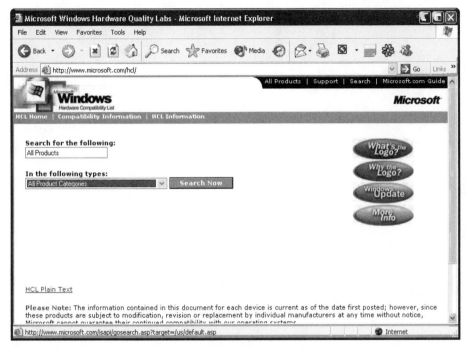

Figure 3.2 *Use the HCL to check compatibility*

Now that you have a better appreciation of the steps you can take in your environment and your PC to reduce or eliminate some problems before they start, it's time to jump forward and begin plotting your recovery strategy covered in Chapter 4, "Assembling Your PC Recovery Resource Kit."

Assembling Your PC Recovery Resource Kit

In the last chapter, you learned about prevention and the ways you can limit the risk of reaching the point where you might need to take action to correct a disaster. Now it's time to think about the inevitable: those times when you need to do some type of recovery work because a problem got past your preventive measures or your hardware just failed.

Toward that end, this chapter will help you create a basic kit that includes hardware, software, and other elements you'll need for serious troubleshooting and repair. We're going to call it a PC Recovery Resource Kit. Thankfully, you won't need this kit every time you work because so much can be done from the keyboard. But it pays to be prepared, especially in the event of a calamity.

Getting the Necessary Hardware Ready

If you've ever seen a huge, elaborate technician toolkit, usually packed in an aluminum attaché case with one or two hundred pieces, complete with a dozen types of screwdrivers and enough other devices to perform a major overhaul on the International Space Station, don't worry; that's not quite what you need. Most PC work can be done with a set of basic tools, many of which can be found in a decently equipped home or office.

Read on to learn what you need.

Assembling Your PC Repair Toolkit

Exactly what you need for your PC repair toolkit may vary because hardware—and the fasteners holding that hardware in place—can differ a lot from PC to PC. For example, some PCs use hex screws to hold their covers or drives in place. This isn't always just poor design—some manufacturers like to use unusual screws and fasteners to discourage people from augmenting or fixing their PCs themselves.

Here's what I consider to be the essential tools for most PC setups, with a couple of highly worthy accessories:

- Anti-static (grounding) strap
- Screwdrivers (Phillips, regular)
- Hemostat
- Mini-flashlight/pen light (optional)
- Two tiny empty containers, one for holding spare screws and small pieces, and one to be used as a temporary holder for screws and fasteners that you remove and must replace during a check or repair situation

I strongly suggest you collect the tools in this list and keep them in a separate case or drawer near your PC, ready for repairs. Some of the best PC repair kits are assembled one piece at a time. Expect to add to yours over a period of time.

TIP *Ever been inside your PC case only to find the toughest task was removing the cover? More than one PC has accidentally ended up on the floor because it was so difficult to remove its cover. Look at the cover opening next time you shop for a PC. Some vendors will swap your PC purchase into a better case for a small fee. If you're feeling ambitious, you can buy a different case design; some covers slide on and off or slide the entire guts of the PC out for you to work on.*

Keep the Tools Separate

You might wonder if you really need to put together a PC toolkit quite like this. After all, you probably have multiple screwdrivers and other tools available in various places in your home and office.

I recommend keeping a separate toolkit for the PC because general-use tools tend to take far more abuse. Tools tend to get tossed into drawers when they're damp, sticky, and even dirty. The same tool you used to take apart the lawnmower may not be the best choice for screwing a PC component into place.

In addition, not everyone who uses your screwdriver will be particularly careful with it, and it's common for screwdriver heads to get damaged. Once a screwdriver head becomes damaged, it leaves marks on anything it touches. On the small PC-type screws, these marks can quickly strip the thread on the top of the screw until you can no longer get a firm hold on the screw. If you replace the screw, you'll just damage the replacement while screwing it into place.

The Right Fit

This may seem like a pesky detail, but make sure you get the right-sized tools for both the job you're doing and for the size of your hands. Over-sized tools present a real problem in the limited space within a computer chassis. If your hand slips while screwing in a new adapter, a smaller screwdriver is apt to do less damage than the same size one you use for putting the trailer hitch on your SUV.

But matching the handle to your own hand is a factor, too. The same tool that works well in my partner's hand often feels too cumbersome in my much smaller hand.

Of course, working with a PC isn't like doing an extensive home repair project. You'll be working with a relatively limited number of screws, depending on what you need to do. All in all, the tools will be in your hand for a short time.

I always judge tools based on my worst-case scenario. This means that I make sure I have the right screwdriver to fit my hand for those times when I really have to work at loosening a recalcitrant screw.

Buying a Packaged Kit

Many online vendors and consumer stores sell pre-assembled PC repair kits (see Figure 4.1), often packed into a vinyl or leather case. For a basic 5–20 piece toolkit, you can expect to pay anywhere from $7–$40.

While some of these toolkits are quite decent, make sure you don't buy one with incredibly cheap tools. Such tools are apt to damage easily, and some of the screwdrivers from such sets actually break while using them. Unfortunately, unless you can hold them in your hand, it may be tough to assess their heftiness.

Another issue with packaged toolkits is that if the package is sealed when you purchase it or if you buy it online, you have no way to gauge the actual fit of the tool in your hand.

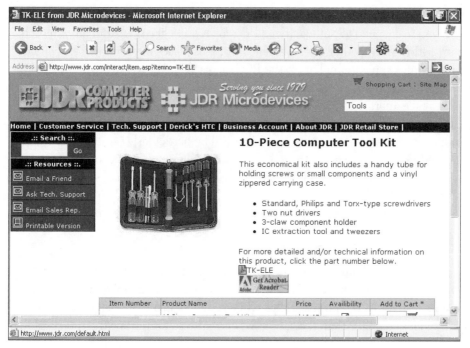

Figure 4.1 *JDR Micro Devices is just one of many vendors selling packaged toolkits.*

Updating Your PC Repair Toolkit

If you're working on your system and discover you're missing something you need for your particular setup, try to pick up the right tool or accessory and add it to your toolkit.

Also, as you use up any extra screws or connectors you may store in your toolkit, don't forget to replenish them. This applies for anything you may add to your toolkit that might need restocking. The last thing you want to do is add to your frustration by not having the right materials on hand when you've been hit by an emergency or disaster.

Keeping Extra Hardware on Hand

Those of you in at least your second generation of PCs usually have some extra hardware components lying around. It's often in the form of a smaller hard drive that you replaced with a larger model even though the smaller drive still works well, or you have an extra stick of memory, an extra mouse, an used cable, or a spare keyboard.

Don't give the old hardware away or hide it away where you won't remember it later on. Selling it is a bad idea, too, because with hardware prices still so low, it's tough to get a decent price for used components. Instead, consider keeping a small set of spare hardware parts or devices on hand. While you shouldn't invest much money or much space in doing so, having a spare keyboard or drive on hand in an emergency can be a real lifesaver.

TIP *Extra hardware can help during troubleshooting. For example, if your main hard drive suddenly isn't recognized by BIOS, you may wonder, "Is the drive damaged, or could something have corrupted my BIOS?" If you have a spare working drive, you can install that instead. If BIOS recognizes the spare drive but not the original, then you know the problem lies with the original drive.*

Take Advantage of Sales

When I can, I take advantage of sale pricing to put a few pieces of hardware aside just in case.

If you have PC vendor fairs or computer shows in your area, as many regions do, they can be an excellent place to shop. After all, you don't need the best equipment sitting on the shelf as a backup part, just something that can pinch hit for you. You can always grab these parts to use as short-term solutions or to use them later in another computer.

For instance, I've done very well just having these working spare parts available:

- Hard drive
- USB CD recorder
- Keyboard
- Mouse
- Memory

Readying Another Critical Device: You

Since you are as critical to the recovery process as virtually anything else is, now seems like a good time to mention a couple of points about how you use—or abuse—yourself.

The best hardware technician in the world can make nasty mistakes and forget crucial things if he or she approaches an evaluation or repair at the wrong time or in the wrong way. For example, it's very important to be able to remember each step you take while troubleshooting. If you don't, you risk either repeating them or never performing them in the first place.

While I assume you're an adult and perfectly able to make decisions for yourself, avoid troubleshooting and repairs when you are

- Exhausted

- Under the influence of anything that may affect your cognitive abilities

- Completely frustrated or tense

- Very distracted by other factors

- Otherwise unable to give the job your full attention

Using the Necessary Software

Hardware tools only get you into the PC and allow you to change the hardware configuration from its physical standpoint. So much of what you may need to work with is rooted in software:

- Disks that help you start your system in an emergency

- Drivers for your hardware

- The Windows install CD

- Needed utilities

- Stored copies of your most important files if you don't have full backups or drive images

Once you read this section, it might be wise to collect a set of essential disks and segregate them in a safe place. Know where they are so you can find them quickly.

TIP *On a shelf near the main entrance to my office is a small, fireproof box that contains the essential material covered in this section. It's positioned near my office so I can grab it quickly on my way out the door in the event of an emergency. Doing this is a lot easier than trying to haul cartons of documents and software during an earthquake, fire, or flood, and ensures that I'll have everything I need to restore to a different PC if my main one is totaled.*

Boot Disks

A *boot disk* is any type of disk from which a computer can be started. The boot disk is specially formatted with system files and contains at least the basic essence of an operating system (or all of an operating system, if you remember DOS).

In this case, I'm talking about a boot disk created and run from a floppy drive. This is very valuable to have on hand when you can't get your operating system to load or you can't get your main hard drive to respond—two of the thornier problems you may encounter.

You may have heard the terms *startup disk* or *start disk*. These two terms are used interchangeably, and they mean roughly the same thing. However, a boot disk usually implies a disk that will boot the computer and display the kind of command prompt you see with DOS. A startup disk, on the other hand, usually tries to get you through the bootup process and into basic Windows.

However, there's a critical difference between what these disks contain. A boot disk has just what you copied to it, including essential system files that allow it to boot. A startup disk, by comparison, contains extra tools such as

ScanDisk   ScanDisk checks for disk problems.

Edit   A DOS editor is required for viewing and editing text and configuration files such as .INI files.

Chkdsk   The Chkdsk utility checks disk integrity and has a repair option.

Extract   This utility allows you to extract Windows files from the large cabinet storage files (ending in .CAB) that are on the Windows CD or that were copied to your hard drive.

How You Use the Boot Disk and the Startup Disk

Let's look at some examples of where and how you might use these two types of disks.

Imagine that you start your PC and find that other functions seem to be working but your hard drive does not appear to be booting or operating properly. You might wonder whether the hard drive failed, whether a virus had corrupted the master boot record or BIOS, or if something happened during your last Windows session.

The first thing you do is turn the system back off and start it up again, since it's possible that the drive didn't power up properly.

If that fails, you go into the BIOS Setup, described in Chapter 2, "How Your Hardware, Operating System, and Applications Work Together," to see whether the drive is being detected there. Remember, the BIOS *must* recognize the drive in order for the drive to work properly with your system. In this situation, let's assume that the hard drive is still seen by the BIOS, which is a good sign; it's probably not a drive failure.

TIP *Always have two copies of either your boot or startup disks. Create fresh copies of these disks every six months or so and whenever you change or upgrade your version of Windows.*

Next, follow these basic steps:

1. Insert the correct boot disk into the floppy drive.

2. Restart the system.

3. Once the system boots to the commant prompt, type this command:

   DIR C:

   If you're able to get a directory listing (what the preceding command does) for your root directory (folder), your drive is probably working fine from an essential configuration standpoint (more good news).

WARNING *If your PC won't boot from a boot disk in the floppy drive, go into BIOS and make sure your floppy drive is listed as one of the possible boot drives, along with your hard drive.*

Some versions of Windows let you load the operating system from this command line. To try this, type

CD C:\\WINDOWS

WIN

These commands select your Windows directory (if your directory is named something other than Windows, type its correct name) and then try to load the executable file that launches Windows.

WARNING *Using the wrong disk can be bad because different versions of Windows require slightly different files and utilities, for example. Always label your boot disks by date and by Windows version and include a short note to remind you what may differ from one boot disk to another.*

You can use a startup disk in a similar manner. But a startup disk is really valuable when the hard drive seems to be working fine but Windows itself won't load—either because you just installed a device or software it doesn't like, you've accidentally deleted a file it needs, or because a virus has disrupted the operating system from launching.

TIP *If you use different color floppy disks, consider reserving one vibrant color—deep yellow or red—for your boot/startup disks. This makes them easy to pick out in a pinch. You can even take this one step farther and use a different color for each major type of floppy you make (such as documents or letters with one color, hardware drivers on another color, and so on).*

Boot/Startup Disks for Windows XP

As you'll learn later in this book, the Windows XP CD can act as a boot disk using something called the Recovery Console. This CD lets you boot your system through your CD drive and then loads a command console through which you can type commands to try to troubleshoot and repair problems.

But let's turn your attention to creating boot and startup disks because Recovery Console can't be used in every crisis.

To create a boot disk that tries to load Windows XP itself requires a little effort since there isn't just one icon to click. To make a boot disk, you need a good blank floppy disk. Then, take these steps:

1. Insert the disk into the A: drive.

2. From the Windows Start menu, choose My Computer.

3. From My Computer, right-click the A: drive and select Format. Confirm your choice by clicking OK. When the disk is formatted, leave it in place in the drive.

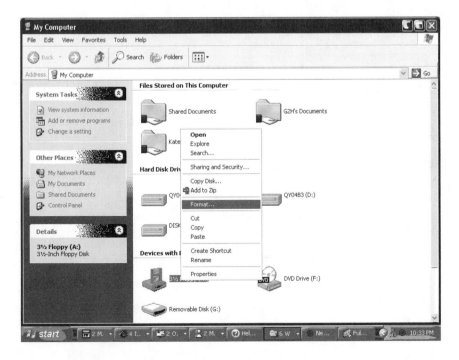

4. From Windows Start menu, choose All Programs ➤ Accessories and then select Windows Explorer.

5. In Windows Explorer, change to the C: drive by clicking the address window and choosing the C: drive.

6. Open the Tools menu and select Folder Options.

7. Choose the View tab, and under the entry marked Hidden Files and Folders, be sure Show Hidden Files and Folders is selected. Click OK.

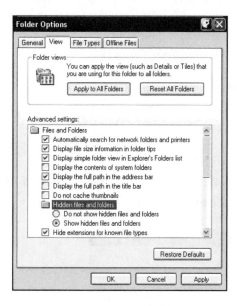

8. In the C: folder, locate each of these files:

    • `boot.ini`

    • `ntdetect.com`

    • `ntldr`

    • If your computer has the capability of booting to two different operating systems, locate the file `Bootsect.dos`.

    • If the computer boots off a SCSI drive, locate the file `Ntbootdd.sys`.

9. For each of the files listed, right-click and press Ctrl+Insert to copy the file. Then, select the A: drive from the address window and press Shift+Insert to paste them to the floppy drive. Repeat until all files are copied.

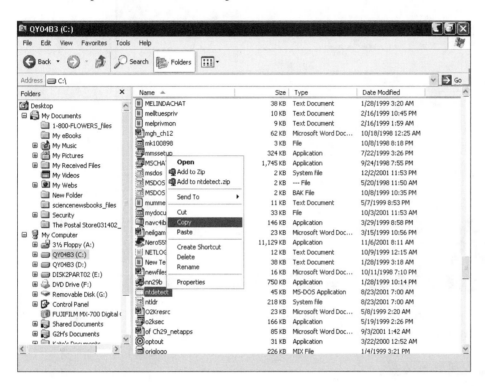

10. Remove the floppy from the drive and label it something like "WinXP boot disk."

If troubleshooting instructions for an installation or repair require a straight MS-DOS boot disk, you can create one easily in Windows XP by following these steps:

1. Insert a blank floppy disk into the A: drive.

2. From the Windows Start menu, choose My Computer.

3. From My Computer, right-click the A: drive and select Format.

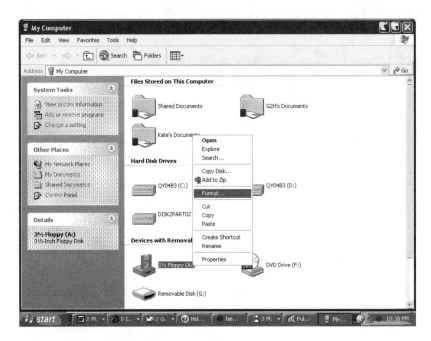

4. From the Format window under Format Options, click to select Create an MS-DOS Startup Disk. Click Start.

5. When the disk is formatted, remove it from the A: drive and label it something like "DOS boot disk."

Boot/Startup Disks for Windows 98

In Windows 98 and earlier, you can create a complete Windows startup disk quickly and easily from the Windows desktop by taking these steps:

1. From Windows Control Panel, double-click Add and Remove Programs.

2. Choose the Windows Startup Disk tab.

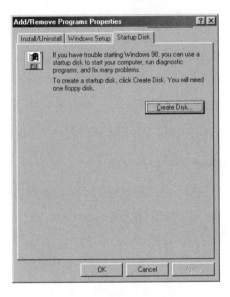

3. Insert a good blank floppy in your floppy drive.

4. Click Create Disk. Click OK.

5. When the disk has been created, remove it from the drive and label it appropriately.

To create an MS-DOS boot disk in Windows 98, take these steps:

1. Double-click the My Computer icon on the Desktop.

2. Insert a good blank floppy in the floppy drive.

3. Right-click the floppy drive (A:) icon and select Format.

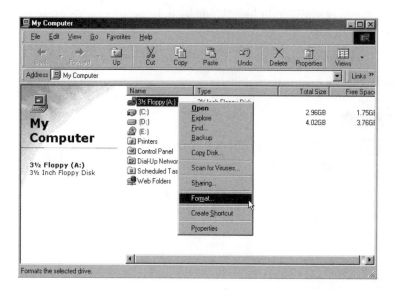

4. From the Format window, choose:

- Under Capacity, click to select 1.44MB (3.5").

- Under Format Type, select Full.

- Under Other Options, under Label, type the name to give the disk and then click to select Copy System Files.

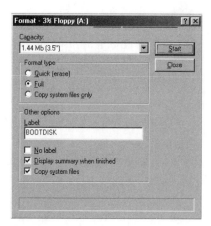

5. Click Start.

TIP *For more information about what files and utilities you should include on boot disks for different situations, visit* www.bootdisk.com.

Master CDs and Data

Include in your PC Recovery Resource Kit all the software and data you might need to return from a complete catastrophe where you might have to start from scratch with a new hard drive, or even a completely new system, including

- Your Windows installation CD

- Disk(s) containing the necessary hardware drivers

- Master install CDs for your essential applications and programs

- Disks or tape cartridges containing your backups, drive images, or copies of critical data files

You don't need a copy of absolutely every application and game you currently have installed, but it helps to have everything available to resurrect your most frequently used programs should the necessity arise.

WARNING *If your current version of Windows is an upgrade from a previous version, you should have both the upgrade CD as well as the install CD for your last full version of Windows; you can't install an upgrade version of Windows on a new or blank hard drive.*

Needed Utilities

You may find that you really need to have a few utilities available in your PC Recovery Resource kit. These utilities might include

- A floppy disk-based anti-virus scanner

- Any bootup utilities your system currently uses

- A simple editor so you can look at text files and make changes to configuration files

- The recovery disk that came with your PC

- A set of diagnostic utilities you really like

Anti-Virus Scanner

When Chapter 3, "Prevention: Limiting Your Risks," talked about prevention, one of the topics covered was using an anti-virus scanner as one of your defenses against damage. However, there are times when a virus may be able to get around your scanner enough to cause problems starting your PC (especially in the case of some of the BIOS-corrupting viruses) or getting Windows to load or run properly. If you don't regularly scan your system for viruses, you stand a greater statistical likelihood of infestation by a virus.

If Chapter 3 didn't convince you, look at acquiring an up-to-date anti-virus scanner—commercial, shareware, or free. Specifically, you want one that supports the creation of a special floppy or CD-based anti-virus disk to use for troubleshooting. You need one that works on another medium besides a hard drive since a real emergency may mean the hard drive isn't available to you. Recall, too, that some viruses act by disabling your installed virus scanner; in such cases, booting the PC with an anti-virus-equipped boot disk might let you back into the hard drive to eliminate the virus.

> **WARNING** *Don't assume you can use free Web-based virus-scanning sites for this task. You can only do that if the system is working well enough to go online, and that may not be the case.*

Special Add-on Utilities

Among the utilities you should have in your PC Recovery Resource Kit is either the master CD or a specially created boot disk for any programs you added to the actual bootup of the computer to help in the startup process.

Sometimes you need this when a system has to run a particular program on bootup to recognize a specific piece of hardware. My satellite modem has a utility like this to ensure that it's available as Windows begins to load.

Another example is if you have a large hard drive that requires you to use a special program to help your older BIOS work with the drive. If you—or a technician—install a large drive and have problems getting the BIOS to recognize the new drive, you're likely using such a special program. EZ-BIOS is one of the most popular among these types of utilities; EZ-BIOS acts as an overlay on top of your older BIOS to remove restrictions in the size of hard drive your PC can detect. Such programs usually require you—at the time you install them—to create a master boot disk with the utility tacked onto the bootup process to make it easier for you to recover from a problem with the hard drive.

Wherever possible, keep the original program/utility disk, any special boot disk it required you to make, and the utility instructions handy. The instructions may provide you with valuable clues on what to do in the event of an emergency. If you've lost the instructions, locate them on the manufacturer's web site, where they are likely duplicated.

Creating the Right Environment for Repairing Your PC

Chapter 3 described the right setup for your PC, one free of the moisture, dust, and clutter that can get in the way of the proper operation of your PC.

Even though you might not need to go inside your PC case regularly, you should designate an area in your home or office that meets the basic requirements for a decent PC repair area. For too many users, failure to have such an area could have one of two results:

- You procrastinate and end up losing more time/productivity with your PCs.

- You try to work in sub-optimum conditions where you can't always see what you're doing, causing other types of disasters to occur.

Let's learn how to do create the right environment.

Components of a Good PC Repair Area

Depending on the type of PC you have and its case design—some are more user-friendly than others—you'll need a fair amount of physical space to open up your PC. You'll need room for the case, the chassis (in which the PC guts reside), and the monitor. Even if you're not repairing the monitor, you may want it close by so you can watch the display to see how a change is affecting the bootup process.

Too often, this is usually more space than many small desks or workstations allow. A good PC repair area should have these qualities:

- Clean and dry

- A stable work surface with adequate room to accommodate the PC, the PC cover, and if needed, the monitor

- Access to a phone line so you don't have to run back and forth between the phone and the PC and to allow hooking a modem to a phone line for testing

- Access to a working electrical outlet (for when you want to test)

- Excellent lighting

- Free of food and drink

- Away from children, pets, and other prying hands

- Tools readily accessible, with documentation and instructions close at hand

- Free of major distractions

A Cautionary Tale: Step Away from the Power Source

There's one another element I'd add to an optimal PC repair work area: a first aid kit.

If you've been inside your PC case, you know it's a sharp, dirty, semi-dark (depending on your case type and lighting), and perilous world in there, replete with near-razor edges, cables, and wires to ensnare you, and things to prick through your skin.

Through the years, I've heard some real horror stories about injuries incurred while working on PCs. I've even driven a few victims to the doctor or emergency room for suturing.

Now, I'm not saying this to scare you. Almost every instance I know about happened not just because of working in a poor space but because of inattention or deliberately choosing not to follow common-sense rules like removing all power from the PC before working on it.

Take the case of a fellow I once worked with who managed to do just about everything wrong when he went to install his first-ever network adapter and hard drive. As soon as he had the cover off, Mark sliced his index finger on the frame of a case. After applying a bandage, he forgot to put his anti-static grounding strap back on so that within a moment or two, he and his video adapter both took a good static Z-I-N-G.

Next, he didn't follow my advice to remove all jewelry and tie back long hair before you work, so as Mark reacted to the static discharge, he caught his college ring on a pin on his video adapter, snapping the pin off. He would later discover the video adapter had problems as a result.

But I haven't gotten to the worst part yet. Mark had never disconnected power to his PC, so when he went to plug the ribbon cable from the new hard drive into the IDE channel on the motherboard, he not only fried the new hard drive. Mark got his finger bandage wet and then managed to get it on a part of the system as he plugged in the hard drive to power. The result made the static zing feel like a simple tickle.

When the emergency room doctor checked him out that evening to make sure he was all right, he asked Mark how he managed to make so many mistakes. Mark replied, "It was too dark to read the instructions."

When More Is Better:
The Bonus of a Second, Internet-Ready PC

If you're fortunate to have another, working, Internet-ready device, particularly another PC, you'll find this is a big boon to you in trying to deal with a dead or disaster-ed system.

With a second available PC, you can

- Try to finish what you were working on before the interruption.

- Go online to manufacturers' web sites and other help sites to research your problem. (See Chapter 15, "Finding Help Online," for more information.)

- Check the second PC to see if everything on the first PC appears to be connected in roughly the same way.

- Troubleshoot using this second working system.

Let me talk a little about that last advantage because it's one that not everyone thinks about when trying to work through a thorny problem.

When I suspect I've got a problem with a device on one system in my home or office, I try swapping that device onto another machine.

Here's an example: If I'm having difficulty determining whether a display problem is rooted in the video adapter or in the monitor, I take the monitor from the problem PC to the other PC and try it there. If the monitor works fine when installed to the second system, I can probably rule out the monitor itself as the source of problems on the first PC. Next, I try the video cable from the second system on the first system to rule out that the cable from the first PC is damaged. Once I clear the cable and monitor as likely suspects, I can look at the video adapter and its driver.

But I also do this with drives, keyboards, printers, and even components you install internally such as video adapters and memory.

While you have to exercise care here that you don't end up with two non-functioning systems, the options that a second PC can provide are broad and very helpful. After all, if you take your PC into a shop, it's possible a technician will test part of your system in much the same fashion. It's a standard troubleshooting technique.

All right. You should now have your PC Recovery Resource Kit pretty much complete, and it should include the following:

- Hardware tools like screwdrivers and an anti–static wrist strap

- Boot/startup disks

- Essential install CDs (such as for Windows and your applications/utilities), disks, and data

Don't forget to remind yourself to keep your PC Recovery Resource Kit well-supplied and updated.

Now it's time to draw up a master plan to prepare for the worst so that you can get back to PC work and leisure after a disaster of almost any type. Let's move to Chapter 5, "Drafting Your Disaster Recovery Plan," to begin planning and implementing this.

Drafting Your Disaster Recovery Plan

One of the many amazing things about the response to the terrorist attacks on New York City and Washington, D.C., on September 11, 2001 is how quickly some of the businesses in and around the disaster areas got back to work in spite of the devastation.

Cantor Fitzgerald, a financial firm that lost most of its New York-based employees in the World Trade Center that day, reopened its operations at another location just one full day after the attack.

When interviewed later on, many of these business people cited two major factors in their ability to do this so effectively:

- They had a disaster recovery plan.

- They practiced what to do beforehand.

Hopefully, you'll live your entire life without experiencing anything of this magnitude at your home or business, but that day of catastrophes taught us all a lesson in preparedness.

Interestingly enough, however, while companies of all sizes usually have detailed manuals about how to protect their computer systems when the great earthquake or great power grid disaster or great asteroid strikes, they usually do not have contingency plans for the most common disaster of all: when a human does something to his or her PC that causes it to fail and lose its proprietary (on that PC only) data.

Read on, develop your personal disaster recovery plan, get started with protecting your data, and you'll have a step up on major conglomerates with billions of dollars in assets and manpower.

Identifying Your Minimum Back-to-Work Needs

You tend to build your home offices and personal PC setups slowly, over time, and this can make it difficult to appreciate not just all you have invested, but all you require of your PCs as well as supply to them in terms of hardware and software.

In this section, you'll be asked to take a good, hard look at exactly what type of setup and services you have now and what you'd need to have available to you should your PC fail.

Wherever possible, think both about what might happen if your PC and immediate work area becomes unavailable and what you might do if you have to set up shop at a different location. The former is much more likely than the latter, but you need to consider both situations when formulating and implementing a recovery plan.

How You Work and What You Have

The best way to determine what you may need in a serious disaster is look at the types of work you perform with your PC and identify the components of your existing system. You can then use this information as the basis for determining your minimum list of requirements for getting back to work.

This may sound very low-tech, but get some paper and a pen or pencil to jot down notes as you read through this section. Use these notes as the basis for a typed-up version of your formal recovery plan. Organizing and putting the details on paper so you can understand and follow them two weeks or two months or two years from now can help you identify weaknesses and keep you focused on the subject at hand.

Type of Work Performed

Pull out your paper and list the five most important operations or functions you perform with your PC. For example, my list would look something like this:

1. Creating documents in Microsoft Word 2002

2. Sending and receiving work-based e-mail

3. Web browsing

4. Software testing

5. Web page design and management

You might be amazed to learn that in this age of Pentium 4s and 2+ GHz PCs, everything I've listed here runs pretty well on an older, slower Pentium 2. I know this because I do this work on a Pentium 2 350 MHz PC, just as I do similar work on much faster machines in my home and office.

Remember this when we talk about your minimum requirements for getting back to work: those minimum requirements may be far less than you think.

Now ask yourself this critical question: How long can I go without a PC before it becomes more than just inconvenient? Some of you may be able to go at least a week; others—like myself—might be affected much more quickly.

Your Current PC Setup

Take inventory of your PC setup by jotting down information on your list about the type of PC you have (for example, Pentium III 900 MHz with 256 MB Rambus memory installed) along with the peripherals you have, including your printer, your scanner, and so on. The following is an example of an inventory list.

- ☑ Intel Celeron 800MHz CPU. Purchased 03-02-00 BIOS is Award (dated 12-30-99)

- ☑ 128 MB PC 100 SDRAM (64 original, added 64 more in 6-01)

- ☑ 20GB WD hard drive (master); added second 20GB Maxtor drive as slave

- ☑ Video, sound, modem, and network integrated into Intel motherboard

Note also what other computers you have available. For instance, if you also have a laptop, this could be useful if your PC or main office space becomes unavailable. A second desktop able to run the same programs, services, and hardware that you run on your main system can be invaluable if it doesn't get struck by disaster as well.

Set this list aside because you'll refer to it again in the next section when you identify what you need to get started again should the use of your PC or office be cut off from you.

This might also be a good time to ask yourself whether your current setup is sufficient for your needs. For example, if you're currently using an older Pentium 2 with 64MB of memory installed and you've been feeling underpowered lately, you may not feel too satisfied by simply replacing that setup with another Pentium II with 64- or even 128 MB should you need or desire to go the replacement route.

Your Current PC Services

PCs today rarely sit unconnected from anything else. Depending on the statistics you read, 60–90 percent of all computers are connected either to another computer, a network of some type, or to the Internet at least part of the time. Many of you now use broadband (high-speed) Internet services and home networks that remain connected to your PCs all the time unless you discon-nect cables. Most of these connections require settings and software that you need to be able to re-establish in the event some major problem occurs.

Writing again to your list, under the category of services, identify all the types of services you use with regard to your PC. These should include

- Phone line connected to your PC

- Internet and online service accounts

- E-mail accounts

- Network protocols

Let's take a look at these services and what you need to know about each one.

Phone Line

If you have a phone line connected to your PC now, you'll probably need access to a phone line later on if you can't use your main PC area. Make a note of this.

Internet and Online Service Accounts

Note on your list all Internet access and online service (such as America Online and The Microsoft Network) account names and passwords that you have.

Place your settings information, account names, and passwords under each service so you have them if you need to set up these services on another computer, or if you've lost them when you restart a disaster-ed system.

If you're using a dialup phone line to access these services, this information can be found under each account in Dialup Networking. To get this information, follow these steps:

1. From the Windows Start menu, choose All Programs ➤ Accessories ➤ Communications.

2. From the resulting context menu,

    • if you're using Windows XP, choose Network Connections.

    • if you're using earlier versions of Windows, select Dial-Up Networking.

3. Right-click the first access account and choose Properties.

4. Click each individual tab and jot down the information.

5. Repeat as needed for additional accounts.

E-mail Accounts

Next, list the same basic information you did under Internet accounts, but this time specifically for the e-mail accounts you use.

Since most Windows users access their e-mail using Outlook Express—part of Microsoft Internet Explorer—I'll show you how to get your e-mail configuration information. If you are using web-based e-mail accounts such as Yahoo Mail or Hotmail, you can usually find this information by visiting your e-mail provider's web site and checking under account information.

To get your information and add it to your list, follow these steps:

1. From Outlook Express, open the Tools menu and select Accounts.

2. From the Internet Accounts dialog box, click the Mail tab.

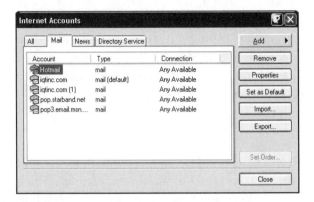

3. Choose the first account you want to check and click Properties.

4. Starting with the General tab and working forward, jot down all the relevant information, including your account name and password, server URL, name of service, POP3 and SMTP mail servers, and so on.

5. Repeat this procedure for each additional e-mail account you have.

TIP *I have a couple of configuration programs for my satellite-based Internet access that have screens containing more than a dozen different settings and IDs I would need to re-establish. Rather than copy all that information onto a sheet of paper or into a protected document, I use screen-shot software to take good-quality pictures of those screens. Then I store these screenshots in my PC Recovery Resource Kit so I can consult them later as needed. Each time my configuration changes—and it does frequently—I simply update these screen shots. Try it!*

Network Information

If you're running a small network, Chapter 14, "Disaster and Recovery Essentials for Your Small Network," will provide you with all the information you need for disaster and recovery. Much of this information also applies to the type of networking you set up as part of a high-speed Internet access account as with cable, satellite, and digital subscriber line (DSL) modems.

Additional Information You May Need

Consider, too, what information you store only on your PC, such as e-mail addresses of work or professional contacts, important phone numbers, and financial data. You need to save a copy of this information, too—either printed out on your printer or copied longhand onto your list (if it's not too extensive). This way, you have this information just in case.

What You Need to Work Again

Now that you have a complete list of what you currently have and what you need, it's time to come up with an "essentials" list of what you would need to get back to work again. Remember, you already have the PC Recovery Resource Kit you constructed earlier, and as this chapter progresses, you'll be adding your protected data to that kit as well.

Bridging the Gap

Recovery is very much about getting from Point A, where you can't function, to Point B, where you can.

The PC Recovery Resource Kit you constructed in the previous chapter can be a critical part of bridging the gap between those two points because it contains tools for doing everything from attempting repairs to having what you need to prep a brand-new system with the data from a totaled PC.

With that in mind, knowing that you can move your protected data as needed, it's time to consider both short-term and long-term strategies for how to cope.

For example, if you know you have a dead hard drive or motherboard, you know you have to replace it. Depending on how you're replacing it, this could take one or more days, during which your main or only PC is unavailable to you. But you also have to come up with ideas for how to handle a more serious problem, such as your home or office being completely unavailable to you and where you may, at best, have just some personal possessions and your PC Recovery Resource Kit at your disposal.

Obviously, the more scenarios you can try to plan for, the better covered you'll be.

Developing a Disaster Recovery Plan

Obviously, the very best result of a disaster is that you, those close to you, and your work and/or living space are functional so that you can continue on as before.

If just your PC won't work, the rest of this book is designed to help you resolve that.

If, however, your PC—or your work space—is going to be unavailable for a period of time, you need to design a contingency plan that gets you back to work as soon as possible.

The easy part is the PC itself, since all you need to do—as long as you have a place to set it up and operate it—is buy a new system and use something like a drive image to set your new system up just like your old one. You'll have different hardware, but your operating system, your settings, your applications, and your data will be all there, the same as before. Drive imaging should be included in your disaster recovery plan.

- But it may not be feasible, desirable, or even possible to replace a PC immediately, so you need to start thinking in terms of "If [this] happens, I can do [that]," for example, "If my PC won't operate today, I can do…."

- "If my PC is unavailable to me for the foreseeable future, I can do [this] in the short term, and move to [this] if the situation persists."

My plan starts off something like this:

- If my PC is unavailable short term, I can move my base of operations either onto my second desktop system or onto my laptop. The desktop system has both its own dialup modem and phone line, plus a high-speed Internet connection, and is connected to my network. The laptop can either use my wireless networking system to access the Internet, or I can install my spare PC Card modem into the laptop, connect the phone line, and use my free Internet access account.

- If my office is unavailable short term under normal circumstances, I can move my base of operations onto my laptop and work from the studio above the garage.

- If my entire home/office property is unavailable and I'm on a deadline at work, I'll take a room at the local business hotel that offers everything I need; I checked—I can even rent a laptop there if necessary, and high-speed Internet access is available.

Include specifics, such as how long you can wait with a dead or unavailable PC before you feel obligated to purchase another one. Also look at some of the additional information provided in this section.

Prepare a rough outline and then synthesize it down into a finished document that you not only copy or back up to protect, but print out and add to your PC Recovery Resource Kit.

TIP *As part of your disaster recovery plan, if your budget permits, start putting aside some money each month into a "PC emergency fund." This can be used to offset the cost of purchasing a new system in the event of a disaster or help you pay for a second system to cover you in the event the first PC fails.*

NOTE *Be prepared to revise your recovery plan as your circumstances—or those around you—change.*

Doing Your Research

You're going to need some additional information that you probably won't find on your PC—except possibly through browsing strategic web sites—and that is too specific for me to provide. Once acquired, these notes should be included in your documented plans.

Insurance Coverage

Some types of disasters may be covered under certain types of insurance policies relating to lost or damaged PC equipment. A standard homeowner's insurance policy would—at best—lump a PC in with other appliances for coverage.

Small business owners and some renters may have a more inclusive policy that specifically lists the overall value of a PC work area. Homeowners may also buy these kinds of policies to add onto their home policy.

If you have insurance, check your policy to see what may be covered. If you have questions, contact your insurance company representative.

WARNING *Beware if you decide to purchase insurance just to cover a home office or other small office. You may see yearly premiums high enough to make a significant down payment on another PC. Check prices and coverage carefully for your area before you make a decision.*

Community Resources

Some communities have special agencies set up just to help people in the event of a disaster, especially local disasters such as a massive fire, flood, or earthquake. What services and help are available can vary widely, depending on the circumstances and the resources available to your community as a whole.

Some agencies may offer temporary shelter, some can point you to others in the community willing to share office space temporarily, and some even offer slight-to-significant financial assistance to help you get back on your feet.

Unfortunately, after a disaster strikes is usually the worst time to try to pull this information together, so check with your city or town government offices for a few emergency numbers you can phone if you find yourself in such a situation. If you've got time, call a few of these numbers ahead of time to determine exactly what services they might be able to offer.

In the most serious of situations, federal assistance is often made available for entire regions that have been classified as disaster sites.

Advanced Research

If you're someone who depends on your PC to make your living, as I do, you may also want to take your research a step farther to see what you can make available to yourself. This may be especially true if you live in an area—like mine here in rural New England—that doesn't offer much in the way of community resources.

For example, if your PC is unavailable for a few days and you don't have a second PC, identify a friend, co-worker, your employer, or other resource who could offer you temporary work space that includes a basic computer setup. They might have a spare PC or laptop you could borrow. In this situation, you can't just assume; you need to ask beforehand to increase the chances of a smoother transition between disaster and recovery.

The same is true if your home or office becomes unavailable to you because of a disaster. If you have a second PC such as a laptop or other mobile computing device but don't have your home/office available, you need a place to charge your mobile battery. A friend or neighbor, for instance, can come in handy for giving you access to power.

There also may be businesses in your area that might allow you to rent space and use their equipment at their location or rent their equipment to take with you for a few days or weeks. Some office supply stores, for example, allow this, as do some printing/office firms chains such as Kinko's. The more advance brainstorming and research you can do, the better.

Assessing Your Plan B Alternatives

For short-term use, there are other options available to you if you can't find a PC or place to borrow for the time it takes you to recover your workspace and working PC.

First, brainstorm the less attractive alternatives. For example, if you can't borrow a PC or space from a friend or family member, you can make use of free Internet access at your local library or at an Internet cafe. With these, you can't go in and load your drive image to get back to work as if it's your own PC, but you can do web-based research and exchange necessary e-mail. It's wise to set up in advance a backup, free web-based e-mail account, such as Hotmail, available at www.hotmail.com, to facilitate the e-mail process when your regular Internet connection and e-mail accounts aren't available.

In addition, many office supply/superstores and copy shops will allow you to use their setups—usually for a small hourly fee. These may give you access to programs and applications you need but can't currently use without your PC.

Look around your greater area to see what else may be available.

A friend told me of a business motel in California that did quite well in the early summer of 2001, when California was being hit by rolling blackouts. This motel advertised a special rate for business people who needed to set up a temporary office to work if their main office was without power. They had printers, fax machines, and many of the extras someone running a busy office might need.

Testing Your Plan

Once you've devised your plan, it's time to test it. Now, you don't need to create a disaster to do this. While it's not necessary to test absolutely everything about your plan, you should drill yourself on important factors so that they stick in your mind. Practice locating the components you need and always make sure they are located within easy access of your PC work area.

As part of the testing process, be sure you cover the following:

- Make certain your PC Recovery Resource Kit is in place and has all the information you need.

- Check the date of your last backups and/or drive image; if they aren't recent, update them immediately.

- Review instructions for recovering backups and drive images.

- Update your plan to reflect any changes to your current setup, what you might need and what services are available to you in a crisis period.

Developing and Implementing Your Data Protection/Backup Plan

Protecting your data so that you have it available should disaster strike is a critical part of the recovery process. After all, you can replace the hardware, the operating system, and the applications on a PC, but you can't usually just go out and buy back the files you've created yourself.

For personal and small business users, there are three practical ways to make copies of your important files and settings:

- Individually copying them to another type of media besides your primary hard drive

- Using a process called *backup* to archive your files together and store them in one or more large backup files that can later be restored

- Using a process called *drive imaging* to make a copy of your hard drive—its operating system, installed applications, and the data

Each of these methods has pros and cons.

Individually copying files can be time-consuming and subject to human error (if you don't remember all the files you need to copy), but it works if you have a small number of files you want to protect in any given time period.

Backups are a time-tested method, and it's a process that can be automated. For example, you can schedule Windows Backup to back up all files created or changed since the last backup you performed (see Figure 5.1). But if you use Windows Backup, you're limited to saving your backed-up files and settings to another hard drive or drive partition or to a low-capacity media such as floppy disks or Zip disks.

NOTE *Floppy disks are probably not practical to use with Windows Backup because they won't have the capacity to store all the files you need to protect.*

Drive imaging is my personal favorite of these methods because it copies everything from Windows, including all your programs and all your data, into an image. But a large hard drive with lots of files and programs could take many recordable CDs to store a single drive image.

As I provide you with more details about backups and drive imaging (copying individual files is probably something you should do almost every day), understand that you may very well choose to use a mix of all three methods for protecting data.

Figure 5.1 *Windows Backup can be set to backup all new and changed files since your last backup.*

Consider the following example: When I'm working on an important file such as this chapter as I write it, I use tools in Microsoft Word to autosave the document every few minutes (in case I don't). But I also manually copy the most recent version of that file to a drive on another computer on my network that acts as a file repository. Then, at least once a week, I perform a backup of my system to record all files that have changed since the last time I backed up my files. Finally, at least once a month, I make an image of my entire primary hard drive so that it reflects all the modifications and additions I've made to my system in the last several weeks.

Using this method, it's been a very long time since I lost a document or needed file on my computer—and I work with hundreds of different files each week. Trust me, I wish I could say the same about my physical paperwork.

My systems have made it through a flood, a small fire, a serious kicking from an angry child, two long-distance moves, countless power incidents, and at least one primary hard drive failure, plus a recent earthquake that measured 5.1 on the Richter scale.

Types of Backups

Do you need to make a full copy of every file on your system every day? Probably not unless you're a major corporation, and then you'd likely be reading one of those dense computer risk management texts instead of this common-sense book.

But you do need to perform backups if you value your files and data. How often and to what degree you back up depends on the amount of work you do that needs protection. If you use your PC casually but the contents of your hard drive are important to you, then do one full backup plus an incremental backup at least once a month, and combine it with copying individual files to a storage medium other than your primary hard drive on a regular basis.

If you use your PC for a mix of business and pleasure, then you may want to back up at least twice a month, if not weekly, and copy your important individual files more frequently. If you create lots of original work each day, you should be backing up in some way every day.

And that's why there are different types of backup methods:

Individual Files   You copy a limited number of individual files.

Full   You back up all or selected files and folders.

Differential   You back up all selected files and folders that have changed since the time of the last full backup.

Incremental   You back up all selected files and folders that have changed since the time of the last backup; changed files are appended (added) to the backup, allowing you to have multiple versions of the same file if needed.

Other Issues in Determining Your Backup Needs

Depending on the type of work you do, it's possible that you create new files each day by writing documents, installing new programs, and saving files you download from the Internet.

Yet even when you don't explicitly create a new file, you're often modifying files on your system without your active knowledge. For example, each time you open your e-mail software and each time you send and receive an e-mail to it, you're changing the index files for your e-mail software. The same is true when you add and remove names from the Windows Address Book you use to store e-mail addresses and names.

Files are also created, for example, when you make modifications to the Windows Registry as you do when you change hardware or software settings and when you get patches and fixes through the Windows Update feature.

So even if you use your PC for purely personal use for an hour or so each day, some files on your system will change almost regardless of what you happen to do on your PC. So if you made a copy of all your files at the end of your day today, you would see changes to some of those files by the end of the day tomorrow.

Determining What You Have

Let's focus on what data you need protected and where it is located, as well as what media you'll be using to store copies of that data.

Identifying Your Important Files and Folders

First, identify the files and folders you want to copy. Your My Documents folder is often a repository for documents you create, for example. If you're storing one-of-a-kind photos in the My Pictures folder, you probably want to copy those files, too.

For other clues, open the applications you frequently use and determine, if you don't already know, where they store the files you create with them. You probably want to protect these files, too. Using Windows Explorer (available under Start ➤ Programs in earlier versions of Windows and under Start ➤ All Programs ➤ Accessories in Windows XP), browse your drive for other files and folders you consider important.

Remember as you work that the more files and folders you have to protect and the larger those files are, the more storage capacity they'll require on the storage medium.

Now, what will you use to store your backups and drive images? Your options are

- Make a copy on the same hard drive in a different folder or partition.

- Copy/back up to a second hard drive—this can be either internal or external.

- Copy/back up to a floppy.

- Copy/back up to other removable storage media such as Zip disks or tape drives.

- Write to a recordable CD—or where available, to a recordable DVD.

You obviously need to have installed hardware to support whatever method you use. So if you want to write your files to a CD—which today often seems like the easiest option—you need a CD-R or CD-RW drive.

But whatever application you use to do backups—or to make copies or to create drive images—needs to support the hardware you're using. You can usually find information on what hardware is supported under Help for the application you are using, as shown in Figure 5.2.

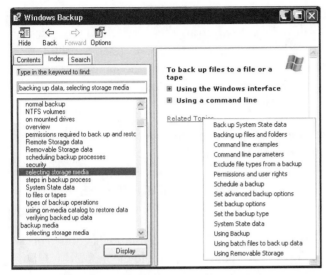

Figure 5.2 *Application Help provides information about supported hardware.*

Make Your Job Easier

Safely protecting your files and other data gets significantly easier if you think logically about where you create and store material you may want to back up or otherwise copy off the main hard drive.

By this, I mean think about where you save critical files to your main hard drive so you can be sure they get copied as part of a backup routine. This is particularly important if you manually select the files or folders you want to back up routinely rather than using an incremental backup where all the files that have changed since your last backup are copied. You'll understand this better as I describe the types of backups.

It Matters How You Store Your Data

Most drive-imaging software allows you to write at least to a recordable or rewritable CD. As DVD recording technology really takes off, you'll see that as well, since even the least capacious type of DVD stores several times more data than a CD.

But most applications permit you to save an image to either another hard disk or to a specially created partition (a way of dividing a large physical drive into smaller logical drives) on your main hard drive.

Because you need to protect your data and be able to recover it as completely as possible, I caution you against storing either backups or drive images *only* to another partition on your primary hard drive. If you lose your primary hard drive or its contents, you've lost both your original setup and data as well as your backup or image. If you have to reformat the drive, the same is true.

If you feel you must store the backups or drive images to your primary hard drive, make a second copy on CD-RWs or other supported media.

TIP *If at all possible, store at least one copy of your most recent backup or drive image away from the building where your PC is located, such as in a detached garage or your workplace rather than in your home. If the worst happens and your primary building is heavily damaged or destroyed, there's an excellent chance the copy will survive.*

Storing backups or drive images to a second hard drive is better because the likelihood of both drives failing at once is relatively small, but storing them to removable media such as CD-RWs is the smartest approach. With removable media, you can make more than one copy and store those copies in more than one place. For example, I keep drive images stored in three different physical locations. Every time I update those drive images, I follow the same procedure.

TIP *Your best efforts at protecting your data will do you no good if you can't locate it later. Label your backups and drive images and store them where you can find them in a crisis.*

Starting Your Backup Routine

Unless and until you decide to go with a separate commercial package, the odds are that you will use the Backup program included in Windows for your backup routine. With that in mind, let's go through the process of performing your first backup. First, however, let me point out some limitations in Windows Backup.

Windows Backup Limitations

One thing to understand about Windows Backup is that it doesn't write backups to every type of drive. It writes backups to recognized drives such as floppy drives, Zip drives, and other hard drives, but it doesn't write to your CD or DVD recording drive. Commercial backup programs usually allow you to write to CD and DVD recorders.

Bear this in mind when choosing what storage media you'll use with Windows Backup, since floppy disks (with less than 1.4MB of storage) and Zip drives (some with less than 100MB but never more than 250 MB) have much less capacity than your hard drive. If your backups are large, consider buying a commercial package or using drive-imaging software; both types of software support CD—and some support DVD—recorders.

Using Backup for the First Time

While the very name of the utility intimidates some people and bores others, Windows Backup is wizard-driven, so it steps you through the process to help. The following steps walk you through a full backup of all major information stored on the computer (the largest type of backup you can do with this software):

1. From Windows Start, select All Programs ➤ Accessories ➤ System Tools ➤ Backup.

2. From the Backup or Restore window, click Next.

3. Select the Back Up Files and Settings option and click Next.

4. On the What to Back Up window, choose All Information on This Computer and click Next.

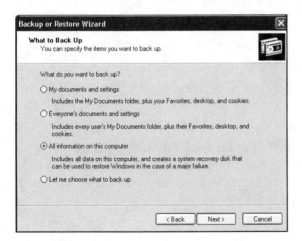

5. In the Backup Type, Destination, and Name dialog box, from the Choose Where You Want to Save drop-down list, select the proper drive where you want to store your backup. Make sure this drive has sufficient space to contain the entire backup.

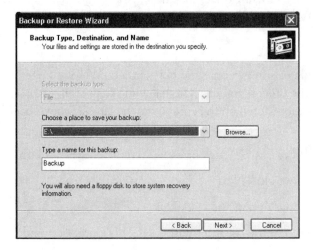

6. On the same window, under Type a Name for This Backup, type the name of the file as you want it to appear. Click Next. Click Finish.

7. When the backup is complete, you'll be prompted to insert a blank floppy disk into your floppy drive to create a recovery disk. Do so.

8. Remove the floppy, label it appropriately, and place this in your PC Recovery Resource Kit.

A Cautionary Tale: Backing Up *Before* an Impending Storm

About a year ago, a fellow who was very busy getting a new distributorship going kept writing to me to ask what he needed to do to protect the hundreds of new records he was creating each day. He had read a column of mine on everyday PC disasters, and he was profoundly worried.

"I can't afford to lose a single byte!" he said again and again.

So we "talked" back and forth in e-mail for some time about his current needs, his expansion plans, his current setup, and so forth. At the end of the regular communication, we set up a decent little plan for him to do a full backup immediately and then do incremental backups each day since he was creating many new files each day. He had the CD-RW writer installed along with backup software he purchased, since he was afraid Windows Backup would be too limiting.

Continued on next page

A Cautionary Tale: Backing Up *Before* an Impending Storm · *(Continued)*

Months went by before I heard from him again, which happened around midnight on a holiday weekend.

"Help! I think I've lost everything here—my database of tens of thousands of records, my forms and invoices…everything."

"What happened?" I asked him, suggesting he restore his backups to regain his records and files.

"Oh, no. I never actually did the backups. I figured I would wait until there was a big storm or chance of a power outage, and then do a full backup. But I didn't have any warning that my wife would get so mad at me she would run the garden hose through the office window and flood the place."

I made some suggestions, but none of them worked. The only avenue available to him was using a professional data recovery service, but a cost estimate from them was extremely high.

"Can't do that," this fellow told me. "But I need the data back. What else can I do?"

Sadly, there wasn't anything else he could do. The backups—or a drive image—would have saved him a great deal of stress, not to mention weeks of reconstructing all those lost records and files. His proverbial ship sailed when he decided to "wait" for the warning of an anticipated disaster before he implemented his disaster recovery plan, and by then, it was too late. In other words, his ship sunk.

Making Drive Images

Drive images, as I mentioned in Chapter 3, "Prevention: Limiting Your Risks," are an excellent way to get a basic system set up again after disaster strikes. For example, if you have to start fresh with either a freshly reformatted hard drive or a whole new system, a drive image taken of your previous setup can help you get back to work a great deal faster than manually installing everything again.

How do you store the contents of an entire hard drive on a recordable CD that has less than 700MB available? Through *compression*, which uses a special formula called an *algorithm* to store an incredible amount of data in a much smaller space.

Two of the best drive-imaging packages are Norton Ghost by Symantec and Drive Image by PowerQuest. Both are priced similarly ($60–70), although you usually pay a few extra dollars for Ghost.

Should you choose to purchase and install a drive-imaging program such as Drive Image, you may find that you are prompted to create rescue or recovery disks to use in the event of a disaster. Often, two disks are created: one that acts as a boot disk and another that contains a floppy-based mini-version of the drive-imaging software itself.

If you don't create these special bootup/recovery disks when you first start the program, please be sure to do so *as soon as possible*. They can be an extremely important part of recovering your system after a failure or disaster.

NOTE *Some companies require you to have these bootup/recovery disks in order to get technical support, meaning if you call for help and don't have these disks made, tech support may tell you to call back after you've made them.*

Choosing a Drive Image/Backup Package

There are several factors to consider when purchasing a drive-imaging program that are also true if you decide to buy a commercial backup program rather than use Windows Backup:

- It must be compatible with your version of Windows.

- It must be compatible with the type of drive you'll record your drive images to; check the compatibility list on the drive image manufacturer's web site.

- It must be compatible with your FAT (file allocation table) type, such as FAT32, which is used by all but much older versions of Windows.

Recording Your First Drive Image

How do you make a drive image? First, install the drive-imaging software in accordance with the manufacturer's directions. Let's go through the process using PowerQuest's Drive Image 2002 (the version to use with Windows XP). Since you've already been warned about storing backups and drive images to your primary hard drive, I'm going to assume you have a CD-R or CD-RW drive installed and the right blank media (CD-R or CD-RW disks) to use with it.

1. From Windows Start ➢ All Programs ➢ Drive Image 2002 ➢ Drive Image 2002.

2. Click Cancel to proceed back the initial wizards screen. (I'll tell you about this after you record a drive image.)

3. Click Setup Wizard. Click Next.

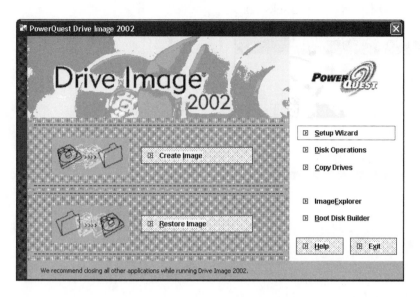

4. From the Setup Wizard, click to select the partition you want to image (the primary hard drive is usually C:\ or Disk 1). Click Next.

5. Under Select Backup Location, click to select An Existing Drive, and then select the location of your CD-R/RW drive. Click Next.

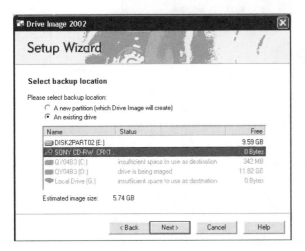

6. From Create Backup Image, click Next.

7. Under the Summary window, check your information, and if it's correct, click Finish. Otherwise, click Back and adjust the settings on the screen.

8. The Setup Wizard then tells you how many CDs will be required to perform the operation you want. For a full drive image at high compression, it may take anywhere between 10 and 20 blank CD-writable disks to record the entire drive image. Click Yes.

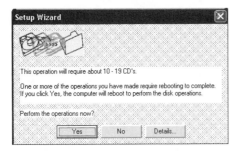

9. You may be prompted at this time to insert the first blank CD-R or CD-RW disk in the appropriate drive, if you haven't already done so.

10. When prompted, remove the first recorded disk of the drive image from your recordable drive, label it, and return it to its case or sleeve, and then provide a fresh blank disc. Repeat as needed until the backup is complete.

NOTE *You have learned how to create backups and drive images. But how do you restore them when you need them? I'll take you through that process in Chapter 13, "Recovering Lost or Damaged Files and Applications." If you've heard that drive images are great but you have to restore the entire image to restore a single file you need, you heard wrong. Recent versions of drive-imaging software allow you to restore individual files from the image without restoring the entire image.*

Using System Restore

Before leaving this topic, let me address a question some of you may have about Windows System Restore and why this hasn't gotten much attention along with backups and drive images.

For those of you not familiar with it, System Restore (see Figure 5.3) is a feature added to recent versions of Windows (Millennium and XP) that allows you to make images of your system, called *restore points*, that serve as markers of how your system is set up at the time they're recorded. The theory is that you can then restore these points when you encounter a problem that messes up your Windows setup. It's like being able to take your PC back in time before a problem occurred.

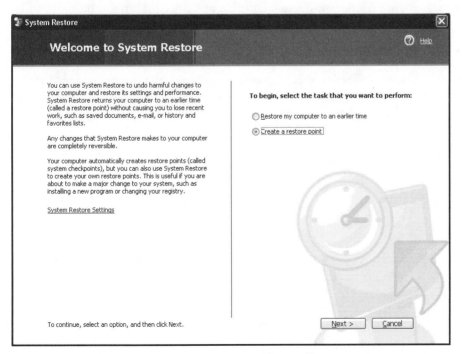

Figure 5.3 *You can create or restore points in System Restore.*

This isn't new software technology; there are a few commercial utilities that have allowed you to do this for several years. System Restore is simply a scaled-down version of those.

While I was pleased to see this feature added to Windows Me and XP, I haven't found it to work well in practice. For one, System Restore usually writes the restore points to your primary hard drive and for reasons I've already explained, storing copies of data in the same place as the original data is a risky way to protect yourself.

Second, many users reinstall Windows in a panic whenever they have a problem; they usually don't try to use the restore points. So the very act of reinstalling Windows may damage those restore points so that they can no longer be used to restore Windows to the previously recorded setup.

Also, System Restore can only do so much. If you change settings or install something that interferes with Windows, restoring one of these points may really help. But it won't do anything to help a serious hardware failure or when your system has reached the point where Windows won't load, regardless of what you try.

Finally, restore points seem particularly susceptible to disruption. Not all of this is poor design, since some users often perform tasks that contribute to the problems, such as trying to delete restore points improperly to save disk space (and the more restore points you have, the greater the disk space it takes).

If you're using System Restore and find it works well for you, keep using it. But use other methods like backups and drive images to store data off that primary hard drive to be sure you'll have your files.

Whether you realize it or not, you've probably already improved your analytical skills just in reading about the major PC components and the way your PC and Windows handles your hardware. Now it's time to pull some of these concepts together and begin developing and refining your ability to effectively troubleshoot problems you may have. Turn to Chapter 6, "Transforming Yourself into a Smart Troubleshooter: Detecting, Analyzing, and Diagnosing."

Transforming Yourself into a Smart Troubleshooter: Detecting, Analyzing, and Diagnosing

If you've watched Saturday Night Live in recent years, you've seen a running sketch called "Nick, the Computer Guy," where users call this computer technician who arrives at their office to berate them for their lack of knowledge. They spit out their problem, he snaps at them, and then he fixes the problem with just a keystroke or two.

What if you could be Nick, minus the attitude?

The truth is, PC troubleshooting usually boils down to common sense paired with a working knowledge of the various components—hardware, operating system, and applications—that comprise a PC.

You don't need to be certified or have a computer degree to extricate yourself and your PC from many of the messes that you or other circumstances get you into. And if you've been using your PC for a few years, you probably already have some troubleshooting skills. Any time you analyze a problem you're having and work systematically through it, you're troubleshooting.

This chapter explains the basic rules of troubleshooting that can help you approach the repair phase of your recovery process. Then you'll learn some of the techniques you can use for spotting the source of a problem, or at least for narrowing it down to a few strong possibilities.

Rooting Out the Problem: Troubleshooting Basics

A good PC technician is two parts sleuth, one part smart user, and two parts person desperate to get the current problem resolved so he or she can get back to work or play. It's how much those first three parts can overcome the final two parts that can ensure your success.

One of the tools a good sleuth has at his or her disposal is the knowledge of the most likely circumstances surrounding a mystery, based on things like statistical averages and past experience. So a PC sleuth should know that some of the most common causes of PC problems include

- Corrupted, incorrect, or bad driver for a device

- Incomplete or bad upgrade

- Poorly behaved program just installed

- Loose or bad cables and connectors

- Corrupted program or program installation

- A temporary problem that can be resolved by a simple restart of your PC

Using this information, a PC detective would

- Check and update drivers.
- Recheck an upgrade or installation and try to repair it, if applicable.
- Check power and cables for looseness or other issues.
- Uninstall and reinstall problem programs.
- Restart the PC to see if the situation resolves.

Rules of the Road

Every troubleshooter, experienced or not, has to follow certain basic rules in working with a PC. Here are 10 of the most important rules you need to follow as you work:

1. Work with adequate lighting.

2. Avoid making snap assumptions.

3. Before you proceed, make certain your data is protected. If you can reach your files and folders, copy or back them up *first*. If you have to troubleshoot to reach that point, do it ASAP.

4. Before assuming a device is broken, check to be sure it's properly connected and plugged into a viable power source.

5. Always check to be sure connections and cables are secure and in good shape. Lots of crimping or gouging of the cable, for example, means you should replace the cable.

6. If you absolutely don't know what to do, *don't* do anything unless you're sure you can back out of it again.

7. Never work inside your PC case with the power connected; the PC must be turned off and the power cord removed from the back of the PC.

8. Never work inside your PC case without being properly grounded using something like an anti-static wrist strap.

9. Never think, "If it doesn't fit, force it." If something doesn't fit, it's usually being installed improperly or is of the wrong connection type.

10. Don't forget to read the instructions. Some of them may be badly written, but they aren't optional. The manufacturer's web site may offer better help.

First Response

If you respond to a problem when you first notice it, you have a better chance at resolving it more efficiently than if you wait. There are a few reasons for this:

- Some of these problems will eventually move from malfunction to outright failure when early intervention could prevent or delay the failure.

- You may not remember the circumstances of the problem's onset once a few days have passed.

- Normal operation of the PC after the problem develops may exacerbate or compound the initial issue.

I ignored this advice recently when I was working on my older laptop and an odd error message popped up on the screen warning me about my battery. I was busy and ignored the error since I knew the laptop's battery had just been recharged. I used the laptop on and off for several more days without ever seeing the error message again. By the time the battery failed—and that was the error message, that the system had detected a problem with the battery—I had all but forgotten about the message and wasted an hour or two trying to figure out why the laptop wouldn't work on the battery power.

Keep a Journal

One of the best things professional repair shops and IT help desks do that most of us do not is keep a record of service on the computers they fix. That record may include hardware added or replaced, along with specific problems and exactly how they were resolved.

Such a record can provide a blueprint for future repairs and upgrades and can remind you how you got yourself out of a particular disaster. For example, if you work through a tough problem with shutting down and restarting your PC, use your journal to note what you did. You can refer back to it later if the problem reappears.

You don't have to make this journal fancy and formal. A thin, spiral-bound notebook or a binder with loose-leaf paper will do. You can make your entries as verbose or as limited as you choose. The important thing is to include enough information so it will make sense to you later, when you may need to refer back to it.

Why not keep the journal on the PC? Well, you want to be able to get to the journal even if the PC doesn't work. Figure 6.1 contains a page from my journal. I keep separate journal sections for each PC I have, and I keep the journal tucked into my PC Recovery Resource Kit when I'm not jotting down entries.

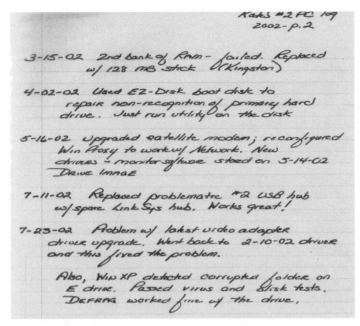

Figure 6.1 *Keep a journal of repairs and changes.*

Use Your Senses

This doesn't just mean common sense, although you need to apply that, too.

First, you need to keep your wits about you. As I mentioned in Chapter 4, "Assembling Your PC Recovery Resource Kit," don't try to troubleshoot when you're panicky, frustrated, under the influence, or past exhaustion. Even the best PC technicians will make mistakes operating under such conditions. Besides the obvious issues, those mental states will prevent you from getting the full benefit from your physical senses: your eyes to scope out the situation, your nose to tell whether you smell something smoking or burning (it doesn't happen often but it does happen), your ears for listening for unusual beeps or strange sounds (especially straining, grinding, or squealing), and your sense of touch for making certain connections are secure and that nothing feels damaged or overheated.

> **TIP** *Cables and wires are important for PC hardware because they provide the physical communication channel between the device and the PC. By using your sense of touch, you may be able to detect a defect or crimping in a cable or wire that you may not be able to spot with your eyes.*

Keep it Simple to Start

In my view, much but not all PC troubleshooting follows a concept typically known as either *Occam's razor* or *the law of parsimony*. The idea is that when you have two or more theories to explain an issue, don't overcomplicate the situation unnecessarily. Instead, assume that the most likely or direct explanation is probably correct until you prove it wrong. When you prove it wrong, then you can move on to the next-most-likely theory.

In my experience—and it's the experience of thousands of other good technicians and PC users—a PC problem is often rooted in the very last thing you did with the PC before the issue appeared.

Always review the last operation or change you made to your system. If you made a change, reverse that change if possible (i.e., properly remove what you installed, switch settings back to their original values). Then re-evaluate your system to see if this resolves the problem. Should this correct the situation, review the change you made and try to identify what you might have done wrong. If the situation doesn't correct, think about the next-to-last change, and so on.

Do No Harm

This is one of the main concepts of modern medicine, and it applies well to PC health, too.

There are two types of troubleshooting situations: those you plan and those you don't. The "Do no harm" concept applies mostly to situations you don't plan and relates to one of the worst types of disasters you can have with your PC, called the *imagined-disaster-becomes-a-reality*. This occurs whenever you panic because of one problem and immediately do something outrageous to break your PC.

One common situation happens when you start to boot up your system and then remember that you want to boot your computer in a different way or go into BIOS. So instead of waiting for your computer to come up fully before you restart, you pull the power cord out of the PC (hitting the power button or Reset button is almost as bad). When users have done this, I've seen PCs get dragged off surfaces as the power cord was pulled or towers topple over and damage the PC contents. I've seen it cause hard drive failures and even video problems as well as Windows difficulties.

Just last week, I saw someone panic when he realized he had not turned off his PC or disconnected power before he removed the cover from his PC and began to uninstall the hard drive. I said, "Wait, what are you doing?" He responded by plugging the ribbon cable he had just pulled back into the powered-up hard drive, killing the drive instantly.

Message: If you do something stupid, stop and think before you do anything else. Instant reactions usually cause more damage than they prevent.

One at a Time

Good PC troubleshooting is done one step at a time.

When faced with a problem, think logically about the possible causes and consider what you can try in order to resolve it. Then try each option one at a time, stopping to evaluate any changes in your system's behavior. If what you tried doesn't have the desired result (i.e., it doesn't fix the problem), reverse what you modified back to its original state and then proceed with your next idea, and so on.

In this way, you avoid creating new problems while trying to resolve the first one. Too often, when you try a whole host of things at once, you can end up with worse results than the original problem. And when you've stacked modification after modification on top of one another, you're not likely to remember everything you did, in what order, and which of those changes caused the new problems.

Here's an example I've heard reported dozens of times in a single week: You just tried to install new office software with special new features (and according to product advertising, they are *all* special new features). But you ran into a problem during the installation, so you ditched the effort and simply deleted the files that had been copied by the CD so far. For the rest of the PC session, you simply browse the Web, downloading nothing and making no other changes to your system. You don't use your PC for a few days but when you next do, you suddenly notice it won't load Windows properly. It acts like it will, but you stay hung at a black screen. You reboot, and the same thing happens. What do you think could be wrong?

If you answered "probably that aborted installation," give yourself 10 tech points, because is the most likely assumption and the first one you should investigate.

In this situation, since you may have made the bad installation worse by trying to manually delete its files, try installing the software again. If necessary, you can properly uninstall it (using Add or Remove Programs in Control Panel) later, but trying to finish the installation may allow you to get past the current situation. Read the software's documentation for troubleshooting tips, and if you're still stuck, you can find help in Chapter 9, "Stabilizing Your Operating System."

You may be thinking, "Wait, it didn't install right the first time, and she's telling me to go back and install it *again*?" Ah, but there's a method to this madness. You can sometimes better correct a bad or aborted installation by doing a completely fresh install and then uninstalling the application. Remember how Chapter 2, "How Your Hardware, Operating System, and Applications Work Together," explained that integration is everywhere in a Windows PC? Once you start a program installation, you may not be able to get halfway through without some changes being made to Windows itself. And this could be the cause of your problem.

NOTE *Fully uninstalling an application through Add or Remove Programs in Control Panel won't cure everything; files and changes made by a program may linger past the program's removal. Your Registry can keep some entries. But you can reduce your problems significantly if you try a full uninstall first, since a majority of programs are written to work with Windows uninstaller.*

A Cautionary Tale: Trying Everything Under the Sun

A long-time associate of mine is more enthusiastic about computers than they are about him. As a result, I frequently get calls to fix problems he's created.

Not long ago, he had trouble with his Internet service provider (ISP), and decided to install one of the free America Online (AOL) CDs he gets in the mail. The installation seemed to go OK, and he was able to set up his account. But something locked up his system during the session, and when he rebooted and Windows loaded, he found he couldn't get online. The AOL software reported one problem, while trying his other Internet account from Dial-up Networking (Network Connections in Windows XP) gave a completely different error. At various times, he received messages about problems with network protocols, his modem, and the COM port the modem was communicating through.

During the next hour, this fellow installed different modems—even modems he didn't have—and deleted ports, removed different devices in Device Manager, and reinstalled Windows at least once. He called for help after the inevitable happened: the "can't get online" problem he started with had quickly evolved into a "can't get into Windows at all" issue. Unfortunately, he had tried so many changes that he couldn't remember the details when he asked me, "So what did I do wrong?"

"You know," I told him, "you tried so many changes without stopping each time to check what you did that I can't even begin to tell you."

We got his problem fixed, but we couldn't step back through the original problem because he had wreaked so much havoc after that. I suspect his original issue could have been fixed in under 30 minutes, but it took me over three hours to get his system back in shape after his try-everything-at-once approach to troubleshooting.

The Best Desktop Troubleshooting Methods

Much of the detective work and troubleshooting occurs not inside the PC case but right inside your Windows desktop. This assumes, of course, that your PC starts well enough to load Windows. If it doesn't, we'll get to that in Chapter 7, "Restarting a Problem PC."

Let's look at some of the ways you can troubleshoot and potentially cure some problems right from bootup and Windows.

Watch Your Bootup Screen

If you're like many of us, you often turn on the PC and then waste a few minutes refreshing your coffee cup or pulling files or papers together while waiting for it to boot. But when you're troubleshooting or even if you just suspect a problem, watch the bootup screen carefully for any errors that may display there well before Windows loads. The BIOS, as part of its work, checks the PC's many components and, if it finds one that is unresponsive or otherwise problematic, it issues a report to your screen. The initial phases of the operating system loading may also report something that can be a critical clue in discovering why something isn't operating properly.

Check Your BIOS

Previous chapters explained how important it is to familiarize yourself with your BIOS while things are operating well so you can better identify a change in your BIOS when a problem crops up. Since the BIOS stores much of the information about the basic hardware attached to your PC—information passed along to Windows—the BIOS is a good place to start when you seem to have a device that's malfunctioning or not seen at all.

To access your BIOS settings:

1. Restart your PC.

2. When the initial screen says, "Press *<this key>* to enter Setup", press the required key(s).

NOTE *Look but don't touch! Until you understand your BIOS and the options it holds (which may be available in your PC or motherboard manual or on the manufacturer's web site), it's important that you look around in BIOS to familiarize yourself with "normal" settings only.*

Review Your Log Files

Whether you realize it or not, different parts of your PC—the hardware, the operating system, and the applications—create log files that provide a summary of any diagnostics performed, how a device loaded up for use, and what device could not be loaded for use.

BOOTLOG.TXT, available in all consumer versions of Windows and located in the root folder of your primary hard drive, is one example of this. Though you'll find it a tough read, this file lists all the devices and services that make up your boot process. Look for text that indicates "FAILURE" or "INCOMPLETE." Figure 6.2 contains a sample BOOTLOG.TXT file, as it should appear without failures or incompletes.

NOTE *The Event Viewer contains a summary of the same kind of information that's provided in* BOOTLOG.TXT. *See the "Using the Event Viewer" section later in this chapter.*

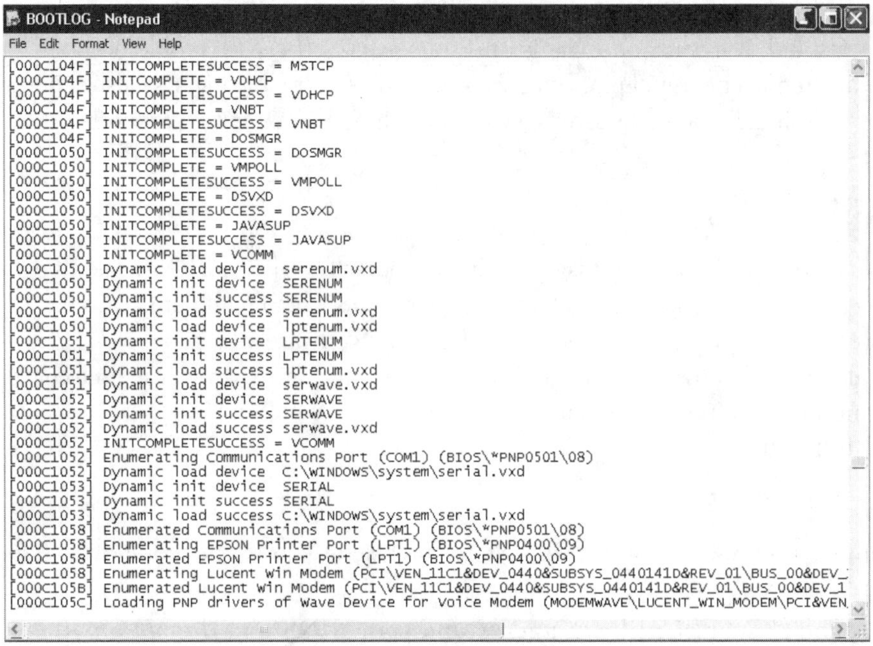

BOOTLOG - Notepad

File Edit Format View Help

```
[000C104F] INITCOMPLETESUCCESS = MSTCP
[000C104F] INITCOMPLETE = VDHCP
[000C104F] INITCOMPLETESUCCESS = VDHCP
[000C104F] INITCOMPLETE = VNBT
[000C104F] INITCOMPLETESUCCESS = VNBT
[000C104F] INITCOMPLETE = DOSMGR
[000C1050] INITCOMPLETESUCCESS = DOSMGR
[000C1050] INITCOMPLETE = VMPOLL
[000C1050] INITCOMPLETESUCCESS = VMPOLL
[000C1050] INITCOMPLETE = DSVXD
[000C1050] INITCOMPLETESUCCESS = DSVXD
[000C1050] INITCOMPLETE = JAVASUP
[000C1050] INITCOMPLETESUCCESS = JAVASUP
[000C1050] INITCOMPLETE = VCOMM
[000C1050] Dynamic load device  serenum.vxd
[000C1050] Dynamic init device  SERENUM
[000C1050] Dynamic init success SERENUM
[000C1050] Dynamic load success serenum.vxd
[000C1050] Dynamic load device  lptenum.vxd
[000C1051] Dynamic init device  LPTENUM
[000C1051] Dynamic init success LPTENUM
[000C1051] Dynamic load success lptenum.vxd
[000C1051] Dynamic load device  serwave.vxd
[000C1052] Dynamic init device  SERWAVE
[000C1052] Dynamic init success SERWAVE
[000C1052] Dynamic load success serwave.vxd
[000C1052] INITCOMPLETESUCCESS = VCOMM
[000C1052] Enumerating Communications Port (COM1) (BIOS\*PNP0501\08)
[000C1052] Dynamic load device  C:\WINDOWS\system\serial.vxd
[000C1053] Dynamic init device  SERIAL
[000C1053] Dynamic init success SERIAL
[000C1053] Dynamic load success C:\WINDOWS\system\serial.vxd
[000C1058] Enumerated Communications Port (COM1) (BIOS\*PNP0501\08)
[000C1058] Enumerating EPSON Printer Port (LPT1) (BIOS\*PNP0400\09)
[000C1058] Enumerated EPSON Printer Port (LPT1) (BIOS\*PNP0400\09)
[000C1058] Enumerating Lucent Win Modem (PCI\VEN_11C1&DEV_0440&SUBSYS_0440141D&REV_01\BUS_00&DEV_
[000C105B] Enumerated Lucent Win Modem (PCI\VEN_11C1&DEV_0440&SUBSYS_0440141D&REV_01\BUS_00&DEV_1
[000C105C] Loading PNP drivers of Wave Device for Voice Modem (MODEMWAVE\LUCENT_WIN_MODEM\PCI&VEN
```

Figure 6.2 *Checking* BOOTLOG.TXT *for problems*

TIP *To find more of the logs created by your system, use the Search tool listed in the Windows Start menu and search your primary hard drive (usually C:\) for any files containing the word log, such as* `*log.*` *or* `*.log`. *Most if not all of your log files are stored as text files that you can open easily using Notepad.*

Scoping Out System Information

Another source for information about what hardware is attached to and seen by your system is the Windows System Information tool (MSINFO32). This tool is particularly useful for looking up additional details about your system and its readout is usually required by technical support personnel.

To run MSINFO32, take the following steps:

1. From Windows Start, select Run.

2. In the Run dialog box, type **msinfo32** and click OK.

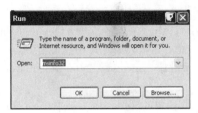

Notice that the System Information window divides the details about your system into several major categories, including Hardware Resources, Components, Software Environment, Internet Settings and (if applicable) Office Applications (for Microsoft Office installations only). Click the + next to each entry to expand it and then select specific listings under each category to get more details.

Of special note, check out System Summary (for basic PC information), the Conflicts/Sharing listing under Hardware Resources, and any listing called Problem Devices located under Components (see Figure 6.3).

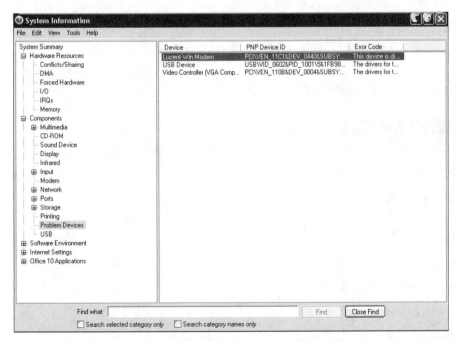

Figure 6.3 *Checking out system information using MSINFO32*

Using Windows Device Manager

Chapter 2 introduced the subject of Windows Device Manager, but let's look at it now from a troubleshooting perspective. It's a great utility to use to check the status of your hardware, to update your drivers, and to remove a device (either permanently or to let it be redetected when your PC is restarted).

If you're not familiar with Windows Device Manager, now is the time to do so. Device Manager is the gateway through Windows into the hardware you have installed, the drivers used to help those devices communicate with the operating system, and the hardware resources (such as IRQs discussed in Chapter 2) assigned to those devices.

Normally, most of the devices you have installed to your PC (and some that are part of the very basic system like the system clock) are listed in Device Manager. When you need to be concerned is when a device you've attached doesn't appear in Device Manager, with some caveats. The caveats exist because some devices, such as individual USB hardware, as well as digital cameras and scanners in many older versions of Windows, may not be listed there. But the ports or other ways they connect to the system (such as the Universal Serial Bus Controllers entry) are.

You should also be concerned when you see devices listed in Device Manager that have either a yellow exclamation mark or a red X. The exclamation mark alerts you to a problem with a device, and the X tells you the problem is so severe, the device has been disabled. Be aware that there are other reasons for a red X, including that you deliberately disabled a device in Device Manager without physically removing the device from your PC.

To check your PC for such problems, follow these steps:

1. From Control Panel, click the System icon.

2. Choose the Hardware tab and then click Device Manager. (In earlier versions of Windows, simply select the Device Manager tab after clicking the System icon.)

3. From Device Manager, click the + next to each listing category to expand it, and look for the yellow exclamation mark or red X on devices.

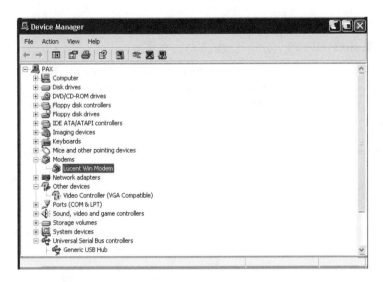

4. If you find such an entry, right-click it and choose Properties to learn the details. Click the Troubleshoot button (if available) to see what Windows reports back to you. Follow any advice offered.

You can also use Device Manager to do an in-session check for changes to your hardware. To do this, simply follow the steps listed previously, but instead of choosing Properties when you right-click in step 4, choose Scan for Hardware Changes.

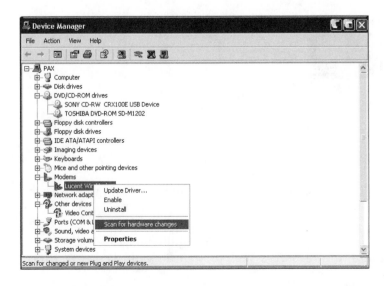

Working Through Problems with Device Manager

Next, let me step you through four of the common ways you can try to get rid of these nasty yellow and red warning symbols using Device Manager.

Removing No Longer Needed Devices

If you're ready to retire or replace a piece of hardware, it's important to remove its driver through Device Manager. This should usually happen just before you shut down the PC to remove the hardware itself (although this doesn't apply to USB and IEEE 1394 devices).

Follow these steps:

1. From Device Manager, locate and right-click the device you want to remove and reinstall.

2. From the menu, choose Uninstall and then click OK in the Warning dialog box. Close Device Manager.

NOTE *Versions of Windows earlier than XP and Millennium, such as Windows 98, require you to select the device and then click the Remove button.*

3. If the device isn't a USB or IEEE 1394 device, go to the Windows Start Menu and select Shut Down.

You can then disconnect power to your PC and go through the steps necessary to remove the hardware.

NOTE *If you continue to load the driver somehow when you no longer have the hardware for it, you will waste hardware resources such as your limited number of IRQs.*

Removing and Reinstalling Devices

One of the first and easiest ways you can try to work around a yellow or red warning symbol in Device Manager is to remove the device listing, shut down and restart your PC, and let the device be redetected with its driver reinstalled automatically. This behaves very much like installing a new piece of hardware, except that you don't have to touch the hardware itself. If the device is detected and a driver is not in the operating system, the Add Hardware Wizard appears.

Here are the steps you need to take:

1. From Device Manager, locate and right-click the device you want to remove and reinstall.

2. From the menu, choose Uninstall and then close Device Manager.

NOTE *Earlier versions of Windows, such as Windows 98, require you to select the device and then click the Remove button.*

3. From the Windows Start Menu, select Shut Down and then Restart.

4. Once Windows restarts, check Device Manager again to see if the yellow or red symbol is now gone.

There is one caveat here: If you have updated the device's driver since you first installed your current version of Windows, you need to have that disk or file you downloaded with the updated driver handy so you can point the Add New Hardware wizard to it.

Updating Device Drivers

Often, the only thing you need to get a problematic device working again is to update its driver. Believe it or not, you see this sometimes even if you simply move devices about on your desktop as you might after an office disaster. (Sometimes though, you need to remove and reinstall such devices and then provide the driver update.) Certain drivers can be installed automatically by the Windows Update utility without any additional work from you.

But when you've visited a manufacturer's web site and downloaded an updated driver for your device or received a disk containing such an update, you can use Device Manager to take you through the updating process.

1. From Device Manager, locate and right-click the device you want to update.

2. From the menu, choose Update Driver.

NOTE *Earlier than XP versions of Windows, such as Windows 98, require you to select the device, click the Properties button, choose the Driver tab, and click Update Driver.*

3. When prompted, provide the location of your updated driver.

Disabling Problem Devices

Here's one last way to use Device Manager to work around a problem device, although this method won't remove yellow or red warning symbols. It may, however, make it easier for the PC to work without tossing out lots of errors.

Let's say you have a situation where one of your CD drives is misbehaving. You can't seem to get it fixed right now, but you're not ready to try more advanced repairs or replace the drive, nor are you ready to remove the drive. However, you want Windows to stop complaining about the drive (assuming it does). The right step might be to disable it in Device Manager.

Disabling a device does nothing to your PC or the drive except tell Windows you won't be using it, which should remove the odd errors. You can do this by:

1. In Device Manager, click the + next to the DVD/CD-ROM drives listing to expand it.

2. Right-click the drive you want to disable and choose Properties.

3. From the General tab, under Device Usage, click the scroll-down list box to choose Do Not Use This Device (Disable). Click OK.

4. When asked to confirm your decision, click OK.

TIP *If you need to try to use this device again, repeat steps 1 and 2, but instead of choosing Properties when you right-click, choose Enable.*

Using Event Viewer

Windows XP keeps three major event logs that correspond to events occurring in and around the key components of the operating system:

Application   The application log records events occurring in and around your installed applications and programs and is stored as `appEvent.evt`.

Security   The security log monitors security-based events and is stored as `secEvent.evt`.

System   The system log records events occurring in and around the overall system and is stored as `sysEvent.evt`.

In most situations, the two most useful event logs for troubleshooting are `appEvent.evt` and `sysEvent.evt`. The application log tells you about problems and successes encountered when installing, loading, and using your programs. The system log provides critical system information about whether key drivers have loaded properly and any difficulties that were encountered in configuring your system for normal use.

1.   From the Windows Start Menu, right-click My Computer and select Manage.

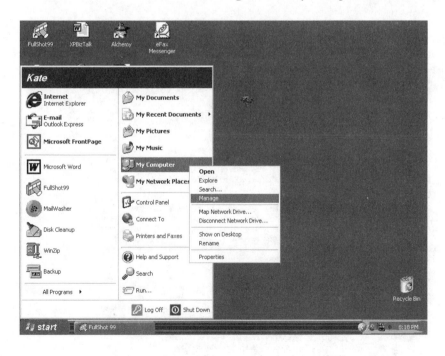

2. From the Computer Management console, under System Tools, double-click Event Viewer.

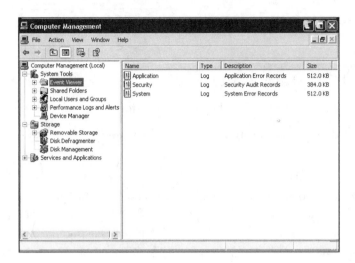

3. As Event Viewer opens, the three components are listed: Application, Security, and System. Click System.

4. Review the long list of entries here.

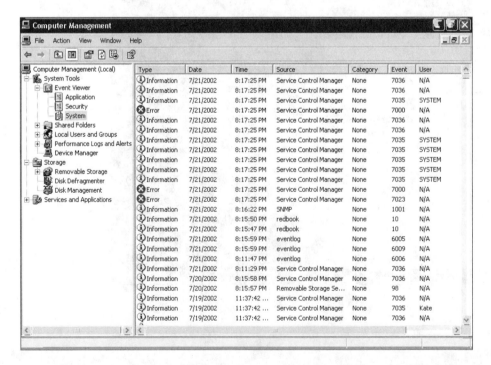

As you review these event logs, notice the three different types of events (under the Type column) that are recorded in this file:

Information (blue "I")   The information category is literally anything that does not fall under Warning or Error, and it includes listings for various types of events, including when the printer is invoked and when your PC loads a driver or a program.

Warning (yellow exclamation triangle)   The warning category records events that are significant enough to warrant your attention (i.e., potential problems) but usually not critical enough to cause a serious problem.

Error (red X circle)   Any entry with this listing represents a potentially serious problem, one that could or did create a data failure, a connection failure, or when a particular piece of hardware didn't load.

Some of the entries in this event log may not make a lot of sense to you because many of these entries refer to processes and services you don't always see or use directly. But you can get more details about each entry by right-clicking the entry, selecting Properties, and reviewing the information provided.

TIP *Still don't know what an entry in the event log means? Some entries you may be able to look up by name using the Search option under Help and Support from the Windows Start Menu.*

Determining a Problem's Origin

One of the most important things you can do while troubleshooting is to avoid missing the obvious clues of a problem, which may include:

- Blinking lights on devices or power lights that should be lit, but are not

- Error codes displaying on a control panel, such as with some printers

- Disconnected power or devices switched off

- Odd noises indicating stress or malfunction

- Error messages or warnings on your screen

When you encounter a problem, scan your immediate work area for any of these clues. Document what you see, hear, or even smell. These clues could provide important information either to you or to the expert help you may end up seeking. Then try to correct the problems. For example, if you notice your PC or printer is unplugged, plug it in. If your printer gives an error code, look it up in the printer manual.

Error Messages and Trouble Codes

Too often, when an error message window pops up on your screen, you barely glance at it before closing it. You just want to get back to work or play, so you're willing to hope the problem resolves itself.

However, the types of error messages Windows and applications display can be invaluable at helping you troubleshoot a problem. This is true even if you don't necessarily understand what the error message means because you can do two things with the full text of an error message:

- You can use resources to look up the error message and what you may need to do to correct it.

- You can supply the full error message to technical support, who may be able to decipher it for you, or at least look it up in their more extensive support databases.

Trouble codes usually refer to special errors that devices, such as printers, may provide in a lit display. These trouble codes can be looked up in the device manual. If you don't have the manual, you can probably look them up on the manufacturer's web site.

You can often look up the name or text of an error message in the Microsoft Knowledge Base, a searchable database of known issues in Microsoft products like Microsoft Windows XP. You'll learn more about Microsoft Knowledge Base in Chapter 15, "Finding Help Online,"

You can also search for trouble codes in Windows Help and Support (or Windows Help in earlier versions). This is a great feature because it not only looks at the contents of the online Help file contained in Windows, but also (with an available Internet connection) searches the aforementioned Microsoft Knowledge Base.

Let's use as an example what might happen when you receive a "low on memory" error message while working on your PC. You would take the following steps:

1. From the Windows Start Menu, select Help and Support.

2. From the Help and Support window, type **cannot find modem** in the Search dialog box and then click the green arrow.

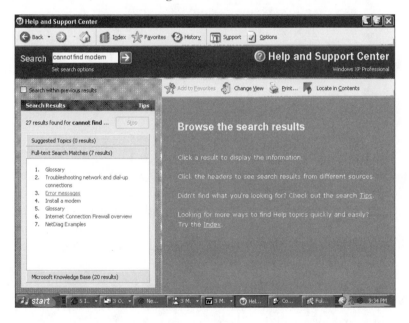

3. A list of results appears in the left lower pane. Click Error Messages on the list.

4. Try to locate the specific error message you're getting and click it; read the error message description to determine the problem and what you can do to resolve it.

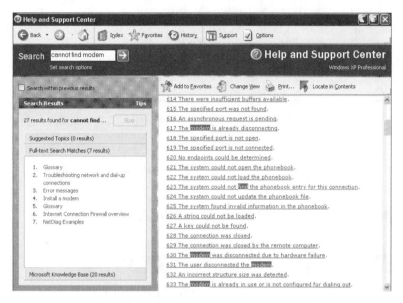

When to Suspect...

As you already know from previous chapters, the integration between your PC, its hardware, its operating system, and the applications you've installed is designed to make new installations go much easier, but it often turns troubleshooting into a hunt for a needle in a technical haystack.

This section provides you with some of the clues you can watch for in trying to determine the source of a technical problem or failure. You'll also pick up some tips on the kinds of spot analysis you'll need to perform as a decent troubleshooter.

When to Suspect Hardware

It's smart to at least suspect hardware if any of the following is true:

- The PC won't turn on, the display does not appear on the monitor, or the hard drive won't engage.

- You have just installed or removed or reconfigured hardware, even if it's a different device that you're currently experiencing problems with.

- The problem appears immediately after you've been inside the PC case or touching or adjusting the connections.

- Your boot screen reports a problem with a device.

- It's a device that would normally be seen in your BIOS but it's no longer listed there.

Don't just think in terms of the main hardware itself when you're experiencing difficulty with external components such as a monitor, printer, scanner, or external drive. Since most of these devices use cables to connect them to the PC and separate power cords to connect them to a power source, the cables and cords could be the source of the problem. The same applies to in-the-case components that require a power connector and/or a cable running between them and another part of the PC, as with internal drives. For example, your hard drive might not be dead if it's not responding; it could be a damaged or faulty ribbon cable connecting the drive either to another drive or to the IDE controller on your motherboard.

An under-powered PC power supply can also mimic hardware failure because the unit just doesn't have enough juice to supply power to every part of the PC. If you've added one or more new devices that require a power supply connection and suddenly can't get all the devices powered up or recognized, this is a possibility.

It's not necessary, however, for a piece of hardware to fully fail before the device becomes unavailable or begins to behave badly. A corrupted or outdated driver can sometimes mimic the effects of a hardware failure. Reinstalling the driver or updating the driver should resolve this. But if you have just updated a device driver and then experience problems with that device, it's likely that the new driver isn't compatible with your version of Windows or something else on your system.

NOTE *A few experienced hardware techs I know swear by using a stethoscope, much like a doctor does. They use it to listen to their power supply and hard drives while in operation so they can appreciate the difference in sound when a problem develops. Use stethoscopes on a power-connected system with extreme caution, however.*

When to Suspect Software

If only one application is misbehaving, the problem is likely the software itself. This could be due to the following possibilities:

- The program became corrupted during its installation.

- Something has fouled the program's necessary files after installation.

- The program may not be compatible with your version of Windows, or with some other program you also have installed.

First, back up any data you have stored as part of the application. Once this is done, uninstalling the problem application (using Add or Remove Programs in Control Panel) and then reinstalling it should correct a bad installation. When you reinstall, make sure you are not running any other applications when you do so. If a problem remains, uninstall the application altogether until you can check with the program's support options (by phone, via the Web) to try to determine what is causing the incompatibility.

Also, some applications, such as recent versions of Microsoft Office, have a repair option built into them that, when used, tries to correct detected problems with the software. You may want to try this option before you uninstall and reinstall.

TIP *If, after installing new software such as a web browser or a game, you find your video display starts to misbehave (doesn't redraw correctly, leaves garbage on the screen), assume it's your video adapter driver, which may need to be reinstalled and/or updated.*

NOTE *If it's your application data (documents, spreadsheets, and so on) that is having fits, you should find some helpful tips in Chapter 13, "Recovering Lost/Damaged Files and Applications."*

When to Suspect a Virus

Oddly enough, computer viruses tend to be not only overly suspected, but also both under- and over-estimated. As a result, many people think they have viruses who don't, and those who are suffering the effects of a virus often don't know they have a virus.

One of the urban myths surrounding viruses is that any misbehaving hardware is the result of a virus. While it's possible for certain viruses to affect your hardware—and indeed, a very small percentage can—most viruses don't. What they can do is corrupt the software and operating system—and even the BIOS—working with that hardware.

A few of the most commonly reported symptoms of computer virus infection are

- You can't boot the PC.

- Your operating system seems extremely confused.

- You receive "out of memory" or other unexpected error messages trying to run programs (anything ending with a *.exe or *.com file extension).

- The virus attaches itself to your Microsoft Office macros.

- Your anti-virus software suddenly won't run.

- You receive an annoying message announcing the virus's presence.

- The virus starts sending e-mail automatically—and attaching itself to these e-mails—to people in your Windows Address Book. (These outgoing e-mails will appear in your Sent folder in Outlook Express.)

The best thing to do—whether or not you suspect a virus—is to check your system thoroughly using an up-to-date anti-virus software package such as the ones discussed in Chapter 4, "Assembling Your PC Recovery Resource Kit."

When to Suspect the Operating System

If you're having problems with just one application, the chances are there's a problem with the application and how it's installed, or something may have affected the integrity of the files used by that application (a virus, a bad spot on the hard drive, or a crash-induced corruption).

However, if you're seeing bad behavior among a group of applications or almost every application on your PC, the problem is most likely rooted in the operating system.

A grunged Windows installation is likely to hang or crash frequently (including the fatal "blue screen of death" errors), fail to shut down properly, produce many error messages, and may experience difficulty trying to locate and open the files you select. It may refuse to correctly install new programs, give "low memory" messages soon after you start your system even with a large amount of RAM installed, and in general, appear to make the entire PC run significantly slower than it did in the past.

Windows can start behaving badly for a number of different reasons, including:

- Corrupted core files

- Incomplete Windows upgrade

- Poor disk maintenance (scanning, optimizing)

- Low available hard disk space

- Problems with the Windows Registry (lots of old entries, bad editing)

- Virus

- Adding one or more badly behaved applications and especially programs that run all the time in the background

If the problem crops up suddenly, you can always restore a previous backup done when your system was working well. Also, if you use System Restore in Windows Millennium and XP—or another product that provides similar services such as GoBack—you can restore your system to a previously stored point.

NOTE *Think a recent Windows Update may be the cause of your current dilemma? You'll learn how to tackle that and other matters in Chapter 9, "Stabilizing Your Operating System."*

In the worst-case scenario, make sure your data is protected using the methods laid out in the preceding chapter so you can start fresh using the guidelines in Chapter 16, "Starting from Scratch the Smart Way." Unless the main problem is with the hardware (a problem with the BIOS, for example), a full reconfiguration should speed your system up considerably and resolve any long-standing performance issue.

TIP *Windows shutdown problems are fairly common. To avoid them, keep the list of programs running on startup down to a minimum, keep your device drivers updated, use Windows Update to keep your Windows installation in good shape, and close all your open programs before initiating shutdown.*

When to Suspect Power Problems

Some power problems you can see. You can see your lights flicker or go dim as a large appliance like a refrigerator or air conditioner begins to cycle up. You may have also seen the lights temporarily grow brighter than normal, as during a power surge.

Any such effect you can see, your unprotected PC can feel because while the power supply affords a small measure of barrier protection between a power flux and PC components, it's not designed to hold back a big fluctuation or surge.

Of course, there are power problems you can't see, too. For example, ever come home to find the PC off when it was on when you left? It's possible some sort of power event—such as power failure—occurred while you were gone. If the PC in turn won't turn on or won't start properly, it's reasonable to assume this power event had something to do with it.

Suspect power also if you—or someone else for you—has been working on components on your PC that directly connect to power (either an outlet or the power supply within your PC). It's possible, in such a situation, to either

- Incorrectly reconnect power after the event, or
- Forget to disconnect power before the event, which can fry many of the PC components

Replacing the power supply itself on a PC is no big deal. I'll take you through the steps for doing that in Chapter 11, "Avoiding Power and Overheating Problems." The real issue is that a power flux can damage your motherboard and almost anything connected to it (which means most of your PC components), and that means you'll need to replace the whole PC, or individual pieces of it.

What do you do when your PC either won't start at all, barely starts before it hangs on an error message, or just refuses to load Windows? Lots of people panic or kick something, but I'll walk you through more helpful responses (such as using a boot disk or Windows Safe Mode) in the next chapter.

CHAPTER 7

Restarting a Problem PC

Q uite honestly, any time you turn on your PC and it won't start properly is a disaster. After all, you have something you either want or need to do and this crucial tool is unavailable. It's not like the PC is the luxury item it used to be; it's basic equipment through which you work, study, create, communicate, and yes, even relax.

Too often, a PC that won't start properly inspires such frustration or trepidation in users that it can be difficult to get a good idea of exactly what behavior the PC is exhibiting. Yet how it behaves can sometimes tell you much about the symptoms that are causing the crisis.

This chapter will help you through the process of performing an initial assessment of your PC crisis, show you how to check and rectify common causes of problems in starting your system, and instruct you about the different ways you can get into Windows if it won't come up normally. Along the way, you'll become familiar with troubleshooting methods you may have heard of before such as clean booting, Windows Safe Mode, and a helpful tool in Windows XP called Recovery Console.

> **WARNING** *If disaster has your PC located in a dangerous situation—where water is present, where electrical wiring may be exposed and/or damaged, and so on—don't try to fix it there. Cut power to the PC by disconnecting it from its power source. Move it to a safer location or wait until the dangerous aspects of your work area have been resolved before trying any of the steps outlined here.*

Assessing the Situation

First, establish exactly what the problem is. Recognize that the first symptom you notice may only be part of a larger puzzle. For example, the odd little extra noise you hear when you start your PC may signal a straining hard drive. But the straining drive could be due to something else, such as a fan that has been clogged and barely functioning for a long period of time, causing a heat crisis for more than just the drive.

By looking not just at the most obvious symptom, but at what else may be related to it, you can keep your eyes open to more complex possibilities when assessing a problem situation.

> **TIP** *Once you've established that there is no immediate danger, try again to turn on the PC. A failing power switch, for example, might require you to press the power button firmly two or three times before you get a response.*

What You Can Determine

When you press the power button, what do you get? Pay close attention. What you hear or see—or don't hear or see—can influence what you do next.

You may need to remove your PC cover first to tell exactly what is or is not happening when you try to start the PC. Remove the cover using the steps described in Chapter 2, "How Your Hardware, Operating System, and Applications Work Together." Don't forget to have the power disconnected for the actual case removal and during any time you have your hands inside the unit. (You will, of course, be wearing your anti-static grounding wrist strap.)

If the PC appears to be completely dead, meaning you have no indication anything is happening when you try to power up the PC, look first at the power considerations discussed in this chapter. If the PC makes some of the usual sounds of booting up but you see no display, check your hardware connections. A loose connection between the monitor and the PC can account for this. This is also a smart time to analyze any changes you made to the PC in the session before this occurred. For example, adding hardware that is either not working or not installed properly could produce this result, especially if what you added was a new adapter in one of the available bus slots on your motherboard.

If the PC tries to boot and you see a display but the PC simply hangs there, going no farther in the boot process, it's time to try the alternative booting methods discussed in this section.

Are you hearing lots of beeps? If this is coming from your PC rather than from something attached to your PC such as a printer or scanner that is fussing because the boot process is stalled, it's likely that the beep codes built into your motherboard's BIOS are alerting you to the type of problem the PC is having. Different makes and versions of BIOS have different beep codes, where four beeps alert you to one situation and six beeps tell you about another. Chapter 2 explained how to determine your make and model of BIOS. Once you know this, you can check the BIOS manufacturer's web site using another PC to see what your beep codes mean.

NOTE *This is an ideal time to review the basic PC bootup process described in Chapter 2. You might get clues there regarding your current situation.*

TIP *Have you had recent problems starting your PC? For example, did the PC not always respond the first time you pressed the power button? This can indicate everything from a bad power connection (where the wires coming from the motherboard to the power switch have been damaged or are no longer properly connected) to improperly installed or connected hardware to a failing power supply.*

What to Do When the PC Won't Turn On

There are two rather ordinary events that you tend to dread disproportionately to their frequency of occurrence: times when your cars don't start and times when your PCs won't start properly. I'll leave the issue of the cars for another book, but there are some important steps you can take when the PC is misbehaving.

A Cautionary Tale: Before You Head to the Junk Yard

The only comment I've ever heard more from PC users than "I have a virus" (usually erroneously) and "But I don't want to upgrade," is this one:

Help! My PC is dead!

But the term "dead" is relative. And believe it or not, at least one U.S. state has a law against shooting your PC when you think its demise has come.

Just as I was writing this chapter, an acquaintance phoned me asking for new PC shopping suggestions. Knowing she had purchased a new PC within the last 18 months, I found myself asking what the problem was with her current system since she kept using the term "replace."

As it turns out, there were several different problems, some of which had begun many months ago. Her power switch had begun to fail (it didn't always respond when she pressed it), her BIOS was giving her odd messages when she booted the PC, and she was developing bad sectors on her hard drive. All of these issues had been exacerbated since she first noticed them, but she did nothing to try to resolve any of them, hoping they might just go away. (I could relate to that philosophy—in my 20s, the car I drove was almost older than I was and operated only under a steady provision of WD-40, duct tape, and prayer.)

However, about a week before her call to me, the PC wouldn't start at all. On a whim, I suggested she check a few things and then gave her the number of a good technician in her area. "Get it checked before you decide to junk it," I told her, deciding not to mention the fact that had she contacted the manufacturer when the initial problem (the failing power switch) first happened, her PC would have still been covered by its warranty.

She phoned back and left a message for me a few days later: her PC was back up and running beautifully again for less than $40. Loose wiring in the power switch just needed to be tightened, the BIOS errors were the result of a prematurely dead CMOS battery that needed a $5 replacement, and her PC manufacturer was sending her a new hard drive to replace the one amassing bad sectors.

While your results may vary, this is another reminder to try to address problems as they arise and that it's worth an effort to check these issues out before you decide the PC must be junked.

Checking Power

The very first thing you need to do when you have a PC that doesn't respond when you turn it on is to check the power and the power connections to the PC.

First, be sure the power cable is firmly connected to the back of the PC and that this cable is plugged into an outlet, surge suppressor or protector, or an uninterruptible power supply (UPS). If it's plugged into anything except a direct electrical outlet, verify that whatever it is plugged into is in turn connected to power, and that the power is on.

A simple way of testing this is to take a working device, such as a lamp, and plug it into the same outlet that the PC is plugged into. Make certain this device is working, however, or it won't be a valid test. If the working device doesn't respond, check electrical devices located elsewhere in that room or in other rooms to see if they have power. If nothing has power, check your circuit breaker panel (or in very old homes and offices, a fuse box) and if necessary, contact your power company.

However, even if you see power working elsewhere, you shouldn't assume that it's not a power issue until you investigate. For example, it's possible that the PC is plugged into an outlet on a particular circuit that has been tripped, meaning it has shut down, while other lights and appliances in the same room are on another circuit that is still engaged and working. In an old house where I once lived, the PC was on a circuit separate from anything else in that part of the house except for one bathroom outlet. Sometimes when my housemate plugged the blow dryer into that outlet and turned it on high, my PC and desk area would go dark. Eventually, I had to call an electrician.

TIP *If you smell anything burning or you hear anything very strange, turn off the PC and disconnect power immediately until you rule out whether the PC is the cause of the smell or sound.*

Checking Connections

Considering that I've had professional PC support technicians—and my own experience—tell me repeatedly that the most common reason a PC won't start or work properly is because the PC is disconnected from working power or a needed component isn't firmly connected to the PC, I always check my physical connections first.

Obviously, the easiest connections to check are the ones outside the PC, and that's where you should start unless you have just been inside the PC case for another reason. In that event, the chances are almost as strong that you may have disconnected an internal component that requires a connection or wrongly connected something.

External Connections

The primary connection to verify is always the power connection, mentioned earlier. In fact, it's not a bad idea to reverify the state of the power connection throughout your troubleshooting and repair work to be sure it's in the same state you remember.

I know lots of friends and colleagues are apt to say, "Oh, I did that with the power turned on and I didn't have a problem." Unfortunately, these same folks aren't apt to help you defray the medical or other repair costs involved when you try it with the power on and your result is far less favorable. Unless you obviously need power (because you're trying to troubleshoot within Windows itself) or you're specifically told to leave the PC on while you perform a step (as when adding and removing USB and IEEE 1394 devices), assume that the power should be not only turned off but disconnected.

But there are other external connections to check:

- the video cable running from the monitor to the back of the PC where the outer edge of your video adapter is installed

- cables coming from external devices such as printers, scanners, mouse, keyboard, drives, cameras, and joysticks

- separate power cords running from some of your external devices to another power source (an outlet, a surge suppressor, and so on)

Be sure that all cables and connectors are firmly attached and show no signs of damage or crimping. Ever get your mouse cord in a knot? Unfortunately, I have. These cords and cables aren't meant to be treated like string; they contain communications channels for the devices to talk to the PC.

Look at power indicator lights (typically green, but sometimes amber or red) on your devices. Anything that should have an illuminated power indicator but doesn't is suspect for a disconnected power source or outright device failure.

Internal Connections

As I mentioned previously, you should suspect an accidental disconnection or misconnection of some component inside the case if you've just recently been inside your PC to add, remove, or adjust hardware. Even if you didn't leave a connection unattached or you accidentally knocked one off, you may have loosened the connector enough to cause a problem.

In this situation, knowing how the inside of your PC should look can go a long way toward being able to distinguish what's different when you have a problem.

TIP *If you're reading this before you experience a problem, consider this: If you have a camera (especially a digital camera) available, take some decent photographs of the inside of your PC from different angles while it's all working fine. Store these photos somewhere you can reach them if your PC becomes incapacitated. Then you can consult them and try to follow cables and connectors in the photos to determine where things should connect and how they should be oriented.*

With that said, however, the kinds of issues you're apt to encounter from a loose or missing internal connection are usually *not* a PC that won't turn on at all. Instead, loose internal connections usually report device failures on the initial bootup screen or later, within Windows itself.

Other Factors

If nothing happens when you try to turn your PC on and you've checked everything else covered thus far in this chapter, broaden your investigation.

Check to see how your PC connects to power. If the PC connects to anything else besides directly into an outlet, it's possible the intermediate device—the power strip that lets you plug additional devices into a single outlet, a surge suppressor, or a UPS—has failed and can no longer supply power to the PC. So check any intermediate devices to see if other working devices operate when plugged into them.

In addition, it's time to check your power supply. When you turn your PC on, the power supply should engage and supply power to various PC components. You should be able to hear it and feel the air moving if you place your hand near the vent at the back of your PC located where the power supply fan pushes hot air from the system. If there is no noise from the power supply, the power supply is likely dead and must be replaced (see Chapter 11, "Avoiding Power and Overheating Problems").

What to Do When the PC Won't Boot

Now let's assume—even though I told you to limit your assumptions—that the PC will start in the electrical sense of the word but won't perform its normal operations or let you into your Windows desktop. This section explains the ways you can spot problems and try to get your system back into working order.

WARNING *Are you having this problem with a new PC or one less than a few months old? If so, exercise your PC warranty and contact the manufacturer's customer support line.*

Common Booting Errors

Thankfully, your PCs are kind enough to *sometimes* tell you why they aren't behaving properly. Decoding what they tell you so you can fix them, however, is sometimes the real challenge. The longer you work with PCs, the better chance you'll have of spending less time trying to research or decode an error message or warning.

Booting errors—as opposed to Windows loading errors—usually report problems with a specific device or with its communication channels into the PC. This hardware may be a device you recognize such as something to do with a drive, or something you may not recognize, including less well-known devices like a drive or device controller, a chipset, or a specific memory address.

When you see a booting error, get the error message down on paper—perhaps in the journal recommended in the last chapter. Try to get the error message word for word because the exact wording can matter if you need to research the error on the Web or call the manufacturer's support line to get assistance.

In addition, if you later do something to try to fix the problem and the error changes or disappears, note that, too. By logging in your PC journal the exact error message and what you did that caused the error, you can reference it the next time such an event happens. If the message just changes (read one way before, another now), this may tell you something about whatever step you took to correct it. It may indicate that you actually caused a new problem in resolving the first one, and you may want to go back and undo the change you made. Or it may indicate that the situation has improved, and you may just need to make an additional adjustment or two to remove the boot error altogether.

If you're seeing a boot error, check your BIOS to be sure your BIOS Setup opens. If it doesn't, it may be corrupted or damaged or the CMOS battery may be so low on power that it can no longer keep the settings intact. Also review your BIOS for any changes that may have been made. (This is another good reason to familiarize yourself with your BIOS Setup when things work so you have a basis for comparison.) Be sure your hard drives are detected, for example. Verify that no device that was previously enabled has been set to a disabled status. If so, this needs to be changed back and your settings saved when you exit BIOS Setup.

Before explaining how to research the error messages and warnings you may see, let's look at the categories of common booting errors.

Keyboard-Based Errors

Keyboard errors can happen for a few different reasons:

- Dead keyboard
- Malfunctioning keyboard (loose keyboard connection to the PC, stuck key or keys, moisture in the keyboard)
- Dead keyboard controller

For a dead keyboard, shut the PC down, remove the current keyboard (it connects at the back of the PC, near where your mouse connects), and replace it with a working keyboard.

A malfunctioning keyboard needs to have its specific problem resolved before it can be expected to work again. With the PC off, disconnect the keyboard and use compressed air or a small blunt device to try to unstick the key(s) or leave the keyboard upside down and detached to remove moisture. Then try the keyboard again. If you can't fix the keyboard (and much beyond what I've already told you, you can't), you need to replace it.

A dead keyboard controller, on the other hand, isn't as simple as buying a replacement keyboard since the controller is located on the motherboard itself. This usually requires replacing the entire motherboard, but consult your motherboard or PC manufacturer to be sure.

There is one more situation in which you could see a keyboard-related error on bootup; this happens when your only keyboard is one that connects through your USB port rather than through the usual PS/2-style keyboard port. Because Windows has to start to load to begin the full recognition process for USB devices, a USB keyboard may not be recognized by a PC before Windows loads. You can usually get around this by simply adding a second standard (non-USB) keyboard to your system. However, you're unlikely to experience this problem except when you first install a USB keyboard. If you don't get the error then, you should be able to use the USB keyboard every time thereafter without an error.

Drive-Related Errors

Be aware that some of the more difficult errors to work around are drive-related errors at bootup. These errors usually occur because the PC cannot get a response from a needed drive such as your booting hard drive or the drive does not recognize that it is attached to the PC.

NOTE *Chapter 17, "Resurrecting a Dead Hard Drive," covers drive-related errors in detail.*

If you've just installed a new hard drive or you've changed your drive configuration, shut down your system immediately, disconnect power, and go inside the case to verify that your connections are correct and firmly seated. If you inspect the hard drive's ribbon cable, notice that one of the wires is red. The red wire must face the power connector. Go into BIOS Setup to be sure that the BIOS sees the drive and correctly reports the size and drive letter of the drive you've installed.

Some drive-related issues happen because some catastrophic event such as a virus or serious crash has corrupted or overwritten the master boot record (MBR) of a hard drive. In this situation, you need to resurrect a viable master boot record to let the drive work with the PC. You'll learn later in this chapter how a Recovery Console command called `fixmbr` can help you do that (and you usually won't lose your data doing so, but make sure your data is protected anyway).

How the drive is installed for use plays a huge role in whether it works, too. Note the following:

The hard drive requires 12 volts from the power supply to start up. It is possible to have a bad power supply when things like the case or keyboard LEDs still illuminate.

In a hard drive, pin 1 on the ribbon cable (the red wire) must face the hard drive's power cable.

The power connector into the hard drive may not be seated correctly. The connector is keyed but not inserted all the way in. (This is one of the most common problems with a hard drive and the easiest to repair.)

If the hard drive is new and you installed it with a new cable, the new cable could be bad. Use the old cable prior to deeming your drive bad.

On certain floppy drives, the red wire may not face the power connector. Check with the floppy manufacturer for more information.

> **WARNING** *If you're getting recurrent drive errors each time you start your system, regardless of the steps you take to try to resolve them, make sure you copy that data off the drive just in case. As soon as you can get into Windows, back up this data.*

Virus Warnings

If you try to start your PC and receive a message warning you about the presence or detection of a virus, stop and think before you panic. As discussed in Chapter 4, "Assembling Your PC Recovery Resource Kit," have your anti-virus scanner available to run from either the hard drive itself (if it's still operational) or from a floppy disk. Run the anti-virus scanner to try to remove the virus before you proceed.

Except for working with the anti-virus disk and any boot disks you may need for the process, avoid inserting other floppies into the floppy drive, especially when you need to turn off the PC. You don't want to risk the chance that you will contaminate other disks, which can either reinfect you later or infect someone else who borrows a floppy from you. Most anti-virus programs have a virus detector that runs on floppies. You start the program, insert the floppy, run the test, and then insert another floppy. You must run this program on all your floppies. If you miss just one, that floppy could contain a virus that will cause you to start this procedure over again. If your floppy or e-mail system contaminates another system, you could be held liable for any damage to that system. You'd rather be safe than sorry.

No Errors Because There is No Display

This is a very common problem. This section describes the steps to take if you have a PC that may or may not be booting up properly but whose display you cannot see (meaning that you can hear it booting but you can't see it).

First, check whether you made any change during the last session that may have affected this. A badly seated adapter that you just installed into your motherboard could account for this problem. Try to restore your system to its state prior to this change and see if you can now see the display.

Next, follow the cable that runs from the back of the monitor to the video adapter connector at the back of the PC. Both ends must be firmly connected. This cable cannot be damaged. A common problem is bent pins in the cable end. If they are bent, try (carefully) to bend them back with small needle nose pliers. If this fails, replace the cable. If the cable is molded into the monitor, bring the monitor into a qualified repair shop.

Then you need to look for a power indicator on your monitor. If it's not lit, either the monitor is not getting power (so you need to make certain it's plugged into a working power source) or it's dead and needs to be repaired or replaced. But if the monitor is showing a lit power indicator, it's not the power, yet it could still be a dead monitor (e.g., picture tube is gone) or something like a dead video adapter or even a dead motherboard. Simply plug the monitor into another PC. If the monitor works, the problem is in your PC (probably in the video adapter). If the monitor doesn't work, either replace the monitor or drop it off at your friendly repair shop. Prior to sending it to a repair shop, ask them for a quote. If they say it's $75 just to look at it and it's a 15" monitor, it's not worth repairing when you can get a brand-new monitor for about $100.

Resources for Checking Errors

Whatever the error you're seeing, it may only make sense to you once you get more information, or at least more information than a small error message or warning box is likely to offer you. Some of the best sources for getting more details—along with possible solutions—for the error you're seeing include

- Help and Support under Windows XP and Windows Millennium
- Your PC manual/documentation
- Microsoft Knowledge Base (`http://search.support.microsoft.com`)
- Software publisher's web site
- Hardware manufacturer's web site

TIP *Some of these options require you to have another computer, or at least another means of getting into your currently disabled computer. This is another great reason to have a second PC available to you, either one you use in your home or office or one you can use at a friend's or associate's.*

Other Means of Booting

Now turn your attention to situations where your PC may start up fine, and boot up without error, but it simply won't load the operating system or won't load it in such a way that you can properly use it.

Some of these solutions depend on a boot or startup disk such as the ones you created or collected in Chapter 2. Other solutions use the troubleshooting tools built into Windows to let you get around a problem so you can reach a point where you can attempt to fix the problem, like Safe Mode and the Windows XP Recovery Console.

NOTE *What if you're receiving Windows Registry errors trying to load Windows? This is covered in Chapter 9, "Stabilizing Your Operating System."*

Using Your Boot Disk

How you start your PC using a boot disk depends on what type of boot disk you have, as you learned in Chapter 4. The usual process is as follows:

1. With your PC turned off, insert the boot or startup disk in the appropriate drive (usually the floppy drive).

2. Turn the PC on.

A system boot disk (usually a floppy) tries to boot your system, but it's likely to leave you at a DOS command prompt. From there, follow the steps outlined in Chapter 4 to try to get into Windows. Realize that if the system boots from the floppy and not the hard drive, the hard drive is the bad guy. The ribbon cable may have slid out, the ribbon cable may have gone bad, the hard drive power connector may have slid out, the BIOS may be set incorrectly (the C: drive isn't on the boot list), or the drive may have gone bad. Check the simplest possibility first—the BIOS setting!

A startup disk, depending on the type, usually facilitates getting you into Windows itself and typically loads a CD-ROM driver in case you need to load your Windows install CD at some point during the recovery process.

If you're using Windows XP, you can also use your Windows XP install CD to boot your system. You insert it into your CD or DVD drive and then try to start your system. You can also couple the Windows XP install CD for startup with the Recovery Console, discussed later in this chapter, to try to fix some of the problems.

Special Boot Disks

Besides your standard boot disk, you may also have special boot disks (discussed in Chapter 4). These may include special recovery disks from manufacturers. Some computers today—including "self-healing" PCs being introduced by IBM and others—have an emergency restore function built right into the keyboard. Use these boot disks according to the instructions provided either with your PC documentation or with your emergency utility package.

Performing a Clean Boot

A *clean boot* is to a way of trying to load a normal Windows session, but minus all the extra functionality that tends to get added to the bootup and Windows startup process over a period of time. A clean boot is useful if you suspect that something loading during bootup or startup is what is causing the problem you are currently experiencing.

The tool within Windows to do this is called the System Configuration utility (or MSconfig), and you can use it to prepare to boot your Windows cleanly by following these steps:

1. From the Windows Start Menu, choose Run.

2. In the Open dialog box, type **msconfig** and click OK.

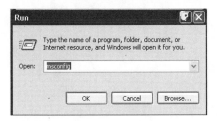

3. Select the General tab, click to choose Selective Startup, and then click to clear these check boxes:

    *   Process SYSTEM.INI File

    *   Process WIN.INI File

- Load Startup Items

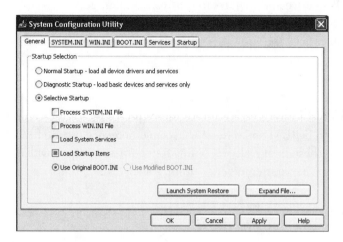

4. Choose the Services tab.

5. Click to select Hide All Microsoft Services and then click Disable All. Click OK.

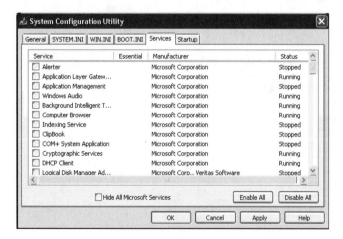

6. When prompted whether or not to restart your PC, click Restart.

7. Once the system restarts, evaluate the startup to be sure it starts fine. If you see messages on the screen, write them down so you can research them afterward. Ditto for any other notable issues.

If the problem with booting resolves once you restart using a clean boot, something in those initial startup files is causing a problem. You can repeat steps 1–2 in the previous sequence and then, for step 3, click to readd one of the services you removed. Do this one at a time. For example, the first time you return to the System Configuration Utility, re-add the process SYSTEM.INI file. Then proceed with your restart and clean boot. If Windows has a problem once you do this, the problem is most likely your SYSTEM.INI file.

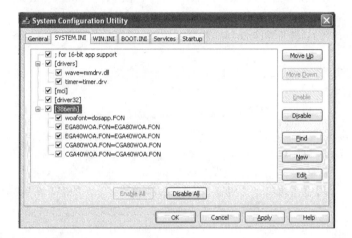

TIP *You can use the SYSTEM.INI, WIN.INI, and Startup tabs in the System Configuration Utility to review what is selected to run from each. Click to remove checkmarks to disable the feature or function.*

Now, until you remove Selective Startup, your PC will always start using this clean bootup method. To return to a normal startup, follow these steps:

1. Run MSconfig.

2. From the General tab, click to select Normal Startup. Click OK.

3. Next, select the Services tab, click to uncheck Hide All Microsoft Services, and then click Enable All. Click OK.

The next time you restart your PC, it will boot up normally.

NOTE *Notice in the General tab of the System Configuration Utility another option called Diagnostic Startup. While this is also a troubleshooting option, part of how it works involves invalidating any restore points you may have created using System Restore. For this reason, a clean boot is probably a safer option for you.*

Using Windows Advanced Options Menu

Although you mostly know Windows through the way it automatically loads as you boot your PC, Windows actually offers some different options for starting the operating system, depending on what you need to do or the situation you face.

You can find the Windows Advanced Options menu (called the Start menu in earlier versions of Windows) by pressing and briefly holding the F8 key when your PC begins to boot and before Windows tries to load.

Look at Table 7.1, which lists the options that may be helpful to you.

Table 7.1   *Helpful Windows Advanced Options*

OPTION	WHAT IT DOES
Safe Mode*	Choose this option to start Windows in a special troubleshooting mode.
Safe Mode with Networking	Select this option to start Windows in this troubleshooting mode, but with basic network support. This option is useful if you're running a network.
Safe Mode with Command Prompt	Same as Safe Mode with Networking, except this option takes you to a DOS-style command prompt for running commands rather than into the Windows graphical user interface (GUI).
Enable Boot Logging*	Use this option to create an extensive log of the boot process (explained in detail in Chapter 6, "Transforming Yourself into a Smart Troubleshooter").
Last Known Good Configuration	Use this option to try to start Windows normally but using the last known good settings, which reverts your system to the way it was during your last saved session.
Start Windows Normally*	Use this option to start Windows as you normally would.

* These options are available in earlier versions of Windows.

Using Windows Safe Mode

Windows Safe Mode is a special troubleshooting mode for loading Windows in the event of a problem and has been available in Windows 98/98 Second Edition, Windows Millennium, and Windows XP.

Safe Mode operates something like its name suggests: It loads Windows in a way that reduces your overall system's dependence on unessential hardware and focuses on core, default drivers to load only the basic devices such as your hard drive. As such, devices like your printer, CD-ROM drive, digital camera, and scanner won't be available in Safe Mode. While this is limiting, it's a much better way to try to run Windows if you suspect a driver or something else you have installed to the operating system is causing your current symptoms.

What does get loaded in Safe Mode is this:

- Default video adapter and monitor settings
- Basic Microsoft mouse driver
- Only essential device drivers
- Network connections, only if you specify Safe Mode with Networking

Windows Safe Mode won't help in every situation. If your Windows installation or hard drive is seriously compromised, for example, you probably won't be able to load Windows even in this special mode. This could occur if essential files have been deleted or corrupted.

Don't use Windows Safe Mode to do your normal work. Safe Mode is generally used to get in, check or adjust a setting, and then restart your system in normal Windows mode.

To load Windows in Safe Mode, follow these steps:

1. From Windows Start, choose Shut Down and then Restart.

2. As the system begins its restart, press the F8 key.

3. From the Windows Advanced Options menu (in earlier versions, the Start menu) that appears, choose Safe Mode.

NOTE *Ever try to upgrade your video adapter and find you have problems with the driver? Safe Mode can be used to set your system back to a basic display driver. Using this basic default driver may better allow you to upgrade the system without problems. Then you can restart your system and install the driver for the new video adapter. Chapter 8, "When Upgrades Go Wrong" has more information about upgrades.*

Using Safe Mode to Reach Windows Troubleshooting

You may have noticed that you didn't get a big, thick manual with your copy of Windows. That's because almost all of the documentation is built into Windows itself or is online on the Internet through Windows. Unfortunately, this isn't too helpful when your PC won't load Windows properly. How do you get to it?

Through Safe Mode, you can reach some of the troubleshooting wizards built into Windows through the Help and Support Center.

Once you have Windows loaded in Safe Mode, take the following steps:

1. Go to the Windows Start Menu and click Help and Support.

2. From the Help and Support Center window, click Fixing a Problem.

3. Click any of the options on the list in the upper left-hand pane to select troubleshooting and help categories. Follow the wizard through its steps.

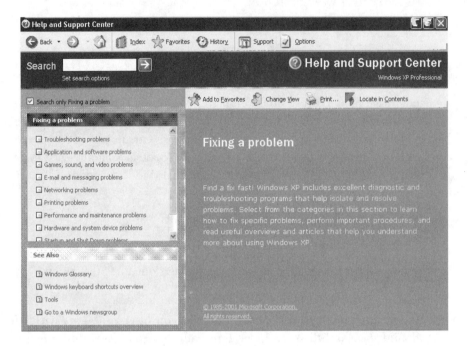

Using Safe Mode to Remove a Problem

One of the best ways to use Safe Mode is to remove either a newly installed or updated driver or a newly installed device or program that may have disrupted Windows enough to cause it not to load—or not to load properly.

For example, let's say a disaster has rendered your current video adapter inoperable. You replace it with another video adapter, which seems to work fine. Then you apply a driver upgrade for the video adapter. When you next reboot, the PC either shows no display whatsoever or the driver you have for it creates a miserable display in Windows.

To resolve this, you can either try to reinstall the driver or roll the driver back to the previous version you were using that worked. You can do this in either Safe Mode (if needed) or in normal Windows (if you can get into it) by taking these steps:

1. From the Windows Start Menu, choose Shut Down and then Restart.

2. As the system begins its restart, press the F8 key.

3. From the Windows Advanced Options menu that appears, choose Safe Mode.

4. Once Windows loads in Safe Mode, choose Windows Start and select Control.

5. In Control Panel, double-click the System icon. Choose the Hardware tab and click Device Manager.

6. Locate your display adapter (what Windows calls your video adapter), right-click it, and choose Properties.

7. Select the General tab and click Reinstall Driver. (To select Roll Back Driver, choose the Driver tab and click Roll Back Driver.)

8. When the Hardware Update Wizard appears, choose Install from a List or Specific Location (Advanced). Click Next.

9. Click Don't Search. I will choose the driver to install. This allows you to choose your setup rather than Windows automatically trying to configure it for you.

10. From the Hardware Type window, select Display Adapters and click Next.

11. Click Have Disk.

12. With the disk containing the needed driver for your video adapter installed in the proper drive, point Windows to the location of this driver.

13. Click OK.

14. From Windows Start, choose Shut Down and then Restart.

This process works for Windows XP, but earlier versions of Windows do not support the extra options like Roll Back Driver. If you're using an earlier version than Windows XP, follow the steps in the previous chapter for removing a device driver in Device Manager and supplying the driver for it when you restart the PC. Restarting the PC should automatically load the Add Hardware wizard when it perceives a "new" device has been installed.

Using Safe Mode with System Restore

Now let's look at another way you can use Safe Mode in disaster recovery.

If you have enabled System Restore in Windows Millennium or Windows XP to create restore points in order to revert your system back to an earlier point of reference, you can use Windows Safe Mode, if needed (since you can restore in normal mode, too), to get your system started and then restore your system to a point when it behaved well. All created restore points should be available to you, provided you used System Restore prior to the current problem. However, it's usually best if you choose the System Restore created closest to the date the PC last worked well.

But there are a few things you should know before you do this. First, any restoration of a previous configuration in Safe Mode can't be undone later through System Restore. Second, System Restore can't create any new restore points while in Safe Mode. In addition, one time when I tried this, I found that it corrupted all restore points except the one I restored, so I had to build fresh restore points from that point forward.

To try to perform a System Restore in Safe Mode, take the following steps:

1. If your system is up and running, perform a shutdown and restart, and restart the system in Safe Mode.

2. Once Windows loads, from the Windows Start Menu, choose Help and Support.

3. From the Help and Support Center window, click Performance and Maintenance.

4. Under Performance and Maintenance, select Using System Restore to Undo Changes.

5. Under Pick a Task in the right-hand pane, select Run the System Restore Wizard.

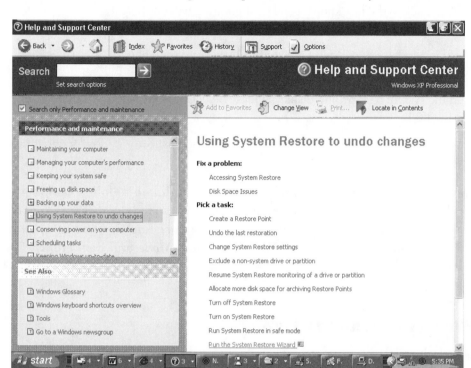

6. Select Restore my Computer to an Earlier Time. Pick the date you want to restore to and the computer will restart.

Using Last Known Good Configuration

Last known good configuration refers to another method you can use to try to roll Windows back to a point before a serious problem developed. This option was formerly available in only professional versions of Windows such as Windows NT 4.0, Windows 2000, and Windows XP Professional Edition.

This option is helpful for situations where a new driver or program may have caused a problem with your configuration or with Windows Registry and does not require you to go into the Safe Mode in order to use it. Nor does it require that you have turned on a feature ahead of time, as with System Restore.

However, last known good configuration is meant as a tool rather than as a magic bullet. It won't work if your Windows installation is seriously damaged or corrupted by a drive problem, a virus, or other means. For example, if you install a bad program that actually removes core Windows files, rolling back to the last known good configuration will not help.

To see if this option can help you with your current dilemma, follow these steps:

1. From the Windows Start Menu, click Shut Down and then choose Shut Down and Restart.

2. When the system restarts and displays Please Select the Operating System to Start, press the F8 key.

3. From the Windows Advanced Options menu, choose Last Known Good Configuration. Press Enter.

TIP *Wondering which solution to use? A good rule of thumb to follow is this: If Windows starts but has problems, use normal Windows mode and then Launch System Restore. If Windows does not start, use the Last Known Good Configuration option. If that fails, try to start Windows in Safe Mode and then launch System Restore.*

Using Windows XP Recovery Console

For those of you who may have been around long enough to hear of DOS, Windows Recovery Console is a command-line console troubleshooting environment that looks very much like DOS. You type commands at a DOS-looking command prompt rather than working in the GUI of Windows.

But it's not quite DOS. There are more limitations and safeguards. For example, some commands can only be used in Recovery Console and you only have access to strategic folders such as Windows.

WARNING *Recovery Console is only available in Windows XP.*

Recovery Console is also not quite like the recovery disks that still come with some PCs as a tool provided by PC manufacturers to help you recover your basic setup after some catastrophic event. Some of these recovery disks can be destructive, especially if you're not sure how to use them, because you can end up wiping your hard drive back to the point you were at when you first bought your PC (another healthy reminder why you need to back up your data to protect it).

Windows XP Recovery Console can be used in two different ways:

- Run from the CD

- Installed to Windows as a startup choice

Be aware, however, that there are times when you may not be able to run Recovery Console the way you choose. For example, a serious problem with your hard drive or Windows might prevent you from being able to load it from the hard drive. You might also face a situation when you can't use your CD or DVD drive to run your Windows XP install CD (or you've misplaced it because you were napping during Chapter 4 "Assembling Your PC Recovery Resource Kit").

TIP *For this reason, I installed Recovery Console to my hard drive and I keep my Windows XP install CD handy. You may find it smart to do that, too.*

The Limitations of Recovery Console

Most, if not all, commands listed for Recovery Console only work in Recovery Console; they usually don't work when run from the command-line console (similar to a DOS window) in Windows itself.

Installing Recovery Console

Should you choose to install Recovery Console to your hard drive, as I suggest, you'll see it's a simple and fast process.

NOTE *When installed to the hard drive, Recovery Console takes approximately 7MB of disk space.*

To install Recovery Console, take these steps:

1. With Windows XP loaded, place your Windows XP CD into the CD or DVD drive.

2. Click Start ➤ Run.

3. From the Run dialog box, type **CD_drive_letter:\i386\winnt32.exe /cmdcons**.

4. Follow the on-screen instructions.

TIP *You'll want your connection to the Internet available when you do this because Recovery Console immediately checks a Microsoft web site and then downloads and automatically installs any necessary updates. While you can press the Esc key to get around this, you probably want the updates.*

Deciding When to Use Recovery Console

Because Recovery Console requires you to work with commands—which not everyone is comfortable using—and because there are some limitations on what you can do using Recovery Console, try to resolve your situation first using the roll back to the last known good configuration option or Safe Mode before you move to Recovery Console.

Launching Recovery Console

How you launch Recovery Console depends on whether you opted to install it to your hard drive or whether you choose to run it right from your Windows XP install CD.

Launching from Windows XP CD

When you use Recovery Console from the Windows XP install CD, the CD can act as a boot disk. It boots and prepares the system with just enough basics to allow you to run Recovery Console to troubleshoot—and hopefully resolve—your current crisis. To do this, take the following steps:

1. Insert the Windows XP install CD in your CD or DVD drive.

2. Shut down and restart the PC.

3. You may be prompted to load certain options to make the system boot from the CD; choose any options you require.

4. Once Recovery Console setup loads, follow the on-screen prompts until you reach the point where you can select R for repair/recovery.

5. Choose the Windows installation you want to recover. (Note that this option is available only where more than one operating system is installed to the PC.)

6. When Recovery Console appears, begin typing commands or type **help** for a list of them.

7. When you're done, type **exit** to quit Recovery Console and restart the PC.

TIP *When you're finished with the Windows XP install CD, remember to return it to your software kit as part of your PC Recovery Resource Kit.*

Launching Installed Recovery Console

To launch the Recovery Console from your hard drive (if installed), follow these steps instead:

1. Shut down and restart the PC.

2. When prompted by the Startup menu, select Recovery Console.

Important Recovery Console Commands

As its name suggests, Recovery Console includes commands designed to provide information when troubleshooting a problem and commands that allow you to fix specific issues. Table 7.2 lists those commands you're most apt to use in a recovery situation, followed by some examples of how you would use Recovery Console to analyze and/or repair a problem. For a complete list of commands available in Recovery Console, use Help and Support in Windows XP to search on the words "Recovery Console." You can then either look at them command by command or review an overview of commands listed under Recovery Console Commands (see Figure 7.1).

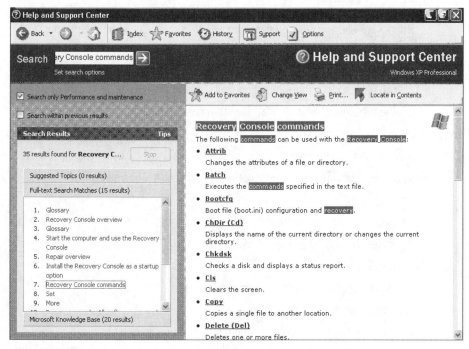

Figure 7.1 *Get a list of all Recovery Console commands.*

WARNING *Use extreme care in properly typing the commands and their switch options (special controls that affect exactly how the command does its job) in Recovery Console. While safeguards and limitations are built into Recovery Console to reduce the amount of damage that can be done, it's still possible to make a serious mistake.*

Table 7.2 *Important Recovery Console Commands*

COMMANDS	SWITCHES	FUNCTION
Chkdsk		Checks the specified disk for errors.
	/p	Checks extensively, but does not repair.
	/r	Checks and tries to recover lost file data.
Del		Deletes a file. This file will not show up in Recycle Bin.
Disable		Disables a specified service or device driver.
Diskpart		Creates or deletes drive partitions. Use this command with extreme care; creating, changing, or deleting disk partitions removes all data contained on the partition.
Exit		Quits Recovery Console.
Expand		Extracts the contents of—or just a specified file from within—a compressed cabinet (*.cab) file, such as those found on your Windows install CD.
	/d	Lists the files contained in a .cab file without expanding the files.
	/f:*filename*	Extracts the specific file.
Fixboot		Fixes—by rewriting—the partition boot sector for your hard drive.
Fixmbr		Repairs—by rewriting—the master boot record for your booting hard drive.
Format		Formats a disk.
Help		Lists Recovery Console commands.
Listsvc		Lists all the drivers and services in use on your PC.
RD		Removes a directory.
Ren		Renames a specified file to a new specified filename.
Type		Types the contents of a text or batch file.
	|more	Breaks a long text file or batch file into screen-sized sections.

Examples of Recovery Console Command Usage

Before seeing the practical uses for these commands, let's go through the steps you take to perform one of these commands. Let's assume that a virus or other problem has overwritten the master boot record, which is keeping your hard drive from booting. You would

1. Shut down and restart the PC.

2. When prompted by the Startup menu, select Recovery Console.

3. Once Recovery Console loads, type this command at the command line: **Fixmbr \device\HardDisk0**.

4. Press Enter.

```
C:\>fixmbr \device\HardDisk0_
```

4. When the operation is complete, type **exit**

5. Once Recovery Console quits, the PC restarts; evaluate the PC's behavior and look for any on-screen error messages to make sure it is now starting properly.

Here are some examples of Recovery Console commands you'll find useful:

Chkdsk c: /p /r   This command performs an exhaustive check of the C: drive, marks any bad sectors, and tries to recover lost file data (although this may not be recovered in any form you can use).

Del bootlog.bak   This command erases the `bootlog.bak` file.

Disable USBdev1.vxd   This command temporarily disables the specified USB device driver.

diskpart /add \Device\HardDisk0 20   This command adds a partition of 20MB (the number 20 specifies the size in megabytes) to HardDisk0.

expand g:\addon\driver.cab /f:widget.sys c:\Windows\system\drivers   This command takes the source file (`driver.cab`) and extracts from it a single file (`widget.sys`) that is then expanded and copied to the `Windows\System\Drivers` folder.

Fixboot D: This command rewrites the system boot sector for the specified drive (D:).

Fixmbr \device\HardDisk0   This rewrites the master boot record for the specified drive (HardDisk0). If you fail to specify the device, the master boot record for your booting drive is rewritten.

Format D: This command formats the D: drive, effectively erasing all its contents, preparing it for fresh use or the installation of an operating system.

Ren C:\utillog.txt utillog.bak   This command renames the file `utillog.txt` to `utillog.bak`.

Recovering from a Bad System Restore

Since I've mentioned System Restore several times in this chapter, it only seems right to talk about another type of disaster that can occur. This disaster happens when you inadvertently convert back to a restore point that you didn't want. For example, this could be a restore point that was created when your PC was having profound problems, and restoring this point revisits all that havoc upon you.

However, you should be able to undo this restore point and select a different restore point, if desired. To reverse your current restore point, take these steps:

1. From the Windows Start menu, point to All Programs ➣ Accessories ➣ System Tools ➣ System Restore.

2. From the Welcome to System Restore window, click Undo my Last Restoration. Click Next.

3. You may or may not see a listing provided by System Restore of the changes between your current system and the previous configuration. If present, click OK.

4. From the Confirm Restoration Undo window, click Next.

Windows should then go through the reversion process and restart your computer. Once Windows reloads, a confirmation appears telling you that the process was complete and you are reverted to your system the way it was *before* you last restored a restore point.

Sadly, some of your biggest PC disasters may occur when you're just trying to improve your systems by upgrading a component such as the BIOS, a driver, memory, or a hardware component with a better product. The next chapter describes the steps to work around a failed upgrade.

CHAPTER 8

When Upgrades Go Wrong

You might think that upgrading some part of your PC will make your life a little easier, perhaps even richer in terms of the capabilities of your PC that you enjoy.

Often enough, this is very true.

But what about those other times when you perform an upgrade that causes you more headaches than it fixes? There will be those times, trust me. It happens to us all.

While some of the snags you may encounter during an upgrade will simply be annoyances or disappointments, some upgrades can lead directly into a full-scale disaster scenario. The PC that worked OK but could work better before the upgrade turns into hefty corpse that won't respond to your most earnest efforts to resuscitate it.

Much of this chapter focuses on working around a monstrous upgrade or upgrade-precipitated disaster, but you should feel free to use this chapter proactively to avoid the common pitfalls that can turn a good upgrade into an unwelcome calamity.

> **NOTE** *You'll hear a great deal about protecting your data by backing it up before you perform an upgrade. While most upgrades go like clockwork, you must be prepared for those that don't.*

Limiting Your Risks When Upgrading

Obviously, the best type of upgrade doesn't involve the words "disaster" or "recovery." Common sense, combined with a little study time and a bit of applied effort, can usually help you avoid the worst catastrophes and the usual pitfalls.

Here are some of the best techniques for ensuring a successful upgrade. Following these instructions can limit your damage or downtime should you encounter an unwanted hitch.

- Protect your data by backing it up first.

- Don't upgrade in a distracting environment; wait until things are reasonably calm.

- Perform one upgrade at a time and verify that the last one is working well before you perform the next.

- Read the documentation that accompanies the upgrade—especially the special notes and warnings. Check the manufacturer's or publisher's web site for additional details or to ask questions before you perform the upgrade.

- Follow the instructions you just read. I know this step seems obvious, but informal studies suggest that even among those PC users who read the instructions, many users continue to perform a task without following the steps they read. Or they omit important steps that prevent easy recovery later.

- If you're upgrading an operating system or a major component like BIOS or memory, check with your PC manufacturer ahead of time to make sure it's compatible with your hardware and operating system.

- If you're installing an operating system or application upgrade, shut down and restart your PC before you start and keep other programs—even those running in the background—closed until you're done with the upgrade and satisfied.

- Double-check your work before you try to use the upgrade.

- If disaster strikes, don't exacerbate the damage. Stop and think. Then, if necessary, restore everything back to the way it was before you started the upgrade to see if your system returns to normal. You can always try the upgrade again—exercising great care to follow the instructions—or wait until you get more information before you proceed.

A Cautionary Tale: Leader of the Pack?

Being at the leading edge of technology can be great fun because you know before anyone else how well that new bell or whistle works. Others prefer to stand back and evaluate your dust as you roar forth into the brave new world of the latest software or the hardware still warm from the manufacturer's production process.

However, leading can turn into bleeding pretty quickly. Being one of the first users to get an upgrade or a new version of something can sometimes have you paying for the right to be a guinea pig of a product that may not have been adequately tested before its release to stores.

As a frequent beta tester (someone who tests pre-release versions of products for computer companies) of operating systems, applications, utilities, and games, I've had more than my share of disasters—from needing emergency BIOS replacements and having to format my hard drive twice a week to watching my crisp computer display turn into abstract art. For this reason, I always caution people against beta testing on their primary PCs unless and until they feel they have the technical acumen to easily recover from a testing-induced disaster.

Being a beta tester also makes me wait when a brand-new product hits the market. Rather than rushing out to buy something I really want, I wait. I take several days to several weeks to check out the reports about the product posted online in technical message boards by those courageous test pilots who *did* rush out to the store ahead of the rest of me. In particular, I read the problem reports and compare the experience the person is reporting against my own system. If any of the circumstances seem to match what I might expect my system to experience, I contact the manufacturer before I proceed.

There's a delicious side benefit to this waiting, besides making yourself better prepared for an upgrade or totally new product: you can save money! Many products fetch the highest price in the first few weeks after release; this is especially true for hot new games and much-hyped new hardware. I've saved as much as 30% off the price—and untold annoyances—by waiting a month or so before trying a new product.

When Your BIOS Upgrade Goes Bad

A BIOS upgrade is a way to update your current motherboard BIOS chip to reflect changes in hardware, operating system, and features since the time your motherboard was manufactured and the BIOS was installed.

In the old days, a BIOS upgrade usually meant physically replacing the BIOS chip on your motherboard. Today, however, most motherboard/BIOS manufacturers allow you to run a program that automatically upgrades your BIOS and its settings, often without doing anything inside your PC case. This type of BIOS is referred to as *flash BIOS* because the chip uses flash memory that can be reprogrammed. The process of upgrading such a BIOS is called *flashing your BIOS*.

NOTE *Some models still require you to set a switch or jumper on the motherboard. Consider this a safety feature to keep you from upgrading your BIOS unintentionally and, more importantly, to prevent a malicious program or virus from damaging your BIOS.*

Let's assume you haven't upgraded your BIOS yet, but you're planning to do so. An important question to ask yourself is why you need to do this, because updating a BIOS—as with so many other issues you've read about—is not a cure-all for all PC ailments.

A BIOS upgrade is sometimes required in the following situations:

- to update your PC before installing a new operating system or an operating system upgrade

- to resolve a problem with existing hardware, software, or operating system that is or seems to be tied to an out-of-date BIOS

- to replace a BIOS damaged by a virus, electrical issues, or some other problem

While a BIOS update, when needed, can do marvelous things for refreshing features and adding functionality to an aging PC or one with a damaged BIOS, my personal philosophy is to leave the BIOS alone until I have a documented reason to change it. This philosophy is borne out of a healthy respect for the serious problems that you can encounter upgrading your BIOS, including (in order of severity):

- You may not be able to use the PC unless and until you can recover your previous BIOS version through stored settings.

- You may not be able to use your PC until you replace the physical BIOS chip.

- You may not be able to use your PC until you replace the motherboard as a whole.

To be fair, these are the same situations you may face if your BIOS becomes corrupted. But in that situation, you have less to lose because you already have an incapacitated PC.

A Cautionary Tale: Watch the Help You Get

Having done this kind of work for a number of years now, I've upgraded the BIOS on many machines of all ages. Using the steps described in Chapter 2, "How Your Hardware, Operating System, and Applications All Work Together," I can readily find the identifying BIOS information to get the right BIOS upgrade.

However, last spring, I had one of those PC-consumer-consciousness type of experiences where you realize some of the people working in customer support for technology companies aren't any more knowledgeable about the product than you are. I had an older machine whose BIOS ID information I never noted elsewhere, and the PC developed an issue that ultimately made IDing the BIOS later a problem. So I went to a few different online vendors who specialize in BIOS upgrades to see which one I needed, based on the model number of the PC and the type of motherboard.

At four different locations, I left my PC information in an online form to see what their specialists told me I needed, along with how much it would cost.

Much to my surprise, almost every site gave me a different answer for the upgrade download I needed. One, I discovered, was definitely not for my type of motherboard, and the other two weren't even for my brand of BIOS, even though the BIOS manufacturer was the one bit of information I could supply. At least one of those recommended upgrades would have caused me more headaches than it could possibly have resolved.

While I ultimately found the right upgrade and applied it successfully, this serves as a word of caution: Go through your PC manufacturer first to determine the BIOS upgrade you need for your system. But you don't have to buy through your manufacturer unless they offer you a great deal. Use the BIOS dealers' recommendations as a second opinion before you buy and compare prices between the dealer and your manufacturer.

What you can't do is assume that the first BIOS upgrade you are told to buy is necessarily the correct one.

How a BIOS Flash Upgrade Should Go

While a BIOS upgrade can amount to a major (and hopefully wondrous) change for your PC, the process by which you apply a BIOS upgrade is often so simple that it can lull you into a false sense of security.

I'll walk you through a normal BIOS flashing process to help you appreciate the details you need to be aware of to do this successfully. Your results are apt to vary because different manufacturers sometimes include extra options or steps, so don't forget to read the accompanying documentation before attempting a flash BIOS upgrade.

First, identify your BIOS or motherboard and obtain not one flash file, but two: a BIOS data file and a flash utility to help you through the procedure. Often, you can purchase and/or download these files online, although there are times when you'll need to order these files and wait for a physical disk(s). In addition, make sure these flash files are correct for your manufacturer and version of BIOS since BIOS updates are not "one size fits all."

Next, your instructions may tell you to run their included utility that creates a special boot disk for performing the upgrade; you'll need at least one good, blank floppy to do this. Other BIOS upgrades will work from a regular boot disk.

> **WARNING** *Don't use a standard boot disk if the BIOS upgrade requires you to make a special disk. You could miss important features or steps.*

At this point, you may need to power the system down and take the usual precautions for going inside your PC case if your documentation tells you that you need to adjust a motherboard switch or jumper.

Instructions may then recommend you go into BIOS Setup (Shutdown ➤ Restart ➤ choose Setup from boot) and turn off all forms of caches, especially any options such as the System BIOS cache and Video cache. Follow the on-screen instructions—it can be important to the success of your flashing. Most of these options are typically found in the CMOS Chipset Features or Chipset Features section of BIOS Setup. Save your changes (if any) and exit Setup.

Typically, you then restart your machine using the boot disk you created, although some upgrades give you the option to use Safe Mode at the command prompt as well. At some point, you're usually asked if you want to save your previous BIOS information. Do so—this could be your saving grace to return to your previous BIOS if the flashing fails. If you don't immediately need the previous settings, store them on a floppy as part of your PC Recovery Resource Kit, clearly labeled and dated.

Consult your instructions for the exact command to run for initiating the flashing process. It usually looks something like the following command for AMI-brand BIOSes (see Figure 8.1):

```
Amiflash filename.bin <press Enter>
```

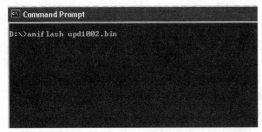

Figure 8.1 *The first step in flashing a BIOS*

In this example, `amiflash` is the name of American Megatrends, Inc.'s flash utility and `filename.bin` is the name of the required data file.

The flashing process commences, and you'll receive some type of message when the job is complete letting you know whether it was a success or not. You can then restart your PC normally.

TIP *Always thoroughly test your system by trying out hardware, software, and a reboot or two following a BIOS upgrade. A bad BIOS upgrade often makes itself known immediately, but smaller problems can be far less obvious. Contact the source of your BIOS upgrade should you experience difficulties.*

Causes of BIOS Upgrading Problems

Two of the most common reasons for problems in upgrading your BIOS are also the most obvious:

- You've used the wrong BIOS upgrade for your make and version of BIOS.

- You didn't follow instructions or didn't understand the directions you did read.

As you read in the "A Cautionary Tale: Watch the Help You Get" sidebar, the former is easy enough to do, and statistically, users are not always apt to follow instructions. But, again being fair, some of the instructions are badly written or poorly translated from another language. (Much of our hardware today is actually manufactured or assembled in Taiwan, China, and Korea.)

Both situations can be corrected by removing the upgrade you applied and reinstalling the previous version/settings. I'll go into that shortly.

Other issues in BIOS upgrade failures include:

- Corrupted or bad BIOS data file or flash utility. Getting a fresh copy of the file should resolve this problem.

- Basic incompatibility. You may need to roll back to the previous BIOS version until a more stable upgrade for you becomes available.

But you'll also encounter a very serious problem—and likely, a dead PC—if your electricity goes out in the middle of a BIOS upgrade. The actual application of the upgrade to the programmable part of the motherboard is particularly vulnerable to power interruptions, and killing power in the middle of this process likely erases the necessary part of the BIOS chip. At that point, rerunning the BIOS upgrade usually won't help. In fact, it may not be possible at all because the PC needs the BIOS as part of its boot process.

If you run into this situation, contact your PC or motherboard manufacturer or your BIOS upgrade supplier immediately. They can advise you what to do, which typically involves at least replacing the BIOS chip.

You can also check out some of the best user information web sites. Wim's Bios Page (www .wimsbios.com) offers invaluable information for those needing to upgrade a BIOS or work past a bad BIOS upgrade. (See Figure 8.2 for a look at the Wim's BIOS Page.)

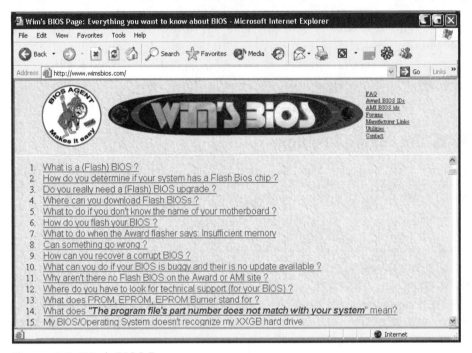

Figure 8.2 *Wim's BIOS Page*

Removing the BIOS Upgrade

First and foremost, consult the instructions provided with your BIOS upgrade on the steps necessary to remove the upgrade and return to your previous BIOS version. Usually this involves booting your PC using the disk (or one of the disks) you made during the BIOS upgrade process, and when prompted, choosing to restore your previous setup. This illustrates why you can't avoid performing setup steps like creating the disk because it's possible you may need it later.

If you can't get your PC BIOS to revert successfully, contact your BIOS supplier immediately to determine what you should do next. There's very little you can do to correct this situation without additional information from the supplier or from your PC manufacturer except run the risk of exacerbating the problem.

When New Memory Causes Problems

As I've explained before, memory can be one of the toughest nuts to crack in terms of trouble-shooting because it displays misbehavior in so many different ways, including:

- Unstable applications

- PC hangs and crashes

- Slowness in multitasking

- PC won't start (or in some odd cases, bad memory can make it tougher to shut down)

- Page faults, blue screen of death crashes, and similar serious errors and warnings

Many of these ways may not give you any hint that it's the memory to blame. Instead, memory crashes applications, garbles files, can confuse your video display, and may tell you other issues are to blame.

However, when you have just recently installed new memory, remind yourself that you've done so should a problem or instability arise. Look at that new memory first when troubleshooting that problem.

NOTE *Windows XP, compared to other versions of Windows, seems to be finicky about having enough memory installed (think 128MB if you have less) and the overall quality of the memory used.*

How Memory Should Be Installed

Many motherboards manufactured in the last 4–5 years have just three memory sockets. Each socket takes one stick of memory, and each filled memory socket makes up what is called a *bank* of memory.

TIP *Remember, when you're installing additional memory, make sure the power is disconnected, take anti-static precautions, and exercise particular care.*

While it may be tough to eyeball this, these memory sockets are usually numbered 0–2, with the first RAM socket ending in 0, as in DIMM0 or RIMM0. Memory should be installed starting with the 0 socket and working forward until you've installed all the memory you need or until you run out of memory to install.

In addition, several technicians I've worked with recommend that you place your largest (in terms of the amount of RAM installed to the stick), fastest RAM—often, this is also your newest RAM—in the first socket, with the next most capacious RAM stick in the second, and so on.

If you're installing new RAM to a system with existing RAM that you're not replacing, take a moment to compare the two—old and new—for any differences. Should the (usually gold) connector edge on new memory look markedly different than the old one, you probably have a different type of memory packaging than your PC uses. Replace it before proceeding.

TIP *Always leave memory and other internally connected hardware in its case or anti-static bag until you're ready to inspect it. If there's a delay between inspection and the actual installation—even if it's just a few minutes—return the hardware to the case or bag until you do the installation. I'll spare you the story about the time I ignored this advice and my cat slipped into my office and became ill on my very new and very expensive video adapter.*

Retaining clips are typically positioned at either end of a memory socket to help secure the memory stick in place. Look at the way the empty socket is situated and then position the new RAM in parallel with the connector edge closest to the socket. Gently but firmly press the memory stick into place in the socket but *do not force it into place*. With some motherboards, the retaining clips automatically snap into place upon proper insertion. On other motherboards, you may need to snap the retaining clips into place. If the retaining clips can't be secured, you have a bad installation. Reseat the memory.

WARNING *The retainer clips used to hold memory in these sockets may sometimes break or become disabled. I do not recommend installing RAM to sockets with broken retainer clips, simply because the memory may pop out if the PC case is moved or jarred, and the possible resulting looseness may affect overall PC performance or cause a permanent motherboard failure. Also, something that makes a connection by hit-or-miss means may be more prone to early failure.*

At this point, you may want to leave the PC cover off when you reconnect power, at least until you've verified that the new memory is recognized and the PC is behaving well after your upgrade.

Memory Troubleshooting Methods

The first place to look for a problem after installing new memory is when you restart your PC after the installation. If your system is configured to display the memory count done by the PC at the time of bootup, the newly added memory should be reported there in the total.

Of course, if your PC won't boot after the new memory is installed, you've got an emergency. But this is problem can usually be resolved by reinstalling the memory. If it's not, it could still be either a poor installation or the wrong memory for what you need. If all else fails, remove the new memory until you can tell which it is.

But let's assume your PC does start up and does a memory count. If your newly added memory isn't included in the total, proceed with Windows loading until you can choose to shutdown. Then disconnect power and perform those other in-the-case steps described first in Chapter 2 to check your installation—a less-than-perfect insertion is always a possibility.

However, once you've satisfied yourself that the installation is proper and yet you still can't see the new memory recognized, consider the following possibilities:

The memory stick is bad.   If possible, try to test it in another PC before returning it for a replacement.

The arrangement of memory isn't ideal.   See the following section, "Rearranging Memory."

The memory is not of the right type.   See the following section, "Rearranging Memory."

The memory stick is "not quite right."   You can buy the right type of RAM for your PC and not have it be quite the quality needed; check with your PC or motherboard manufacturer for recommendations.

In addition, there's also the remote chance that the memory socket itself is not making proper contact with the motherboard. Very occasionally, one or more memory sockets just fail while one or more is left functional. At this point, consider either a motherboard or a full PC replacement, depending on your situation.

Rearranging Memory

If the way you've arranged memory in your system doesn't work, it's time to try something else. Swapping out and rearranging memory is one time-honored way of troubleshooting different arrangements to see if one combination works when another combination doesn't work.

Let's look at the two most common scenarios: adding more memory to existing memory or replacing all currently installed memory with fresh memory.

If you've added more memory to existing memory and you still see just the amount of memory that was installed *before* the upgrade, first check your installation. Then swap the memory around to see if installing the same memory to a different socket may let it be detected and available for use.

In this first situation, let's assume you have one stick of 128MB memory already installed in your PC to DIMM0. Then you add a second 128MB stick of new memory into DIMM1. When you start your PC again, all you see is that original 128MB. With the PC disconnected, remove both sticks of memory while remembering which stick is the new one. Since the first 128MB stick was working before you added memory, it's probably reasonable to assume it's working now, and *that* is what is supplying the 128MB of detected RAM.

So next, install only the new stick of RAM, occupying the DIMM0 socket formerly occupied by the original memory. Then reconnect the PC and try to boot. If you get a memory error, the new RAM may be incompatible (or again, badly installed). But if the memory is seen and adds up to 128MB, wait for Windows to load and then shut down the PC, disconnect it, and try adding the old memory to DIMM1. You should see your whole 256MB of memory when you reconnect and restart the PC. If not, repeat these steps until you exhaust all the possible combinations. Should none of the combinations work, determine the exact type of memory you need and be sure to get that type.

When you're replacing memory, you can try similar schemes. A few (usually much older) motherboards require memory to be installed in pairs, meaning you need at least two sticks installed. But be sure to check with your PC or motherboard manufacturer directly should you have any lingering questions.

TIP *Some motherboards limit the amount of memory that can be installed to a single socket. For example, if you want to install 256MB of memory into your system and your motherboard only recognizes a memory stick of 128MB or less, you'll need to purchase two sticks of 128MB to get your 256MB total.*

Making Sure the Memory is the Right Type

Don't simply assume that the "standard PC memory" you purchased is the memory you need. Today, there are a number of different ways you can verify the type of PC memory you need for your PC:

- Check your PC manual. This information should be listed and correct, provided you haven't already changed/upgraded memory previously.

- Contact your PC manufacturer or check the PC manufacturer's web site for specifics on your PC model, such as the one you can find by visiting **www.dell.com** and clicking on Memory Lookup (see Figure 8.3).

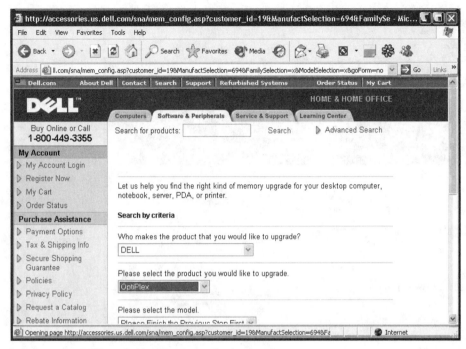

Figure 8.3 *Dell's web-based memory lookup tool*

- Check the memory that's already installed. This can work, but you have to know what the different memory types look like already.

- Remove a stick of your current memory and take it to an electronics/computer store to match.

- Go into a computer or electronics store and ask for their *memory match* calculator, a little touchpad device that lets you look up your memory type by manufacturer and PC model name and number.

- Look this up by your PC brand and model using online vendor sites such as Crucial Technology (`www.crucial.com`), Kingston (`www.kingston.com`), and Viking Components (`www.vikingcomponents.com`). (Figure 8.4 illustrates Kingston's online memory lookup tool.)

Figure 8.4 *Kingston's web-based memory lookup tool*

NOTE *While I used to tell people that it can be tough to install the wrong memory into one of your PC's internal memory sockets, I've since seen how many ways people can force the wrong memory to fit. Some users consider any connection with the motherboard socket, however small, to constitute properly installed memory, and that simply is not so. If the memory doesn't fit fully and firmly into the socket, either you've installed it wrong or it's not the correct memory packaging type for your PC and its motherboard.*

When You Run into Problems Upgrading or Replacing a Motherboard

Replacing a motherboard is no simple task. I tend to think of it as the PC equivalent of heart transplant surgery because there are so many connections into and out of the motherboard, just as there are with a heart. In fact, it may be one of the toughest upgrades or replacements a PC owner can perform.

Part of what makes replacing a motherboard so difficult is that the documentation accompanying a new motherboard is often poorly written or translated. For example, I bought an off-brand motherboard two years ago and got a package that contained only Asian-language instructions. When the company sent a replacement in English, it made almost as little sense to me as the Asian version.

In addition, I've found that diagrams of the motherboard represented in the documentation get reversed too often, which makes it no fun trying to orient yourself and the motherboard during the replacement procedure.

While I'm not trying to frighten you away from replacing or upgrading your motherboard, consider the task carefully before you undertake it yourself. Some users find it much easier to pay a decent PC support technician to do the job for them. A PC support technician is more likely to have testing tools that can make evaluating the source of a motherboard problem more scientific than the more hit-or-miss way you can test power and capacity on your own.

Unfortunately, it's hard to do a proper motherboard installation justice in the space available in this chapter, let alone cover all the troubleshooting necessary if problems occur. Here are the most common problems that can occur during a motherboard upgrade or replacement:

You omitted steps.   Follow the directions with great precision because there are no extra steps.

Bad motherboard installation.   The actual process of seating the motherboard in its frame without shorting or otherwise damaging the motherboard against the sides or stays within the PC case can be very tricky. Go slowly and watch your placement.

Connections are loose or wrong.   This is a very common problem. Even though I've done this work for many years, I don't do enough motherboard installations to always remember each detail. So I often take small strips of masking tape to label each connection. Before I apply the tape, I jot down the identifying connection in shorthand on the small strip of tape. This makes reconnecting everything correctly later much easier.

The BIOS update didn't take.   Many motherboards either include a BIOS update disk or provide instructions for obtaining an update, since these products may sit on the shelf at the factory or store through a few version updates. Try the motherboard directly after installation before you run this BIOS update. Then follow any advice in the update instructions for rolling your BIOS version back to the original one if you experience significant problems after updating.

You don't have the right CPU.   CPUs and motherboards must be matched to one another. For example, a CPU made by Advanced Micro Devices (AMD) may not work for a motherboard designed to support an Intel Pentium series CPU because the CPUs are packaged differently for installation into the system. You can't just assume that the great motherboard you see on sale will work with your existing CPU. For this reason, many people upgrade their CPU at the same time they upgrade their motherboard. Both CPU manufacturers and motherboard manufacturers typically include a list of recommended products on their product web sites, so check there before performing an upgrade or replacement.

It wasn't (just) the motherboard that was dead.   If you replace the motherboard and still hit the same errors or problems, look at what the errors or problems are telling you. It's not uncommon to replace a motherboard thinking it's damaged when it may actually be a dead CPU.

Similarly, you can have a situation where both the CPU and motherboard are damaged and need replacement. Just replacing the motherboard may not fix the entire problem.

TIP *Replacing or upgrading your motherboard is one of the situations in which reinstalling your operating system after the upgrade is often a good idea, especially if you notice your operating system loads more slowly or behaves as if it is confused.*

When You Have Problems Upgrading or Reinstalling Your Operating System

If you take the time and effort to poll most computer users of any type, you'll probably find that problems upgrading or reinstalling your operating system ranks as one of the top frustrations. Some have called this *PC purgatory*. Invariably, you have to solve the problem you're having just to get back to the point where you can use your PC; doing this is often easier said than done.

Much of the hands-on type of work involved in stabilizing your operating system for an upgrade or proper installation is covered in Chapter 9, "Stabilizing Your Operating System." But let's look at some quick issues not discussed there.

The Myth of Curative Reinstalling

One common myth with operating systems is that no matter what may go wrong with your PC, reinstalling the operating system will fix it. Wrong! While there are times when reinstalling Windows may help (for a large number of missing or corrupted files, for example), it won't solve most issues. In fact, at best, it may roll you back to old hardware and software drivers and pre-fix versions of Windows updates as if you had never applied updates at all. At worst, it can take a system that was working and turn it into one that doesn't.

In addition, there's a tendency among less experienced users to think, "If the first reinstall didn't work, maybe the fourth or fifth will." Well, if it was going to fix the problem, it probably would have done it the first time.

This isn't to say that you can't reinstall Windows or that reinstalling Windows isn't sometimes necessary. In fact, you'll find situations in this book when I recommend it. But don't think of reinstalling Windows as a magic pill for all that ails your PC. Sometimes that pill can taste pretty bitter.

NOTE *Windows XP limits the number of times you can reinstall this version of Windows on your system without actually calling Microsoft support for assistance (registered XP users get two support calls only). Some applications now also limit the number of times you can reinstall the product. Much of this effort is based in antipiracy measures to prevent endless unauthorized copies, creating untold numbers of pirated installations.*

Common Causes of These Problems

An unbelievable number of factors can contribute to nasty, system-affecting moments while trying to upgrade or reinstall Windows—from hardware to drivers to applications to a silly glitch on your desktop before you start the upgrade or reinstall the operating system.

How You Upgrade

Absolutely nothing else should be running on your desktop—either directly or in the background—when you begin an operating system upgrade or reinstall. It's also wise to restart your PC before you start the upgrade or reinstall to be sure nothing is left in memory that might be compromised or that may affect the setup process.

Remember in Chapter 7, "Restarting a Problem PC," learning about how you can clean boot Windows? If you run into problems trying to run Setup from the Windows install CD, consider clean booting and then running Setup. Upgrading Windows may be possible once certain device drivers and extraneous features have been temporarily disabled, as they are with clean booting.

Articles available in the Microsoft Knowledge Base (`http://search.support.microsoft.com`) can be invaluable when you're troubleshooting a problem upgrading or reinstalling Windows. For example, if you search on article number 310064, you'll discover a thorough article with suggestions for working through difficulties upgrading to Windows XP Home Edition from Windows Millennium or from Windows 98. Article 307551 provides an excellent overview on what to do if your PC stops responding during the Windows XP Setup process.

Outdated BIOS

An older BIOS, particularly one that is dated two or more years before the release of an operating system upgrade, can prevent your operating system upgrade entirely or disable features and devices that previously worked.

Incompatible Hardware

Hardware compatibility has forever been an issue with upgrading an operating system, as well as with Windows stability and performance, as we first talked about in Chapter 2. Without a device driver specifically written with a particular version of Windows in mind, you may be locked out of certain features of that device, or you may be unable to use it at all. But incompatibility can extend to performance issues a device simply doesn't achieve the speed it did under a previous version of Windows, for example. You may also increase the likelihood Windows will either not start or not shut down properly, and that you may be hit by far more lockups and crashes, and general instability because of these incompatibilities, with or without on-screen errors or warnings to alert you to the situation.

Use hardware manufacturer web sites and the Microsoft Windows Hardware Compatibility List site (www.microsoft.com/hcl) to determine whether your hardware is compatible with the new operating system version before you upgrade. If it's not, you may want to remove or replace the incompatible hardware before you try to upgrade or reinstall.

When Reinstalls Don't Help

As previously recommended, don't simply keep reinstalling Windows if the first attempt or two doesn't resolve a problem you're having. You may need to start fresh by reformatting the drive and doing a completely fresh installation of Windows (and your device drivers and applications or try to pinpoint and fix the source of your problems.

> **NOTE** *For information on starting fresh with a new installation of Windows, see Chapter 16, "Starting from Scratch the Smart Way."*

System Requirements

While today's super-charged PCs usually exceed the minimum system requirements for installing the latest version of an operating system, always check these requirements against your system before trying to upgrade. Be aware of the fact that minimum requirements aren't ideal—you really need more than the minimum requirements to work and play most effectively.

This is especially true if you're working with an older PC. I find, for instance, that a Pentium II 350 MHz system is really about the oldest PC to which I can comfortably install Windows XP.

If your system is more than 3–4 years old, consider upgrading your current operating system to a later version than you have, but not to the latest version, which right now is Windows XP.

The Premature Upgrade

One common situation is when someone has serious problems with their current installation, so they think installing a newer version of the operating system will correct it. Sure, it's possible that's all that's needed. However, many times, installing a new version of Windows on top of an unstable current version nets you an unstable new version or real headaches in getting the upgrade process to even complete. Wherever possible, get your current version of Windows into proper running shape before you try to upgrade.

> **NOTE** *To learn more about curing Windows instability and/or effecting a good upgrade, see Chapter 9.*

When You Encounter Problems Upgrading or Reinstalling Your Applications

Before you finish up, turn your attention to the issue of problems upgrading or reinstalling your applications, since they play such a major part in the real work you do with your PCs.

Common Causes of Application Installation Problems

One of the most common culprits in a faulty application installation relates back to what else is running on your desktop at the time of the installation. Background anti-virus software, memory and disk utilities, and other software can present major problems with new installations, but the problem is not limited to those types of applications. For this reason, close everything possible before you start such an installation.

If you haven't used Task Manager before, acquaint yourself with it because it's a simple way to close unneeded applications. Throughout all versions of Windows, you can access Task Manager by using the key combination Ctrl+Alt+Delete.

> **WARNING** *Press Ctrl+Alt+Delete just once. Pressing it twice reboots your system.*

Let's go through the steps for shutting down unnecessary programs:

1. Press Ctrl+Alt+Delete.

2. Click Task Manager.

3. For Windows XP users, choose the Applications tab, select each program listed, and click End Task until all applications are closed.

If you're using another versions of Windows, select every item listed except Explorer and Systray and click End Task.

4. When done, close the Task Manager window. You may now begin your application installation.

What Else to Try

Some applications, like Microsoft Office, include a repair feature that allows the application package to try to fix itself at your behest. Check your application's Help section to see if yours does.

For example, to try to repair a Microsoft Office XP installation, you would

1. From Control Panel, click Add or Remove Programs.

2. Click Change or Remove Programs.

3. Select Microsoft Office XP from the list of installed programs and then choose Click Here for Support Information.

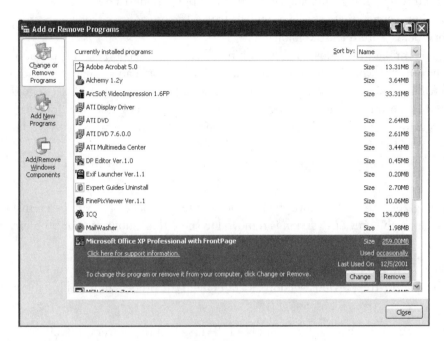

4. Click Repair.

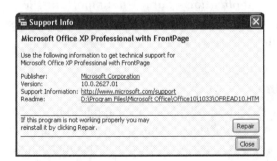

5. When prompted, insert your Windows Office XP install CD into your CD or DVD drive and click OK.

Consult the application software's web site and your PC manufacturer to see if there are any known issues with your application. The Microsoft Knowledge Base is another good source of information on known problems between the most popular applications and the Windows operating system.

Uninstalling Previous Versions

If you're having difficulty upgrading a previous version of an application to a new version, try uninstalling the previous version first. This is especially true if the previous version you're using is either very old or a beta or pre-release version.

Now, before going through the steps for you to uninstall an earlier version of an application, understand that this may not work in all cases. For example, many application upgrades require you to have the previous version already installed on your computer to allow that PC to upgrade successfully. There is a reason for that—you usually pay far less for an upgrade than for a full version, so if the previous package wasn't required, everyone would buy the cheaper upgrade rather than the full version.

You have some options uninstalling a previous version, depending on how the application is designed:

- Install the upgrade and then remove the previous version. (If necessary, you can reinstall the upgrade after the previous version is removed to see if that stabilizes your problem application.)

- You may be able to uninstall the previous version and then simply supply—when prompted to do so—the previous version's install CD in the process of installing the new version.

- Remove the previous version and then apply a full version of the newer product.

WARNING *You should always back up an application's data—the important files you use or have created under the program—before either uninstalling a previous version or applying an upgraded version.*

Steps for Uninstalling a Previous Version

While I'm providing instructions here for removing a previous version of an application—if needed—to successfully upgrade, you can use these same steps to uninstall a problem application and then reinstall it again fresh. Follow these steps to remove a previous version of an application in Windows XP:

1. From Control Panel, click Add or Remove Programs.

2. Click Change or Remove Programs.

3. From the list of installed programs, carefully select the previous version you wish to remove.

4. Click Change/Remove. When prompted, confirm the removal.

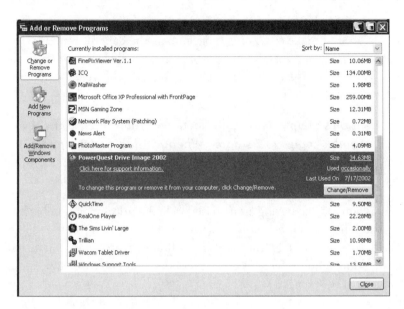

If you're using an earlier version of Windows, use these steps instead:

1. From Control Panel, click Add/Remove Programs.

2. On the Add/Remove tab, all your 32-bit installed programs are listed. Locate and high-light the previous version or the application you want to remove.

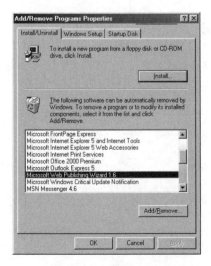

3. Click Add/Remove. You'll be asked to confirm your removal.

Backing Up Application Data

If you've been following my recommendations, you've already started a regular backup routine as part of your disaster recovery plan. But make extra sure to back up all the data files you have for any application you're about to upgrade or reinstall. This ensures that you'll have valid copies of these files stored elsewhere in case there is a catastrophic problem during the upgrade or when you uninstall and reinstall the application.

NOTE *Check your application's Help section and documentation in case the program has an easy way to make copies of its data. When available, this approach may be a faster route than backing up the data formally. However, it won't protect other data on your system in the event of a catastrophe.*

All too often, the problems you may be having aren't based in bad hardware or a problem software upgrade but in an instability in your operating system. Such a situation can have limited effects, or it can make almost everything you do from startup to shutdown an exercise in misery. This is not a situation you should tolerate for long because it reduces your ability to work and places your PC's health and data at risk.

Chapter 9 will describe the common symptoms of an unstable Windows installation and show you some of the ways in which you can try to get it back under control.

Stabilizing Your Operating System

There are several features and functions that you enjoy with your PCs that you could actually do without if you needed to. You don't usually need sound, for example, and few people have ever died from their inability to play computer games.

Yet the one feature you can't live without is a stable operating system because it serves as the foundation for almost everything you do, regardless of how you use your PC or how the PC is equipped.

When the operating system is unstable, you might experience some of the following symptoms:

- Programs may close as soon as you open them or fail to open at all.

- You're unable to use onboard tools such as MSINFO32 and Disk Defragmenter (called Defrag in some versions of Windows).

- Good passwords may fail.

- If the system lets you work at all, you may feel insecure about your ability to save your work properly.

- Often-changing error messages may block your ability to perform the simplest of tasks, use important hardware such as your printer or CD drive, or force Windows to either reboot or shut down altogether.

If this sounds like a nightmare scenario, it really is. It's a disastrous situation that usually gets worse as time goes on, where one problem or Windows crisis ends up causing another problem, and so on.

This chapter will explain the most frequently reported causes of operating system instability and describe the tools you can use to assess and report the difficulties. You'll also learn how to weigh your options for how to proceed to get back to the point where you can work effectively.

Common Causes of Windows Instability

You'll discover that many of the usual suspects in PC problems are also most likely to create instability in Windows. These include the following, many of which have been covered in earlier chapters:

- Improper or corrupted original Windows installation

- Continuing to run a beta or pre-release version of Windows well past the time the full version is released

- A history of unsuccessful upgrades (you've tried and failed to upgrade Windows)

- Hardware and drivers that are not compatible with your current version of Windows

- Using the wrong driver for a piece of hardware or software

- Failing or failed hardware

- Conflicts between different hardware components (for example, a sound card and network interface card sharing the same resources), usually seen as a yellow mark on a listed device in Device Manager

- Conflicts between two or more applications that are running

- Poor system maintenance (You don't defragment the hard drive, you don't clean up temporary files on the drive, or you don't use ScanDisk in earlier versions of Windows or Chkdsk in Windows XP.)

- Bad Registry editing (This often happens when someone reads about a performance tweak they can make to the Registry that ends up costing them overall performance rather than improving it.)

- Overheating

- Overclocking (a process by which you adjust hardware and software settings to try to maximize the speed and performance of your system)

- Trying to run a second operating system from the same hard drive as your first operating system without partitioning the disk

- Corrupted BIOS

- Virus

TIP *If you notice a problem first outside of Windows like a damaged cable, a problem with memory counting up at bootup, or a strange sound within your case, investigate and resolve this situation as soon as possible. If Windows begins to behave badly before you correct it, assume until proven otherwise that the problem you've seen may be at fault.*

Reducing or Eliminating Instability

If you've read Chapter 3, "Prevention: Limiting Your Risks," you already have a solid blueprint for reducing your chances of encountering a serious instability or incompatibility issue with Windows. This section zeroes in on ways you can work within Windows to try to resolve problems beyond those you've learned about in earlier chapters. Some techniques, such as using Windows Update, can prevent these pesky problems from appearing.

Table 9.1 lists some of the common problems you may see with Windows and suggests ways you might resolve them.

TIP *To make Windows XP as stable as possible, the Windows Hardware Compatibility List (WHCL) must be used because they have been tested by Microsoft specifically for use under XP.*

Table 9.1   *Windows Problems and How to Investigate Them*

PROBLEM	WHAT TO INVESTIGATE/DO
Display degrades as you work	This problem is often the fault of an out-of-date video adapter driver. It can also indicate low desktop resources. First, restart your system. If that doesn't resolve it, check for a video driver update.
Freezing when you try to run programs	This could be the result of low hard disk space (you would need to make some available), failing or incompatible memory (see Chapter 8, "When Upgrades Go Wrong"), corrupted applications (reinstall them), or a virus (perform a complete virus scan).
Invalid page fault errors	See the "Dealing with Windows XP Stop Errors" section in this chapter.
Missing file errors	This is most likely tied to a file you deleted without properly uninstalling or removing it from Windows. You may need to reinstall the program the file is part of or the file itself or copy back the file from your backup copies.
Pointing device won't cooperate	This could be dirt inside the mouse or trackball or on the mouse pad; clean these items thoroughly. It could also be tied to an out-of-date video adapter driver or an unresponsive program running in the Windows background.
Registry errors	If these errors prevent you from getting into Windows, you may need to reboot using the Last Known Good Configuration option in Windows XP. From the command prompt, run the Registry checking tool Scanreg by typing **Scanreg /fix**.
Same program crashes each time	This could be the result of a bad program installation. Try removing the program through Add and Remove Programs in Control Panel and then reinstall the program.
Slowness	This could indicate many things: low available disk space (have at least 300MB free in Windows XP and no less than 100MB free for earlier Windows versions), low desktop resources (a restart should refresh them), running the system with too little memory (add more), or a badly fragmented hard drive (use Disk Defragmenter). Also look at what programs are running in the Windows background and terminate.
Stop Errors	See the "Dealing with Windows XP Stop Errors" section in this chapter.
Windows keep closing on their own	First, restart your PC to be sure this isn't a transient problem. Windows could also be corrupted or low on available memory, or there could be a conflict between programs you're running.

NOTE *If Windows only misbehaves on very hot days in the room where you work, you should suspect that the system is overheating. If you don't have air conditioning or other means of cooling the room, shut down your PC and let it cool for a few hours or until the temperature drops a bit. You may want to move the PC into a room where the temperature changes are more moderate.*

The Quest for a Well-Running PC

While I know many people hold a different view, I've always been amazed at how much abuse Windows can take before it starts to pitch a real fuss.

As long as I try to correct problems as they crop up, I can go a few years, a few versions, and lots of testing in between periods of instability that require much effort to resolve. Trust me: I wish the rest of my life ran so smoothly.

But I don't ascribe this to luck or to a perfect operating system. Knowing that the work I do (beta testing software, deliberately trying to "break" things so I can document them) can be abusive to a well-running system while realizing how much I need my PC, I follow this healthy PC diet and exercise regime:

- I regularly clean up unneeded files and unused programs.

- I don't panic because I keep my data regularly backed up, and I frequently update both my disaster recovery plan and my PC Resource Recovery Kit.

- I carefully choose the software I install.

- I research a program's or device's compatibility with my operating system and other components before I buy and install it.

- I read about my Windows Update selections before I install them, and I watch how Windows behaves after installing each update.

- I follow the excellent maintenance procedures described in Chapter 3.

- I fix small problems as they occur.

Using Windows Utilities to Address Operating System Instabilities

Chapter 8 described the methods you can use to get into Windows such as Safe Mode and the Last Known Good Configuration option when Windows won't load properly. This section explains the tools and techniques provided by Windows to help you address serious operating system instabilities.

Short-Term Pain Relievers

No, this section's not talking about headache potions or analgesics, but ways you can reduce the amount of instability your system displays until you can find the source of the current problem.

One major form of relief can sometimes be found by turning off the massive customization many users do on their systems. Features such as the following may tax an operating system that isn't running well:

- Animated cursors

- Special backgrounds

- Fancy screensavers (or even the use of a screensaver at all)

- Heavy use of streaming audio and/or video from web-based broadcasts

- The use of "system enhancement" software such as *RAM boosting*, software that tries to manage your memory for Windows to give you more bang for the amount of memory you have installed

Windows Help (or Help and Support in Windows Millennium and Windows XP) can step you through the process of disabling features like screensavers and animated cursors. Documentation for the extra software you're running should offer tips for disabling and/or removing it.

NOTE *Important reminder: Make changes to your system one at a time, with a reboot after the change.*

Reverse Recent Changes

I've already mentioned that you should always consider the last change you made when trying to identify what's wrong with your PC.

However, if simply undoing that last change doesn't correct your situation, you should undo all recent changes, including the installation or removal of programs, hardware, and the modification of settings. This is where the PC notebook I've recommended since Chapter 5, "Drafting Your Disaster Recovery Plan," comes in handy. Keep undoing these changes until you notice an improvement in Windows stability. You can always add these changes back again later, performing them one at a time and stopping (and reversing again) should the problem resurface.

Reinstalling Windows

One of the first "quick" solutions people tend to use to try to solve a problem with Windows is to reinstall Windows. This is usually accomplished by simply re-running the Setup program on your Windows install CD, which installs a fresh copy of Windows over your existing version. Before you do this, however, go back to Chapter 8 and review the myth of the curative reinstall and the situations that are most likely to benefit from a reinstallation of Windows.

Should you decide to reinstall Windows and you encounter problems doing so, use the Custom option in Setup to specify that Windows be installed into a different folder than your existing Windows installation. While this won't preserve the settings that would normally be carried from the previous version of Windows into a new (re)installation, the Custom option may allow you to get back to work in Windows when other options fail.

Using Windows Updates

Every version of Windows since 1998 has included support for Windows Update, a feature Microsoft calls its online extension to its operating system. Windows Update can be found at `http://windowsupdate.Microsoft.com` and is a web-based feature that checks your system and operating system-component versions against Microsoft's ever-growing list of driver and program updates. These updates may include:

- Service packs (a collection of many different bug fixes and enhancements that appear between Windows versions)

- Hardware and software drivers

- Security patches for Internet Explorer and other features.

You can also check your update installation history through the Windows Update site.

If you've used Windows Update before, you may not realize that Windows XP can be set up to automatically download and install whatever software the Update site determines you need. This makes it ultra-convenient, although I'll talk in a minute about why I discourage automatic updating.

The very first time you run Windows Update on a new version of Windows, you'll be asked to download and install a utility called Windows Update Control. This is required before you can visit the site and determine what updates you need.

Windows Update Control serves several purposes:

- It helps you identify future problems you may face. For example, Windows Update Control tells you there's an update available to work with a problem shutting down the system and properly saving data to disk using IDE hard drives in Windows 98.

- It recommends important files that can affect problems you may currently be experiencing.

- It keeps your system current with the latest fixes and files.

The Windows Update service for Windows XP distinguishes between three major types of files they offer:

Critical Updates and Service Packs   These are files deemed important for your overall operating system operation and security.

Windows   These are files recommended for your Windows version.

Drivers   These are the available device or software driver updates.

A Cautionary Tale: Updated Into Oblivion

While I've spent many years supporting tens of thousands of users with Windows problems, I've almost always enjoyed a very stable Windows environment.

So one of the joys—and headaches—of writing this book was the need to create situations for myself that would render Windows unstable so I could recover from them. Here's one that occurred with Windows Update that took more than a couple of days to fully resolve.

I used Windows Update to manually check for available updates for my PC. I decided to forego my usual great caution and just accept for installation everything the Windows Update site suggested. One of these updates was a new driver for my ATI Radeon video adapter, notable because ATI video driver changes can be tricky. Remember how I said you may sometimes want to use Safe Mode to change to default video drivers before you apply a new adapter-specific driver? ATI adapters and drivers usually fit this bill.

Normally, I would never automatically update a driver for my ATI Radeon without extra care and due diligence. But this time, I decided, "Let's give it a try!" After all, I have the experience to overcome anything it might do. Or so I thought.

I downloaded the driver from the Windows Update site, and it installed automatically. No problems were immediately detected until Windows Update recommended I restart the PC. When I did, a lot of my Windows text (on menus and screens) disappeared. OK, I thought, let me shut down and restart my system in Safe Mode and go back to default drivers until I can load the previous driver for my video adapter.

Windows had other ideas. First, Windows wouldn't restart in any mode (including Safe Mode). Then, when it did, it immediately gave me the blue screen of death, even in Safe Mode, so I couldn't reach the controls necessary to remove the disastrous driver upgrade. So I brought the system down and removed my ATI video adapter altogether, substituting a basic video adapter I knew worked well with Windows XP. Now, Windows Registry errors kept me from entering Windows, even in Safe Mode.

Continued on next page

A Cautionary Tale: Updated Into Oblivion *(Continued)*

Perspiration beading on my brow, I decided to use Windows XP Recovery Console to try to get into my system to effect repairs. Remember, I knew that at the very least, a very bad driver upgrade was keeping me from working. Only my Recovery Console was set to work only with a password, and the correct password I supplied was being refused…again and again. But I needed to get into Recovery Console to fix my system, so I jumped on another Internet-connected PC in my office to check the Microsoft Knowledge Base. This informed me that I needed to reformat my system to get back to Recovery Console and reset the password.

<insert scream here!>

A week later, I was almost back to the point where I was before my Windows Update/driver debacle. A drive image performed just before chaos descended protected my data, but this situation is an example of how ugly things can get if you perform updates thoughtlessly and without observing proper precautions. In this situation, critical tools like Safe Mode, booting using the Last Known Good Configuration, and the Recovery Console option in Windows XP were all rendered unavailable. A bad driver probably didn't cause all the damage, but it seemed to precipitate other problems once Windows choked on the driver. It took me from a well-running system to a nightmare in just the time it took to download that update.

Mind you, this is an extreme example. I've worked with Windows Update for four years, and I've seen nothing else create this level of chaos. But be prepared for potential problems; you can't afford to assume that everything recommended by even informed sources will do well on your system.

Turning Off Automatic Updates in Windows XP

You may have already guessed that my preference with Windows is to use Windows Update, but to use it selectively. The most selective way to do this is to turn off automatic updating. This doesn't mean to stop using Windows Update. You just need to remember to run it yourself at least once a week, or whenever you think you have a problem that an update might address (for example, because you've read about it in a technical message board or it was suggested by a Microsoft Knowledge Base article).

To run Windows Update manually, choose Windows Start ➤ Programs ➤ Windows Update. To turn off automatic updates, take these steps:

1. Choose Windows Start ➤ Control Panel.

2. Double-click the System icon.

3. Choose the Automatic Updates tab, and under Notification, click Turn Off Automatic Updating. Click OK until done.

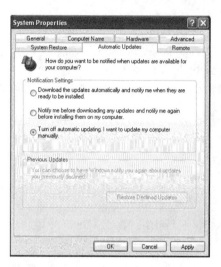

Wait! What if you think you simply won't remember and don't want to set it up through automation? Then you can follow the previous steps, but under the Automatic Updates tab, choose Notify Me Before Downloading Any Updates and Notify Me Again Before Installing Them on my Computer.

Removing an Applied Windows Update

In Windows XP, all of your major Windows Update installations are listed with other installed programs under Add or Remove Programs in Windows Control Panel.

To remove an update from Windows XP, take the following steps:

1. From Windows Start ➤ Control Panel ➤ Add or Remove Programs, select and highlight the update you wish to remove.

2. Click Change/Remove.

3. When prompted, click OK to confirm. You may be asked to restart your system.

Likewise, Windows Millennium and Windows 98/98SE store critical updates (such as the upgrade to 128-bit encryption for Internet Explorer-secured financial transactions) in the program list available under Add or Remove Programs from which you can later remove them.

You can also often remove applied Windows updates right from the Windows Update site product update pages for each update you install. Click Show Installed Updates, as illustrated in Figure 9.1, locate the update you want to remove, and look for and click the Uninstall option in the far right-hand column (see Figure 9.2).

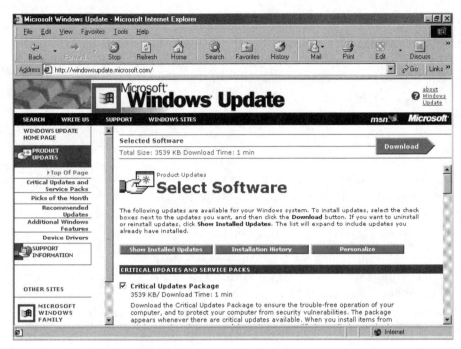

Figure 9.1 *Displaying installed updates for Windows*

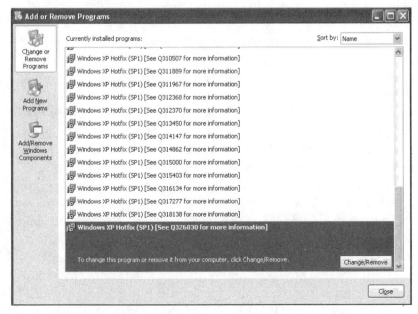

Figure 9.2 *Removing installed updates for Windows*

Error Reporting

For years, users have been looking for a simple way to tell Microsoft when they're having a problem with their product. Calling on the phone is an option, and it's a good option because you can get (almost) immediate feedback, but it can get expensive. You can also send comments to Microsoft using various areas on their main web site (`www.Microsoft.com`).

But Windows XP is the first version of Windows to include error reporting directly from the operating system and the applications installed to it. There are two main situations you may encounter in which you're apt to run into this error-reporting option:

- When an application crashes or prematurely closes and Windows informs you of the same. As it does this, Windows XP usually gives you the option to click a button to send a report of the problem you experienced. If you choose to send the report, it is then transferred to Microsoft. If you click Don't Send, no report is tendered.

- After a blue screen of death telling you that Windows has encountered a problem and the system will be shut down. Associated with this, you'll also see a memory dump occur before the system shuts off. If you're lucky and the system restarts properly for you, you may immediately see a box telling you, "The system has recovered from a serious error." It then gives you the Send/Don't Send choices, as before.

The Value of Error Reporting

This error-reporting capability offers two major benefits, one that may serve you directly and one that may eventually help you.

The first benefit is that by using error reporting, Windows will sometimes (usually as the result of a crash), after receiving your error report, give you feedback on the nature of your problem through a web-based feature called the Windows Online Crash Analysis. This may provide specific help, such as informing you that an out-of-date driver or application is responsible for the crash you're having, or it may be less specific, such as telling you that a device driver is causing a problem for you and suggesting ways to narrow down the culprit. Sometimes, the crash analysis window provides you with a link for downloading a recommended update. This can be invaluable, saving you potentially hours of troubleshooting.

The second benefit is that it's useful for Microsoft to collect data related to problems experienced with their products, including Windows. Hopefully, such information can be used to help improve and enhance the product so that you have less need to use the error-reporting capability.

However, like all good things, this crash analysis isn't perfect either. For example, with a recent problem, Windows Crash Analysis pointed me to a decoder update that I already had. Uninstalling and reinstalling the update did no good; I kept getting the same erroneous feedback. I subsequently learned from the manufacturer that the decoder update recommended by Windows wasn't even the correct one for my DVD/video setup and could cause a serious compatibility issue.

Still, in my testing, the feedback from Windows XP error reporting usually gives me at least enough information to begin sorting out the problem. I encourage you to give it a try the next time the error-reporting option pops up on your screen.

Using System Restore

If you're already using the System Restore feature available in Windows Millennium and Windows XP (discussed in earlier chapters), you can always try restoring your system to an earlier point before the instability developed. However, to do this, there are three requirements:

- You must have System Restore enabled; turning it on after a problem develops that you need to recover from won't work.

- You must have a restore point that dates back to a time prior to the current crisis.

- You need to be able to restore the previous configuration successfully, and as I've told you before, that is not always the case with System Restore. It may be worth a shot, however.

If you're able to get into Windows, simply run System Restore (discussed in Chapter 8) as you would normally. If you can't get into Windows, take these steps:

1. Restart your system.

2. Before Windows starts but fails to load, press and hold the F8 key.

3. When the Advanced Option menu appears, choose Last Known Good Configuration; this rolls you back to a prior restore point.

Let's assume you're lucky and you can roll back to a previous restore point. You must then be careful not to repeat whatever process or modification caused the previous instability. That means you need to be able to identify exactly what caused the problem or come up with a list of possible culprits, and either resolve or avoid the previous situation.

WARNING *Since new restore points being recorded will eventually overwrite the oldest existing restore points, you don't want to wait too long before you try to restore.*

Reverting to a Previous Version

If your Windows instability appears immediately following an update of your operating system, it's smart to consider whether the new version is at fault. In this situation, you have two basic options available to you:

- Try to isolate and resolve the instability itself. This may be simple, or it may demand hours of troubleshooting.

- Return to the previous version of Windows installed on the PC until you can find out the cause of your problem(s). This should put you back where you were before the upgrade, whether you want to go there or not.

Of course, this assumes you have a previous version of Windows installed. That won't always be the case. Formatting the drive, setting up Windows on a new drive, or deleting your previous version of Windows after installing the new version can make your prior Windows version unavailable so you can't revert back to it in a jam. Also, if you're running an older version of Windows using FAT (or FAT16), having recently upgraded to a version using FAT32, you won't be able to revert automatically; you'll have to format the drive and start fresh.

In these situations, it's wise to have a recent drive image that was created before you upgraded Windows. You can follow the directions for your drive-imaging software to restore the image containing your last best working Windows environment.

Removing Windows XP

Let me explain how Windows XP allows you to uninstall all current versions of Windows to revert to a previous one; most other versions of Windows behave similarly.

As part of Windows Setup, uninstallation files for the new operating system are created at the same time you're upgrading your version of Windows, unless you're seriously hurting for available disk space, in which case these uninstallation files may not be created and kept. However, not having the uninstallation files means you can't simply remove the last version of your operating system so you can return to your previous one. This makes it much tougher to return to your previous Windows version without reformatting your drive and starting all over again. Thus, you definitely want to be sure you keep at least 500 MB free beyond the size of the new operating system installation to accommodate these files.

TIP *Always back up your data before you upgrade and before you remove an upgrade.*

Providing that you have an earlier version of Windows on your PC to roll back to, take these steps to remove Windows XP:

1. Shut down and restart your PC in Safe Mode.

2. Choose Windows Start ➤ Control Panel.

3. Click the Add or Remove Programs icon.

4. Locate and select Uninstall Windows XP in your program list. Click Change/Remove. When asked to confirm your selection, click OK.

Dealing with Windows XP Stop Errors

Stop errors in Windows XP—part of the so-called Windows blue screen of death phenomenon that halts your Windows session—are some of the most frustrating errors you may experience, especially if you receive them frequently and the content of the stop error message changes from crisis to crisis. These aren't entirely new to Windows XP; you just know them by different names, such as invalid page faults, from earlier versions of Windows.

Like other types of error messages, it's important to get the exact text of the error on this screen. This can matter in determining what is causing the problem; even if the message doesn't make sense to you, a technical support representative may be able to look it up, or you can check it against the database at the Microsoft Knowledge Base. Windows XP stop errors are typically caused by issues with either hardware or software. These can include:

- Outdated or corrupted hardware or software drivers

- An incompatible device that Windows cannot work with

- Badly-behaving applications or utilities

- An improper or corrupted Windows installation

- Failing or incompatible memory

- Windows installed to a system with a corrupted or out-of-date BIOS

- Hard drive problems (including those related to overheating)

- A virus

The first thing to suspect is any hardware or software you've recently added or modified. If possible, return your system to the way it was before you made the change, either by removing what you installed or resetting changes in the configuration. If this modification was the cause of the problem, switching back should resolve it. If not, leave this change undone until you can figure out what is causing the system halts.

The frequency with which stop errors or invalid page faults occur is important. Most of us get into a strange situation now and again that might cause a single stop or invalid page fault error. A restart of your system is often all that's needed to clear it. But when the error recurs, especially if it recurs after a restart, you've probably got more than a transient problem on your hands.

Exactly when errors occur matters, too, because you can sometimes detect a pattern. For example, if every time you use your scanner you receive an invalid page fault or stop error, look at the scanner, its TWAIN driver (the drivers used by acquisition devices like scanners and digital cameras), its software, or the way Windows is trying to use it. Something is amiss.

More headaches occur when you can't see a discernible pattern. In these cases, you just may need to observe the situation longer. For example, if doing various tasks in Windows produces the same types of problems (crashing, slowdowns, errors), look first at what software is always running at the time this problem expresses itself. Maybe your out-of-date virus software or your last-version-of-Windows disk utility is running in the background each time, and this is the cause of your problems. Once all this is checked, it's time to look at critical hardware, such as memory, your hard drive, and even your motherboard and CPU, because a problem or impending failure with any of those can produce significant Windows instability.

In the worst scenarios, you'll find Windows reporting a problem with memory management in this blue screen, while telling you about an IRQ problem in another. Like the previous situation, you need to investigate what software is always running when this occurs. Once software is ruled out as a cause, investigate hardware problems as the possible cause.

> **NOTE** *Are you so frustrated with unresolved Windows problems that you just want to pack it in or get a fresh start? I can't help you cut your ties to your PC, but I'll tell you about "Starting from Scratch the Smart Way" in Chapter 16.*

One More Before We Go

Here's a tip offered by the wise technical editor on this book, Don Fuller, that covers another area in which Windows built-in assistance can really lend a helping hand.

"When I first installed XP, I ran into severe problems. I [received] blue screens about 200 times in the first three months. The machine I installed XP on was previously running Windows 2000 Professional Server with no problems. The blue screens were random, with no specific error. There is a feature hidden in XP that was the charm. Go to Start ➢ Help and Support ➢ Use Tools… from Pick a Task menu ➢ My Computer Information ➢ View the Status of my System Hardware and Software. In the Hardware section under Update, I had an update required on both my video card and sound card. Although I was using the vendor-recommended drivers, they were not WHQL. (For a stable XP environment, WHQL drivers are the only way to go.) The instability was caused by these two drivers and the relationship between both drivers. I eventually found WHQL drivers for both cards; I had to replace the sound card–a SB PCI 128–because the SB PCI 128 Live was supported, not the one I had. The problems were finally resolved. This feature saved my neck and I'm sure it will save someone else's."

Hardware failures, brought about by the ravages of time and overwork or because of a natural disaster, are a sad reality of working with computers. Failing hardware—hardware that is not quite ready to give up the digital ghost—can contribute to instabilities such as the stop and invalid page fault errors you've just read about.

Chapter 10, "Understanding and Troubleshooting Hardware Failures," will explain some strategic hardware-specific troubleshooting that can help you both in disasters and in your everyday work. Chapter 10 will also talk about repairs and replacements you can do yourself.

CHAPTER 10

Understanding and Troubleshooting Hardware Failures

PC hardware is something you want to be able to take for granted; you just want it to work so you can largely ignore it the remainder of the time.

But hardware can only be ignored for so long; eventually, you'll experience a device failure that is more serious than losing a mouse or a keyboard. That failure may prevent your PC from starting or from being used satisfactorily, and could endanger your unprotected data.

Two of the pitfalls of the relative affordability of PC hardware today are

- Many components formerly made with metal or other decent materials are now made with cheaper plastic and other less sturdy stuff.

- Most of this inexpensive hardware does not go through the rigorous quality assurance and inspection that the industry used to employ.

What this means for you is that even a brand-new PC or component may arrive defective out of the box, even if it doesn't show signs of a broken part or other obvious damage.

It also means that many hardware components on your PC may not be of sufficient quality to be worth repairing. For example, floppy and CD-ROM drives that you used to try to repair 10 years ago are typically replaced these days. If you develop a problem with your new hard drive or still-under-warranty monitor, the manufacturer will probably tell you to send your current unit back for replacement rather than repair. These lean prices contribute to a climate where fast, free, and good technical support is not easy to find when you run into problems with your hardware. But, hopefully, throughout this book, you've picked up tips, tricks, and troubleshooting techniques to help you resolve many of the disasters that might afflict your hardware.

This chapter, at about the midway point of the book, seems like an ideal time to delve more deeply into hardware failures, both real and imagined. I say imagined, because many problems can mimic a hardware failure when the hardware is fine except that it has been badly configured, become linked to the wrong driver, or is fighting another device for the CPU's—or the operating system's—attention.

In particular, this chapter highlights critical failures, meaning when can't-do-without hardware such as memory, the motherboard, video, and the CPU. You'll want to couple this information with material you've already learned about in earlier chapters, particularly Chapter 6, "Transforming Yourself into a Smart Troubleshooter: Detecting, Analyzing, and Diagnosing," and Chapter 7, "Restarting a Problem PC."

> **WARNING** *If you suspect a critical hardware failure is imminent, back up your data immediately. If the problem becomes so severe that you need to replace your system, you'll be glad to have your data safely together in one place.*

Working Through Hardware Failures: Symptoms and Solutions

As you go through some of the symptoms and realities of hardware failures, along with problems that mimic hardware failures, keep in mind the important troubleshooting techniques you've learned already. You definitely must

- Keep your eyes, ears, and your nose open to symptoms such as error messages and on-screen warnings, unusual beeps or other noises you haven't heard from your PC before, and burning or odd smells coming from the PC or its components.

- Be prepared and available to cut power to the system quickly if the need arises.

- Work through problems one modification at a time to make sure you don't exacerbate existing problems or create new ones.

- Try to have another Internet-ready PC available to you to get online to get answers to your questions if your main PC is down. Don't be afraid to use public resources like your local library to access the Internet.

In addition, there are two other important issues to keep in mind as you work through hardware failures:

- I follow a great technician's advice to me when I was first learning the ins and outs of PC hardware: "Suspect a driver problem before you suspect a hardware failure, unless you have definite evidence of damaged hardware." This makes sense because replacing or updating a driver is generally far easier than checking the physical hardware itself. If you resolve the problem with the driver alone, you don't have to monkey around with the hardware or its resources.

- Remember to use your BIOS Setup and Windows Device Manager to check the status of a device. A device or connection disabled in BIOS normally won't be available in Windows, so make sure that a device you want to work is not disabled in the BIOS. While not every device on your system is listed in Device Manager, the important ones are.

NOTE *Why aren't your motherboard and CPU listed in Device Manager? Well, many parts of your motherboard, including important controllers and buses, are listed under resources used. But if your motherboard or CPU is seriously malfunctioning, you probably won't be able to get into Device Manager to check their status anyway.*

More About Device Manager

Since I've so often touted Device Manager as a central location for troubleshooting—and you really can't avoid Device Manager when working with a potential hardware failure—let's explore more about its usefulness when coping with a disaster-ed system. Specifically, let's look at two situations you may encounter:

- What to do when an Unknown Device listing appears in Device Manager

- What to do when a device on your system returns an error code

Working with Unknown Devices

As if some of the details in Device Manager aren't mysterious enough, you may find yourself one day looking at an entry in Device Manager—typically highlighted with a yellow exclamation point—that reads simply, "Unknown Device." What this means is that Windows recognizes that a device is attached, but it's not sure what that device is. If you right-click an Unknown Device listing and choose Properties, you probably won't get any information giving you a clue as to what device it is. After all, if Windows could tell you anything about the device, it wouldn't be unknown. Right?

Device Manager may report a device as unknown for a number of reasons:

- Windows can't find any driver for it.

- The only available driver is for a much earlier version of Windows, such as Windows 95 or 98.

- Windows can't read the hardware's proprietary identifier (every PNP device should have one).

- The device has been fundamentally changed in some way since it was manufactured and configured for use (because of damage or because of modification by the user).

- A problem within the operating system is preventing Windows from seeing the device and its driver properly. However, if this is the case, you should see other signs of instability or corruption in Windows.

- Software is somehow interfering with the process. Often, this isn't so much the usual applications you install to your PC but software-created virtual drivers for a particular piece of hardware that don't allow Windows to view the actual identifier on the device (USB and IEEE 1394 devices sometimes fall into this category).

If Device Manager reports a device as unknown, review these issues and see if anything about your PC setup fits these risk factors. For example, are you experiencing an instability with Windows that might account for its failure to recognize a device installed to your system? If so, try to correct the Windows instability first, and then see if Windows can properly identify the device.

Look at any devices with which you've recently experienced problems. Check the status of each of these devices in Device Manager to rule them out as the possible source of the Unknown Device listing.

NOTE *It's more important to notice when a formerly properly identified device suddenly reverts to an Unknown Device listing than it is if a newly installed device is unknown because the former situation tells you that something has occurred to change the device's status. Since we're discussing disaster recovery, a physical disaster (natural or human) has to be considered a possible cause. It could be a matter of an out-of-date driver, but it may also indicate a device that's just operational enough to be seen, but not working well enough to report its identity.*

The Process of Elimination

What happens if you have no prime suspects when you discover an Unknown Device listing? The standard answer is to employ the process of elimination: Go through Device Manager, expand each category, and check to make sure that every device that was listed there before is properly listed there now (another strong reason to familiarize yourself with Device Manager before you hit a disaster or distress). To do this, take the following steps:

1. From Control Panel, double-click the System icon.

2. Choose the Device Manager tab. (Under Windows XP, choose the Hardware tab and then click Device Manager.)

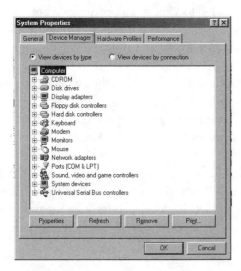

3. Click the + sign next to each major category to expand it.

4. Verify that all known devices are listed.

Should you find that a device that was formerly listed—such as a video adapter or a modem still in use—is now no longer listed (and you haven't removed it), you may very well have the source of your Unknown Device listing.

A Real-Life Example

Let's look at an example of a situation where Device Manager entries are affected after a calamity in your system. Let's assume that your main PC is connected to a surge suppressor to protect it from power instability problems, but that your monitor is not so protected—it's plugged directly into a wall outlet. A surge hits somewhere along the electric lines and sends a serious charge throughout the homes and offices in your area.

Your surge suppressor should curb or completely assume the blow from the surge and try to keep its worst effects from reaching your PC power supply and beyond. But the monitor, unprotected, isn't so lucky. As a result of the surge, the monitor can't be turned on. Unhappily, you replace the existing monitor with another working monitor and attach it to the connector on the edge of the video adapter at the back of your PC. You successfully start up the PC and see the display. Windows automatically loads the driver needed for your new monitor. Yet when you look in Device Manager, you suddenly see an Unknown Device listed. Well, you think, you just installed the replacement monitor, so maybe it's that. You check the Device Manager entry for the monitor, however, and it's fine. Then you go to the Display Adapter entry and notice that your video adapter—which certainly appears to be working because you're able to see video—is no longer listed there. In fact, nothing may be listed under Display Adapter.

Bingo. You've just discovered the identity of your unknown device. The problem with the monitor has somehow affected the video adapter—or Windows—enough to affect Windows' ability to display the correct information for your video adapter.

Reinstalling the driver for your video adapter should resolve the problem. If it doesn't, the power surge could have extended its damage—at least in terms of being able to properly recognize the device—to the video adapter through its direct cable connection to the affected monitor. Should reinstalling the correct version of your video adapter's driver not resolve the situation, contact your video adapter manufacturer. If it's under warranty, the manufacturer may agree to replace it; if not, they may be willing to replace it at a reduced cost (and that's nice, because the manufacturer really isn't responsible in a situation like this).

Getting the Scoop on Device Manager Error Codes

Device Manager typically provides an error code and a brief explanation when Windows detects a problem related to a specific device. However, this brief explanation may not be enough to tell you what you need to do to correct the problem.

Earlier versions of Windows—specifically, Windows 95 and 98/98 Second Edition—often just posted these errors, followed by a number (for example, Error 630). These numbers may be reported on the screen when you're trying to use a problem device.

For example, when Windows Millennium was first released in 2000, everyone was looking for help with a Code 22 error in Device Manager. The problem was that Code 22, all by itself, sounded like an error but it wasn't; it was just letting you know about resources assigned to PCI devices (and many expansion boards are PCI-connected). So unless someone had a Code 22 error that coincided with problem with a PCI device, there was much alarm about fairly little.

These error codes are listed, if they are reported, under the properties for each device in Device Manager. To find out the meaning of a specific code, take these steps:

1. From Control Panel, double-click the System icon.

2. Choose the Device Manager tab. (From Windows XP, choose the Hardware tab and then click Device Manager.)

3. Click + to expand device category listings to show each device.

4. Right-click a specific device and choose Properties. The error code, if provided, should be listed on the General tab.

Researching the Error Codes

One of the first places you should go to further research an error code in Device Manager is the Microsoft Knowledge Base I've mentioned so frequently. Once there, you can search by specific article number if you've been provided one, such as article Q310123, which lists Windows XP Device Manager codes. Or you can search on keywords, such as "Device Manager codes" or "Device Manager error."

TIP *In Windows Millennium and Windows XP, you can also perform this search through your Internet connection by going through Windows Start ➤ Help and Support.*

To research error codes for Windows 95 and 98, take these steps:

1. With your connection to the Internet already established, load your web browser.

2. Type in the address for Microsoft Knowledge Base: `http://search.support .Microsoft.com`. Click Enter or Go.

3. From the Microsoft Support Web page, click Search the Microsoft Knowledge Base.

4. From the Microsoft Knowledge Base search page, under Select a Microsoft Product, locate your version of Windows from the list of supported products.

5. On the same page, drop down to the section labeled Search For, type in the keywords for your problem (for example, "Device Manager errors"). Click the green arrow.

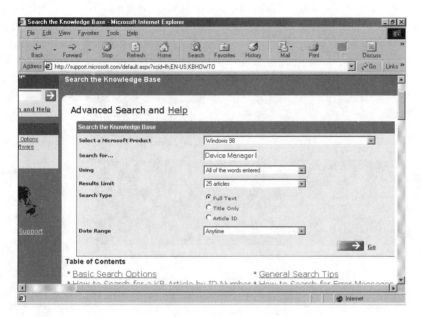

6. From the resulting list, select the article entitled "Explanation of Error Codes Generated by Device Manager" and begin reading.

To do this for Windows XP, follow the same steps, substituting Windows XP for the selected Microsoft product. Also, in step 5, choose the article by the exact same title, "Explanation of Error Codes Generated by Device Manager." However, the resulting article is specifically for Windows XP; the content is different from the article for Windows 95/98, as you can see in Figure 10.1. (The Windows XP Device Manager error codes are listed in the article Q310123 that was noted earlier in this section.)

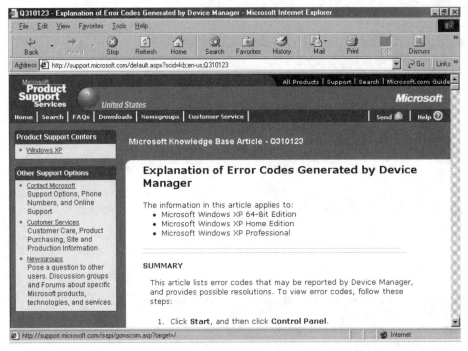

Figure 10.1 *Microsoft Knowledge Base can provide details on Device Manager error codes.*

Drive Failures

One nice thing about most drives other than your booting hard drive is that there is usually very little they can do by themselves to make your system fail. You need other drives, such as a floppy drive, when your booting hard drive won't boot.

Since this topic is the entire focus of Chapter 17, "Resurrecting a Dead Hard Drive," you can either jump ahead if you need the answer to a specific problem, or wait until you get there. I'll give you one clue, however: Always check the BIOS Setup. Most if not all of your drives should be listed there.

Motherboard Failures

Some motherboards will appear to fail all at once. You turn on your system, you hear the power supply engage, and maybe (but unlikely) you see some display alerting you to a problem, but nothing else happens. Many motherboards, however, begin to fail over time, affected to some degree by how many times you restart your PC, run them in extremes of heat, cold, or moisture, or press too hard when you install components such as memory and expansion boards. In my experience, I've seen original IBM PC motherboards that are still working today, and I've seen plenty of motherboards manufactured just in the past year or two that have already died.

Some of the initial and less-than-obvious symptoms of a failing or malfunctioning motherboard include

- Hesitancy or other problems when the PC is first turned on.

- Your PC may reboot itself or just go dead in the middle of a Windows session.

- Windows may be far more unstable without any seeming cause.

- Windows may begin to report ever-changing error messages or may fail to load at all, even when using Safe Mode; these problems may begin slowly and then increase.

- Devices appear and disappear at random (this can be in BIOS or Device Manager, usually the latter.

Unfortunately, most of these early symptoms can result from other failures, too, making identification of the problem more difficult. For example, a virus, overheating, or a serious disk error could spontaneously reboot your system, and as you learned in Chapter 9, "Stabilizing Your Operating System," many different problems can contribute to serious instability in Windows. For this reason, try the barebones setup test discussed later in this chapter to see if the motherboard performs better once most of its extra components are removed.

There are also times when a motherboard is more likely to fail suddenly rather than slowly. Most of these times relate to a situation that physically stresses the motherboard, including

- After a physical move where the PC case was not well protected from being bumped or jostled (This can also affect components and how well they're seated in the motherboard.)

- Following a difficult motherboard or motherboard component installation, where you may have flexed the motherboard too severely or shorted the motherboard or one of its components

- After an electrical event such as a nearby lightning strike or power surge while the PC was in operation and unprotected (and even if it was protected, depending on the severity of the event and the quality of the protection)

- After operating under stress for a prolonged period of time such as in extremes of temperature and humidity

- Following many years of service

Unexplained Hot or Dead Zones

Dead men may tell no tales, but dead hardware sometimes does.

Motherboards are just large printed circuit boards. Take a good look at one, and you'll see that it's covered with sockets and slots and ports that allow you to install hardware and wiring and communications running throughout so that the different components can talk with each other.

One of the ways a motherboard may begin to fail is when it develops *dead zones*, areas where hardware that is plugged into or built into the motherboard may not work any longer. A variation on this is when hardware installed to a problem zone works intermittently, yet the PC runs and there are no identified conflicts or problems except this intermittent failure. In this second situation, the same memory stick in the same memory socket in your motherboard is recognized one time, not the next time, then is recognized again…ad infinitum. Once you've verified that the memory is of the right type, that the stick is good (for example, it's always recognized when it's installed in another socket), and that you have it properly installed, you're running out of possibilities: it's probably a damaged motherboard.

NOTE *Some people can run a damaged motherboard for years without ever seeing the full board fail. But there is a fire risk with some types of motherboard failure. If you don't replace it immediately, make sure the PC is at least turned off when you're not around.*

Neither of these situations is good. The first situation alerts you to expect a full motherboard failure sometime down the road. The second situation not only does this, but it may also indicate a voltage problem or damage that could result in fire or the premature death or damage to other hardware installed into the motherboard.

This voltage issue brings up another problem that you may be able to spot—and avert a later disaster—by watching for certain conditions with your motherboard whenever you're inside the PC. (Remember to disconnect power and wear an anti-static device whenever you're inside your PC case.) This is especially true when swapping out hardware, as you'll read in "A Cautionary Tale: There's Hot, and Then There's HOT!"

If you have any of the following warning signs, turn the PC off and disconnect power, and then have the motherboard checked and/or replaced:

- Obvious signs of damage (fractures, charred areas, or melting of wires) or warping

- Sparking or smoke coming from the motherboard itself (A smoking power supply or component may not affect the motherboard unless you continue to run the PC with this problem.)

- Having to replace too much hardware over a period of a year or two (However, this is more likely to be the result of power problems; anything damaging expansion boards and other devices installed directly to the motherboard is hurting the motherboard, too.)

- Having to replace a component like a modem because of lightning or power-surge damage but your system remains affected by what may seem like odd, disconnected hardware problems

- Serious problems after an electrostatic discharge (shock or zap) within the case, such as you might have if you forget to ground yourself

- Same as above, but you notice hesitations or "dead" behavior after you install something into or remove a component from the motherboard while the PC is powered up

WARNING *Look for anything out of place with your motherboard like two pieces of metal touching one another—a situation that can produce an electrical short. A common area for such problems is the way the motherboard is positioned in the PC case; if one of its edges inappropriately touches one of the metal standoffs in the case frame, the board can short. In addition, check for foreign objects or a large accumulation of dust that can be removed with compressed air (not blowing with your mouth, because it's moist).*

A Cautionary Tale: There's Hot, and Then There's HOT!

As I told you in the last chapter, part of my work in preparing this book was to re-create some of the disasters we're discussing.

One of the unwitting victims of all this research was my poor P2-350 motherboard, pressed into service on 9/11/98 and committed to a PC hardware recycling program on 8/24/02. That motherboard helped me through the writing or editing of a dozen books, thousands of hours of online research and providing technical support, a few dozen beta tests, and way too many hours playing "The Sims." Ironically, the motherboard lasted a few years longer than the company that sold me my system.

It didn't go out with a bang, either. Instead, I spent a week trying to resolve some really bizarre Windows stop errors (discussed in Chapter 9, "Stabilizing Your Operating System") that I had assumed were caused by some of my testing. Then one day, I tried rearranging my memory to see if a failing memory stick was at fault.

Continued on next page

A Cautionary Tale: There's Hot, and Then There's HOT! *(Continued)*

I installed a brand new stick of working SDRAM into my system, but found I got no display—and no beeps—when I powered the PC back up. After I powered it down again and disconnected the power to the PC, I removed the new stick of RAM I had just installed. I discovered that the heat from the connector edge of the stick was severe enough to warm the entire stick.

Thinking I must have installed it improperly since less than 60 seconds of operation shouldn't result in that level of warm up, I tried another stick of memory, being extra careful with its installation. I got the exact same result. However, this time, I could smell the overheating and was pleased to get the system disconnected again before I had an electrical fire—the situation seemed ripe for one.

When I had the board fully checked a few days later, only some of the board was getting power, while part of the board was showing a real flux in voltage. Because I stopped using the motherboard immediately upon discovering the overheating, I probably saved many of the components installed into it. So I opted to replace just the motherboard itself.

FYI, the occasion made me stop to consult my PC journal, calculate how much I had spent on the system both to purchase and to power, as well as to repair through replacement components and operating system upgrades. All total, that PC cost me about $1.58 a day, or less than the price of an Egg McMuffin or a cup of Starbuck's coffee. Not a bad investment. Plus, since I've got drives and many other parts I can still use from it, the cost over the PC's life should decrease from even that paltry $1.58.

Central Processor Unit (CPU) Failures

Plain and simple: If your CPU doesn't work, neither will your PC. The power supply should engage when the PC is turned on, and the motherboard and other components should roar to life. But if the CPU isn't available because it has been removed, poorly installed, or has failed, you won't get farther than the POST process. The CPU isn't optional equipment; it's core equipment.

If you try to start your PC one day and receive an error message on the boot screen related to the CPU, you have no choice but to go inside the case. Take these steps:

1. Turn off the PC and disconnect power.

2. Remove the PC cover.

3. Ground yourself using your anti-static wrist strap according to its directions.

4. Locate your CPU.

5. Check the CPU's seating. It doesn't hurt either to check other aspects of the mother-board and its components to be sure there is no damage or loose boards or connections.

6. You may want to leave the cover off while you reconnect power, turn the PC on, and try to boot it again.

If the installation is correct and the CPU was working previously without any intervening event that may have damaged it, you may indeed have a dead CPU. You'll need to get either an exact replacement (meaning the same CPU type, speed, and package type such as a PIII 800 MHz) or another CPU that can fit the range of CPUs supported by your motherboard. Your motherboard or PC manufacturer often provides a list of these on its support web site or by call-ing their Customer Service representatives.

Checking the CPU Fan

In evaluating a CPU, it's important to check the status of the CPU's fan since a malfunctioning or non-operational CPU fan can damage or destroy a CPU because it fails to remove the heated air around the processor. Before this happens, such heat can also shut down your system. Many—but by no means all—motherboards include a thermal sensor feature that automatically shuts down your system when the interior temperature near the sensor reaches a designated peak tem-perature (which hopefully is below the point at which wires melt and chipsets fail). Thus, if you've had unexplained shutdowns or other problems you've wondered might be related to overheating, check the CPU fan *before* you wake up to a dead CPU.

The best way to test a CPU fan—like other fans on your system—is simply to eyeball the fan while it's in operation. For example, follow the last set of steps for checking your CPU and, after completing step 6 with the cover off, look at the CPU fan (but keep hands and face away) to be sure its small blades are turning.

While the CPU fan is a separate piece of hardware, it is mounted or otherwise attached to the CPU packaging. Because the fan is separate from the CPU, it's easy to remove the CPU fan for cleaning (compressed air works great), as you can see in Figure 10.2. Built-up dust and debris can slow or stall the fan blades. Just cleaning alone can often turn a malfunctioning fan into a working one. If cleaning doesn't help, you can usually replace a CPU fan for less than $20, depending on the features of the fan (some get quite elaborate) and the type of CPU packaging involved.

Figure 10.2 A Pentium II/III CPU fan removed for cleaning

TIP *Unless you're positive the CPU fan works, replace the CPU fan at the time you replace the CPU. It's always possible that the fan at least contributed to the CPU's failure, and you don't want a replacement CPU to fall prey to the same fate. Also, if you change your motherboard and CPU as part of the replacement process, you may need a different CPU fan because of CPU packaging differences between Pentium II/IIIs and Pentium IV systems, AMD Athlon and Duron vs. earlier AMD CPUs, and so on.*

Power Supply Failures

Power supplies typically die one of two ways: slowly or instantly and forever. While the power supply is statistically most likely to fail completely when it's been turned off (or when you attempt to turn it on again), it sometimes fails right in the middle of a session. In most cases, your PC seems to switch off and usually won't respond when you try to turn it on again. If it does try to start, you may smell smoke or overheated parts.

If the power supply doesn't engage, the power supply may be well on its way to burning out, if it's not already dead. If the power supply starts but the fan doesn't move, turn the PC back off immediately, disconnect power, and use a can of compressed air to clean any debris and dust from the fan before trying again.

Those of you who are familiar with power supplies for other types of devices may already know that the fan in a PC power supply can usually be removed, cleaned, and oiled to grease recalcitrant blades (a droplet of 3-in-1 Oil usually works for me) or replaced. Then the entire power supply can be mounted back inside the case and reconnected to the rest of the system. This is a bit too advanced for me to recommend to everyone, so I'll let the adventurers among you proceed at their own risk with this caveat: The fan should not be reinstalled until it is fully clean and dry, and you must exercise extreme care in reassembling the fan into the power supply and in reattaching all the connectors from the power supply to the other parts of your system that require them.

Chapter 11, "Avoiding Power and Overheating Problems," explains how to install a new power supply should you need to replace or upgrade your current power supply.

TIP *Don't underestimate the ability of an overtaxed power supply to cause problems on a PC. On a standard 200-watt PC power supply packed in many computers, it's possible to run out of juice before you run out of devices you can install into your PC that need a connection from the power supply. Chapter 11 contains more information about this.*

PC Memory (RAM) Failures

Since Chapter 8, "When Upgrades Go Wrong," offers some useful suggestions for memory troubleshooting, let me turn my attention here to the two issues that were not addressed there, but which often come up in questions I receive from users with problems:

- What to do when a memory socket on your motherboard fails

- What it means if you experience repeated memory failures

Broken Memory Socket

If your memory socket becomes damaged in the process of installing new or additional RAM, you want to finish your task without installing RAM to the broken socket. Then reconnect power and try to start your system.

A broken socket by itself probably won't hurt your PC. Most of the ways it can break are mechanical; for example, the retainer clips break. A broken socket is really just an inconvenience that robs you of an available memory socket.

Depending on how ambitious you feel and how much you want to restore your damaged memory socket, you can sometimes obtain a fresh memory socket from your motherboard or PC manufacturer. On many motherboards, tiny screws hold the socket in place, and removal of these tiny screws allows you to pull the old socket free and screw a new one into place. But you must have the right socket, and not all motherboards make it possible for you to replace these sockets.

You may find it easier to simply populate your remaining working memory sockets with more capacious sticks of memory (say, 128MB each rather than 64MB, providing your motherboard permits this) than it is to repair a busted socket. Even with small and slender fingers, replacing a memory socket is a challenge, as you can see in Figure 10.3. Those tiny screws can fall and disappear into a nest of cables or fall onto an expansion board and scratch one in a delicate spot.

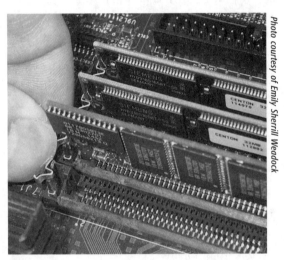

Figure 10.3 *PC memory sockets and installed RAM (SDRAM)*

TIP *Here's a tip offered by Don Fuller, technical editor on this book: When I build a PC, I always put in two memory sticks. If I'm going to install 256MB, I'll use two 128MB sticks. If one stick fails, I can remove it and the PC is still operational. This allows me the time to procure another stick at hopefully a better price and leave the client's machine operational.*

Repeated Memory Failures

Have you experienced failure of different sticks of installed RAM more than twice on your PC? If so, the problem may lie either with the type and quality of RAM you purchase or with your system itself.

First, look at the RAM you buy. Does it all come from one manufacturer? If so, you probably want to

- Verify that you are buying the correct type of RAM for your system, as discussed in Chapter 8.

- Try buying RAM from another manufacturer to see if this resolves the fast failures.

Dirty or irregular power or a bad motherboard can both play a role as well. However, these factors are less likely culprits than the memory itself *unless* memory isn't the only component on the motherboard you're replacing (due to failure) more than once or twice during the average 2–3 year life span of a new PC. (The PC itself usually lasts much longer, but until PCs become easier to upgrade, users are tossing them after a few years as obsolete.)

Video/Display Failures

Most people assume that when they first power on their PCs and fail to see a display, something is terribly wrong with the video itself. But as you've read in previous chapters, it's not uncommon for an improperly installed or incompatible device to prevent the PC from booting to the point where a display appears or to interfere with the display that should appear. Thus, if you've just installed a new or replacement component to your PC, check this installation first.

Well, almost first, since the leading cause of reported video failure is actually a tie between

- The monitor not being turned on or not being plugged in to a good power source

- A loose or disconnected cable running between the monitor and the video adapter

Check both of these situations first. Other possibilities include

- A serious driver problem

- An improperly installed video adapter

- A damaged or dead video adapter

- A malfunctioning monitor (A dead monitor usually won't have any power, while a malfunctioning one may show a lit power button, but no actual video.)

- A bent pin on the cable connector running from the monitor to the video adapter (These bent pins can sometimes be carefully bent back into place. Often, the bent pin just snaps off and you need to replace either the cable or the monitor if the cable is permanently attached to the monitor (some repair shops can re-pin the connector for you).

- A damaged or dead motherboard, especially if the video chipset is integrated into the motherboard rather than available as a separate add-in expansion board

TIP *If the monitor works well enough to do its self-test (see your monitor documentation) and reports that it is working well, you should assume the problem is with the video adapter or with the system itself.*

Video and Overheating-Induced Failures

Today's best video adapters—and even some average ones—are powerful beasts that can provide you with luscious game play and DVD playback quality. The electronics required to empower these adapters are often a miracle of modern engineering in terms of all that they fit onto those small printed circuit boards. As you'll recall from Chapter 2, these video adapters often have their own graphics processor, acting as a video-specific brain, and many other strategic components, including anywhere from 8MB to 128MB of memory.

Unfortunately, serious heat can build up around the video adapter as a direct result of its functions and features. While several top-of-the-line video adapters feature an on-board fan to move hot air away from the graphics processor and some also offer a heat sink used to reduce the heat generated by sensitive components, either your video adapter may not have this heat-reduction hardware or it may be insufficient to do the job. For example, if your video adapter is just one of a number of different boards installed in your motherboard's expansion slots, it may have a tough time pushing that hot air away from such a crowded space, even with a fan present.

While overheating is one of the major topics of Chapter 11, you need to factor in this possibility when troubleshooting video failures. An overheated video adapter that has not yet been permanently damaged by excessive heat may work fine whenever the unit has been turned off for a period of time (to cool things off) and then started back up again. But the situation may degrade again once the ambient temperature around that video adapter climbs past acceptable levels. If that's the pattern you see in a suspected video adapter failure, you need to improve the circulation inside your system.

TIP *Your video manufacturer's web site may contain helpful suggestions for reducing heat-related problems.*

A Cautionary Tale:
In the If-it-Ain't-Broken, Fix-it-Until-it-is Department

Remember that earlier in this chapter I discussed the issue of the Unknown Device listings in Device Manager and how to troubleshoot them. That discussion reminds me of an older system in my office that has listed its installed video adapter as an Unknown Device since the PC was upgraded to Windows XP last year. I know exactly what the problem is: The video adapter in that PC was made by a company that went out of business in 1999, so it hasn't had a driver update since Windows 98 was new.

If I replace the video adapter with one that can be updated, that Unknown Device entry would disappear like yesterday's weather. But the video works decently, and I've had no problems beyond that entry in Device Manager, so I'm happy to nurse this situation along until I retire the system before it's time to upgrade my operating system again.

What makes this a cautionary tale is that the only times I have had problems with my Unknown Device display is when I've tried to cure it: by going back to default video drivers, by trying to use a very similar device driver, and by trying to install the last available driver for that video adapter. In fact, these so-called cures caused me several headaches until I set things back to the way they had been.

The message here is two-fold. One, not all errors and problems that appear in Device Manager will affect your ability to work with your system. Two, you must sometimes pick your fights with recalcitrant devices and drivers. If you've got a situation that isn't ideal but yet is still stable and workable, think twice before fixing it.

Modem Failures

While a modem isn't core equipment in the way that a CPU or motherboard is, it's become important to business, home, and school users simply because users want and need access to the Internet. A modem is the most common way to do that through the PC. So let's take a few moments to discuss the serious problems that you might encounter with modems.

Modems are one of the most frequently replaced components in a PC—and not always because they're broken. Instead, the difficulty with which some modems are configured—or respond badly to your attempts to change their configuration—cause many people to decide they just can't deal with a modem problem in any other way except to replace it. What they don't realize is that the next modem may be even more challenging to get working properly and at the same speed.

But if defective modem hardware isn't responsible for all modem failures, what is? The list is long—with many items on it tying back to the difficulties of modem configuration—and includes

- Using the wrong driver for your modem

- Using the wrong driver version for your version of Windows

- Improper connection of the phone line or satellite/cable/DSL high-speed connection cables/hardware

- Failure of the support software for the service, such as corrupted Dial-up Networking in Windows or misconfigured high-speed provider software

- Resource conflicts, where the same resources used by the COM port providing communication with the modem are being used by another device in your PC such as a sound or network adapter

For these reasons, it's important that you cover the following bases as you troubleshoot an apparent modem failure:

- Obtain and install the latest driver available for your modem and operating system version.

- Verify the phone/high-speed access connections using your documentation (and by a call to the provider, if necessary). In addition, make sure that there is "live" service (a dial tone on that phone line, or a live cable, satellite, or DSL feed).

- Make sure you're using the proper software (and the correct version of it) for the type of connection you're trying to use, and verify through your provider that it is configured correctly. (This information is often available at a provider's web site.)

- Check Device Manager for devices with a yellow exclamation point or red X mark; they could be the source of the conflict with the modem's COM port. Resolve them using the techniques discussed in Chapter 6.

Before discussing the use of the Windows diagnostic tool with a modem, remember to use the resources for understanding error codes discussed earlier in this chapter. Table 10.1 in the next section lists the most commonly reported modem problems and what you should do to try to resolve them.

Windows Diagnostic Testing for Modems

Windows includes built-in diagnostic testing for a modem that has been installed into the operating system. Always use this tool when you suspect a problem related to your modem. To do this, take these steps:

1. Go to Windows Start ➤ Control Panel (Windows Start ➤ Settings ➤ Control Panel in earlier versions of Windows).

2. Double-click the Modems icon.

3. Select the Diagnostics tab.

4. From the Diagnostics tab, select and highlight the modem/COM port you want to test and then click More Info.

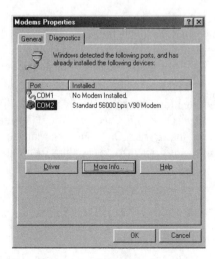

5. A message appears on your screen telling you that Windows is communicating with your modem. When complete, a brief report appears, letting you know everything tested fine or that there was a problem. Click OK.

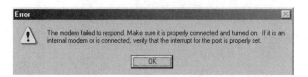

Table 10.1   *Common Modem Issues and Their Solutions*

MODEM ISSUE	TROUBLESHOOTING/SOLUTION
Could Not Open Port error.	This is usually the result of a conflict between devices. Use Device Manager to look for conflicts between the COM port used by the modem and another device. Also, a communications program—such as America Online software or other software—loading in your Startup folder could be opening the port and then making it unavailable later. Remove such programs from Startup.
Modem fails; gives errors after a Windows upgrade.	Locate and install the latest driver available for your modem for your version of Windows. If you're using a high-speed modem, check with your provider. You may need to reconfigure your high-speed setup or install new utilities based on your upgrade, and you may be unable to use your Internet service until you do so.
Modem was installed but disappeared.	This is most apt to happen with Winmodems. Check Device Manager to be sure you no longer see the modem listed. Then use the Add New Hardware wizard (available under the icon of the same name in Control Panel) to install the modem driver again. If necessary, point to your modem driver rather than letting Windows try to detect it (which you should try first).
Replaced modem; PC won't boot.	The first thing to check is the modem installation. Then make sure you didn't loosen other installed boards and other components during the installation. Try different internal slots (if it's an internal modem) or a different external COM port (if it's an external modem). If necessary, remove the new modem and set it aside until you contact the modem manufacturer for assistance.
Trying to replace my integrated modem with a full modem; I only see the old one.	You probably need to disable the integrated (on the motherboard) modem in the BIOS before you can successfully use the new modem. Check with your PC manufacturer or motherboard manufacturer on the specifics. Often, just removing the integrated modem as it's listed in Device Manager can accomplish this. Then restart your system with the new modem installed.

NOTE *Let me remind you once again that it's better for the environment if you don't simply "toss" your PC or its parts into a landfill. As you learned in Chapter 3, "Prevention: Limiting Your Risks," some of the materials that comprise your PC are pretty toxic. Users throw away so many PCs that dead PCs are being shipped to other countries to be deconstructed. Check to see whether your community has a PC recycling/collection effort that can reclaim some of the materials from your old equipment to reduce the load on landfills.*

Advanced Power Management Issues

Having already broached the subject of power management in Chapter 2, let's focus on the ways in which power management may interact badly with your hardware.

As you recall, power management's job is to let the parts of your system go into a lower power consumption mode when you're not actively working with it. Sometimes this can lead to you thinking a device is malfunctioning when Windows has put it into a sleep mode from which Sleeping Beauty…oops, wrong story…your hardware cannot awaken.

A common example of this is when your screensaver kicks in after the configured number of minutes of keyboard inactivity. Power Management should terminate these suspended modes as soon as you press a key or move your mouse. The problem occurs when you return to your keyboard and find yourself stuck in the screensaver or in some way prevented from returning to your normal session without restarting your PC. A hard boot may be required to break out of it. Enough of these forced restarts, and you start to sense a disaster in the making. You might start seeing fragmented files if you had data open and unsaved on your desktop. You could develop a bad sector on your hard drive. Even shy of a disaster, it's not good to have to work this way; those computers who do display these types of lockups tend to do it frequently.

Hardware drivers are a common source of such problems. For this reason, you should see a noticeable improvement in such problems after updating a driver. Interestingly enough, it doesn't have to be a driver for the specific device involved in the suspension, such as a monitor or hard drive, that causes the problem. I had a USB graphics tablet, for example, that frequently caused these problems with Standby mode whenever it was plugged in and in use before the system went idle.

Sadly, just updating a device driver isn't always the answer.

An out-of-date BIOS is another possible cause, requiring a BIOS update. Malfunctioning hardware itself could also be the cause, the solution for which is to isolate the device and replace or repair it.

One thing to consider here—at least as a short-term workaround until you can update, upgrade, or otherwise resolve your dilemma—is to disable power management. On my system, for the best effect, I usually need to disable power management both in BIOS Setup under the Power Management category and also within Windows, as discussed in Chapter 6.

Advanced Hardware Troubleshooting Techniques

What happens if you're still stumped as to what device is causing the problems you're experiencing? This section tries to answer that question by describing two advanced techniques that involve a lot of hands-on, detail work. Beware, they're not for the faint of screwdriver.

The Barebones Setup Approach

One tried-and-true method used in deep hardware troubleshooting, such as you might have with a suspected motherboard or CPU failure, involves stripping your system down to its most essential components and then testing it. This works especially well when you're trying to rule out certain components as the cause of your current crisis.

If you're uncomfortable with expending this much effort, take the PC into an authorized service shop or hire a technician to do this. Don't berate yourself if you do: it's a slow, painstaking process that I don't expect everyone will want to undertake. Yet it can be very valuable in giving you diagnostic feedback and a better understanding of how all those parts fit together. But be aware that this same barebones setup is likely to be used by the technician in troubleshooting your problem.

> **WARNING** *Before you start, make sure you have a working mental or physical diagram of what is connected to your motherboard—along with how each piece connects—so that you can put it all back together when you're done. If you diagrammed the inside of your PC when I recommended it in Chapter 2, you should be all set. If not, do it after you open your PC case and before you start working, putting the diagram right inside your PC journal for later consultation. You may also find such a diagram in your PC manual. Small pieces of masking tape that you can write on can be used to label wires and connectors as you work.*

How You Accomplish It

OK, let's pull out that PC toolkit and prepare to label.

To strip your system down to a barebones setup for testing, perform these steps:

1. With the PC turned off and disconnected from power, first remove all externally connected components, including your mouse, printer, and so on. Set these aside. Note: Some users would remove the keyboard, too, but I suggest you don't.

WARNING *Make sure to use a standard PS/2-style keyboard rather than a USB keyboard since a USB keyboard may not be recognized immediately upon bootup but after Windows loads.*

2. Use your screwdriver to remove the screws (if any) holding your PC cover in place. Remove the cover and set it aside.

3. Don your anti-static grounding wrist strap and follow its instructions for grounding it with another object.

4. Remove all installed expansion boards and unplug connections for all major devices *except* for the following:

    *   The power supply as it connects to the motherboard and other components listed here

    *   One known working memory stick (If possible, substitute your current stick for a stick from a working PC or a brand-new stick that's rated to work with your motherboard.)

    *   Your CPU and its fan

    *   Known working video adapter

    *   Known working drive (A single hard drive with operating system is preferable but even a floppy drive with a boot disk inserted should work.)

5. Reattach the PC monitor to the video adapter connector at the back of the PC.

6. Recheck the components in step 4 to make sure that only the essential components are ready for use, and that each is properly and fully installed.

7. Remove your hands from inside the case and restore power.

8. Turn the PC on.

As the PC starts and while keeping your hands *out of* the interior of your system, listen to the boot process.

Next, while working cautiously around the open and running PC, answer these questions:

Can you hear the power supply and feel air moving past your hand as you place it near the exhaust fan at the back of the PC? If not, see the section "Power Supply Failures" earlier in this chapter.

Do you see the CPU fan turning? If not, turn the PC back off immediately. A defective CPU fan may have fried your CPU already in earlier sessions. See the section "Central Processing Unit (CPU) Failures" earlier in this chapter.

Do you see a display on your monitor? No? Check the section "Video/Display Failures" earlier in this chapter.

If you see a display, do you see the memory count on your screen or some other indication the PC sees your memory? If not, consult the section "PC Memory (RAM) Failures" earlier in this chapter.

Is there an error message displayed about your CPU? If so, you may have found the source of your trouble.

I don't see the problem now. If the computer works as it should (given what limited resources it now has), you should feel comfortable in assuming these core components are operational—at least for the time being. (See the following note for more details.) At this stage, you can power down and disconnect the PC (don't forget to ground yourself), and begin adding back other components one at a time and then powering up and testing the PC's operation.

NOTE *Unfortunately, this process does not guarantee that one or more of these core components isn't malfunctioning or is about to fail. For this reason, I often leave things apart and retest the system at least twice more, spread out over a period of several hours (when possible). It's easier than seeing a positive result, assuming all is well, and putting my PC back together, only to see the same problem later.*

Revert to Default BIOS Settings

Another hardware troubleshooting technique often used in conjunction with the barebones approach involves resetting the options configured under BIOS Setup back to the default factory settings. To pair them, simply perform the steps following step 7 in the instructions for the barebones approach.

The idea is that something you may have changed in your BIOS Setup may be causing the problem rather than just faulty hardware. And remember, BIOS and Windows control much of your hardware. When they control it badly, it can look very much like a hardware malfunction.

TIP *If the BIOS settings won't revert to their default values, this tells you something all by itself. It more than hints that you may have a corrupted BIOS—which may or may not be linked to a damaged motherboard—that must be repaired or replaced (see Chapter 8).*

How You Accomplish It

To reset your BIOS settings to default, take these steps:

1. Restart the system and follow the on-screen instructions to enter BIOS Setup. This typically requires you to press the Delete key as the system powers up.

2. In the CMOS/BIOS Setup, check for a Reset to Default option or something similar. Choose it.

3. Under the listing called System Chipsets or Advanced Chipsets, locate the setting for BIOS Shadowing. Follow the on-screen instructions to disable this.

4. Before you exit, note the changes you've made (I would jot these in my PC journal, if I were you) so you can reverse them later, after your problem is resolved.

5. Save your changes and then exit BIOS Setup.

6. Restart the system and check to see if the problem has improved or is resolved.

TIP *Disabling BIOS shadowing and caching in BIOS Setup can sometimes help you through a difficult upgrade of either hardware or your Windows operating system. You just restore them to their original state once the upgrade is successful.*

You learned in Chapter 3, "Prevention: Limiting Your Risks," that temperature and consistency of power are very important to your overall PC health. Chapter 11 explores this topic in more detail since you can't afford to take either situation for granted.

Avoiding Power and Overheating Problems

I'll bet you've noticed that the issue of lightning, dirty power (which I'll tell you about in the first section), and overheating has come up often in this book when discussing types of disasters. This is because these factors join bad drivers, old hardware, unstable operating systems, and just plain user errors in creating some very nasty situations.

The challenging part of power and overheating problems is that you normally won't witness the problems themselves, but you'll get saddled with the aftermath of their harmful effects. You might not even realize the event has occurred, so you may end up feeling like you're doing battle with a phantom. Nor can you completely avoid power and overheating problems, since you must use power for your PC and one of the by-products of power is heat. Heck, one of the worst by-products of trying to cool something is usually more heat. Go stand next to the outside vent on your air conditioner if you have any doubt.

Chapter 2, "How Hardware, Your Operating System, and Applications Work Together," gave you a preview of the extra components (for example, fans) that are installed to combat the worst effects of overheating from the heat-producing components in your PC. But you may have noticed that there wasn't much built into your PC to protect it from unruly power fluctuations that might occur when your local power transformer blows, someone runs their truck into a utility pole, or lightning hits close to you.

This chapter will help you understand the symptoms and solutions related to electrical and overheating problems. Many of the steps you can take are easy to implement and monitor, and many of the protection devices can be surprisingly affordable.

Let's plug in, shall we?

The Shocking Truth: Electricity and Your PC

The electrical utility poles (or underground utility cables) along your road or street can carry whopping amounts of power, starting at around 7,200 volts and moving upwards; 7,200 volts represents something called a *phase*, and utility poles may carry multiple phases. The power coming into your home or small office is most likely a 240-volt current. It usually arrives in two wires carrying 120 volts each, plus a bare ground wire. By itself, 120-volt current can power many of the normal appliances and devices in your home, including your PC. Heavy-duty appliances such as a refrigerator, an air conditioner, a large copying machine, or major power tools may need the full 240 volts.

Along with the number of volts, regulating that voltage is an issue because it doesn't always flow at a nice, even rate. If you graphed the power state for one of your 120-volt lines, you'd see that it fluctuates wildly, creating an often-dramatic sine wave pattern of peaks and valleys. And this is operating under normal conditions, not taking into account events such as brownouts, blackouts, and power surges that can make that pattern even more dramatic and variable.

This isn't a random accident: this is what is known as *alternating current (AC)*. But beyond the variation naturally built into alternating current are added variables based on factors such as distance from a power sub-station, the quality of the lines carrying the power to you, and even the wiring in the building you're living or working in. The use of other appliances, large and small, also affect that electrical stability. By the time all these other factors come into play with the energy being delivered to your modest little outlet, your power can be pretty dirty.

What is "dirty power"? Those peaks and valleys I said you would see if you graphed your electrical flow aren't all nice and neat and uniform. As a refrigerator or freezer case kicks in, as you turn a big appliance off, or as a malfunctioning electrical appliance such as a toaster misbehaves, you can see those peaks turn into a series of shuddering spikes. Bad or older wiring can produce some erratic behavior in power flow, too. Such conditions are often referred to as dirty power, because fluctuations exceed normal operating ranges.

How bad can it really be, you may wonder. After all, other appliances plugged into regular wiring in your home or office seem to keep working through these fluctuations.

It's a good question without a simple answer. For instance, some devices are engineered to be more tolerant of these power highs and lows. Really, any electrical device that didn't take into account some of these fluctuations probably wouldn't last long.

This brings me to an important and often-overlooked point: You don't have any accurate way of judging—barring a rare situation where a power surge kills a piece of equipment or an appliance—how much your dirty power contributes to early appliance failures in your living and work spaces. I can't say with any certainty that the television I had to replace after eight years might have lasted 12–15 years had it been protected from these fluxes. What you do know is that, among unprotected equipment especially, such fluxes can damage appliances and equipment; it's the degree and the volume that I must leave to the engineers to debate.

However, I wouldn't be doing this topic justice if I didn't talk about the role that circuit breakers (for most of us) and fuses (in older buildings) play in protecting you from the problems that can arise from electricity and the devices that require it.

Power lines from external poles or underground cabling typically come into the house through the circuit breaker box or the fuse box. Each of these boxes acts as a buffer between your building's wiring and the rest of the power system. For example, when you have some types of power surge, your circuit breakers or fuses should take the brunt of the force. The circuit breakers will trip, requiring you to reset them, while the fuses will likely blow, demanding that you replace them before you can restore power.

Likewise, circuit breakers or fuses protect you from the worst effects of an electrical problem that may occur within your home or office. Without circuit breakers or fuses, a broken wire can much more readily start a fire or potentially electrocute you.

Yet these intermediaries won't protect you from everything. If they did, you'd never see your lights flicker. A lot of damage can still be inflicted on delicate electronics by serious power variations, which is why surge-protection devices for consumer electronics and appliances appear to be gaining in popularity. After all, no one wants to buy a new 40" TV and lose it the next day, as one of my friends did, to an electrical storm.

> **TIP** *Having worked in locations where fuse boxes were used and locations where circuit breakers were located, I strongly recommend upgrading a fuse box-based building with circuit breakers. Circuit breakers make it substantially faster and easier to cut power in an emergency, they can be reset (rather than replaced as fuses need to be), and you won't burn your hand trying to remove a hot fuse (which can create an electrical fire).*

Let's look at the issue of power—both dirty and otherwise, although many argue that all the power you use is pretty dirty—and its relationship to your PC. The first stop in this discussion is the PC power supply, the vital intermediary between your wall outlet and your motherboard and other components.

> **NOTE** *For those of you with a better understanding of electricity than most, please understand that I kept this topic purposely simple.*

A Cautionary Tale:
Building a Healthy Respect Based on Intense Pain

When I was a young teenager, my parents' old home was poorly wired and we had a number of incidents related to lightning. After years of going out and standing in the middle of a field to watch violent electrical storms because the power of them fascinated me more than scared me, I happened to be turning off a brass floor lamp one afternoon when lightning entered the house. Sometime after I discovered I had traveled about five feet across the room from the zap I received as the lightning centered itself on the metal lamp I was touching, I developed a healthy respect for lightning.

Later, when I first started working with PC hardware, I had a similar learning curve with the electrical side of computers. I was pretty sure those instructions telling you to "power off and remember to ground yourself" were for nervous people who weren't careful as they worked.

My foolhardiness was bolstered by the fact that I had managed to get away with swapping several pieces of hardware in which I'd bent the rules about grounding and power disconnection; the hardware was fine afterwards and so was I. Sure, powering down, disconnecting, and grounding doesn't take much time. But in the days before hot-swapping hardware, you had to power down, install, and then power up again to have every newly installed device recognized (as you still do for many devices today).

Continued on next page

A Cautionary Tale:
Building a Healthy Respect Based on Intense Pain (Continued)

Then one day, after this string of irrational successes, I was working on my PC with the cover off because I was testing. I happened to notice a string of dust hanging from the power wires just above the memory sockets. Without thinking, I stuck my hand inside the live, powered PC to grab the string. But the string got wrapped around something, so I ended up pulling harder than I might have expected. When it finally came loose, my hand slipped, hit the edges of my installed memory, and I heard a popping noise in the PC somewhere around the time my ears began to ring thunderously.

Gee, I guess there's a reason you're not supposed to do that!

The good news is that my ear-ringing stopped after a few days, and that only my PC memory was damaged. The bad news is that PC memory at the time was far more expensive than it is now; a problem with chip supply that year had lifted the price to more than $40 per megabyte, and I had to replace 16MB.

Some lessons are just more expensive than others.

Role of the Power Supply

The PC's power supply sits between your home or office current and the PC electronics itself. It expects a reasonably steady flow of 120 volts operating at roughly 60 cycles to empower it so it can provide power to the rest of the PC.

But the power supply isn't just a simple intermediary. Instead, part of a power supply's job is to convert the AC flowing to it into direct current (DC) required by your PC components before it pushes that power out into the system through the connectors plugged into components such as the motherboard and the drives.

Like other devices, the power supply has a degree of fault tolerance built into it that allows for some fluctuation in power before it begins to affect the flow of power to the PC. But most power supplies aren't designed to withstand massive fluctuations. When hit by them, a power supply may simply shut down (either temporarily until you restart the system or permanently because it sustained damage). Or it may continue to work, but the clock may have started ticking on the day that power supply will fail. Subsequent power problems may hasten this date along.

I'll tell you more about differences in power supply quality in a moment.

WARNING *Why is it so important for you to unplug your PC when you work? Whether you realize it or not, even when your PC is turned off, a small amount of current continues to pass from the PC power supply to the motherboard. The amount may sound minute compared to the zap potential when the PC is turned on, but it's enough to cause damage to the components. You might not enjoy it too much either.*

Some Symptoms of a Failing Power Supply

While many times a PC power supply seems to fail quickly and without prior notice, you can often pick up subtle and not-so-subtle symptoms before the actual failure occurs. Some of these symptoms include

- The PC doesn't always turn on the first time you try it.

- You find yourself pressing and holding the power button to keep the power supply engaged long enough to let the system start.

- The PC resets itself spontaneously.

- You hear a strained, grinding, or otherwise strange sound that seems to be coming from the power supply when it's operating.

- You notice a strange drop in overall PC noise level that seems to resolve, only to happen again. This may mean the power supply stops and restarts, which it should not.

- You feel little or no air output from the power supply fan located behind a grill at the back of the PC.

- Devices directly connected to the power supply may seem to appear and disappear without signs of a device conflict or other problem. For example, a CD drive may disappear in Control Panel without any other reason, only to reappear again later.

WARNING *Don't assume a power supply is dead until you make certain everything is properly and firmly connected and the PC has power available to it, yet the PC won't turn on. If you suspect a dirty power supply fan and can see that it's dirty, you'll find instructions for cleaning the fan when we discuss fans in the section "PC Overheating: When Things Get Too Hot."*

Not all of these symptoms are only attributable to a dying power supply. Other problems, including operating system instability and a damaged motherboard, can, for example, cause a PC to reset itself spontaneously. A loose power switch can give you trouble when turning a PC on. But consider the status of the power supply when you notice these symptoms, especially when you notice two or more symptoms.

TIP *If you experience any of these symptoms, or other symptoms you think may be related to your power supply, consider purchasing a replacement power supply before the old one fails. You can't always buy the right power supply just anywhere; the wattage must be matched or exceeded and more importantly, the mount holes must align between the case and the power supply (meaning that you must buy the right power supply for the form factor for your system). If you bought your PC pre-assembled, check with your PC manufacturer to make certain you get the correct type. This information may also be available in your PC manual.*

Evaluating Capacity

Many PC systems today ship with a 200-watt or 250-watt power supply, which is usually more than enough for the components installed into them. Where you begin to exceed a standard PC power supply is when you begin adding additional devices that consume a higher than average amount of wattage.

But how much wattage is enough? The rule of thumb with power supply capacity is that you need more wattage available than your connected PC hardware consumes. This means that if you're running equipment that requires about 200 watts of power and your power supply is 200 watts, you're hitting the power ceiling. In high-demand situations, some devices appear to fail temporarily because too many pieces of equipment are vying for power.

Table 11.1 lists some major PC components and the number of watts of power each device requires. While these are rough numbers that are based on available product information, they give you an idea of how these devices begin to cut into what sounded like a more-than-adequate power supply capacity. Notice that for many devices, these numbers are expressed as a range. Yes, many times these devices will only consume the number of watts represented by the low number of the range. However, you have to accommodate the possibility that each device might somehow hit the peak wattage demand at the same time. Then you must tack on a bit more working wattage room, both for safety's sake and for the potential that you'll add more equipment to your system, which in turn drives up your power requirements.

So if you're barely skating by on a 200-watt power supply and you're about to add a drive or two (say, a hard drive and a CD/DVD burner combination), you may want to upgrade to at least a 250-watt or preferably, a 300-watt power supply. That extra bump to 300 watts should buy you the power expansion room you need for the length of time you're apt to operate your present PC.

TIP *Should you go as high in power supply wattage as you possibly can if you decide to upgrade or replace? Not unless you anticipate adding a great deal of extra hardware. If you're like many people, you may run out of room to add devices before you exhaust the capacity of a 300-watt power supply. While it's true that a higher capacity power supply doesn't always cost you more to operate in terms of power consumption, it can be overkill.*

Table 11.1 *PC Hardware Wattage Requirements*

DEVICE	TYPICAL WATTAGE REQUIRED TO OPERATE
CD drive (48x)	7–30 watts (Depends on the CD formats supported.)
CPU	18–50 watts (Depends on the CPU type and age; a Pentium III often takes 20–30 watts, while some Athlons require 40 watts or more.)
Fans	Variable; a case fan often needs 12 watts.
Floppy drive	4–5 watts
Hard drive (IDE/ATA)	5–20 watts per drive (Often, the higher the drive RPM, the higher the wattage used.)
Memory	10 watts per 128MB (some higher, some lower)
Motherboard (bare)	20–35 watts
Network adapter	4–5 watts
SCSI host adapter	20–30 watts
Sound (card) adapter (PCI)	5–20 watts
Video adapter (AGP)	18–35 watts
Video adapter (PCI)	4–15 watts

These are rough estimates; check the technical specifications for your devices, which are usually available in the product documentation.

Replacing a Power Supply

Before you decide to upgrade or replace a dead power supply, identify what you need. This involves

- Knowing the capacity you need.

- Knowing the form factor of your system. The form factor relates to the size of the motherboard and the type/shape and placement of the power supply. The form factor can usually be found printed on your existing power supply, in your computer or motherboard documentation, or by calling your manufacturer. Most systems today take some variation of the ATX form factor, but AT, LPX, and NLX form factors are also found.

- Verifying that the power supply is set to U.S. power settings. Many power supplies sold today are manufactured both for use in the U.S. (which uses a 115-volt standard) as well as for use in other parts of the world where a 230-volt setting is used. Most power supplies sold here are set for the U.S., but you occasionally get one that is set for 230 volts.

NOTE *It can be tough to verify that a power supply is set to U.S. power standards. For this reason, purchase a power supply from a store or company that routinely sells them and that knows the products they sell. This tends to ensure that you're getting what you expect. If you buy from a company outside the U.S., you increase the risk of getting a supply set for non-U.S. use.*

Once you obtain your replacement power supply, verify that you got the correct unit. This information may be available in the accompanying paperwork, but verify it against the information available on the metal information plate on the power supply itself. This information should include the power supply's manufacturer, wattage capacity, serial number, and other details.

Differences in Power Supply Quality

For most users, a power supply is pretty invisible; it's secreted within the case. Users may be completely unaware of its rated capacity in watts. They also may not realize that there can be a big difference between the quality of one power supply vs. another. For example, if you were to compare two different makes of a 250-watt power supply, you might find that one is substantially heavier than the other. The lighter unit may have less power-handling hardware, such as fewer transformers, and may or may not be able to withstand what the heavier unit could. However, this isn't the supermarket where you can easily compare cantaloupes; you generally won't shop for a replacement power supply based on its weight. So understand that you may be doing more than saving money when you try to get a good deal on a power supply purchase; some of the missing hardware may result in a power supply more apt to fail under stress.

A decent quality, known brand with a good reputation and a warranty is generally all you need.

By default, most new PCs ship with an adequate-but-not-exceptional power supply unless you order a custom PC and specifically request a higher quality power supply.

Buying Refurbished Equipment

I can be something of a bargain junkie, as I bet many of you are. In a tight economy, it certainly makes sense to watch where you spend your money.

Frequently, and especially with devices I use occasionally but not all the time, I'll consider purchasing a refurbished model of a product to save a bit of money. (If you're not familiar with the term, a refurbished or reconditioned product may have been returned as defective, but it was tested, presumably fixed, and sold again with clear labeling indicating it's not a brand-new product.) I've had excellent success with refurbished products, including PC expansion boards, peripheral devices like printers, cameras, and monitors, and consumer electronics such as video cameras.

But one place where I won't cut corners is essential equipment like a PC power supply. While I've purchased refurbished power supplies in the past, I did so at a time when they were far more expensive than the average $20–$40 you spend for one today. One of these refurbished units I bought arrived at my door looking like it had been through a major catastrophe, while another arrived with such damage to its metal casing, I assumed an elephant had used it as a stepstool.

Sure, most of them worked well (I returned the other two), but this is one area where saving a few dollars makes little sense when you consider the importance of the device you're buying.

What I do, however, is keep a working refurbished power supply on hand as a temporary solution if my main power supply fails. This way, I have something to fall back on to run my PC should it take a few days to get a replacement unit, but I don't have to depend on the used power supply for any prolonged period of time.

Installing the Replacement

Since most of us will at some time need to replace a PC power supply and a dead power supply is a disaster all in itself, let's walk through the steps of replacing one. But before you grab a screwdriver, do at least two things:

- Read the power supply instructions and read your PC documentation as it relates to replacing parts.

- Look at the current power supply (see Figure 11.1) and how it is currently connected

The trickiest part about replacing a power supply is simply making certain that you reconnect the new power supply up to everything the old power supply was connected to. If you don't, you can have a serious problem with the replacement power supply or with another component that you might erroneously think is caused by a device failure.

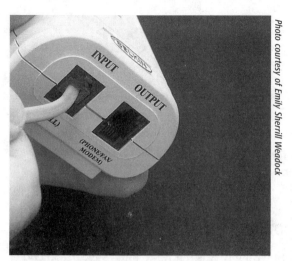

Photo courtesy of Emily Sherrill Weadock

Figure 11.1 *PC power supply*

First, get a roll of write-on tape or tiny sticky notes, along with a pen or marker. Use these to create labels for the connections to help you re-establish the proper connections later on. Then, with the power disconnected, the cover removed, and while wearing your anti-static wrist strap, take these steps:

1. Re-review the current setup.

2. As you note each power supply connection, place a piece of tape or sticky paper labeled with the connection's identity on each connection on the old power supply. Make sure you note the orientation of the wide (typically white Molex) connectors that plug into the motherboard. Reversing these connections can damage the motherboard permanently.

3. Once complete, I unplug each connection between the power supply and the PC.

4. Using the screwdriver with one hand and using your other hand to balance the unit's weight (especially important when you reach the last few screws), remove all the screws holding the power supply in place. Set the old power supply aside, but where you can still see it to review those connection labels.

5. Orient the new power supply so it's positioned in the case exactly as the old one was. Screw it into place using the screws you removed from the old unit.

6. Using the labels on the old power supply as a guide, begin connecting the new power supply to the various components like your motherboard and your drives. Make sure all the connections are firm and secure.

7. Review your work and your documentation; adjust as necessary.

8. Leaving the cover off until you're sure everything works, reconnect the power and start the PC.

WARNING *It's not uncommon for a new component such as a power supply to emit a slight smell for the first several minutes to an hour after it's pressed into service. But if you notice a strong smell that seems to increase in intensity or if you see smoke, turn off the PC and disconnect power immediately. Then contact the power supply manufacturer or the dealer/seller you purchased it from.*

Home/Office Wiring and Other Appliances

Many old homes and office buildings may contain wiring that is not up to today's electrical code. Obviously, you can have a problem with wiring last updated in 1940 or 1960 because in those days, there weren't anywhere near the appliances or power demands that exist today. Overloaded wiring, as you already know, is a huge fire risk that too often becomes reality.

However (and considering the number of my friends who have purchased new or almost-new homes in the last year who immediately had to call an electrician to correct problems), not all modern-day wiring is an exercise in perfection either.

Nor do many of us, as electrical consumers, help. Rather than call in an electrician to add more outlets, some of us happily buy huge, honking power strips and set them up throughout our homes and offices. A room that was wired to allow plugs for 4–6 devices suddenly finds itself sporting plugs for 30. Repeat that in a number of rooms and, depending on the state of your wiring, you may overtax your resources and potentially increase your chances of fire. You may also be introducing a lot more dirtiness to your home or office's power than was present before. Your PC won't like that, and neither will your consumer electronics and appliances.

TIP *Is there a working smoke detector in the area where your PC is located? If not, there should be. Unless the PC is located in an area where a false alarm could be tripped easily (around fireplace or kitchen smoke, for example), it's wise to have a smoke detector positioned within 10 feet of the PC. Since PC smoke may not be voluminous unless more than a single component is involved, it may be harder for it to trigger the alarm from a distance. Remember to change the battery each year and test the unit regularly.*

An electrician once described to me a simple test of overall building wiring. He said to spend a period of time (optimally as much as 3–6 months) during which you buy average (not cheap, not fancy) lightbulbs for your incandescent lamps, preferably during a time of the year when your area is prone to storms. Then chart how many lightbulbs you replace in your home during that period of time, especially where you have to replace the same lightbulb more than once in that period. If you notice that only one lamp seems to go through lightbulbs quickly, there may be a problem with either the lamp itself or the wiring in the outlet supplying the lamp with power. If instead, only lamps in a particular area of your house seem to need frequent lightbulb replacement, you've probably got a problem with wiring in a particular zone. For this, have your wiring professionally evaluated. However, he said, if you're frequently replacing lightbulbs in various rooms throughout the building, get an electrician in there pronto (don't wait for the rest of the test period to run out), and limit your use of electricity to serious need only until you do so.

If you need to call in an electrician, show this professional where your PC is located and ask whether he or she sees any potential problems with other devices being used on that zone. Large appliances such as refrigerators, freezers, and air conditioners tend to cycle; you may notice this in the form of flickering lights. In some cases, you have enough fluctuation in your power during such a cycling-up period that you can affect PC performance and the long-term health of your power supply (and other components, too).

What's a zone? Unless you're in a situation where you have just one or two rooms, your area is likely divided up into electrical zones. Each zone has circuit breakers or fuses assigned to it in your circuit or fuse box. If your zones are labeled, check this utility box to find the zone covering the area where your PC is located. You may be able to determine from that what zones cover your large appliances. If possible, avoid having your PC on the same circuit with your dishwasher, or other similar appliances.

WARNING *Never use a PC with an extension cord, especially not a common household, non-grounded extension cord.*

Some Symptoms of Power Problems

If you've been on the planet for a few years, you may have noticed that electricity can do odd things all on its own, and when paired with your electronics, the list of potential problems gets even longer. However, there are some common symptoms that indicate you're having power problems or that you've just suffered a power event:

- You walk away from your PC with it running and return to find it off, especially if the PC is off but other peripherals connected to it are still on.

- You experience what seems like a fast replacement rate on hardware components, having to replace memory or expansion cards more frequently than you might anticipate.

- You experience a hardware failure or malfunction after a major power event such as a power surge.

- Your PC or PC display misbehaves when a motorized device is used nearby.

- If you use a power strip to connect your PC, and you have to replace it more than once in two years.

- You turn on your surge protection device to turn on your PC and it fails.

- You notice a certain burning smell only when you turn the PC off.

The Best Methods for Troubleshooting Power Supplies

Statistically speaking, the PC power supply is the most often replaced component. Because of this, you always have to consider this possibility when you have a power-related problem that is affecting system operation or even the ability to turn the unit on.

One of the best ways to test a power supply is also one of the least pleasant. You need to have another PC that uses the same form factor of power supply, and you must remove the suspect power supply from the first PC. Then try installing it into the second PC (which also means temporarily removing its power supply) to see if you have the exact same problems. Obviously, this process is simpler if you have a spare power supply, as mentioned earlier in the discussion about refurbished equipment.

Another technique is to test to see whether you're exceeded the capacity of your power supply. You do this by removing power connections to non-essential devices such as a second CD or DVD drive. If removing a few connections suddenly resolves your problems, the power supply could still be on its way to failing, with this test giving it a brief reprieve. However, it's more likely that this test indicates you need a higher wattage power supply.

When you question whether interference or problems related to a non-PC device may be causing your power problems, unplug all non-essential devices or appliances in the room or zone where your PC is located. If the problem resolves, add back these other devices and appliances one at a time until you see the problem recur. This should identify the source of the problem, and you should move the other device or appliance to another electrical zone in your home or office.

If unplugging all the non-essential devices in the room doesn't stop the problem, now unplug everything except the PC (and monitor). If it doesn't improve then, check the PC itself for problems or call an electrician, especially if other devices in the room also show symptoms of interference.

Using PC Power Protection Devices

Now that I've scared you with dire predictions of electrical woes, let's turn your attention to ways you can protect your system—and your ability to keep using it—from the very power it so desperately needs.

Power protection schemes and their associated hardware components exist at all places along the spectrum, from basic and inexpensive to advanced and costly. In fact, some of the protection equipment used by consumers today was largely only used in the corporate world less than a decade ago. But all computers need power protection. While you might be able to avoid a virus or dodge someone trying to access your computer remotely using good security practices, it's hard to protect your hardware from power problems without buying a little more hardware.

Let's talk about the two most common forms of power protection: surge suppressors and uninterruptible power supplies. Both of these are used in addition to your PC power supply. One special note about both devices: Surge protectors may need to be changed out after a major power event like a serious surge, while an uninterruptible power supply will need a new battery at least every few years. Build these tasks into your regular maintenance routine, but on an annual schedule.

Surge Protectors/Suppressors

If you don't know what a surge suppressor is, you probably know it by another name, since it has many, including surge protector, spike arrester, spike suppressor, transient suppressor, and even lightning arrestor.

WARNING *A surge suppressor is sometimes called a lightning arrestor, but it really doesn't protect from lightning, which can produce a much stronger voltage flow than most electrically based surges. You still need to have standard grounding (a lightning rod and/or a grounding wire) installed at your home or business. In addition, you still need to unplug your PC and its peripherals, including a phone line used for a modem, to protect them from power during a lightning storm.*

More important than the name is the fact that many folks tend to confuse surge suppressors with power strips. They look alike, and both plug into a wall outlet and then allow other devices such as your PC, your monitor, and your printer, to be plugged into them. Both have a kill switch, allowing you to kill power quickly to the devices installed into it. However, I've seen many power strips without any true surge-suppression capabilities. This seems to be truer for the off-brand power strips sold at deep-discount stores.

What differentiates a surge suppressor is included hardware (a varactor diode) that tries to localize and minimize the damaging effects of a power surge. The varactor diode channels any voltage that exceeds the anticipated household 120 volts back into the wall outlet's grounding wire, allowing the requisite 120 volts to keep flowing to your PC power supply. A decent surge suppressor is designed to die in the line of duty, if necessary, to keep your system from suffering the same fate.

You'll find wide variations in the prices and features of surge suppressors, including the number of devices that can be plugged into it. Some manufacturers offer warranties that can offset your damage should the unit fail. Most of the price differential has to do with the level of protection the suppressor offers, although a suppressor by itself can't protect you from every potential power mishap. It should, however, take the brunt of power fluctuations, providing a needed buffer between your PC and its power source.

NOTE *While I believe you do get what you pay for with protection devices and that many of the more expensive devices are actually the better ones, I recommend that you have some protection, even if cheap, over none at all. A $7 clearance sale Curtis surge suppressor once burned itself out (literally, with just a bit of flames near the kill switch for heightened drama) to spare my testing PC from a mighty surge after a tornado touched down near my home.*

Uninterruptible Power Supplies (UPSs)

An uninterruptible power supply (UPS) provides a battery power assist or backup to anything connected to it during times when your regular power isn't available. Figure 11.2 illustrates a UPS manufactured by American Power Conversion.

Usually, the battery life provided by the UPS gives you a little extra time past the point of power failure in which you can finish and save your work and shut down the PC properly. This can avoid the effects of power-related crashes and lost work.

But don't plan to work for a few hours into a total blackout; the battery life on these units is finite, and the more you have plugged into a UPS that's installed between the power source and your PC, the shorter that grace period will be. Less expensive, less capacious units tend to give you a few minutes, while costlier ones allow you to work for 15 minutes or more.

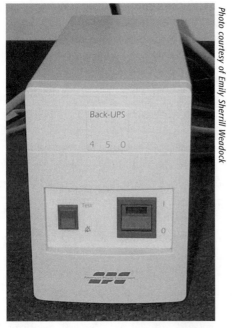

Photo courtesy of Emily Sherrill Weadock

Figure 11.2 *An APC uninterruptible power supply*

Many makes and models of UPS come with warranties to offset your costs should your system be damaged while using the UPS, even the less expensive consumer ones that start at around $100. They also include some of the same protection hardware as surge suppressors.

There are two major types of UPSs:

Online   The most expensive type, it's called online because it's always operational even when your power is available and operating properly. This avoids any lapse of time during which the PC may be waiting for battery power to kick in.

Standby   Like the online type, a standby UPS monitors the power situation but it waits until it detects that power is unavailable before its battery power kicks in, which can lead to a slight (several millisecond) delay.

NOTE *I experience far fewer problems and far fewer device failures on systems that I protect using a good surge protector coupled with a good UPS. I don't think it's a coincidence.*

PC Overheating: When Things Get Too Hot

Almost every major component on your PC is designed and manufactured with a specific operating temperature range in mind. Exceed that temperature, and you may not have the effectiveness you have within the proper heat range. Exceed that temperature regularly, and you not only invalidate the product warranty, you're apt to kill the component, either now or later.

Of course, different devices have different heat thresholds, but many devices begin to experience difficulty once the operating temperature climbs past 150 degrees Fahrenheit. (Actually, this is often a range between 120–175 degrees, or about 50–80 degrees Centigrade). While the room where your PC is located may be a comfortable 72 degrees, inside that case the temperature can easily soar past 150 degrees.

Some estimates, including one available at PC Power and Cooling (`www.pcpowerandcooling.com`), a widely respected online vendor for cooling devices, report that for every 18 degrees you push a PC component past its heat threshold, you cut the life expectancy of that component by as much as half. Even if the real numbers are far lower, it could still spell an uncomfortably high amount of device failure.

While overheating has serious long-term effects for PC life and use, there are immediate short-term effects, too. An overheated PC is an unstable one, and the quality of the data written to such a system can become highly suspect. Files you think you've saved may not be there when you return from a quick restart. What you type at the keyboard may turn into a nonsense of jumbled characters and symbols on the screen, making you think that perhaps your keyboard has shorted.

NOTE *According to PC Power and Cooling's web site, the five hottest components within a PC are usually the CPU (always the hottest), the video adapter, the motherboard's core-logic chipset, the installed memory, and then the hard drive(s).*

What's Making the PC Overheat

Before I list the factors that cause a PC to overheat, let me remind you that you can cut down on the occurrence of these problems by following the preventive measures described in Chapter 3, "Prevention: Limiting Your Risks."

The following are the most common causes for PC overheating:

- Blocked intake and exhaust vents

- Operating the PC in a very warm environment

- Dirty or malfunctioning internal fans

- Heavy dust accumulation on internal components

- Overcrowding of equipment within the case

- Adding several "hot" components without augmenting internal cooling

- Overclocking (the process of changing hardware settings to "push" hardware beyond its rated speed/operation)

Symptoms of Overheating

Overheating can actually cause some rather bizarre and not-easily-explained phenomena. Here are just some of the symptoms you might see with either acute one-time or chronic overheating:

- A PC that was operating fine when you first turned it on begins to develop increasing problems. For example, you type one thing but the monitor displays another, opening or saving files to a disk gives you drive errors, or hardware "disappears." A restart of the PC does little or no good.

- You place your hand near an exhaust point, such as at the location of the power supply fan, and notice little or no air being pushed out against your hand. Under ideal conditions, the fan output here isn't exactly robust, but you should feel a steady flow of warm air.

- If you turn the PC on, it appears to start normally and then resets itself after a short period of time, usually the time it takes for the PC to warm up.

- You notice parts of the case, especially where drives are located or the side where the motherboard sits, become extremely warm to the touch.

- You go inside your system—with power disconnected and properly grounded—and note that components are (or almost are) too hot to touch.

- There may be a smell—often a compound of smells related to overheated components, grease, and dust—that may or may not seem like burning.

- You receive an on-screen warning about internal temperature. This is a feature with some motherboards and accessories you may add, but not available or enabled on every system.

Tips to Avoid Overheating

The best way to limit the chances of your system overheating is to follow the maintenance recommendations offered in Chapter 3:

- Keep your PC work area clean and free of dust and debris.

- Keep the PC vents free of blockage.

- Keep air circulation within the PC optimum by keeping air paths open and fans working and free of dust.

If your PC is located in a room that tends to get very warm despite drawing curtains or blinds against the sun and you have no air conditioning present, try to schedule your PC time away from the hottest time of the day. For example, I live in an area where air conditioning is rare. In the hottest times in summer, I adjust my schedule to get on the PC early in the morning and return to it later in the evening, leaving my PC turned off or in low-power mode during the mid-to-late afternoon hours. This schedule also helps me avoid the late afternoon thunderstorms that frequent our summer days.

On the flip side, it's not good to fire up your PC when it has been sitting in a very cool or cold room, since the warming of such cold components can cause condensation and shorting. If your PC is located in a room that doesn't get much heat until you arrive at your desk, consider turning on the heat first and allowing the temperature to slowly rise into a normal range well before you turn on the system.

You'll find more ideas when I talk more about the ways a PC tries to cool itself and how you can augment this cooling process.

PC Air Circulation and Vents

In standard PC architecture that includes PC case design, fresh air comes in the vents located at the bottom of the PC. This air should then move towards the back of the PC case and then be drawn upward until it exits the exhaust fan vent at the top rear, like with the power supply fan. Along the way, this fresh air flows past the hot components and helps push the hot, stale air found around these components away and out of the PC.

You can prevent air blockages within your PC by keeping cable bundles grouped together and positioned out of the way and keeping vents clear. However, most PC case designs—compounded by the devices you pack into them—allow for the creation of no-breeze or so-called *dead zones*, areas where air simply does not move. In dead zones, heat can build to much higher temperatures than in areas where air is moving to push the hot air away from components.

Of course, there are some areas of the interior of the PC where this isn't so critical. In other areas, like around filled drive bays containing your hard drive, CD drive, and floppy drive, or around a full row of installed PCI cards, warm-to-hot stagnant air can have troubling symptoms and sometimes dire consequences.

Depending on your situation and whether you can establish that internal overheating is a factor in your problems, augment your current in-case air circulation by adding additional PC fans, checking the status of your CPU heat sink, installing some type of heat monitor, or even changing your PC case.

TIP *Find yourself with a fair amount of debris building up in your PC, drawn in by the intake vents? Many smart folks get thin filter material such as the type you might find in an air conditioner or air cleaner and cut it to fit the size of the intake vents. Then they affix this filter material to the inside of the vent (only on the intake vents) to help trap ash, dust, and other debris before it gets sucked into the system. Heat-safe tape applied around the edge of the filter against the case worked well for me in the days when my PC sat near a woodstove.*

The Role of PC Fans

Take a good look around your PC case, and you may notice that yours may not have that much in the way of intake vents bringing air into the PC or exhaust vents located at the back of the PC. If you depended solely on these glorified holes for air circulation within your PCs, it would be like sitting your CPU under a skylight in an aluminum trailer positioned in the desert during the high sun of a summer afternoon with just little vent windows at the front and back providing any cooling.

Fans are installed to move air away from the hottest components and to force that warm air out of the PC. Most PCs include at least two fans: the power supply fan that pushes exhaust out the back of the PC and the CPU fan, both of which have been discussed in this book. Some devices that you install may have their own fans, like the one built into my ATI Radeon video adapter.

As you read, think back to the preventive environment described in Chapter 3. Internal fans can do a great job, but if the air coming into the PC from the room is overheated, you're going to increase the temperature inside the case. You can help your PC fans—and your PC itself—by keeping the area around your PC reasonably cool. If you can't keep it cool, limit the amount of time the PC is on when room air is very warm.

WARNING *Excessive internal heat around PC drives can actually distort and warp the drive platters that store your data.*

Types of Fans Found in a PC

Besides the types of fans already mentioned, there are other fans that are not commonly installed in brand-new systems (especially budget ones) but are available for purchase separately. These include a fan that installs to one of the available slots in your motherboard, much like a sound adapter or internal modem does. This type of fan falls into the category of system or case cooler.

Other fan types include special fans designed specifically to cool drives (drive coolers) and to cool expansion cards (card coolers or graphics coolers). Both drive and card coolers are great in defined situations, where a specific device (a drive or an installed PCI card) tends to run hot or is affected by the heat being produced by something positioned close to it.

There are other specialty fans, including those with double fan assemblies, elaborate coolers, and something called a peltier cooler. A *peltier cooler* is a fan/heat sink combination that uses a peltier element that acts as a heat pump as it draws very hot air away from the hottest components, such as a CPU. This is ideal for the component being cooled, but a peltier cooler actually heats up the rest of the case because it's more effective in drawing heat from its target and tends to be a power hog, too.

NOTE *PC cooling specialty sites and stores offer a host of articles, tips, and step-by-step instructions on adding both system and spot-specific coolers to your system. These include PC Power and Cooling and The Heat-Sink Guide* (www.heatsink-guide.com).

Checking Fan Function and Cleaning

I recommend that you check your fans for dirt and debris whenever you're inside the PC case. Wherever possible, fans should be removed for cleaning so that you don't end up sending the debris from the blades onto the other components inside the case.

Chapter 10, "Understanding and Troubleshooting Hardware Failures," explains in detail how to check and clean your PC fans.

Adding Fans

Positioning of fans is critical to achieve the results you want. After all, it's always possible that by trying to spot-cool one hot device, you may cause unintended problems for another device that becomes blocked by the effort and equipment used to cool the first device.

When adding fans, do your homework before you install them. As I mentioned in the last tip, most of the online cooling sites offer good recommendations for fan placement. They also offer step-by-step instructions for novel solutions, including how to drill a blowhole in your PC case to increase air circulation and allow another place for hot air to escape.

The Role of Heat Sinks

A *heat sink* is simply an aluminum alloy compound used in conjunction with a processor to draw the heat away from the processor and send that heat out into the circulating air of the PC case, where it can be pushed out through back vents.

The heat sink is affixed to the CPU through the use of a special thermal compound you can get wherever you can buy a CPU or other chips. (You may see other high-heat components such as a video adapter's graphics processor use a heat sink as well.) If you buy a PC pre-assembled, all this is done for you. But if you have to replace the CPU later on or, as sometimes happens, the thermal compound breaks down, you must reattach the heat sink before you run the PC.

> **TIP** *If you have to replace a heat sink, don't slather on the compound thinking if some is good, more is better. Cover the core with thermal compound and leave it at that.*

A dirty heat sink is a less effective one. If the interior of your system tends to accumulate much dust, dirt, or ash, clean a heat sink before you attempt to re-affix it. This can be done using rubbing alcohol and a dust-free cloth; pay close attention to removing the previous application of thermal compound. Leaving bits of old compound in place when you apply the new compound may interfere with an optimal attachment.

PC Temperature Monitors

Along with fans, heat sinks, and special cooling arrangements, you can buy temperature monitors that permanently mount within your PC or hand-held probes that you can hold or place.

Such monitors can be valuable if you suspect overheating or you know that your system has had issues with overheating in the past. They are much more reliable than leaving your cover off and carefully placing your hand near an area to test heat; measuring equipment is less subjective than you are. In addition, the very act of removing the cover to test temperature makes it less accurate because you're no longer testing the enclosed environment of a closed case; removing the cover can immediately drop the temperature several degrees.

Temperature monitors can be purchased in just about every price range (from about $20 to well beyond $100) from the same types of places, both online and locally, that sell PC fans and CPUs. Radio Shack is a good place to look for the probes themselves.

Before you shop, however, check your PC documentation and BIOS Setup to be sure you don't already have a temperature monitor built into your motherboard. While you're in BIOS Setup, make sure that the temperature monitor/alarm is enabled or it won't help.

Watching What You Install

Now that you have a better grasp of the issues related to internal PC temperature and the consequences of overheating, you can appreciate why it's important to consider the effects on temperature when you add new equipment to your system.

Obviously, the more congested with internal hardware your PC becomes, the more likelihood your system may experience heat-related problems due to increasingly limited air circulation. This doesn't mean you must forego adding equipment. Think carefully about a device's placement and the type of device it is because some devices will heat considerably more than others.

Certain devices are more prone to heat than others. These include:

- Large, high-speed drives

- Certain video adapters

- Certain CPUs

- Peltier coolers and other types of special targeted coolers

You also want to think about your PC case. While many users keep the same case throughout the life of a PC, you can upgrade your PC case to accommodate increasing internal hardware demands. More room coupled with a better-designed case layout may promote better air circulation and reduce overheating.

If you spend any time looking at PC cases on the Web, you'll be amazed at the possibilities out there. Many PC cases offer not just extra room, but easier access (for example, a front panel for installing external components) and even fashion. One I saw in England offered a lava lamp effect built into the case. I'm not at all sure that will help with overheating, but it might take your mind off your slow Internet connection.

A Cautionary Tale: The Brewing Storm in the Basement

Power problems can be tough to figure out. While you might be aware that using the modem during a lightning storm can result in later hardware problems, you might not know about the other power-related problems you can face.

When I ran a busy online hardware help forum for The Microsoft Network, we had a woman who kept having hardware failures. Since she had only recently purchased her system and it was still within its warranty period, I suggested she contact her PC manufacturer to tell them she wanted a full evaluation of her system to see what might be causing the problem.

The manufacturer took the unit back, scoped it out, and found nothing wrong. But the company tried to give her good service, so they shipped her a new unit.

Within a few weeks, she was back in my help forum telling me she was having failures yet again. I asked her about storms in her area because I knew she lived in a storm-prone area of Florida where many of the utility lines are overhead and susceptible to weather-related damage.

Sure enough, she had been hit by bad storms that had been disrupting power for many weeks. Based on that, I recommended that during such storms, she turn off the PC, completely disconnect (remove the power cord, disconnect the phone line from the modem) her PC, and get a good surge protector to place between her house wiring and the PC.

She was back pretty quickly with a sudden memory failure after another storm. Yet she told me that she had the surge protector in place and had been keeping the PC disconnected during storms. But then she provided the clue I needed: her surge protector had burned out when she turned the PC back on after the storm.

I'll spare you all the sordid details, but the culprit turned out to be bad wiring in her basement, which was on the same circuit as the room where she kept her PC. While she was disconnecting the PC during power fluctuations and storms, a huge, old freezer in her basement had problems cycling back up after a storm. So each time she turned on her PC within a half hour after the storm, the PC was being affected by spikes that the freezer was sending along the wiring.

An electrician fixed her problem for less than the cost of one of the drives she lost when the problem first began.

Sluggish PC performance ranks right up there with Windows instability and hardware failures and interferes with your ability to work and play with your PC. In Chapter 12, "PC Performance: Diagnosing, Monitoring, and Troubleshooting Problems," I'll show you how to monitor and troubleshoot performance-related issues.

PC Performance: Diagnosing, Monitoring, and Troubleshooting

Almost as reliably as your new car depreciates in value the instant you drive it off the dealer's lot, so too does your PC performance begin to slide the moment you take it out of the box and turn it on.

Some of this degradation is to be expected. After all, the first time you turn it on, everything is fresh and new. The only installed applications are the ones that came with the system; you haven't yet had a chance to upset the operating system by adding incompatible hardware or programs that were written back in 1986. Your hard drive hasn't had a year or two of files tossed at it and the random PC crashes that make the hard drive scramble to write work before data is lost. In addition, it will take several more months before dust begins to clog your internal PC fans.

Fast-forward a year, and you've got a much different picture. Everything inside your PC may have a thin patina of dust and grime. That 20GB hard drive you were sure would last a long time is almost full, and your power supply is out of available connectors to install another drive. Even if you have an available connector, your drive bays are full, too. Your sound card sputters, your video adapter is woefully out of date, causing you problems viewing web pages and playing video games, and Windows seems to take forever to load. When it finally loads, it quibbles about the low amount of free disk space and, to make matters worse, your Startup list for Windows is so large that you only have 50 percent of your available desktop resources on startup.

This, my friends, is another type of disaster. It's less dramatic than your power supply catching fire or lightning zapping your printer, but it's a functional disaster nonetheless because it badly affects the proper operation of your system. Your PC is supposed to be a tool, after all; it's not supposed to contribute to your misery.

This chapter zeroes in on PC performance: for hardware, for your applications, and for Windows.

Measuring PC Performance

One of the toughest things about measuring performance of any kind is that it can turn into an exercise in subjectivity. How slow *is* slow, anyway?

I might say my system is slow if I sit staring at the Windows hourglass for an operation to complete, even after I restart my system. You might say your system is slow when you sit at the Windows logo screen for an extra ten seconds. We're both right because it's based on our own knowledge about how our individual PCs respond.

Whether you realize it or not, *you* are a critical part of evaluating how well or how badly your system responds to your demands. No one knows your PC or your needs better than you do. You have a sense of how long for example, it should take your printer to start printing once you click the Print button or how quickly Windows normally loads (or shuts down).

This chapter discusses the common causes of performance problems and the measures you can take to restore your system to better overall operation. But I urge you to bring what you've learned in this book so far, together with your common sense and personal experience, into your troubleshooting and maintenance procedures for improving performance. An experienced technician may know all your components' capabilities and limitations better than you do, but you know your normal PC operation in a way that no one else does.

> **WARNING** *Beware of messages that pop up on your screen while browsing the Web that suggest some site has performed a free check of your system and now recommends you boost your PC performance (or Internet connection speed or the amount of RAM you have installed) by buying their product or service. First, no legitimate site should be performing such an evaluation without your authorization, and second, it's almost always a lie to promote their services. While many of these services do almost nothing to help, others can actively damage an otherwise healthy PC by either recommending or implementing a tweak or program that may damage your Registry or worse. Don't bite.*

Have a Stopwatch? Time it!

This may sound strange, but one thing I do when I buy a new system is literally pull out a stopwatch. I measure how long it takes the system to get to the initial bootup screen, how long it takes to get into Windows, and later, how long it takes to shut down. I then jot these times down in my PC journal.

After I begin adding applications and hardware, I measure these times again to see how they may have changed (and hopefully, to figure out what, if anything, seems to be adding serious time to the process). These new times are recorded, too.

Then, when I have a serious performance problem with my system and I want more information than a subjective, "I think it's starting a lot slower," I can refer back to the times in my PC journal.

This isn't science, but it provides one more system marker, for troubleshooting and for tracking the evolution and the slow decline of the PCs I use at home and work.

When a Damaged PC Misbehaves But Doesn't Always Fail

PC performance usually begins to slip slowly over a period of time. This can make it seem insidious to you later because it creeps up on you until one day you shake your head and ask, "What's wrong with this system?"

If instead, you see your PC performance take a sharp dip quickly (for example, from one session to the next there is a sharp decline in responsiveness), the first thing to consider is whether some type of failure, misconfiguration, or change in your system may be responsible for this behavior.

The first place you should look, as always, is at any modifications (additions, removals, or tweaks) that you've made since your system last performed well. Because of this, it's important that you address situations like this as soon as you spot the symptoms; the passage of time may dull your memory (unless, of course, you're using the PC journal recommended early in this book and you're making entries faithfully).

Next, try the techniques described in the section "Performance-Related Maintenance" in this chapter to see if you begin to see an improvement in your system because of these actions. If not, you may have a basic instability in your operating system (see Chapter 9, "Stabilizing Your Operating System") or a hardware failure (see the section "Using Device Manager" in Chapter 6, "Transforming Yourself into a Smart Troubleshooter" or Chapter 11, "Overcoming Hardware Failures").

With an unstable Windows environment, you're likely to see error messages in conjunction with the performance loss. This isn't always true, but it's often the case. With a hardware failure, it's possible that your PC has become underpowered because your memory failed, overheating is affecting performance, or a hardware conflict exists (two devices using the same resource).

In extreme cases, you can start fresh by reformatting your system and reinstalling Windows (see Chapter 16, "Starting Fresh the Smart Way").

Common Symptoms and Their Culprits

When PC performance begins to sag, you can usually feel it, even instinctively. A few of the most frequently noted symptoms are

- Prolonged time between the moment you press the power button and the time Windows loads (or reloads)

- Sluggish shutdowns

- Slowdown in disk operations, including the opening of file screens through Windows Explorer or the Search feature

- Programs taking longer than usual to load

- Difficulty in changing your focus among different windows open on your desktop

There are so many potentially contributing factors to ailing PC performance that they merit a book of their own. Some of the most common issues responsible for slowdowns include

- Poor disk maintenance practices

- Poor system organization (You don't watch what is installed or you don't remove from your hard drive programs you no longer use or data you no longer need to keep.)

- Underpowered or overworked PC (not enough disk space, too little memory, and so on)

- Viruses (Remember, many viruses annoy more than destroy.)

- Poorly configured or missing Windows page file for virtual memory (explained later in this chapter)

- Hardware issues, including bad drivers, device conflicts, or failing (but not quite failed) devices

- An imbalance in resources (For example, you're running many background programs by choice, and the balance of processing power is going to the foreground programs such that you have an imbalanced load. Just like your washing machine, Windows works best and makes less noise when you watch what you load and how you load it.)

The Best Methods for Monitoring and Modifying System Performance

This section covers the following topics:

- How to set realistic expectations for the times when you compare the performance of one PC to that of another PC

- The tools Windows offers to monitor system performance

- The Windows options provided to modify performance

- What benchmark tests are and how they can be used (and abused)

Realistic Expectations

Before delving deeper into PC performance, let's discuss the need for realistic expectations when evaluating your system.

Don't mix apples and oranges. If you want to compare the performance of your Pentium III 750MHz machine with 128MB of SDRAM memory installed to another PC, don't evaluate it against an Athlon XP 2.4GHz PC with 256MB of DDR-RAM. Try to compare it to a system of a similar type that is similarly equipped on at least these key points:

- Similar CPU (same type—for example, Pentium II, Pentium III, Pentium IV, AMD Athlon, AMD Duron—if not the same speed in MHz or GHz

- Similar amount and type of memory

You may run into situations when you want to evaluate your system against a more powerful one to see whether some task would perform faster on the better-equipped PC. But the rest of the time, you'll want to compare like systems.

A Cautionary Tale: Getting Up to Speed with Upgrading Computers

"Why isn't a 2GHz PC 10 times faster at everything than a 200MHz PC?"

Someone asked me that in an e-mail recently, lamenting the fact that she had finally replaced her aging Pentium MMX system with a Pentium IV and didn't quite understand why everything wasn't "so much blazingly faster than before." She ended her note with a plaintive, "Shouldn't I return my new system as defective?"

Explaining the many reasons why a PC that sounds like it runs 10 or 5 or 2 times as fast would take a whole book of its own. What's important is that the Pentium IV runs faster, boots faster, loads Windows more quickly, handles types of hardware that an earlier Pentium (Pentium, Pentium MMX, Pentium II, Pentium III) may not, and takes into account many of the ways in which computer use has changed in the past few years.

However, with all the talk of faster speeds and evolving needs, one important fact often gets missed: Many of the ways you use your computers today don't specifically require a PC with a 2GHz CPU or 512MB of installed memory. Some of your most common activities—creating and editing documents, going online, browsing the Web, playing games, participating in Internet chats and messaging, sending and receiving e-mail, and downloading files—won't change remarkably whether you're using a Pentium II-350 MHz or a Pentium IV 1.8 GHz. Mind you, the overall experience of doing these activities may improve slightly. But for most of those tasks, you'd need a faster Internet connection more than a faster processor to get the desired effect.

Should she return her new system as defective? No. From all the information she supplied to me on follow-up e-mails, it sounded like her Pentium IV was running exactly as it should. It was just not running at quite the speed of light she expected.

Windows Tools

Let's discuss the tools provided by Windows to help you identify, monitor, and troubleshoot performance problems. You'll spot some tricks to try to adjust performance, too.

Using Performance and Maintenance under Help and Support

The Help and Support tool available from the Windows Start menu has a Performance and Maintenance section. This section contains suggestions and step-by-step tutorials for optimizing your PC's efficiency and explains how to do the maintenance necessary to keep your PC in good shape. (Some of this information is discussed later in this chapter in the section "Top Ways to Improve Your Performance.")

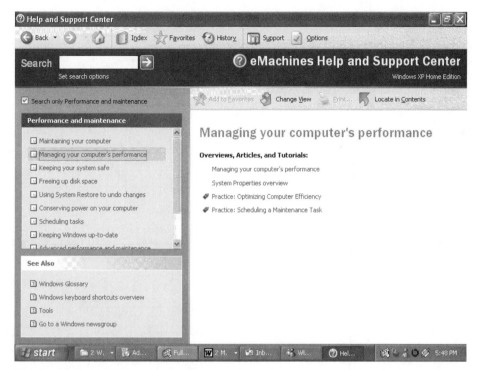

Figure 12.1 *Click a topic to get more information.*

Balancing Performance between Foreground and Background Programs

You probably already know that the term *foreground programs* refer to active, open windows on your desktop. *Background programs* often run outside your sight (and sometimes without your apparent knowledge) although they may—or may not—appear as icons in your Systray.

An imbalance in the processing time allocated to each type of program (foreground vs. background) can lead to performance problems as Windows struggles to try to handle an imbalanced load.

You can adjust the performance balance as needed (or simply to troubleshoot) by following these steps:

1. Double-click System in Control Panel.

2. Choose the Advanced tab and then click Settings listed under Performance.

3. Select the Advanced tab (again).

4. Under Processor Scheduling, click either of the following:

    • Programs—if you need to give more processor time to your active Windows running in the foreground

    • Background—if you want to try to equally divide resources between the foreground and background

5. Click OK.

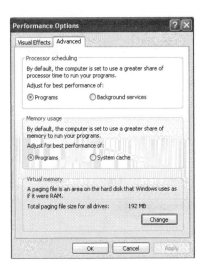

Memory Usage Issues

Similar to adjusting the processing time balance between background and foreground programs, you can decide whether to optimize the use of your installed memory for your programs (usually preferred because that's where you probably spend most of your time working). Or for best use of your system cache (which may be preferred in some circumstances which is useful if most of your work isn't in using applications actively but running applications that may sit idle or just calculating things for a prolonged period of time).

By default, this Windows performance option is set to optimize memory use for programs. To change it, take these steps:

1. Double-click System in Control Panel.

2. Choose the Advanced tab and then click Settings listed under Performance.

3. Select the Advanced tab (again).

4. Under Memory Usage, click System Cache. Click OK.

Page File Issues

The Windows *page file* is the available area of your hard drive that gets lumped into one huge, hidden "file" named `pagefile.sys`. `Pagefile.sys` acts like memory (hence the name *virtual* memory) for use by the system when your available physical memory is otherwise occupied with other jobs. The Windows page file may be familiar to you under different names, including the paging file, the virtual memory file, or the swap file.

How large this file is depends on a few factors, but primarily on how much physical memory you have installed on your PC. The formula Windows uses by default is that size of the page file should be equal to 1.5 times the amount of installed memory. Thus, if you have 128MB of installed memory, your page file is likely between 180MB and 192MB in size.

Often, people try to adjust these settings either up or down just to see what gives them the best "feeling" in terms of overall desktop performance and how fast you can open and close different files in different applications.

By default, Windows manages the page file (its size and location) for you. Yet it allows you to adjust the size of this page file; you can make it larger or smaller, depending on your particular needs and any performance issues you may see. However, adjusting a page file too far in either direction may negatively impact your performance. If you choose to adjust the page file, you may need to try different settings until you find the one that feels best to you from a performance perspective.

To check your page file settings or to make adjustments to it, follow these steps:

1. From Control Panel, double-click System.

2. Select the Advanced tab and then click Settings listed under Performance.

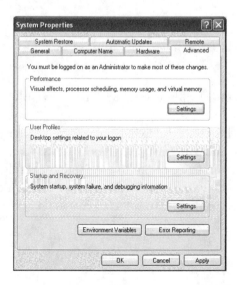

3. Choose the Advanced tab again and click Change listed under Virtual Memory.

4. From the Virtual Memory window, select the drive where your paging file is located and check the information available.

5. If you wish to make a change to your page file, click Custom Size and then specify the size (in MB) that you want to use instead.

6. Click Set and then click OK.

Depending on the changes you make, if any, you may be prompted to restart your system. You also have the option to store this page file on another drive besides the drive that contains your Windows installation. Doing so *may* improve your performance.

WARNING *Place the page file on another hard drive, not on another partition on the same hard drive as the partition that contains Windows, for the best results.*

Using Performance Tools in Windows XP

Windows XP Home Edition includes a performance-monitoring tool called System Monitor formerly available only under Windows NT/2000 systems. This tool serves as the first of three components in Windows XP you should become familiar with regarding system performance:

- System Monitor

- Performance Logs and Alerts

- Task Manager

Using System Monitor

System Monitor is a very useful tool for doing a spot check of how your system is currently behaving.

One caution, though. While System Monitor can be wonderful in helping you identify bottlenecks (periods when the system is working too hard and data can't pass through at its normal speed), you should run System Monitor *before* your performance begins to sag. Note the results of that test in your PC journal so that you have an idea how your system performs normally. Such a study is called a *baseline* and is ideal for comparisons against later results, when you do have a problem.

Take these steps to open System Monitor:

1. From Control Panel, double-click Administrative Tools.

2. Double-click the Performance Shortcut.

3. From the Performance window, select System Monitor.

The default view for System Monitor contains color-coded graphs for a specific item, called a *counter*, listed at the bottom of the screen. Each counter gets its own color on the graph to make it easier to distinguish between them.

Let me explain counters. Windows breaks down a number of the PC and operating system's parts and processes into groups called *performance objects*. These performance objects include but aren't limited to

- Cache

- Logical disk

- Memory

- Network interface

- Physical disk

- Processor

- Processor performance

- System

Under each of these objects are listed specific characteristics of each object's workload/ responsibilities; these are the *counters*. The counters allow you to narrow your focus to only those areas of a device's or service's performance that you are most interested in tracking.

This analysis works in the following way: System Monitor samples your system demands related to the specific counters chosen at specific intervals of times, which you can adjust as needed. To change the sampling rate, choose the counter measurement in System Monitor and press Ctrl+Q. Under the General tab near the bottom there's an entry entitled Sample Automatically Every: <Number> Seconds; modify this entry as needed. However, the shorter the sampling time is, the more desktop resources will be pulled just to monitor the counter. In addition, excessively long sampling times may make it difficult to get the best picture.

To see an example of this, let's look at the Logical Disk performance object and its counters, which include

- % Free Space
- Avg Disk Write/Bytes
- Disk Write/Sec
- Disk Reads/Sec

If you don't understand a specific counter, you can select it in the list and then click Explain.

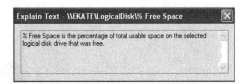

You can choose to add all counters or select specific counters from the list. Each counter you select is tracked by System Monitor in the Performance graph window.

How can you use these performance objects and counters to monitor and troubleshoot specific problems you're experiencing? Let's learn how to add counters.

WARNING *Choose your counters carefully and with restraint. It's possible to slow your performance down markedly by monitoring too many processes at once. All your system resources start going to the monitoring process, which in turn affects your ability to work normally. It also results in skewed usage figures since you don't usually run all these performance-checking tools.*

Using System Monitor Counters to Track Memory Issues

You can track memory using the System Monitor counters by following these steps:

1. From Control Panel, double-click Administrative Tools.

2. Double-click Performance Shortcut.

3. From the Performance window, select System Monitor.

4. From the System Monitor display window, click the + icon on the toolbar. (You can also type Ctrl+I.)

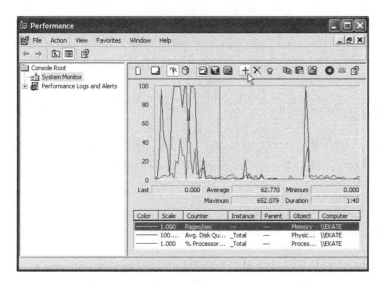

5. The Add Counters window appears. Click to select Use Local Computer Counters.

6. Under Performance Object, click the list box and select Memory.

7. Next, click Select Counters From List. Then click to select Available Bytes from the list box. Click Add.

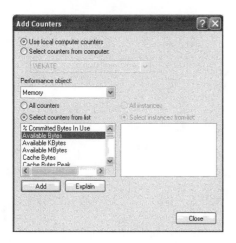

8. Repeat step 7, but this time choose Pool Nonpaged Bytes/Sec. Click Close.

You can now view the results on the graph in System Monitor. You can also set up performance logs and alerts to automate this process; this topic will be discussed momentarily.

Look for a significant instance where the number of available bytes is at its lowest. By rule, available bytes should never be below 4 MB while Pages/sec should not be above 10 on average. This situation may indicate you have a memory bottleneck, which may be caused by too many applications and programs running at once or could be the result of insufficient memory for all you are trying to do. This is also true for high Pages/Sec peaks.

TIP *Search on "Performance" or "System Monitor" under Help and Support in Windows XP to see other examples of using System Monitor counters to track disk, processor, network, and printer bottlenecks. Feel free, too, to mix and match your counters to see what counters give you the best information for the problem you're watching.*

Using Performance Logs and Alerts

NOTE *Most of you don't have time to sit and watch the System Monitor utility. This is where the Performance Logs and Alerts feature is useful because it allows you to log the results of your monitor/counter sampling. In addition, if you set it up to do so, this feature can alert you when a critical issue is noted.*

Here's are the steps you take to set an alert:

1. In the Performance window, click and expand Performance Logs and Alerts.

2. Right-click Alerts and select New Alert Settings.

3. Name it anything you want and click OK.

4. Click Add.

5. Select Use Local Computer Counters.

6. Under Performance Object, select Memory and under Select Counters From List, choose Pages/Sec.

7. Click Add and then Close.

8. In the Limit box, enter 10. In the Interval box, select 3.

9. Click OK.

You've just set an alert that will log an entry in the Application log in Event Viewer if your Pages/Sec counter exceeds 10 within three seconds.

NOTE *Setting up System Monitor and Performance Logs and Alerts most effectively really can't be done justice in a book on disaster recovery. One great source of more information on this topic is found in* Mastering Windows 2000 Professional, 2nd Edition *by Mark Minasi, another Sybex title. While that book is about Windows 2000, the information about System Monitor and such is very similar to that found in Window XP's.*

Complete information on how to set up additional alerts is available under the Performance Alerts and Alerts section in the Performance window. To reach this window, take the following steps:

1. From Control Panel, double-click Administrative Tools.

2. Double-click Performance Shortcut.

3. From the Performance window, select Performance Alerts and Logs, which expands in the right pane to a list:

   - Counter logs

   - Trace logs

   - Alerts

4. Choose Alerts, right-click it, and choose Help, which opens the Help window.

5. In the Contents Tab, select Performance Logs and Alerts, then double-click How to.

6. Double-click Work with Logs and Alerts.

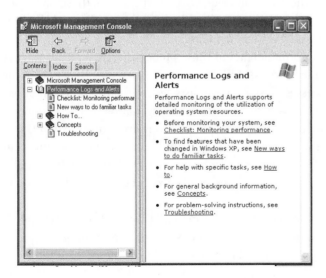

NOTE *Remember to review these logs later to get the benefit of their information. Once you create logs, you can view them under System Monitor by typing Ctrl+L.*

Using Task Manager

Although you've heard about Task Manager before, let's revisit it from a performance perspective. Task Manager—formerly just a single window from which you could log off, shut down, or end a particular task—has evolved under Windows XP Home Edition to include extra tabs that can be used to track performance.

To access Task Manager, press Ctrl+Alt+Delete *once*. You should see five tabs: Applications, Processes, Performance, Networking, and Users. This section focuses on two of them: Processes and Performance.

NOTE *Non-XP users can still use the single-window Task Manager to end tasks that refuse to close on their own.*

Processes Tab

The Processes tab lists all the processes currently running on your system at the moment you check it. Depending on what you have open on your desktop or running in the background, this list may show dozens of entries under Image Name. Some of those entries may be listed more than once such as SVCHOST.exe and rundll32.exe, two important Windows programs.

Unfortunately, it may not be clear to you what all of these entries are, although you may recognize some. Explore.exe is part of the process running your Windows desktop, iexplore.exe is Internet Explorer, and taskmgr.exe is the Task Manager. Often you can look these processes up using the search function under Help and Support or directly through the Microsoft Knowledge Base. You can also check the Microsoft TechNet database (http://technet.Microsoft.com) for information about these processes.

You'll find other information listed in the Processes window as well, including the name of the user who's logged in and using these processes. Task Manager lists the username and whether or not a given process is a System, Local, or Network Service. Task Manager also lists the amount of CPU usage (under CPU) and the amount of memory each process consumes (under Mem Usage).

You can use the End Processes button to terminate a highlighted process, but you only want to do that once you're sure what a specific process is and why you want to terminate it. Not all processes will end quietly and cleanly; terminating processes like explore.exe will force you to restart your system.

Consider the Processes Tab in Task Manager as an informational tool that serves several useful functions. It helps you become familiar with the processes you are running and pay particular attention to those processes that require a large amount of CPU processing. The exception is the System Idle process, which may consume up to 99% of processes listings but is simply telling you that the CPU is waiting for work to do.

Performance Tab

The Performance tab in Task Manager gives you an encapsulated view of the two main components of your system's current operating capacity: CPU usage and PF Usage (or page file).

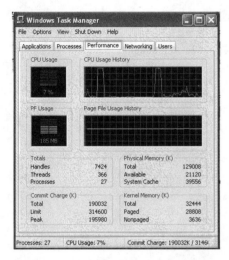

Under CPU Usage, you should expect to see the graph run low, between 0 and 20% of capacity, with occasional spikes when the CPU is very busy. If instead, the CPU Usage graph runs high (70–80% or higher) and stays there for prolonged periods of time, look at what's running on your system at that time. Certain programs like benchmark tests can tie up the CPU in testing for long periods. Normally, however, your CPU should not be running flat out because this load will begin to interfere with other tasks you need to do that also demand the CPU's time. When the CPU Usage graph is high, other tasks must now wait for the CPU to become less busy.

Under Page File Usage History, this marker should report the size of the page file and its usage demand. Normally, this should stay fairly flat and even, with just some small variations. However, if you've adjusted the size of your page file (discussed earlier in this chapter), watch for changes here. The page file size could require enlargement because the system is working too hard.

Graphics (Video) Acceleration

All versions of consumer Windows support the capability to change the rate of graphics acceleration used by your system. Graphics acceleration, put simply, tries to help your system adjust its performance based on specific video (graphics) demands placed on it. This capability of adjusting graphics acceleration is often used to try to troubleshoot video problems, crashes, and system sluggishness.

To change the rate of graphics acceleration on your system, take the following steps:

1. From Windows Control Panel, double-click Display.

2. Choose the Settings tab and then click Advanced.

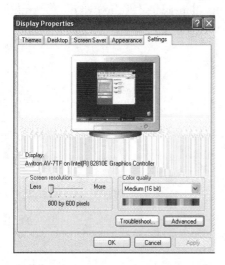

3. Click Performance tab or Troubleshooting tab depending on the version of Windows you're using.

4. Under Hardware Acceleration, click to move the slider bar down one notch (usually from Full toward None). Click OK until you exit. You may be prompted to restart your system.

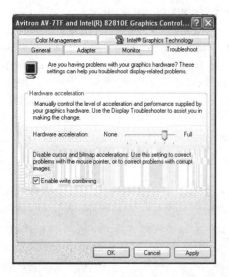

5. Following the restart, re-evaluate your system performance. If it appears improved, you can leave the Hardware Acceleration setting as is. If performance doesn't seem to improve, repeat the first four steps to move the notch one place closer to None, and repeat the restart and re-evaluation. If performance still is not improved, return the Hardware Acceleration setting to its original value.

Benchmarks

You may have heard the term *benchmarks* used in relation to PC performance. You may have also had benchmarking recommended to you as a means for evaluating your system's performance.

A benchmark is simply a performance test that scores a PC's speed and then rates it against statistical averages of how other PCs or components perform. "Test" may be the wrong word, since a series of tests are typically performed as part of a benchmark analysis. For example, you might be testing the CPU's ability to perform a specific series of instructions and then scoring how well it performs as part of a benchmark analysis.

Some of the best-known benchmark tests include the following:

- Dhrystones tests general computing instructions.

- Khornerstones tests CPU and I/O operations.

- Whetstones tests floating-point calculations, both 32-bit and 64-bit operations.

- WinBench comes in versions that test particular capabilities of your PC such as video and audio.

- PerformanceTest tests overall system performance and specific benchmarks such as video and memory

- HD Tach tests your hard drive.

- Mem Tach tests your memory.

All of these benchmarks are typically available to download from sites such as Cnet's Download.com (`www.download.com`) or Major Geeks (`www.majorgeeks.com`). Most of these benchmarks are freeware, which means you can use them without cost, or shareware, which means you can try them for free, but if you want to keep using them, you should register them for a specified price.

How Benchmarks are Used and Abused

If you're tempted to use benchmarks to test your system's performance, there are some things you probably need to understand first.

Benchmarks for computers are similar to standardized testing in American schools: You want to have some means of measuring aptitude and performance, but you realize the test results may only tell you so much. Just like with students in schools, some computers give test results that exceed how they perform in actual daily operation. Conversely, some systems that don't test well in benchmarks still perform decently for what you need to do with them.

You need to know what a benchmark measures. A benchmark series that only tests your memory won't be of much use to you in assessing your hard drive performance. In addition, make sure to read the documentation that accompanies any type of benchmark so that you can understand what is being tested and how to interpret the results. Not all benchmarks use standardized reporting. For example, a score of 300 might sound good until you realize that most other like systems rate at least 500 on another company's benchmark.

Too often, people who start using benchmark tests get into a cycle of trying to improve their system's test score for the score itself, sometimes to the detriment of how the same system behaves in day-to-day work. Users sometimes read about a tweak or a pushed setting they can try to improve their benchmark rating and they implement it. They might wind up with an outright disaster (hardware fails, Registry errors) or a disaster in the making (changed settings may drive up internal temperature, impact the video display, or create drive errors).

A technical administrator I know felt that the use of benchmarks became such a distraction and caused so much collateral damage because users reported problems that didn't exist that he stopped the general use of them altogether. Instead, he runs three different benchmarks at the time a PC is first pressed into service, then repeats those same tests at the six-month, one-year, and two-year marks. He reviews the changes in the system recorded at each marker point to look for specific issues his technical support department needs to address for its users.

"Mine is Bigger (or Better) than Yours"

Although I spend a fair amount of time working with PC hardware—sometimes mine, often someone else's—I only rarely perform benchmark testing. Usually this occurs because I'm testing hardware or applications or when I'm looking for a specific problem because I want to see what the benchmark results tell me that I may not be able to see on my own.

I find benchmark tests to be only so useful. While I can see their value in a spot application such as when you're testing a dozen like computers to see which one scores best or worst in certain areas, I don't usually recommend their use.

Other Ways to Improve PC Performance

You've learned about some of the adjustments you can make to try to improve your PC performance. In addition to those already covered in this chapter, let's look at some other steps that may improve your PC's performance or, better yet, prevent you from experiencing many performance problems at all.

Make Sure Your PC is Sufficient for the Job

Here's a plain and simple truth about PC hardware: If you don't have the resources you need to do your work, your PC's performance and your productivity will suffer greatly. You're unlikely to find enough tweaks and worthwhile "booster" programs to make up the slack. A booster program, in this case, is any type of utility that says it will enhance overall performance, such as Internet connection speed, memory utilization, and so on.

These are some questions you should ask yourself when you evaluate whether your system is sufficient for its responsibilities:

Is my processor powerful enough?   The answer is probably yes, unless your system is very old or you absolutely must do many tasks at once that may stress a processor earlier than a Pentium II.

How much memory is enough?   Never believe the minimum memory requirements listed for Windows and applications you install. Running with a bare minimum amount of memory is a performance-killer in most situations and truly limits what you may be able to do.

While many Windows 95 installations may do fine with just 64MB of RAM installed, you should have 128MB for any situation in which you run professional-type applications such as Microsoft Office. Most consumers rarely need more than 256MB installed unless they're doing heavy-duty video editing or original, detailed graphics work.

How much hard disk space is enough?   If you've been using your PC for more than six months, you should already know there is never enough hard drive space. Seriously though, you will need as much as you can imagine, and then some.

However, you must always have at least enough available disk space for the Windows page file, which means about 200MB minimum for 128MB of installed RAM. Once you begin running out of space for the page file, Windows becomes increasingly erratic and runs out of resources to run your programs. Capacious hard disks are so cheap now that it's hard to justify this happening.

How much PC power supply is enough?   The simple answer is a 300-watt power supply for most PCs, and 400-watt units for users who love or need to install a lot of extra hardware to their PCs. But if your PC came with a 200-watt supply and you aren't adding much else to the system, you'll probably get by just fine unless and until something kills your current power supply. Then you might want to replace it with a more powerful model. After all, even if you plan to buy a new PC when the time comes for a serious upgrade, you can always harvest the better power supply from your current PC to keep it on the shelf for a day when you need it.

When is it time to think about replacing the entire PC rather than just upgrading parts to improve performance?   This really depends on what you currently have, how many components you need to replace to upgrade your current system, and how the prices for replacement parts compare to the price of the new system.

Right now, budget PCs without a monitor start at around $400–$500. For a Pentium IV system of 1.8GHz or better, with a monitor, prices start at $700. If it costs you at least half as much to replace the components in your existing system as it costs you to replace the entire PC, I suggest you buy a new system if you can.

Performance-Related Maintenance

You'll need to perform the maintenance described in Chapter 3, "Prevention: Limiting Your Risks," to reduce the chances of a badly fragmented hard disk, a hard disk containing cross-linked files, or a surplus of unwanted temporary files. In addition, backups of documents and other files may seriously hurt your overall system performance. Note that I'm talking about temporary backup files, not the important data backups that I've recommended throughout the book.

Performance-related maintenance tasks should include the following:

- Running Disk Defragmenter

- Running Disk Cleanup

- Deinstalling applications you no longer use

- Running Check Disk (CHKDSK) utility in Windows XP (or ScanDisk in other versions of Windows)

- Regular virus scans

- Moving large stores of data you rarely if ever access to a removable medium such as a recordable CD. Make a couple of copies and properly mark these copies before you delete these large hard drive-based data stores.

NOTE *Remember the type of work-area maintenance described in Chapter 3. You may find your performance doesn't suffer quite as much if you respond proactively to keep dust, debris, and moisture away from the area in and around the PC.*

Consolidate and Streamline

Often, your PCs end up being masterpieces in progress. You get a system and then begin to swap out one device for a better one while adding components you didn't have before, such as an IEEE 1394 adapter (so you can plug in your digital video camera or an external IEEE 1394 drive), a digital camera, or a printer or two.

Sometimes, these additions begin to add up, in terms of power requirements (see Chapter 11, "Avoiding Power and Overheating Problems") and hardware resources like IRQs and I/O addresses. Such a system may have devices installed that are no longer used because another device has been added that performs the same function. In other words, you augmented your PCs, but you didn't do it with great forethought or intelligence.

When performance begins to suffer on your system, it's smart to analyze your PC to see which hardware components you use and which components you don't need. Then, do a systematic removal of what you no longer need, or at least reconfigure your PC in a way that makes more sense in terms of resources. Consider everything from available drive bays and connectors from the PC power supply to desktop resources and hardware resources.

TIP *Actually, it's even wiser to perform such an analysis every six months or so, depending on how frequently you add new hardware to your PC. You don't have to wait until you experience a problem to prevent a future one.*

Let's talk about this in more detail, using examples of what you may face with your own PC.

Removing Unused Devices

Take a cool, objective look at your system and see what devices you've installed that you no longer use. Then remove them, both physically and by uninstalling their drivers in Device Manager. These unused devices might include

- The dialup modem you stopped using two years ago when you got broadband service. You kept the modem thinking it was a backup but you never use it.

- A SCSI host adapter you installed ages ago for an older scanner or other device, but you no longer connect any SCSI devices to it.

- USB devices (see the next section).

About USB Devices

Let's talk in detail about universal serial bus (USB) devices because there are a few misconceptions about these devices, along with a lot of barely used USB devices loading up with the PC each time you start it.

Chapter 2, "How your Hardware, Operating System, and Applications Work Together," when I discussed USB devices, I don't think I mentioned that you can have up to 127 USB devices connected simultaneously (at least, by specification). This is true, but there are a few caveats:

- USB devices generally need to get power from somewhere, either through a separate power cord that plugs into an outlet or surge suppressor or through the PC's power supply.

- These USB devices will gladly share the same hardware resource (IRQ), but you can tax your system by installing (and keeping installed) too many USB devices at once.

- Unless you uninstall a USB device, it continues to use most resources except power.

It's been my experience that users prefer to buy USB devices that don't require a separate power cord. This is understandable since the area around your PC tends to be a jumble of cords and cables.

However, it's not realistic to install and run 10 USB devices at once—all without separately supplied power—without draining your power resources through the PC and its power supply. Granted, your PC has a limited number of available USB ports, but as you've already learned, you can add a powered USB hub that plugs into one of those available ports and then supplies connections (along with some power) to other USB devices plugged into it. You can plug in these hubs until you run out of USB ports, but do you really need to do that?

To that end, think carefully about what USB devices you want to have connected to your PC all the time. If you have many USB devices, the number of obligatory ones is still probably pretty small. I have more than a dozen USB devices. To limit power consumption and to free up some room in my too-often-cluttered workspace, I unplug unneeded USB devices until I need to use them again. They store beautifully on a shelf below my main work area and are less prone to damage or accidentally dropping because they are out of the way of the desk-area traffic.

However, just unplugging an installed USB device consumes all the resources the device needs, including the loading of its driver. This is very helpful if you have something like a USB scanner or a printer or camera that you might use a few times a week and like to unplug between uses.

For other devices that are apt to be used far less infrequently, I actually uninstall these devices from Windows Device Manager simply because I rarely use them and don't want their drivers loading each and every time I boot my PC. An example of this on my system is a USB-connected microscope with a fancy Wacom graphics tablet. By uninstalling it, there was a side benefit with my Wacom tablet because its driver can sometimes interfere with my PC's normal shutdown process.

Not all such devices can be uninstalled. But those devices that use special software installed with the USB device may be listed under Add or Remove Programs in Control Panel. This special software allows you to uninstall the device software just before you unplug and remove the device.

Consolidating Drives

One area in which consolidation can be very helpful is with multiple drives. Many systems today have had at least two different drives added since the PC was first pressed into service. There is nothing wrong with this per se, but if you're out of drive bays and power supply connectors because you've built your system up incrementally, it may make more sense to rethink your approach. Extra physical drives push up internal temperature, demand more power, and take up more room.

Here's an example. One of my associates was complaining the other day that he had a great new hard drive, but no bays were available and there was no room left to install another IDE/ATA controller into his motherboard. He had no desire to move to a SCSI-based system, where it becomes easier to attach multiple drives to a PC. When I asked what he had installed, he told me that he had a 20GB hard drive, a CD-ROM drive, a CD-RW drive, and a DVD-ROM drive.

Now, this fellow isn't someone who needs to use both CD-type drives at once, although some people do. Even if he did, his DVD player reads and plays his CDs fine. This means he can remove his CD-ROM drive, freeing up enough room for that new hard drive.

But he can take it one smart step forward: He can remove both his CD-RW drive and DVD player (which he can move to other PCs he has) and install a DVD/CD-RW combo drive, which couples DVD and CD playing/recording. With this, he frees up hardware resources, he frees up a drive bay and a power supply connector, and his PC case becomes less congested.

I don't want to leave you with the impression that there's a direct correlation between reducing the number of devices you've installed and overall system performance. But it makes sense that reducing overall resource demands may contribute to a system that starts a little faster, has better internal air circulation, and requires a little less power.

Watching Startup Issues

One of the most effective ways you can wear down your PC's performance and shorten the length of time before you have to restart your system is by having many programs loading at Startup. That's not something you want to do even if you have a large amount of memory installed.

Loading many programs in Startup may:

- Seriously reduce available desktop resources for your Windows session.

- Interfere with the installation of other programs and driver updates as these programs run in the background (and may or may not be obvious to you as you work).

- Interfere with other desktop processes, including running other applications and games.

- Lead to system instability (if one or more programs in Startup has a tendency to misbehave).

To view all the programs that load at Windows Startup, including those you may not see in your Systray (the bottom-right corner of your desktop next to the time of day), follow these steps:

1. Right-click the Windows Start button and choose Properties.

2. Choose the Start Menu tab.

3. Choose Classic Start menu and then click Customize.

4. Click Advanced, which opens a Start Menu explorer window.

5. Click the Programs folder and then click the Startup folder for a list of programs that load at Startup.

To move an item from your Startup folder (where it automatically loads each time Windows starts) to your Start menu (or to another folder), take these steps:

1. Follow the previous set of steps.

2. At step 5, locate and select the program you want to remove from Startup and drag this program to another folder such as Start Menu.

This book has talked about saving your data and trying to restore your system back to normal operating function. But what do you do about recovering files and applications that may have been lost to you due to some type of disaster? That subject is up next in Chapter 13, "Recovering Lost or Damaged Files and Applications."

Recovering Lost or Damaged Files and Applications

I 've yet to find a Halloween horror tale or scary movie that equals the gut-wrenching terror one feels when a much-needed file is missing in action, so damaged it won't open at all, or opens to a screen filled with unrecognizable garbage characters. Clearly, the old horror masters such as H.P. Lovecraft, Edgar Allen Poe, and Mary Shelley never owned a PC.

You may experience such problems as an isolated incident (one important file won't open), or as a cluster, where all files of a particular type appear to be damaged. You might also see that only files created on or near a specific date are affected.

Regardless of the situation, you're in a mess. You feel you must either accept the loss of the file as gone forever or you're stuck redoing hours', days', or even weeks' worth of effort. Or you could sit and bemoan the fact that you never did that backup of your files you kept procrastinating.

None of those options sounds ideal, do they?

But you can sometimes turn a no-win scenario around by knowing some of the tricks of the trade in file recovery.

In previous chapters, you and I have discussed

- Your PC, its hardware, and its relationship with the Windows operating system and its installed applications

- How to protect your system and your data

- How to stabilize and resolve various problems you're likely to experience—either as part of a disaster or as a situation that quickly degrades into one

Let's tackle the vexing problem of file and application recovery since this is one of the most common, time-consuming, and aggravating issues you may face as a computer user.

The Symptoms of File Damage

The symptoms of a missing file are pretty obvious (you won't be able to find it), but the symptoms of file corruption can run the gamut. Some of the symptoms of file corruption include

- A file that won't open when you click it; the operation either puts you at an hourglass or does absolutely nothing.

- You see the file you want to open in a folder list but when you try to open it, you're told the system cannot find the file or it's not a valid file.

- A file opens with a wide range of error messages, not all of which indicate corruption.

- A file opens to display what appears to be garbage characters as if you opened the file using the wrong program (see Figure 13.1).

- As the file is opening, a low memory warning appears, or you're told you cannot open the file because you have too little available memory.

- Windows prompts you to tell it what program to load this file with, when the file is of a type already associated with and recognized by that program (such as **.doc** files in word processors).

- Your application exits spontaneously every time you try to open a specific file or group of files.

- Your application, previously open and working fine, displays odd behavior each time you open a particular file.

- You have problems saving other files from an application that are open at the same time as a corrupted file.

- Closing a suspect file seems to improve the performance of the application.

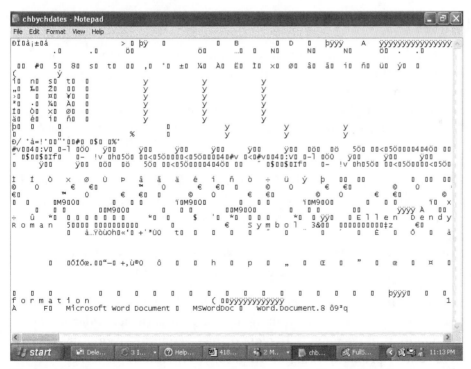

Figure 13.1 *File corruption may make the content look like "garbage."*

TIP *Before you assume a file is corrupted, shut down and restart your system. Then try to load the appropriate application by itself, without loading any data files. Restarting the system reduces the odds that an instability on the desktop is causing the problem. If the application itself won't open, you may need to uninstall and reinstall it.*

Why Files Disappear or Become Corrupted

Unfortunately, so many different issues can factor into the disappearance or corruption of files (and applications), it makes you wonder how 99.9 percent of your files are always there and intact. Yet a well-running system rarely experiences file problems, telling you a great deal about the importance of stability and overcoming small problems before they grow into much larger ones.

Let's look at the major causes of the disappearance and corruption of files.

Computer Viruses

Your primary concern with computer viruses is that some of them may corrupt the core files that run a particular application, which may affect how the application behaves (or if it opens at all) and may damage files you create using that application.

Sadly, today's virus-ware now includes programs that attack other types of file formats besides those that actually execute your programs (*.exe and *.com files). For example, Word macro viruses are special viruses written to exploit the Visual Basic programming that can be added to Word and other applications to perform specific functions. Word macro viruses are abundant in corporate settings where users indiscriminately pass the infection back and forth between each other unchecked. Some of these viruses automatically send copies of themselves to contacts stored in an e-mail program's address book, which is even worse than those bad fruitcakes that re-circulate at holiday time.

But you can prevent this damage from viruses. Your risk should be pretty low if you follow the recommendations described in Chapter 3, "Prevention: Limiting Your Risk."

NOTE *Here's a bit of irony. My virus scanner has notified me 11 times that some-one has sent me a Word document containing a macro virus (which pales in com-parison to the hundreds of documents I create or receive in any given year). Ten of those files were sent by people working at Microsoft Corporation, the folks who produce Word and work to keep it safe and secure. Granted, these viruses occurred a few years back and stopped as soon as I brought it to someone's attention, but...*

Improper Shutdown

Chapter 2, "How Your Hardware, Operating System, and Applications Work Together," described the role of proper startup and shutdown, along with some of the problems caused by an improper shutdown. The effects of such a shutdown can be devastating on some types of files that may be open on your desktop, including documents you're working on at the time. These files may not be written properly to disk, may not reflect changes you made since the last time you saved the file, and could become corrupted. Always be sure you shut down your system properly whenever possible.

Even if you never shut down your system improperly, power outages can turn your PC off prematurely. If you have files open at the time of an outage, they might be corrupted when you reopen them after the system reboots.

If your system simply won't shut down as it should, resolve the problem as quickly as possible (information about this can be found starting in Chapter 3, "Prevention: Limiting Your Risks"). In the intervening time, make sure to close all your open files *before* you shut down to reduce the chance that open, working files may be damaged.

Operating System Instability

An unstable operating system creates a ripe environment for file corruption because it can cause you to crash out of an application in which you're working or it can freeze the system in mid-session, requiring you to reboot your PC without saving your open work.

The first step is to stabilize Windows using the recommendations described in Chapter 9, "Stabilizing Your Operating System." Until then, take extra precautions to protect the files you're working on by saving your files frequently during a session, by saving extra copies of your files, or by performing more frequent backups. Avoid installing any new applications or upgrading existing applications until the operating system is stable.

Problem Applications and Utilities

Another potential cause of file damage can be linked to unstable programs you run on your system. These can be applications that seem to generate corrupted files, applications that conflict with the operation of other programs, or applications that affect your system and the way it stores files or maintains file integrity.

You may see file damage when

- installing older software

- installing or using utilities written for an earlier version of Windows (more likely if the utility was written to work with systems running FAT16 file systems, such as pre-Windows 98 systems)

- programs with existing problems are installed onto your PC

With outdated software, the solution is usually as simple as upgrading to a program that's compatible with your version of Windows. Doing so becomes more important if you begin to see nasty side effects of the incompatibilities such as file corruption. This is a situation you can't tolerate for long.

For unstable software, check with the publisher of the package to see if they have recommendations to help you overcome your current problems. You'll need to fully document the symptoms when you see them and record any error messages you see. Until then, consider uninstalling the unstable software or keeping that program closed when you're working on open files in other programs.

Unfortunately, there are times when corruption won't be limited to one or a handful of files. In extreme cases, all files created using an application may be damaged.

If all files are corrupt in an application as soon as they are created, the first thing to suspect is the application itself has become corrupted and cannot write legitimate data to disk that can be read again. You'll see the same effects when the application isn't compatible with your version of Windows.

Your chances of recovering files corrupted in this way is low, so always make sure to test the files you create with a new application before you get too far in your work. At the very least, this limits the amount of work you could lose.

In such situations, uninstall the unstable application using the Add and Remove Programs feature in Control Panel. Once properly uninstalled, restart your system and then attempt to reinstall the application. Be sure to create some test files, save these files to disk, shut down and restart again, and then try to open them. If they open now, you may be OK.

WARNING *After the reinstallation, back up the files you create at least once a day until you feel comfortable that the original problem has been fixed. Then you can move to a less rigid backup schedule, if you desire.*

But if reinstalling doesn't produce better results, uninstall the program (or at the very least, stop using it) until you contact the program's publisher to see if they can determine the source of the incompatibility. It could be that the unstable application conflicts with something else installed on your system, or with your version of Windows. In either case, you don't want to risk your work by committing it to software that trashes files.

TIP *Always check for Windows version compatibility before you buy and/or install software, just as you do with hardware. There are just enough differences between some versions of Windows and the file systems they use to cause serious data issues in some applications.*

Formatting and Recovery Tools

For all intents and purposes, formatting your disk wipes it clean of data. But this isn't entirely true. Expensive professional software packages and data recovery specialists can often look beneath a reformatted disk to extract files and information that you can no longer see. Often, however, these services get priced out of the realm of mere mortals, even if you can claim the cost as a legitimate, tax-deductible business expense.

The same is often true with the recovery disks that many manufacturers distribute with a new PC. Many of those disks work by replacing the current contents of your hard drive with a drive image of what your system looked like when it was configured at the factory, in terms of the operating system and installed applications. When you're desperate and you use the recovery disk, you may not notice the fine print on the screen warning that you're about to lose everything you've installed since you first turned on the system. And, sadly, a few recovery disks I've seen did not even warn you at all; those users didn't know the implications of using the recovery disk and got a nasty surprise.

Along with recovery disks, you can lose all your current files if you don't save them off your hard drive before you run a "go back to a previous PC time" program. Such programs allow you to revert your system to the way it was before harmful changes may have been made. System Restore does not typically replace the files you create in your programs; it focuses instead on critical system files. However, some utilities that work similar to System Restore may, so check their documentation. Utilities such as GoBack allow you to preserve the files you've created or stored since the last time you made a system snapshot.

Likewise, you can have the same problem restoring a drive image. Always back up your good files before you use any of these techniques so that you don't lose valuable data.

Other Contributing Factors

Several other problems can contribute to lost or damaged files, such as

- Power-related problems (see Chapter 11, "Avoiding Power and Overheating Problems")
- Dirt and debris in the system (see Chapter 3)

- Programs running in the background at the time a file is being written to disk, such as virus scanners or anti-crash software (the latter is software which says it protects your system from unwanted crashes)

- Having your disk (usually removable) in close proximity to serious magnetic exposure, as you might see when putting floppy drives on a stereo unit

- Using disk utilities while also trying to save open files

The Best Practices to Avoid Losing Files and Applications

Now that you're a quasi-expert in the causes of lost or damaged files, let's go over the best practices you can employ to try to keep the situation from happening in the first place:

Back up! I know I've said it so often, but considering how few people actually do it, it bears repeating. Just backing up your daily files off your main hard drive can save you from much aggravation and inconvenience.

Read the documentation. Always read through the documentation—either hard copy or online through a Help index—for an application to see what recovery methods may be supported *before* you get into a bad situation.

Go solo. When you're working on something critical, avoid having any more applications open than you absolutely need. The fewer applications that are open if a problem occurs in Windows, the better your chances that data can be written to the disk without (too much) distortion.

Also, unless you absolutely need to be connected to the Internet while you work (always a possibility), either terminate your connection, or, if you have a continuous connection with cable, DSL, or satellite access, keep your Internet applications closed. Problems from simple glitches to malicious behavior on the part of others using the Internet can make a crash while connected more likely.

Enable auto-save. Check to see if the programs you use have an automatic save feature like Microsoft Office does. Then be sure to configure it to save your work every 5–10 minutes.

TIP *If you work or type very fast, set up automatic saves to occur more frequently. I can easily type 100 wpm, which could make for a lot of work lost if I waited 10–15 minutes between saves and something happened to the file before the next time it was saved.*

Stabilize your applications and operating system.   If you're having problems with an application you're working in or with Windows itself, exit your work or avoid reopening it until you resolve the instability.

Avoid saving the only copy of a file on a system or a drive you already know is experiencing problems. If it's your only system and your only hard drive, save a copy of the file to a floppy or a Zip drive, or if it's very large, save it onto a CD.

Don't make major changes in the middle of a project or session.   All too often, you hear a tragic story about someone who was rushing to meet a deadline of some kind (writing a big paper, drafting an article, creating a wonderful piece of original art) who takes a break from that project to install a new application or make major changes to his or her machine. My favorite story involves a writer (thankfully, not me) who decided to take an hour's break from a career-altering deadline to install an operating system beta test. Multiple disasters later, he was three weeks late and lost an important job (he didn't like to back up either).

Protect your PC from unexpected power losses.   Add an uninterruptible power supply (UPS) to your system to prevent situations where you lose power without the ability to properly save your work. Depending on the UPS capacity you get, you might even have time to make an extra copy of your work.

Scan for viruses.   While viruses and Trojan horses used to target only executable files (those with the `.exe` or `.com` file extensions), many viruses today wreak havoc with more file types, including macros and VBA programming.

When receiving files from others, always scan these files before you open them or save them to a disk.

Watch how you delete.   If you like to use the Command Console in Windows XP (or a DOS window for earlier versions of Windows), beware of deleting from the command prompt. Files deleted this way will *not* appear in the Recycle Bin and are much tougher to resurrect later if you find you've erased the wrong files.

The Issue of Time

The sooner you try to recover a lost file or application, the better. Every moment that passes, each operation you run, and each additional disk write that is done after a file is lost decreases the likelihood that you'll be able to recover that file.

Unfortunately, however, you may not discover a file is missing or corrupted until days or weeks after it happens. Make a point of identifying your most important files and go to the trouble of checking on them to be sure they are present and they open properly. Conscientiously back up your files off the main hard drive.

When personal computers were relatively new, you often heard the saying that a hard drive was like an electronic filing cabinet. In many respects, this is still quite true, especially since many users keep vital information that normally *only* exists on paper tucked instead into the 1s and 0s that populate the binary world of our PCs.

But the file-cabinet comparison is only accurate up to a point because you can exercise more control over the organization of your physical filing cabinet and how things are placed in it than you can effectively impose on your hard drive. The physical condition of the hard drive itself, combined with the properties of the operating system and the file-indexing system (usually the file allocation table or FAT with Windows consumer versions), control the actual "filing" process. You can tell Windows where to save a particular file but how that information is written to the platters making up your hard drive is pretty much out of your hands.

In addition, it seems easier to make digital bytes disappear than to make a piece of paper disappear. I say this with only a bit of sarcasm, because it's really quite true. Unless you consciously throw away a piece of paper (or even burn it), you're apt to see that piece of paper resurface every time you move things around in your home and office (probably making you think each time, "I really ought to throw that away or file it"). With your PC, you don't have to hit the Delete key to make a file disappear. You could save it to the wrong folder or location (in which case it's there but missing to you) or another situation might cause the file to temporarily disappear, such as a poorly behaved application you're using to create or modify that file, or difficulties with your PC where the PC crashes before the file is properly saved.

Over time, the contents of a single file can get spread out, or *fragmented*, across the platter of a drive, making the file slower to open or problematic once you do get it loaded. You may even see some of the types of corruption mentioned earlier in this chapter in a fragmented file.

The same holds true for your applications. The files that support the application may get fragmented. An application that ran so well when it was first installed may load more slowly or display odd behavior (for example, it can't find a file that is obviously present). This problem sometimes cannot be corrected by regular disk maintenance. In the worst case scenario, it's better to back up the data, then uninstall and reinstall the application—effectively rewriting it to the disk—to get it to work the way it did before.

When you do something like accidentally delete a file in Windows, which (unless you configure it otherwise) goes into Recycle Bin, the physical placement of the file on the disk may move. This means that the original space it occupied may be overwritten by other files as they are in turn written to disk. And if you erase files outside Windows, from Recovery Console or from the Command prompt, for example, these files don't go to the Recycle Bin. Their space may be immediately overwritten by other files.

Using Windows Tools to Organize Your Disk and Locate

One of the best ways to reduce the chances that your operating system and hardware may conspire to help you lose files or experience file corruption is by using the Windows maintenance tools. These tools keep your disk organization relatively clean and running well. Windows Search (in Windows Millennium and XP) or Find (in earlier versions of Windows) are powerful tools for helping you locate seemingly missing files or temporary files that may store the work you did to an open file just prior to a system crash.

Disk Maintenance

It's important to maintain your hard drive using the Windows tools already discussed, including

- CHKDSK for Windows XP or ScanDisk for earlier versions
- Disk Cleanup
- Disk Defragmenter (defrag)

Chapters 3 and 9 provide the details on how to use these utilities and explain why they can make such a difference in good PC operation and performance.

Using Search to Locate Older Copies

Having problems locating a file or older versions of a file that you now can't open or use? Take advantage of Windows Search to help you look for it, including the advanced options that help you find a file whose name you may not know.

Searching for a Known (or Mostly Known) Filename

If you know part of a file's filename, take these steps to locate it:

1. Choose Start ➤ Search ➤ All Files and Folders.

2. From the Search window, click All Files and Folders, unless you know that what you're looking for is a document or a picture, as listed on the Search menu.

3. Under All or Part of the File Name, type the filename you want to look for. Click Search. You can use wildcards such as * and ! to fill in for text you don't know.

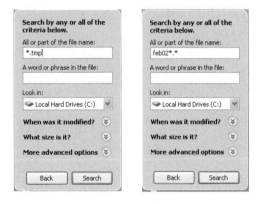

All files located that match your search criteria should appear in the right-hand pane.

Search works a bit differently in earlier versions of Windows. For those operating systems, take the following steps:

1. Choose Start ➣ Find ➣ Files or Folders.

2. Choose the Name and Location tab. In the Named text box, type the filename (or part of the filename with wildcards) of the file.

3. In the Look In box, you may want to specify where to look for the file; for example, your C: drive or another drive, if you're sure it should be found on one drive over another.

4. Click Find Now.

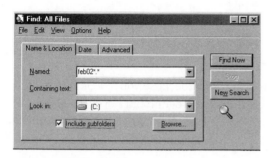

Searching for a File by Words or Phrases It Contains

If you don't know the filename but you know some unique words that may appear within the content of a file, you can search on them by performing these steps in Windows Millennium and XP:

1. Choose Start ➤ Search ➤ For Files or Folders.

2. From the Search window, click All Files and Folders.

3. In the A Word or Phrase in the File dialog box, enter the words you want to search for. Choose words as unique as possible to help narrow down the choices.

4. Click Search.

To do this in earlier versions of Windows, take these steps:

1. Choose Start ➤ Find ➤ Files or Folders.

2. Choose the Name and Location tab, and under Containing Text, type the significant keywords found within the file you're looking for.

3. Click Find Now.

Searching for a File by Date

Suppose you don't know the filename or even the file's format because you're looking for a temporary backup copy of a file that was automatically created by a program but never saved to an actual working filename. If you don't know anything more than the approximate date on which the file was last created or modified, take the following steps under Windows Millennium and XP:

1. Choose Start ➤ Search.

2. From the Search window, click All Files and Folders. This step is important because the file you're looking for may not be recognized by Windows as a particular file type.

3. Under Search by Any or All of the Criteria Below, choose the drive(s) under Look In, and then click When Was It Modified to expand this listing.

4. Under When Was It Modified, click Specify Dates, and then provide the date range to look in. For example, if you know the file was open on a given day, enter that day's date.

5. Click Search.

As you can see from the results shown in Figure 13.2, a great many files can be generated just in the course of a single day, depending on the kind of work you're doing and the type of applications you have open. In this instance, I've spotted a temporary file (.tmp) that may contain most of the contents of changes made to another document since it was last properly saved. For example, I might be able to see that the size of the file roughly matches the size of the file I was working on, and this TMP file was written to disk within minutes of when I was working on the other file. If I right-click that entry and choose Properties, I'll learn more about the file itself.

TIP *Most temporary files are saved with extensions such as* .bak, .old, .bk1, *or* .tmp. *Check your software's documentation to see if it specifies whether temporary files are kept (usually the case) and how you can identify them.*

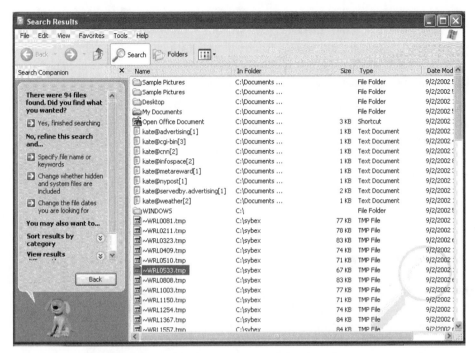

Figure 13.2 *Finding a* `.tmp` *file that may contain my lost document*

To do something similar in earlier versions of Windows, take these steps:

1. Choose Start ➤ Find ➤ Files or Folders.

2. Choose the Date tab, select the date type (Modified, Created, or Last Accessed), and then set the range to check.

3. Click Find Now.

A Cautionary Tale: Open and Look

Here's a situation I face with an older program I still use that I know isn't terribly compatible with my system. I know this because it crashes frequently and a promised update to the program never appeared. This program lacks any kind of recovery process, but it does automatically save my work at 10-minute intervals. In between, the file gets stored in temporary versions whose names end with a unique file extension, a fact I wish I was able to glean from its poor Help file or manual.

Continued on next page

A Cautionary Tale: Open and Look *(Continued)*

The first few times I got caught in a crash, I lost several minutes of work each time (and remember, I write and type very fast). Finally, I got smart and began to use the Windows Search tool to look for all files modified on the day I had the problem. By opening all the files I couldn't identify, including dozens of temporary files, I discovered the program was indeed making interim saves of my work.

From then on, whenever I lost several minutes of work, I began looking for these temporary files to try to grab back some of the lost work, which I then cut and paste into the last saved version of the file. Since I can't stop these crashes as long as I continue to use this outdated software, I'm very glad I found a solution that saves me some of the ill effects.

Working with Damaged Files

Don't just assume that a damaged or corrupted file is completely useless. In my own experience, in at least 50 percent of the cases, I've been able to recover at least some if not all of the file; this success ratio increases with straight text files and some documents such as Word and Works files, WordPad, and so on.

This section explains some smart yet easy-to-use techniques for recovering your work from temporary files.

Work-Arounds Don't Always Work

Before going into depth on this subject, let me add that even if you're successful using these techniques to rescue work from corrupted files, it won't always work. You have to back up your files, and you should do it while they're in good condition so you have another copy to fall back upon should you encounter a serious problem that corrupts them.

This raises another issue. You now know that there are different levels of backup, including one that simply replaces files that have changed since the last time you backed up your files. Some backup programs overwrite the initially stored versions of files with the updates. Obviously, this isn't great if your original file worked fine and was backed up in that condition, but now a corrupted version on your system replaces it in your backup files.

For this reason, check your backup software's documentation for ways to configure the program to keep different file versions separate from one another. As an additional backup, you can also make a separate copy of critical files onto a separate disk each time you update these files. This way, you may have a few versions of a file you can use, if needed, to re-create a fully updated file that can be saved without any corruption.

Recovering Core Windows Files

One mini-disaster that befalls many users is core Windows files that are suddenly missing. These are files that prevent Windows from loading and files that you won't miss until you load a utility like Control Panel and receive an error message. In either case, Windows won't be happy or run properly until you're able to resurrect these missing files.

One of the most frequent causes of such errors is using a disk cleanup program that may unintentionally remove a file or utility you need. But sometimes you can do a number on Windows just by improperly removing applications.

How you recover these critical files depends on what types of files are missing and what protection methods you're using. You could

- Restore a backup made at a time before this problem happened, as long as the backup includes the core Windows files.

- Restore a drive image you created of your system at a previous time. This works best only if the drive image is very recent and you've made few if any changes to your system since then.

- Use System Restore if these are files that would be covered in a restore point (usually the case with core Windows files).

- Replace your missing Windows file with a fresh copy extracted from the compressed cabinet (.cab) files on your Windows install CD.

The first three of these methods require you to have these features and functions in place before you try to use them. For example, if System Restore isn't enabled, you can't restore a restore point.

Extracting Individual Files from the Windows Install CD

Let's spend a moment talking about how to extract files from the Windows Install CD, since the procedures have changed in Windows XP. However, the command syntax is the same.

The files comprising your Windows installation are (mostly) stored in compressed cabinet files on the Windows install CD. You must use a special command, Expand (in Windows XP) or Extract (in earlier versions of Windows), to extract these files out of their compressed state and put them in place of your missing core Windows file on your hard drive.

While you can do this from the command prompt (the MS-DOS prompt under Start ➤ Programs ➤ MS-DOS or Start ➤ Programs ➤ Accessories in earlier versions of Windows), Windows XP limits the use of this command to the Recovery Console. (Chapter 9 discusses the use of the Recovery Console in detail; you must restart your system and load the Recovery Console)

It also helps to know in which cabinet file a particular file is stored. This information can sometimes be gleaned from an error message or looked up in the Microsoft Knowledge Base.

The command syntax for Extract and Expand is as follows:

```
Extract/Expand [source location:\filename] [/f:filespec] [destination]
[/d] [/y]
```

where

- **source location** is the exact name and location of the cabinet file containing the file you want.

- The **/f:filespec** option lets you specify the file you want to extract.

- **destination** is where you want the file copied to.

- The /d switch allows you to list the contents of the specified cabinet file without extracting any of its files.

- The /y switch blocks Windows from prompting you whether or not you want it to overwrite existing versions of the same file.

For example, let's say you need a copy of the file **cdrom sys**. Its name tells you it's part of hardware operations, so in looking at the available cabinet files on your Windows install CD (mostly found in the **i386** folder), you decide that **driver.cab** is probably the best place to begin your search for this file. Of course, in their compressed format, such files have slightly different names, usually replacing the last letter of a filename extension with an underscore (_) character. So you need to look for a file named **cdrom.sy_**, not **cdrom.sys**.

The command to check the contents of this **.cab** file looks like this for most versions of Windows:

```
Extract /d [drive letter]:\i386\driver.cab |more
```

or

```
Expand /d [drive letter]:\i386\driver.cab |more (Windows ME and XP)
```

NOTE *The |more option is used to break long lists into individual screens.*

After entering the command, check your results to see if the file is indeed listed there, as it should be.

To extract the desired file from your Windows CD `driver.cab` file and install it with its proper, full name to the `Windows\System32` folder, type one of the following commands:

```
Extract [drive letter]:\i386\driver.cab /f:cdrom.sys
C:\Windows\System32\Drivers
```

or

```
Expand [drive letter]:\i386\driver.cab /f:cdrom.sys
C:\Windows\System32\Drivers
```

Here's a common example. Whether you realize it or not, all the icons that appear in Control Panel are backed by files with the `.cpl` file extension. At times, these `.cpl` files may disappear or become corrupted, and you suddenly find you can't open that option in Control Panel any longer.

NOTE *Copies of your `.cpl` files are stored on the Windows install CD in the i386 folder.*

Let's say you need to replace the `inetcpl.cpl` file that opens Internet Options in Control Panel. Use one of the following commands to replace this file:

    Extract [*drive letter*]:\i386\inetcpl.cp_ C:\Windows\System32\inetcpl.cpl

or

    Expand [*drive letter*]:\i386\inetcpl.cp_ C:\Windows\System32\inetcpl.cpl

Recovering Core Application Files

Should you run into a situation where you try to launch a program or application and an error message appears telling you that a core file is missing, your options are usually as follows:

- Reinstall the application.

- Copy specific files from the application's install disk. See the software's documentation to determine how best to do that.

- Restore these files from a previous backup or drive image. See your backup or drive-imaging software documentation for details on restoring individual files.

It's always possible that simply running the Setup or install program for the application will restore the required core files. This method also usually retains the settings you've customized since you first installed the software.

However, in more stubborn situations, it may be necessary to do the following:

1. Use the Add or Remove Programs feature in Control Panel to remove the damaged application.

2. Choose Start ➤ Shutdown ➤ Restart.

3. Once the system has restarted and with nothing else open or running on the desktop, reinstall the application.

Working with Corrupted Zip Files

Zip files are compressed files ending in the `.zip` file extension. (Special types of Zip files that can be unzipped simply by running the file may end in the extension `.exe`.) Zip files are usually collections of multiple files—or sometimes just one large file—that have been compressed using a special formula to make them much smaller than their original file size.

The leading cause of corruption of Zip files has to do with how they are transmitted: usually over the Internet. You see them most often with files you download. Line noise or other problems with your Internet connection may damage files in transit as they are being downloaded to your PC. The best recourse is to simply re-download them.

If you download the same file more than once and keep getting a message about a corrupted Zip archive when you try to unzip the file, check the file size of at least two copies you've downloaded. Is the corrupted file size always the same? This may indicate that the corruption is on the other end, meaning that the supplier of the Zip file is giving you a damaged copy. If this is on a web site, drop an e-mail to the webmaster (often, this is webmaster@website.com) explaining the problem. If the Zip file was sent to you in e-mail by a friend or associate, tell the person about the problem and ask them to re-zip the file and resend it.

However, if you're always seeing different file sizes on these corrupted Zip downloads, your Internet connection may be experiencing serious problems. The best way to test this is to download another type of file from another site. If you can download fine from another site, you may again be seeing corruption from the source rather than from anything your connection is causing.

I mentioned a moment ago that Zip files can be created with .exe file extensions. These are known as self-extracting Zip files because you simply click the file to run it, which automatically launches the unzipping process whether or not you have Zip file management software (such as WinZip or FreeZip) installed on a PC.

Should you receive a self-extracting Zip file and you get a "corrupted header" error message when trying to open the file, this probably means the Zip file was created on a system infected with a certain type of computer virus. The very act of trying to open the file, however unsuccessful, could potentially infect your system.

To avoid this, always perform a virus scan on all Zip files you receive, regardless of the file extension. If you fail to do so and you receive a "corrupted header" warning on such a file, immediately run your virus-scanning software and isolate the file that gave you this error. If possible, contact the source of the Zip file to notify them about your results and encourage them to scan their systems.

NOTE *If all Zip files report corruption, even ones that you know open fine on another system, consider the possibility that your Zip file management software has a problem. Uninstall and reinstall it.*

Recovering Accidentally Deleted Files

The first place to check for unintentionally deleted files is the Recycle Bin in Windows. Unless you've disabled this feature, this is where all files deleted within Windows come to rest before they are permanently removed from the system.

In fact, unless and until you go into the Recycle Bin and use the Empty Recycle Bin function, you should be able to find the deleted files there. Sometimes, however, the files are removed from the Recycle Bin because it is configured to keep only a percentage of your available disk space free to act as a repository for "almost gone" files and it automatically empties out some entries.

To recover a previously deleted file from Recycle Bin, take these steps:

1. Click the Recycle Bin icon on the Windows desktop or choose Start ➤ My Computer ➤ Recycle Bin.

2. Locate the deleted file you wish to restore in the list of files.

3. Right-click the file and choose Restore.

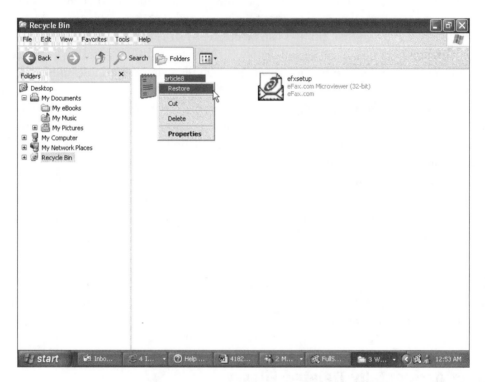

Once the Recycle Bin has been emptied, your files are effectively gone. Review the list of deleted files before emptying the Recycle Bin to be sure you're not deleting something you might need later.

NOTE *There are some exceptions to Recycle Bin and deleted files. For one, any files deleted outside Windows (for example, from the Command Console or when using the Recovery Console) won't be listed there. Also, when deleting a file, if you click No when asked if you want to send the file to Recycle Bin, the file is simply deleted and does not appear in your deleted file listing.*

There are some freeware and shareware utilities that try to restore accidentally deleted files or try to recover files already emptied from the Recycle Bin. These utilities are available for download at sites like Download.com (`www.download.com`) and Tucows (`www.tucows.com`). I've tried the following utilities with some success:

- Fast File Undelete (DTI Data; $29.99 shareware; all Windows versions) (`www.dtidata.com`)

- GoBack Deluxe (Roxio; $40 shareware; all Windows versions) (`www.roxio.com`)

- PC INSPECTOR File Recovery (Convar Europe Ltd.; Shareware demo; Windows 95/98) (`www.pcinspector.de/file_recovery/UK/welcome.htm`)

- R-Undelete (R-tools Technology, Inc.; $29.99 shareware; all Windows versions) (`www.r-tt.com`)

Techniques for Working with Damaged Files

There are tricks you can use in working with corrupted files to try to get some or all of the basic content of the file saved even if you can't salvage the whole file. How well some of these tricks apply to your situation depends on what type of applications and file formats you use. For example, it can be very difficult to cut and paste parts out of a damaged graphics file and still wind up with something that resembles what you first created. But you may be able to use the cut-and-paste technique effectively with word-processing documents.

Before you start, check the Help file and documentation for the program you're using. See if the program includes recovery/repair options, something like the recovery options Microsoft Office provides (I'll explain those in a moment). Such a feature can often be the best tool for working with a damaged file. The availability of recovery options is a good thing to consider when buying new applications.

Make sure you're opening a damaged file using the right application. Loading a file to a program that doesn't support the file format can look very much like a corrupted file ("garbage" on the screen) even though the file itself is fine when opened by the correct application. You may want to restart your system and try to load a file again to make sure some problem in your current Windows session isn't temporarily affecting your PC's ability to work well with open files.

WARNING *Some of the methods described here will result in the loss of specific formatting within a file. Usually, it takes a far shorter time to reformat the file than to re-create the meat and potatoes of the file. Always check file formatting carefully after any salvage operation.*

Cutting and Pasting into a Second File

Let's assume that you can open a file but each time you save it, the file corruption remains.

If the file contains text or objects that can be cut and pasted, use this technique to cut chunks of content from the damaged file and paste them into a new file within the same application. Figure 13.3 shows a file that you can use this technique with.

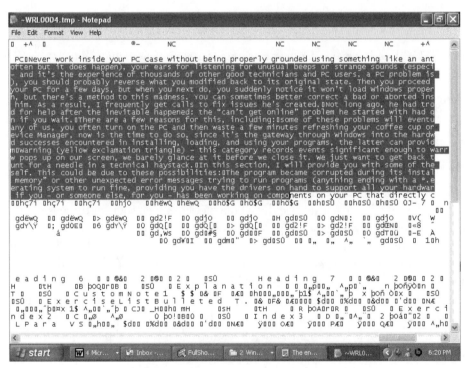

Figure 13.3 *Choose carefully what you copy when cutting and pasting data into a second file.*

As you work, take care that you don't copy any of the "garbage" or symbol characters that were not part of your original file. Moving those with you could carry the corruption into the new file. Also, if the data ends a few lines before the actual end of the file (meaning that something like carriage-return characters separate the start or the end of the file from the top or bottom of the file as you view it), don't copy these carriage-returns because they might be a source of the corruption. They may contain hidden header or footer information that has been corrupted.

You can use this same method to extract content from the temporary files talked about in the "A Cautionary Tale: Open and Look" sidebar.

When you're satisfied that you have copied out all the data you can, save the new file under a different filename. Then close both the file and the application. Shut down and restart your PC, reopen the application, and try to open the new file. If the new file opens fine, you've successfully recovered its contents. You can then make any needed changes to the formatting.

Saving as Text

Can you open the file at all? If so, and if it's a word-processing document, try saving the file as straight text (usually an option under File ➤ Save As). This removes any special formatting you've already established for the file, but you can rescue the file's basic contents (the text). Here's an example of how to do this using Microsoft Word:

1. Launch the application and then load the file you're having problems with.

2. Choose File ➤ Save As.

3. From the Save window, click the list box under Save as Type, and select Text Only. Click Save.

TIP *If your application allows you to save in rich text format (*.rtf), you can choose that instead of Text Only. RTF preserves some of the formatting lost to text-only saves.*

Trying to Open with Another Program

Do you have another program that can open the type of file you're having problems with? If so, try to open the corrupted file with that program. Formatting as well as programming differences between the two programs may allow a recalcitrant file to open in the second program but not the first. If the second program opens the file, try saving another copy of the file but with a different filename than the first. A strange character in the filename sometimes prevents a file from being properly opened by certain programs.

Trying to Open the File on Another PC

If you have another PC available to you with the same application installed—or another application that will open the same file type—copy the file to a floppy or send it across the network. Then try to open the file on the other PC. If the file opens fine on the second PC, there may be a problem with that program on the first PC. But it could also reflect slight changes between the systems that permit the second PC to open the corrupted file.

Once the file is open, save another copy of it, preferably with a new filename. Then reverse the process and try to open the new copy on the first system.

Working with Damaged Files in Microsoft Office

Since Microsoft Office, or one of its main components such as Word, is so widely used, let's discuss the recovery options within Office that can help you salvage some or all of a damaged file.

If you're using an older version of Office, you won't have these advanced recovery options available to you. But for other users, these options can often make the difference between a few minutes of fixup vs. re-creating an entire file from scratch.

Office 2000 was the first version of Office to include features for repairing a damaged file. Office XP includes significant improvements to these features. But the true gem of both versions is an auto-recovery option you enable to save copies of your work and to recover the last versions automatically for you in the event of a crash or power outage that closes out your open Office files.

For this, you need to enable the auto-save feature, because it works in concert with the recovery feature in Office to store copies of your file frequently and automatically as you work. Once Office—and especially Word—loads again following a crash, the recovery feature tries to load your files from those saved copies.

To enable this feature, take these steps:

1. From Word, click Tools ➤ Options ➤ Save.

2. Click to check Always Save Backup Copies (Office XP/Word 2002 users will see Always Create Backup Copy).

3. Click to check Save AutoRecover Info Every and then specify the time period (I would recommend every 3 to 6 minutes). Click OK.

While this works in Office 2000, it's improved greatly in Office XP to the point where it's rare for me to lose more than a few sentences after a system crash. (As you may recall from some of the disasters I created in Chapter 9, I had a number of opportunities to try this out.) The moment I load Word after such a crash, a Document Recovery window pops up showing me the files it has recovered. I usually don't need to do a thing except check the recovered documents and save them as needed. I wish all programs were so accommodating.

One last thing about the Document Recovery window in Word/Office XP: You can select a recovered file from this window and click Show Repairs to learn exactly what changes were made to the file in trying to recover, repair, and make it available to you. The information located here may give you hints as to problems in formatting, for example, that you should check in the document before you save it again.

If all else fails, purchase and download software specifically written to extract data from damaged Office files. One of the best-known sites for this type of software is Office Recovery (`www.OfficeRecovery.com`). At this site, you'll see that not just Microsoft Office is covered; you can get tools to help with programs such as Outlook Express and Microsoft Money.

Using Microsoft Office Application Recovery

New in Office XP is Microsoft Office Application Recovery, a tool designed to get into a non-responsive Office application and recover the files that are currently open. This tool works not just for Word, but also for Excel and PowerPoint as well.

If you get into this situation with one of the listed Office programs, simply run the Application Recovery tool by choosing Start ➢ All Programs ➢ Microsoft Office Tools ➢ Microsoft Office Application Recovery.

This won't necessarily work every time to recover all open and unsaved work, but it's certainly worth a shot, especially if you're inclined to simply restart the machine and potentially lose that open work anyway.

Application Recovery Options

Most of the methods you would use to stabilize, uninstall, and reinstall applications have already been covered, both here and in earlier chapters.

However, I encourage you again to check your application's documentation (including online Help files) for tools that may be included to repair or recover a misbehaving program. If all else fails, have your application install disks handy if you need to do a full reinstall, as described in Chapter 4, "Assembling Your PC Recovery Resource Kit."

For example, check applications like Microsoft Office and notice that Office 2000 includes a repair utility that may not require you to reinstall Office (although the repair utility does a bit of that for you). To run the Detect and Repair utility, follow these steps after you close all your open Office files:

1.   From Word ➤ Help, choose Detect and Repair.

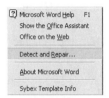

2.   From the Detect and Repair window, click Start.

The Windows Installer launches to reinstall and repair the application.

Keep a Copy of Special Downloads

Today, many applications—and their upgrades—can be purchased and downloaded directly from a web site. Often, though, you get your downloaded copy but no install disk. In fact, you save a little money off an application's retail price because of this.

Obviously, however, this becomes a problem if this is your only copy of the file. What if you experience a problem on the hard drive where you've stored your copy before you get a chance to back up this file as part of your maintenance routine?

You may be out of luck unless you can reach someone at the web site where you purchased the program. Call their customer service number to see if they can help. Usually, you'll have to provide some proof of purchase. While the web site may have sent you an e-mail with registration information, what if you can't access your e-mail because of the disk problem?

Let me share what I do to try to prevent this problem from happening. Whenever I purchase and download an upgrade or new program or application, I take these steps:

• I immediately make at least one additional copy of the program by copying the file to another hard disk.

• I jot down in my PC journal the registration information (usually a product key) I received from the web site when I bought the software or in an e-mail sent by the company.

• At least once or twice a month, I burn such downloads onto a CD, the contents of which I clearly label on the writable CD itself, the paper sleeve, or the CD jewel case.

A Cautionary Tale: When "Borrowing" Software Can Bite

It's time to address a difficult subject, often ignored when discussing the horrors of lost applications as if the phenomenon I'm about to discuss is some rare occurrence when it's not.

This issue is software piracy, as it's called by the software industry, or software "borrowing" for those who like a softer phrase for a serious matter. It involves obtaining, installing, and using an unauthorized or illegally distributed copy of an application, violating the application's end-user licensing agreement (EULA). Such EULAs often state that you can install the application on one PC, but they prohibit you from making copies to give away or sell.

I happen to believe the vast majority of you reading this kind of book are scrupulous about making certain that the only software you have has been properly obtained and is fully legal.

But I'm not going to talk about the legal issues in software piracy because they're well known, if not always well understood or observed. Instead, I want to address the issue of how difficult your life may become if you rely on borrowed applications to do important work.

Forget that illegal software often gets distributed with viruses and sometimes even "spyware" that sends information back to the pirate distributor. Forget the problems you can face in installing this software given some of the anti-piracy measures now being used to thwart illegal distribution like Microsoft Windows XP and Office XP's enforced registration.

What people who use borrowed software need to worry about is, "What do I do in an emergency?"

If you don't properly purchase software, you can't call for technical support. If you get such software on a disk, you can't replace the disk if it's damaged. You generally won't have a product key with which to reinstall it (or the one you got with the borrowed software has been long since lost), so you'll likely be locked out of reinstalling it. Most programs now only let you delay providing the product key for a limited amount of time (30 days or less) before they stop operating or will no longer run.

The bottom line is that it's tough enough investing your time and effort and trusting your precious files to an application as it is. Adding an extra layer of potential problems—not to mention possible legal ramifications—by borrowing software just doesn't seem worth it, not if you value the work you do.

The use of networks to connect two or more PCs at home or the office is becoming very common, and they can add a layer of complexity to both preventing and troubleshooting disasters you may experience. Turn to Chapter 14 to learn more.

Disaster and Recovery Essentials for Your Small Network

Ten years ago, we talked about how wonderful it would be when most homes had a personal computer. Today, many homes and small offices now have two, or three, or even more computers. Because of this, home and small networking has grown tremendously because users need a way for multiple computers talk to one another and to exchange files easily. This is important because many files today are larger than the capacity of a floppy disk. Who wants to burn a CD every time you want to move a file to a different computer? Networking also allows all the PCs to work with a single device such as a printer and to share a single Internet connection.

In fact, the ability to share a single Internet connection is one of the leading reasons home and small business users have networks. Otherwise, you'd need to have a separate Internet account and connection for each PC, and that's not just expensive, it's usually unnecessary. If broadband Internet access in the form of high-speed cable, DSL, or satellite service is not available, each PC needs its own phone line to dial out. Two or more computers can share a dial-up phone line Internet connection, but the maximum 56K speed divided among them may make that an unsatisfactory solution.

An estimated 7+ million U.S. households are now networked, along with millions of small offices. The number of home-based networks is expected to triple in the next few years. Networks aren't just for geeks with too much hardware anymore.

This chapter assumes you're one of those millions who has a network in place. I'm just slightly ahead of you, with three local networks serving my home and office complex. I'll tell you what you need to know but can't find in your networking manual and online support about protecting your network in the event of a disaster. I'll also explain how to troubleshoot problems if you do experience a disaster. This chapter includes the most common types of disasters—the ones users sometimes cause themselves.

NOTE *For complete details on setting up your home network, check out* Mastering Home Networking *by Mark Henricks (Sybex, 2000) and* Home Networking Visual JumpStart *by Erik B. Sherman (Sybex, 2000).*

The Lowdown on Small Networks

At its most basic level, a network's job is to allow two or more computers to communicate with each other, despite small or large differences among them. Special software known as *network protocol*s allows that communication; protocols provide a mutual language that each PC can communicate through. Several different protocols are used, but TCP/IP (Transmission Control Protocol/Internet Protocol) is the one you're apt to hear most often. TCP/IP is used the most for the types of networks—including Internet connections—described in this section.

The type of network most home and small office users have is called *peer-to-peer*, which simply means "from user to user" because that is how it operates. Each PC in a network, referred to as a *node*, is of equal status, and each PC can be configured to share files and devices with one another while working and behaving independently. This differs from the *client/server* networks often used in corporate environments. In a client/server network, each computer is a client that is served by a central computer acting as an administrative server. The server has e-mail, files, applications, and other features that it offers to the clients.

NOTE *Ever wonder about the term* local area network (LAN)? *It means what you'd expect: a network spread out over a small geographical area, as opposed to networks that exist over a huge geographical area or entire cities. Most home users and small offices use Ethernet LANs that use Ethernet adapters connected by Ethernet cable (either CAT-5 or coaxial cable). However, more and more lately you hear about* home area networks (HANs), *which are a subset of LANs.*

What You Need to Know About Your Network Before Disaster Strikes

Home and small office networking kits, along with advances in the Windows operating system, make it incredibly simple to set up your first network, even if you have little or no experience. But it's important to take a few precautions to make sure your new network is prepared for any possible disasters.

This simplicity is a huge plus in terms of convenience. In fact, it makes networking seem deceptively easy, when it's one of the more detail-sensitive areas of computing. Communication between computers is as complex and prone to error as human interaction, but you'd never realize it from these easy network kits.

The same is true with Windows, where networking is well supported in both professional and consumer versions of Windows. New PCs often come with a network interface card (also called a network adapter or an NIC) or network functions built right into the motherboard. So it's possible to have a network where you only need to know where to plug in the network cable.

Windows XP Home Edition recognizes network hardware and connections and configures them automatically for you, as illustrated in Figure 14.1. For instance, when I placed a new Windows XP PC into service recently, all I did was plug the Ethernet cable into the pre-installed NIC at the back of the PC, When I turned the system on, Windows XP found the existing network and plugged me into it without so much as a blink.

Figure 14.1 *Windows XP makes networking very easy.*

Yet like all conveniences, the simple network technology comes with a price. It's a price you may pay later when you encounter a problem and begin to understand that you don't know terribly much about your network setup because your kit didn't explain the background information and technical terms you need to know when troubleshooting. Unless you have some idea how everything was configured for your network when everything worked, how will you know when something has changed (and changed in a way that prevents proper connections)?

This chapter gives you basic information about simple networks and how they're typically set up. It also explains how you can restore your working settings after your system experiences a disaster.

Preparing Yourself

Before you start, pull out the PC journal you've been keeping since Chapter 2, "How Your Hardware, Operating System, and Applications Work Together." This journal is a great place to document the hardware and software configuration of your network now, while everything works and communicates well. Later, when you're recovering from a disaster or just performing basic troubleshooting, you'll find your recorded information invaluable in verifying that every part of the network—from its hardware to its protocols to its file and printer sharing—is configured properly. Trust me, a few pen or pencil strokes can make all the difference in your future network health and your sanity.

If your journal is a sectioned notebook, use a separate section just for your network; this distinguishes it from all the other data you record in your journal. If your Internet or network connection details change later on, be sure to re-record these settings into your PC journal. You don't want to reconfigure the system using the old settings or you simply won't connect.

Have your networking kit documentation handy. This may help you spot the differences between the type of networking setup discussed in this chapter and what you have.

TIP *If you haven't done so already, remember to add any disks or documentation for your network to your PC Recovery Resource Kit, as prescribed in Chapter 4.*

Your Networking Setup Options

While this chapter focuses on traditional small network setups, there is actually quite a range of hardware and networking options now available. For example, you may have

- An external network adapter that plugs into an external USB port rather than into an available slot in your motherboard

- Networks that depend on existing phone or electrical lines to supply the physical connection between computers

- A wireless networking setup, where you have a wireless access point (a small box with indicator lights, cable connection, and antenna) that connects a non-cabled computer to the network by means of radio airwave transmission

All of these options depend on basically the same software configuration, so the primary differences are with the hardware.

Refer to your networking kit documentation, if you're using such a kit, to learn more about your particular setup.

The Hardware and Its Connections

To understand a typical network hardware setup, let's assume you have three PCs. Each PC on the network has either a network adapter installed to it or network capabilities built directly into the motherboard. Into each network adapter is plugged a cable (Cat-5, the most common cable type, or coaxial). The cable in turn connects the PC into the network by means of support hardware such as a *hub* (see Figure 14.2), which allows for four, eight, or more simultaneous network connections. These connections are referred to as *ports*; hubs are referred to as four-port, eight-port, and so on. The hub acts as a traffic manager because all the computers are connected to it and all data comes in and goes out of it.

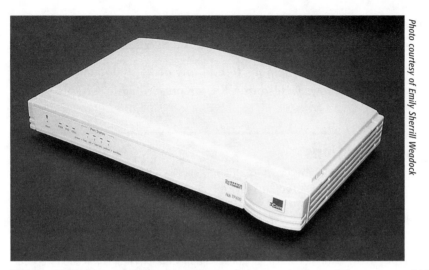

Photo courtesy of Emily Sherrill Weadock

Figure 14.2 *Network hub with indicator lights on the front (The ports are hidden at the back.)*

NOTE *CAT-5 cable is terminated (meaning the ends are sealed) by modular RJ-45 plastic jack-style connectors that look similar, but not identical, to the RJ-11 plastic jack connectors used with modern telephones.*

On some networks, you won't have a hub but a switch, illustrated in Figure 14.3. A *switch* (also called an Ethernet or LAN switch) functions very much like a hub. However, a hub has to share the available bandwidth for the network among all the PCs, but a switch allows the full bandwidth to be available to each system. Put simply, this usually makes for a faster network.

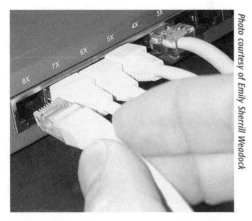

Photo courtesy of Emily Sherrill Weadock

Figure 14.3 *Network switch with cables*

NOTE *You may hear the term* router *used in connection with small networks. Routers are used to forward data along large networks that may be divided into* segments. *In a home network, the segments might represent the upstairs and downstairs PCs. However, most simple networks don't use routers.*

When you have just two PCs, you can set them up using a hub or a switch or you can connect the two PCs directly to each other—one network adapter to the other—using a crossover cable (Cat-5).

NOTE *Even with just two PCs, I still recommend you get a hub. It gives you room for expansion, and the feedback provided by the hub's indicator lights tells you if it's working, what's connected, and what's actively communicating. This information is extremely helpful when you're trying to troubleshoot your network or recover from a disaster.*

The final term you need to be familiar with is *gateway*. On a small network, a gateway acts to connect all the PCs on your network to the mother of all networks, the Internet. The gateway is usually one PC directly connected to the Internet that other PCs on your network rely on for their Internet access.

Use your PC journal to diagram your basic network setup, including what components you have and where each piece plugs in. Identify the type of network adapter each PC has; you can find information about this in Device Manager by taking the following steps:

1. From Control Panel, double-click System.

2. Choose the Hardware tab and then click Device Manager. (In earlier versions of Windows, simply choose the Device Manager tab.)

3. From Device Manager, click the + sign to expand the entry labeled Network Adapters.

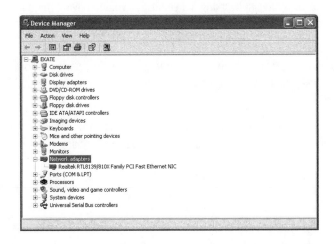

4. Verify the information on the screen and document the network adapter type in your PC journal.

While you're there, make sure there is no red or yellow mark on the network adapter listing that indicates it has been disabled or has a conflict. You can click the entry to check its properties and to be sure it is reported as operating properly. You can also click Troubleshoot from the General tab to troubleshoot any problems you may see.

A Cautionary Tale: Don't Let Me Scare You

If all my talk about the complexity of computer communications in this chapter puts you off the issue of networking and makes you long to turn to the next chapter, don't give in to the urge. I can speak with some experience because I used to be network-phobic. After struggling through a number of tough network installations in the day when Novell was the king of computer networking, I steadfastly avoided having my main work PC on a network because I felt it added a layer of complexity I didn't need. I joked that my fear came from being bitten by an Ethernet card as a young child, but I digress.

Then, one day, I encountered a situation where I needed to move many large graphics files back and forth among three different computers, and, of course, the best way to do that was over a network. Since I took the plunge, I've been very pleased.

Once you have everything in a network configured properly and working and you've documented your network setup and the troubleshooting techniques, you're ready to put the network back to working communication in the event of disaster.

Continued on next page

A Cautionary Tale: Don't Let Me Scare You *(Continued)*

So yes, a networked group of computers can be a little more trouble than non-networked systems, but they can also be very useful. You can always unplug a computer from the network if you want to temporarily remove it from the rest of the network.

The Software Configuration

Before setting the software configuration of your network, there are a few important points to understand because they may come up while troubleshooting.

Each computer on a network has at least two unique identifying points:

- The Media Access Control (machine access code) or MAC address. The MAC address is a unique serial number burned into your installed network adapter.

- An Internet Protocol (IP) address. An IP address is a designated Internet address for your network so that the Internet knows where to send files designated for that address.

Beyond that, each computer has a unique name that's created when the system is first set up. To view your computer name from Windows XP, take these steps:

1. From Control Panel, double-click System.

2. Choose the Computer Name tab.

3. Verify the name of the PC you're working on. If necessary, click Change to change either the computer or workgroup name.

Under earlier versions of Windows, take the following steps:

1. Open Control Panel and double-click Network.

2. Select the Identification tab and modify the names, as needed, for Computer (the PC you're using) and Workgroup (the name of your network).

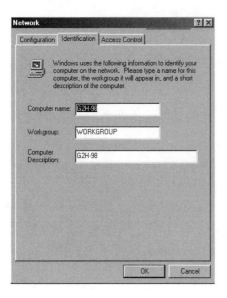

3. Click OK.

Sharing Folders and Printers Among PCs

The way you enable other PCs on your network to open and execute files on another system is by sharing folders. By default, such sharing is turned off, so you need to turn it on if you want this capability available.

You can share the entire contents of a disk drive and all its folders, or you can just share a particular folder. You can also share a printer that's connected to just one PC on your network.

To share folders and/or a printer, enable File and Printer Sharing for your system if it's not already set (Windows XP sets this automatically, but other versions may not, depending on how you had your system/network configured before you installed them). To do this, take the following steps on Windows XP:

1. From Control Panel, double-click Network Connections.

2. Under LAN or High-Speed Internet, double-click Local Area Connection.

3. Click Properties and choose the General tab.

4. Be sure that File and Printer Sharing for Microsoft Networks is installed. If not, click Install and then click Service. Click File and Printer Sharing for Microsoft Networks to check it and then click Install.

For earlier versions of Windows, take these steps instead:

1. From Control Panel, double-click Network.

2. Check to be sure File and Printer Sharing is listed. If it's not listed, click Add and then add this listing.

After you reinstall Windows or even if you add a new hard drive and you want to share it, you should

- Check to be sure that the folders you shared are still enabled for sharing.
- If you format and do a fresh installation, set up initial folders to share.

To set these up initially, perform the following steps or use the steps described earlier to share a folder or drive:

1. From Windows Explorer, locate the folder you want to share.

2. Right-click that folder and choose Sharing and Security (or Properties and then the Sharing tab).

3. Under Network Sharing and Security, click to check Share This Folder on the Network.

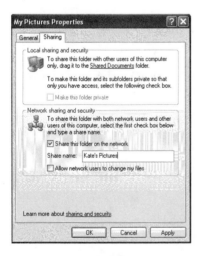

4. Under Share Name, enter a unique name for this folder to help distinguish it for those looking at the folder from another PC on your network.

5. Click Allow Network Users to Change My Files if you want others to be able to modify your files from their PCs on your network. Click OK.

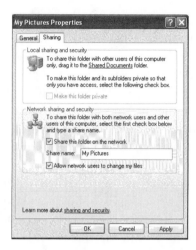

If you've previously shared a printer on your network and you're now having problems printing (usually, the job simply sits there, not printing), verify that the printer is still shared by taking the following steps:

1. Choose Start ➤ Settings (or Control Panel) ➤ Printers (or Printers and Faxes).

2. Locate the printer you want to share, right-click it, and then choose Sharing.

3. From the Sharing tab, verify that Share This Printer is selected (the Share name can be changed, as desired, by clicking on the name and modifying it). If not, click to select it. Click OK.

NOTE *You can follow the same basic steps to share a printer, too.*

Sharing an Internet Connection on the Network

It's useful for network troubleshooting to understand what happens when you share an Internet connection over your network. Usually, the situation is this: One computer is set up as the gateway, meaning that it has the Internet connection installed to it. The gateway is configured to communicate with your Internet service provider (such as America Online, EarthLink, or MSN) and to provide a threshold through which other PCs on your network can connect to the provider. Each other PC on the network has a network adapter installed and connected through a cable or other means and is configured to look to the gateway as the provider of its Internet connection.

Special software is used to allow this communications-sharing relationship to happen. Many Windows customers since Windows 98 use Internet Connection Sharing (ICS) built into Windows. Other users, including myself because my satellite Internet service software doesn't work well with ICS, use a *proxy*. A proxy allows an Internet connection coming into one PC to act as a proxy so that the other PCs in the network can communicate with the Internet.

Recording Your Configuration Information

Again, it's important to document your network settings before you experience problems that affect your ability to connect from one PC to another or from one PC out to the Internet. Before you start, be aware that the information you jot down for your gateway PC (the one with the direct connection to the Internet if you're sharing a high-speed connection) may be far more detailed than that of the PCs sharing its connection, which may automatically acquire their settings.

The steps for recording your network configuration go like this:

1. From Control Panel, double-click Network or Network Connections.

2. For those with earlier versions of Windows, proceed to step 3. For those with Windows XP, double-click Local Area Connection. From the General tab, click Properties.

3. Choose the General tab under Local Area Connection properties and view each of the items listed there: Client for Microsoft Networks, File and Printer Sharing for Microsoft Networks, QoS Packet Scheduler, and Internet Protocol (TCP/IP).

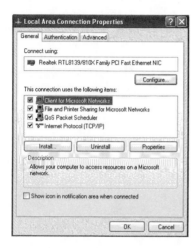

4. Select Internet Protocol (TCP/IP) and click Properties.

5. Review each tab. Any information listed under the tabs in Internet Protocol (TCP/IP) is especially important, including the information you see by clicking the Advanced button.

6. Repeat for each PC on your network, documenting it as you go and clearly marking which settings belong to which PC.

To get a snapshot of your connection details, take these steps on Windows XP:

1. From Control Panel, double-click Network Connections.

2. Double-click Local Area Connection.

3. Choose the Support tab and click Details.

4. Jot down the connection information listed here into your PC journal.

```
Network Connection Details                    [?][X]

Network Connection Details:

Property              Value
Physical Address      00-40-2B-33-47-D0
IP Address            192.168.0.2
Subnet Mask           255.255.255.0
Default Gateway       192.168.0.1
DHCP Server           192.168.0.1
Lease Obtained        9/8/2002 2:13:41 PM
Lease Expires         9/12/2002 2:13:41 PM
DNS Server            192.168.0.1
WINS Server


                                      [ Close ]
```

An Ounce of Prevention

Just as you learned about keeping your physical computer setup safe from external damage, dry, and clean in Chapter 3, you must do the same for your network, even if it branches out from one room to other rooms in your home and office. Make sure you have

- Adequate power protection (covered in detail in Chapter 11, "Avoiding Power and Over-heating Problems")

- A way to kill power quickly in the event of a storm or other disaster such as fire or water

- A way to keep your hardware out of high-traffic areas

Besides these measures, there are a few more factors to consider.

If you have network cable that runs across a large room or into multiple rooms, secure the cable so that you and others won't walk on it or become tangled in it, that you aren't dragging wheeled desk chairs over it, and that a powerful floor-cleaning device can't damage it. I'll spare you the story about how my floor wax buffing machine turned one cable into expensive but colorful spaghetti.

Always use good-quality pre-crimped network cable or buy the crimping tool (along with some extra cable and RJ-45 connectors) and learn to do it properly yourself. You need some hand-arm strength and an eye for detail to punch them together properly, but the more you do it, the easier it becomes. It's important to know that your cable is apt to take a hit before anything else on your network, simply because it often gets itself into harm's way or wasn't crimped properly.

Your life will be much easier if you buy equipment listed in the Microsoft Hardware Compatibility List (`www.microsoft.com/hcl`) and rated to work with the networking supported by your version of Windows. This way, you'll waste less time troubleshooting incompatibilities while you're wondering if your problem is due to defective hardware or a bad configuration.

Extend that care to your system itself and beware what software you install. Many high-speed Internet access carriers, for example, require you to use special software to configure and connect with their service. Installing conflicting software can make your life miserable. I've run into software that couldn't be entirely erased without starting my system from scratch; that's a problem to avoid when you can.

The Essentials of Network Troubleshooting

When you encounter a problem or experience a disaster on networked PCs, it's important to figure out whether the problem is limited to one node on the network or whether the problem is network-wide.

The most logical way to troubleshoot this is to first look individually at each PC on the network using the technical troubleshooting techniques described in other chapters like Chapter 6, "Transforming Yourself into a Smart Troubleshooter." As part of this, you should disconnect each networked PC from the network to test it separately.

Once you've determined that each PC appears to be running well on its own and the configuration information looks right, then look at the network itself.

What to Check First

As usual, the most obvious issues are the first you should check. These include

Network cable   This is especially important when you're using new, untested network cable or older and much-trod-upon network cable that has worked in the past. Always check the quality of your cabling whenever you have a problem. A crimp, a cut, or other damage to the cable and its connector could keep the networked PCs from communicating with one another.

TIP *Always have spare cables and connectors on hand. They'll allow you to add another machine to the network and to swap out a cable for troubleshooting. However, make sure the spare cable works before you use it for a test.*

If you made the cable yourself using CAT-5 cable, a device called a *crimper*, and a connector such as an RJ-45, be sure you have the orientation correct. If the connector is put on backwards (and it can be), it won't work.

Cable to network adapter   Verify that the cable running from the hub or switch or other PC to the network adapter is free of damage and is firmly connected to the network adapter.

Cable to other devices   Repeat the previous step to be sure the cables and connectors to other devices are fine.

Status of all devices   If you're using a device like a network hub that allows you to plug several computers/network devices into a single box, a router, a wireless access device, or other device with power/communication lights, make certain these devices are plugged into power, turned on, and their lights are flashing. If all lights are flashing except those linked to a specific computer, for example, look first at that computer rather than at the entire network.

TIP *The flashing lights that indicate data activity on network hardware really help in troubleshooting. Bad cable, for example, often results in no light being displayed.*

Your network software configuration   Next, look over the software configuration for your network. Compare it to the information you recorded in your PC journal while everything worked well.

The automated troubleshooter   If you're using Windows Millennium or XP, use Help and Support's automated troubleshooter to scan your system and try to resolve the problems it sees in the configuration. To use this tool, follow these steps:

1. Choose Start ➤ Help and Support.

2. Click Use Tools to View Your Computer Information and Diagnose Problems.

3. Click Network Diagnostics.

4. Click Scan Your System.

5. Review your results, looking for anything marked Failed.

The Windows Network Troubleshooter   Follow these steps to run the Windows Network Troubleshooter:

1. Choose Start ➤ Help and Support.

2. Click the Networking and the Web option under Pick a Help topic.

3. From the Networking and the Web window, choose Fixing Networking or Web Problems.

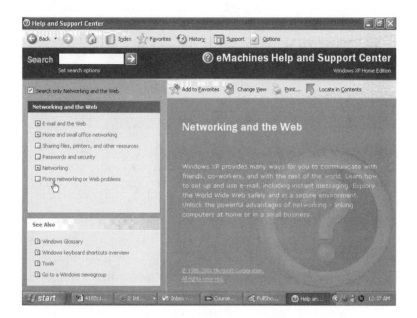

4. Click Home and Small Office Networking Troubleshooter and choose the symptom you're experiencing.

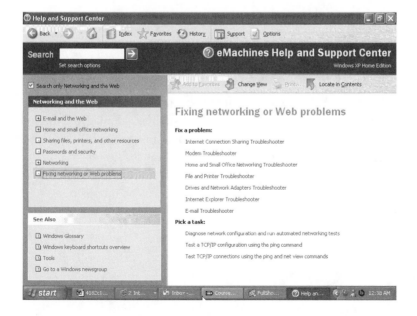

Your network's diagnostics   Many home network kits and network adapters ship with a CD that contains the drivers and required software. They also include special network diagnostic tools for checking your network connectivity. Check your network hardware documentation or the manufacturer's web site for more details.

Your network adapter driver   Be sure to keep your network adapter driver up to date, especially if you're upgrading your version of Windows or making some other substantial change to your PC.

A Cautionary Tale: Don't Assume

The issue of drivers reminds me of something that happened on one of the extra PCs on my network. After upgrading the operating system, which updated my network adapter driver, Windows Update proudly announced to me that I needed to update my driver (again). I thought, "Been there, done that." And I ignored Windows Update's recommendation.

A couple of weeks later, when next I rebooted that system, I noticed I was having problems with the network. It could communicate with the Internet and it could see other computers on my office network, but it was S-L-O-W and seemed to get "lost" frequently (it couldn't find files I knew were there). Someone else had been using the system, so first I scanned for viruses, in case the other person had brought along an infected floppy.

Then, after wracking my brain for several minutes, I remembered the Windows Update driver recommendation and retrieved it. Once the new driver was installed, the network problems completely resolved themselves.

Repairing Network Connections in Windows XP

New in Windows XP is a tool that can help repair certain minor but important problems with a network connection. This clearly won't correct hardware matters such as a damaged Ethernet cable or a non-functioning hub, but it's worth a try for more minor issues, such as a connection that needs to be reset. To use this tool to repair your connection, follow these steps:

1. From Control Panel, double-click Network Connections.

2. Double-click Local Area Connection.

3. Choose the Support tab and click Repair.

4. Check the Repair status window and click OK when the process indicates that it's done.

Checking Network Connectivity

The `ping` command is the most common way to check whether a particular IP address is a viable connection. The `ping` command sends a packet of information from one computer to another across a network and then waits for a reply, as if the other computer said, "I got it, thanks!"

NOTE *You can find more information about Network Connectivity issues and related matters under Windows Help or Help and Support, depending on your version of Windows.*

To use the `ping` command, you need to know the IP address (discussed in a moment) of the computer you are trying to reach. For example, you might need to check the connection between your PC and a PC in your house that acts as the gateway for your Internet connection. Or, you might need to check if the gateway PC is communicating properly with another PC, so you'll need the IP address of that other PC on your network.

Here's how to use the `ping` command:

1. Choose Start ➤ Run.

2. Type **cmd** and click OK or Run to launch the Command Console.

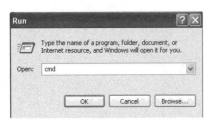

3. At the Command Console prompt, type the following:

ping *xxx.xxx.xxx.xxx*

where **XXX.XXX.XXX.XXX** is the IP address (such as 192.168.0.1)

```
C:\WINDOWS\System32\cmd.exe                                    _ □ x
Microsoft Windows XP [Version 5.1.2600]
(C) Copyright 1985-2001 Microsoft Corp.

C:\Documents and Settings\Kate>ping 192.168.0.1
```

4. Press Enter and view the results that appear on the screen.

```
Pinging 192.168.0.1 with 32 bytes of data:

Reply from 192.168.0.1: bytes=32 time<1ms ITL=128
Reply from 192.168.0.1: bytes=32 time<1ms ITL=128
Reply from 192.168.0.1: bytes=32 time<1ms ITL=128
Reply from 192.168.0.1: bytes=32 time<1ms ITL=128

Ping statistics for 192.168.0.1:
    Packets: Sent = 4, Received = 4, Lost = 0 (0% loss),
Approximate round trip times in milli-seconds:
    Minimum = 0ms, Maximum = 0ms, Average = 0ms
```

If you're seeing lost packets (the number of packets sent is less than the number of packets received), something may be interfering with the data moving along your network. This could be due to several factors:

- A network cable malfunctioning because your foot is now standing on it

- Lots of other activity currently on your network

- A possible bad configuration

If none of the packets sent are received, check the configuration of the computer you're pinging and make sure all the settings are the same as when it worked (as recorded in your PC journal).

You can also perform the **ping** command using a computer's name. You take the same steps as if you're using the IP address, but substitute the name of the computer for the IP address.

All versions of Windows support a number of network-checking command-line tools, like ping, that help you troubleshoot your TCP/IP connections, including the following:

IPConfig   Use IPConfig to display the current TCP/IP configuration settings; run the IPConfig /all command to get a detailed report, as illustrated in Figure 14.4.

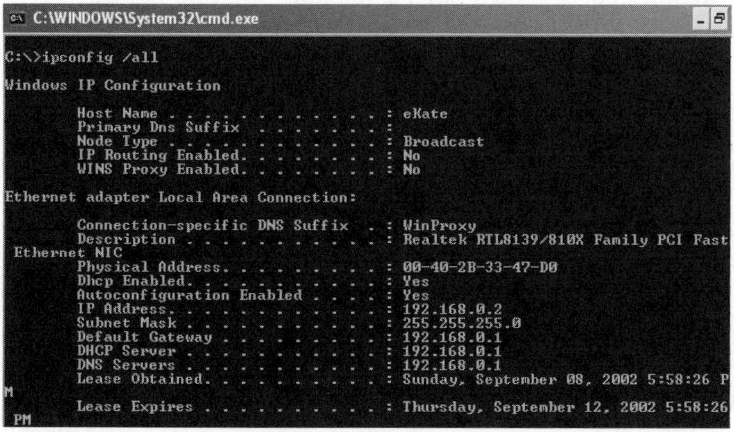

Figure 14.4 *Results of using the* IPConfig /all *command*

Tracert   The Tracert **IP-address** command allows you to examine the route a packet takes to and from the other computer.

TIP *Search on TCP/IP under Help and Support (or in Windows Help for earlier versions) to learn more.*

Common Network Mini-Disasters

This section explains how to approach the most common mini-disasters you may encounter with your network or its components.

When Your Network Adapter Isn't Detected

Getting your PC to detect a network adapter is usually one of the easier steps involved in having a network. There are at least three possible scenarios and solutions:

New Network Adapters

If the network adapter is brand new to the system and was never installed before, check the physical installation of the network adapter. You can try moving a PCI-connected network adapter into another open PCI slot, but make sure the adapter is firmly seated and secured into place (usually with a screw).

If the network adapter is built into the motherboard, check the BIOS to be sure this feature isn't disabled. If it is disabled, enable it and try again.

Should these steps fail, use the Add Hardware wizard in Control Panel. Choose the option to tell Windows what device you are installing and then provide the driver for your network adapter to see if the PC will detect the new adapter.

In addition, check Device Manager to be sure you haven't exhausted your available supply of IRQs because a network adapter usually takes one IRQ. However, since it's PCI, it can typically be shared with another PCI device. If you're out of IRQs, you may have to remove a device that uses an IRQ the network adapter can use. Try a different network adapter before you do this; it might be more tolerant of sharing an IRQ with another device.

Existing Network Adapters

You encounter a thornier problem when you have a network adapter in your system that was working, but now it's no longer detected or it's marked as disabled. It doesn't respond to your best attempts to restore it to service.

Was the network adapter installed at the time of a disaster? If so, the network adapter may be damaged and require replacement. Your best indication of this is if you install a new network adapter and it's detected immediately.

NOTE *Make sure any new network adapter you buy is compatible with your version of Windows and with the type of network you're running.*

If you're unaware of any precipitating event that caused the network adapter to disappear or become disabled, update your network adapter's driver. You may also want to

1. Remove the network adapter entry in Device Manager.

2. Shut down the PC, disconnect power, remove the cover, and ground yourself.

3. Remove the installed network adapter.

4. Reconnect power and let the system start without the adapter or its driver, then shut down the PC again, disconnect power, and replace the network adapter, perhaps in a different slot.

5. Restore power one more time, turn the PC on, and see if the network adapter is now detected.

Integrated Network Adapter

As mentioned earlier, check the BIOS Setup to be sure the network adapter has not been unintentionally disabled. If it is, you need to re-enable it and see if the on-board network function now works and is detected. You should also reinstall or update the network adapter driver.

If none of these steps fix the problem, it's possible that the integrated network feature is damaged. You may be able to restore network connections by installing a separate PCI network adapter and disabling, in the BIOS (just to be sure it doesn't "recuperate" enough to interfere), the on-board adapter altogether.

In the worst case scenario, you may have to replace the motherboard.

When Your First, Second, and Third Network Adapters Aren't Detected

Here's a nasty situation that occasionally happens after a disaster has forced you to buy a new system or replace an existing network adapter. You install a network adapter. You can't seem to get it to work, so you try another, and then another until you begin to wonder, "What are the odds I have so many defective network adapters?"

Statistically, your chances of that are pretty low (although not non-existent). Instead, it's time to think about more likely possibilities, such as

- Your hardware configuration may have changed. If so, set up your system as close as possible to the way it was before, using the same make and model of network adapter.

- You're using the same bad cable each time. If so, swap the existing cable for another length of cable that you know works.

- Settings already configured in your system, usually through Windows, aren't releasing the information about your original network adapter and/or other hardware, so it can't accept the new one.

The first two situations are self-explanatory, so let's talk about the third situation because it involves some painstaking troubleshooting. The best way to troubleshoot configuration is to take the following steps, which assume you've already documented your working networking settings:

1. Shut down and restart your system in Safe Mode as described in Chapter 6.

2. Choose Start ➤ Settings ➤ Control Panel ➤ System ➤ Device Manager (or Start ➤ Control Panel ➤ System ➤ Hardware ➤ Device Manager in Windows XP). Check each entry for duplicate or non-existent devices and remove those you find.

3. Shut down the PC, disconnect it from power, and remove the network cable from its connection at the back of the PC. Open the case and, using your anti-static wrist strap, remove your network adapter. (If the network adapter is integrated into the motherboard, check your documentation for instructions on disabling it.) Set the adapter aside in a safe, clean, dry place or return it to its original anti-static bag.

4. Restore power to your PC and turn it on.

5. Once the system reboots normally, check Device Manager again, looking particularly for conflicts or failures identified by yellow exclamation points or red X marks.

6. Shut down the PC once more, disconnect power, ground yourself, and carefully reinstall your network adapter (or enable a motherboard-based network option). Reconnect the network cable to it, as illustrated in Figure 14.5.

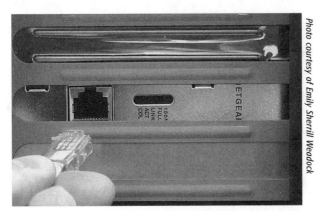

Figure 14.5 *Connecting the Ethernet cable to the adapter connector at back of PC*

7. Now, reconnect power and restart the PC. (You can replace the cover before this step or wait until you're sure everything works.)

8. Configure your network settings again, per your journal's recorded information.

When You Can't "See" a PC on the Network

When you can't "see" a PC on the network, the first things to look for are

- The PC you can't "see" has a network adapter installed and Device Manager lists it without red or yellow marks on it indicating a problem.

- This same PC is configured properly.

- The network cable connecting this system to the rest of the network works.

Wake-on-LAN

One great tip I read recently (at www.practicallynetworked.com) suggests a problem I've never run into but other people have told me they have: a problem with *Wake-on-LAN (WoL)*, sometimes called Wake-on-Ring.

The WoL feature is another part of power management that's designed to wake a dormant system whenever there is activity on the network. Many new PCs have at least one WoL-compatible PCI slot on the motherboard or they have it programmed into the networking hardware that's built into the motherboard.

The problem comes when you have WoL enabled (usually, this is a Power Management option in the BIOS Setup) but

- You use a network adapter (or its driver) that doesn't fully support this feature.

- Your operating system's version of the WoL feature doesn't match the functionality of your PC's.

These situations can lead to a network adapter that isn't recognized by the rest of the network or that can't maintain a connection with the rest of the network.

You may want to disable WoL in your BIOS Setup unless and until you have a network adapter that is better suited to working with this feature.

When You Can't Get Any PC to Connect to the Internet

If you can't get any PC on your network to connect to the Internet, it's probably because you haven't configured the gateway correctly. The gateway, as you'll recall, provides the Internet connection to the other PCs on your network.

Double-check that all of your settings are configured exactly as you documented them when the systems were able to connect to the Internet. Then, once you have the gateway PC communicating with the Internet, check to see if the other PCs now connect, too. If not, point them to the correct IP address for the gateway PC called the default gateway (often, this is 192.168.0.1). You can check your default gateway by looking on your primary connection system (the PC directly connected to the Internet), and by checking properties under Connections/LAN under Windows XP, use the Windows Start ➤ Run and type in WINIPCFG.

Also, are you using Internet Connection Firewall (ICF) or another firewall? (A *firewall*, in this case, is software written to block unwanted access to your PC or home network from outside parties.) You should not have a firewall installed on any system on your network except the gateway PC, and even then, you must take particular care to configure it to allow the right mix of protection and access. You may want to disable your firewall until your connection is working properly. Then re-enable it with care.

When You Can't Get One PC to Connect through the Network to the Internet

If you can't get one PC on your network to connect to the Internet, then a bad configuration is the most likely culprit. If you have more than one PC that gets its Internet connection from another PC that's directly connected, compare the configuration of the one that can't connect against the one that does. A damaged or bad cable could also be at fault.

Again, make sure you're not currently using a firewall. If you are, disable it first to see if this is the cause of your connection issues.

When You Can't Access Another PC's Files or Printer

If you can't access the files or printer of a PC on your network, the mostly likely reason is that File and Printer Sharing for Microsoft Networks hasn't been enabled on the other PC or you've forgotten to share these folders or devices. Review the issues discussed in the section "Sharing Folders and Printers Among PCs."

When You Suspect TCP/IP Is Corrupted

Once you've checked all your hardware and software, you may wonder if somehow your TCP/IP setup has become corrupted. Because the Network Connection window contains options such as Install and Uninstall, you may think that you can uninstall your TCP/IP protocol. But you'll find that you cannot uninstall it because it's one of XP's core components. (In earlier versions of Windows, you can remove TCP/IP and reinstall it from the Network icon in Control Panel and you may want to try this if you suspect that TCP/IP may be corrupted, which it might be if you receive error messages related to TCP/IP.)

However, you can reinstall—and thereby reset—TCP/IP using the NetShell utility that's included with Windows XP. Take the following steps and use the Command Console:

1. Choose Start ➤ Run.

2. Type **cmd** and click OK to launch the Command Console.

3. At the Command Console prompt, type the following command:

```
netsh int ip reset C:\logs\newtcp.txt
```

4. Press Enter.

Note that the name **newtcp.txt** in the **netsh** command is the name of the log file created by this operation. You must specify a name for the log file for the command to execute, but you can use any name you like. I created a **Logs** folder just to place extra log files like this that I generate during troubleshooting. Such log files can be opened using any text viewer like Notepad or WordPad.

> **NOTE** *This steps performed above will reset Windows Registry entries for TCP/IP in a manner that approximates the results you would get if you uninstalled and reinstalled TCP/IP.*

One important tool at your disposal in resolving both PC and small network disasters is your access to the Internet so you can check information. In the next chapter, I'll tell you about some of the types of online help available through the Internet, and how to find what you need.

CHAPTER 15

Finding Help Online

If you're new to using online technical support, you may think that the Internet is just bursting with the type of information you need. This is true, but only to some extent.

The dot-com failures and the tough economic climate in technical companies of the last few years have shrunk the free, expert-help web sites that were so popular in the late 1990s. Many companies, even those that conduct much of their support and sales online, have cut back on online technical support. Online services like CompuServe and MSN, which used to maintain active resources for users with questions, no longer have them or have reduced them to shadows of their former selves.

Making it harder still is the fact that much of our computer hardware is not manufactured in the U.S. What this means is that you may find yourself referred to a web site for product details that appear only in Taiwanese or Chinese. And it's not like this material was easy to comprehend in English or gets easier if you have to read the labels on a diagram written in another language.

Even when you can find a good site, you may have to be a subscriber to access the best material or it's been written for someone with a graduate degree from Caltech. After all the years I've been doing this type of work, my eyes rapidly glaze over if I'm trying to learn one thing and I get treated instead to a long, highly technical discourse on voltage.

But there is good material to be found—in some cases, more than you'll have time to sift through. There are still some support sites that strive to answer your most difficult questions in a matter of hours. Other sites may offer a wealth of info on configuring a device or troubleshooting an installation; you just need to know where to find them and how to use them to your best advantage.

The better prepared you are with information about your technical problems, the better the quality of help you'll receive. Attitude matters, too, because it takes time to find what you need, and you have to be willing to do some reading and note the suggestions you find.

This chapter explains the places you can go online to get assistance, what you need to know, and what features you'll typically find at these sites. In addition, this chapter looks at some of Windows XP's new options for online assistance.

Before You Ask, Be Prepared

Although Chapter 18, "Knowing When to Call Professionals," talks about this subject in more detail, let me offer a suggestion before you look for online help, especially if you're planning to use newsgroups or the technical help chat rooms at manufacturer web sites and online services. This suggestion also works well before making calls to customer service.

Prepare a brief statement (2–5 paragraphs is usually best) in which you talk about

- What kind of system you have

- What operating system and version you use

- The symptoms you're experiencing (including the exact wording of any error messages or on-screen warnings)

- What you may have done (added, changed, or removed) since the last time everything worked properly

- What else you've already tried and what results you got from those attempts

- Any other relevant information such as previous problems of a similar nature

Being prepared will make it easier to provide the facts to those assisting you, while making it less likely you'll forget something important. And if type up your problem in a program like Notepad, then you can simply cut and paste the information into a post that you leave at several different help sites.

Here's an example of a well-detailed posting to a message board asking for help:

Hi and hope you can help.

My Celeron 1.4GHz running Windows 98 has three drives installed, including two hard drives: a 60GB IBM and a 20GB Seagate.

Now the 60GB drive is seen and works fine and is the larger drive. However, the smaller drive is only seen as being 8GB in size rather than the 20GB it actually has.

Both drives are FAT32 and if my BIOS can see the first, larger drive correctly (and it does), I don't understand why it's got the other drive wrong.

One other thing: the 20GB Seagate came out of a PC that was totaled in a flood. The drive was checked by a technician after the disaster and checked out fine. Here, it's detected and works fine except for the size issue.

Any ideas?

Thanks.

Information You Should *Not* Give Out

When asking for help in chat rooms or posting online in message boards and newsgroups, there is some information you should *never* give out, especially in public areas. This includes

- Your home telephone number

- Unique identifying information such as your name, your home address, and *never* your Social Security number

- Your product serial number

- Your banking/credit card number

First, you may not know exactly who the person is on the other end of the line (online or telephone). Second, there are companies that exist just to extract private information from online postings to sell to marketers and other businesses.

Types of Online Resources

In the old days, the places to go online to get technical help were the tried-and-true online services like CompuServe and MSN, and for a few years, America Online, before it stopped providing support for products other than its own software. In addition, users frequented bulletin board systems (BBSes) where you used your modem to dial into company numbers (often at long-distance prices) to check information and download drivers.

Today, of course, almost everything is centralized on the World Wide Web, where you'll find three major types of online technical resources:

Manufacturer-based   These sites are usually run by the company manufacturing or distributing your product. These sites are almost always free.

Other commercial/public   Many online technical communities are offshoots of online services, publishing companies (such as ExtremeTech run by Ziff-Davis and ZDNet run by CNET), or peer sites that are partially supported by manufacturers and/or advertisers. These sites typically don't require a membership fee, but may insist that you register (provide your name, address, and e-mail) before you post questions or access its content.

Peer-to-peer   Peer-to-peer sites take a more person-to-person approach in offering technical help. They provide text help for hardware and software troubleshooting and answer questions in message board or chat areas on their personal/small office web sites. Most of these are free, but a few involve users who bid for help ("I'll pay $5 to the first person who can tell me how…") or users who pay a small subscription fee.

Let's look at what you can expect to find on manufacturer-based web sites. Then I'll explain how non-manufacturer sites differ slightly.

NOTE *As I talk about the features of technical support sites, please understand that these sites differ widely from each other and they change their formats frequently. You might find one that has a live, help chat room one month and then discover that feature is no longer there the next month.*

Manufacturer-Based Online Support

Some of the best manufacturer sites look rather boring when you first open them in your browser. Some of the flashiest sites actually have the least to offer, perhaps because they spent their budget on fancy web effects rather than on smart people to write useful help.

But don't let first appearances form your judgment when you visit manufacturer web sites looking for technical support. Dig beneath the surface and be prepared to spend time looking around to see what may be available.

The exact names of the features may vary from site to site, but most manufacturer sites offer the following:

- Online product registration

- Product information and manuals

- Drivers and downloads

- Frequently asked questions (FAQs)

- Support options, including

  - Message boards or newsgroups

  - Live chat

  - E-mail to a technical-support representative

  - Online analysis

  - Other support options

Besides these, most sites contain a Search option that allows you to search the site based on a word, phrase, or even a product name or model number.

NOTE *While many users think immediately of hardware when considering manufacturer sites, most major products—from Windows (*`www.microsoft.com/windows`*) to specialty software—have sites offering some level of help.*

Online Product Registration

Online product registration offers you a slight advantage over filling out, stamping, and returning those product registration postcards included with most electronics and computer hardware. Many manufacturers allow you to register your product online during your first visit.

A few companies require you to register a purchased product before you get full access to the rest of their web site. The overwhelming majority, however, make their sites public, so you don't have to show proof of purchase to use them.

Product Information and Manuals

For most hardware and software products, the days of fat manuals with detailed diagrams and useful suggestions have long passed. Extensive product documentation costs money to develop, print, and ship, so this was an early casualty in the war to make PCs cheaper. To be fair, most companies realized that many users don't bother to read the manuals.

Fear not, however. Some of those same companies have realized that it's far less expensive to publish their manuals and product specifications online at their web sites, viewable using something like Adobe Acrobat Reader, software that's often installed already on new PCs or can be easily downloaded. You'll often find more extensive information in the online manual than you will with the product itself. So even if you get a manual with your product, check the online version, which may have been updated since yours was printed. Figure 15.1 contains one of Western Digital's online manuals.

TIP *Obviously, the manufacturer's site is the best place to check if you've lost the manual you received with the product.*

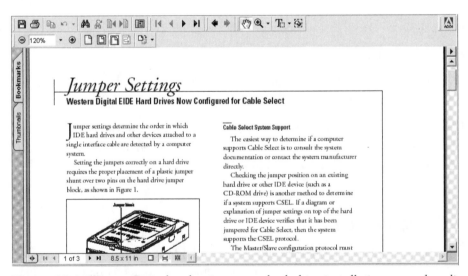

Figure 15.1 *Western Digital makes it easy to check drive installation manuals online.*

Drivers and Downloads

Recall that Chapter 2, "How Your Hardware, Operating System, and Applications Work Together," explained that PC hardware may sit on a shelf for months or longer before you bring it home, which can present a problem when the driver(s) packed with that device become seriously outdated.

The manufacturer's web site is an ideal place to download the most recent driver version. And sometimes you can also find updated companion software there for download as well. Figure 15.2 shows the downloads available at Creative Labs' technical support site.

Before downloading a file from a web site, take these precautions:

- Make sure what you download and install is for your exact product and is compatible with your version of Windows.

- Read any instructions or notes posted on the site regarding what you download.

- Carefully follow the instructions for installing it.

When the product is software, many manufacturer sites let you, as a registered owner of the product (or someone who wants to try it out), download a full working copy or a trial demo of the most recent version of that software. You can also get patches and add-ons, depending on the site, the product, and the manufacturer.

Figure 15.2 *Use the Download Drivers section on sites like this to find drivers and software.*

Frequently Asked Questions (FAQs)

Found on technical sites all over the Internet and on manufacturer sites, Frequently Asked Questions (FAQs) lists are just what you might guess: a list of the questions asked most often about a particular subject. Most sites offer many FAQs, covering a wide variety of issues on the same topic.

The quality of FAQs varies, but they can be an excellent resource for problems you're currently having and problems other users may be having with a particular product or feature that you should be aware of. Sometimes it's easy to see that the questions being answered in the FAQs are ones that could have been answered from reading the product documentation. Other questions may alert you to incompatibilities between this product and others, to early warning signs of failure, or to limitations of the product itself.

Other Support Options

You may run into other features at manufacturers' web sites, including message boards or newsgroups, chat, an e-mail link to customer support, and online analysis.

Message Boards or Newsgroups

A message board is often likened to an electronic bulletin board, where questions, comments, and announcements are posted as individual messages in a special area of a web site. As these messages generate new comments and questions (in the form of replies), these individual messages become tied together into a *thread*, a progressive text conversation. Major threads are grouped into folders to organize what is often a very busy manufacturer message base.

There are message boards everywhere:

- manufacturer web sites
- online services like America Online and MSN
- government web sites
- newspaper and magazine sites
- simple "home" sites

On a manufacturer's site, your posts are apt to be answered by customer service representatives for that company. On non-manufacturer sites, a mix of different people (knowledgeable and not) respond to user questions.

Later in this chapter, in the section "Asking for Help in the Expert Zone," you'll see the details of one message board.

Understand that different sites use many different types of message board software, so how you use them may change from site to site. Always look for a Help or Message Board Tutorial link in a message board area for instructions. Most boards have certain rules that are clearly posted, for example, no profanity or no advertising.

Newsgroups are also collections of messages, much like message boards. However, unlike message boards that are based on web sites, newsgroups follow a specific non-web format for message exchange. This means you need a newsreader rather than a web browser to read newsgroups (Outlook Express has a newsreader, for example). You need to configure your newsreader to look at a particular newsgroup server to send and receive messages for that newsgroup.

However, newsgroups aren't the most common way people share messages today; message boards dominate. Those web sites that offer newsgroups tend to offer them in a web-based format.

Live Chat

You often see live chats on computer shopping sites, where you can talk with a customer representative about a purchase you're considering. But several manufacturers and technical support web sites offer a chat room feature as well.

A chat room, if you've never been in one, is simply a program that opens up a direct or indirect connection between two or more persons who can then type back and forth in the same window. This is faster than exchanging e-mail or using a network messaging program like ICQ or Windows Messenger.

E-mail to Support Representative

Most manufacturer web sites allow you to e-mail a question directly to support staff. Unfortunately, this isn't always the fastest option to use for help. Support staff answer e-mail messages around their other duties, so it can takes days or weeks to get a response.

If you need a faster answer, try posting to appropriate message boards in the hope that other users will jump in and help you within a matter of hours (most respond within 48 hours). However, if you need an immediate answer, call the manufacturer's technical support phone line.

Online Analysis

A few manufacturers and technical sites offer a feature that can test certain problems on your PC, including your Internet connection, modem speed, hard drive speed, or video capability. This analysis evaluates how well their product (or someone else's product that you're considering replacing with their product) performs.

This analysis can be similar to the benchmark tests I told you about in Chapter 12, "PC Performance: Diagnosing, Monitoring, and Troubleshooting Problems."

Other Support Options

Finally, most manufacturers' sites offer a variety of ways to contact the company for more assistance, including fax numbers, other contact e-mail addresses, or special phone numbers for serious problems and/or product returns.

Finding Your Manufacturer's Technical Support Site

Since it's in a company's best interest to be easy to find, always try the most obvious domain name. For example, you can find Dell Computer at **www.dell.com** and IBM at **www.ibm.com**. If your manufacturer doesn't make it easy, use a web search engine such as Google (**www.google.com**) and search on words you think will identify it, such as the product name and/or the company name. Table 15.1 provides a list of some major computer manufacturers and their web sites.

Table 15.1   *Major Computer Manufacturers' Web Sites*

MANUFACTURER	URL
3Com	www.3com.com
Advanced Micro Devices	www.amd.com
ATI Technologies	www.atitech.com
Compaq	www.compaq.com
Creative Labs	www.creativelabs.com
Dell	www.dell.com
eMachines	www.eMachines.com
Epson	www.epson.com
Gateway	www.gateway.com
Hewlett-Packard	www.hp.com
IBM	www.ibm.com
Intel	www.intel.com
Logitech	www.logitech.com
Quantum	www.quantum.com
U.S. Robotics	www.usr.com
Western Digital	www.wdc.com

Technical Web Site Support

Now that you know the most common help features on manufacturer sites, let's discuss other types of sites, including peer-to-peer and professional and/or commercial sites. Many of these sites offer the same features as manufacturer web sites, including

- Product information (usually for more than one company's products)

- FAQ lists

- Message boards and/or newsgroups

- Drivers and downloads

- Live chat

Figure 15.3 shows you how similar these technical sites are to the manufacturers' support sites. At this free help site, Tech Support Guy, thousands of users have posted questions and received assistance for their problems with various versions of Windows, hardware components, and software utilities.

Figure 15.3 *Busy message bases at the Tech Support Guy forums*

The main difference between the manufacturer sites and the other technical sites is that while the manufacturer focuses on its own products, a non-manufacturer site addresses a wide range of products, if not everything about a PC. Thus, you're freer to discuss other manufacturers' products, and often, comment more honestly than you might on the manufacturer's board itself.

Other differences may include special content, such as

- Product reviews and anecdotal experience (pro and con).

- PC industry analysis where users write about different issues like where PC hardware or operating systems are headed in the future.

- How-to articles and tutorials covering a broad range of topics like "How to protect your PC from a storm" or "How to set up your first small network."

- Recommended downloads where collections of utilities that the site's staff considers particularly useful are made available for direct download. Or, the site provides links to other sites for downloading them.

What to Expect from a Technical Support Web Site

How do you tell a good technical support web site from a bad one? Sometimes, your gut instincts alone will alert you when the site seems right for you; for example, you sense you're talking to computer professionals rather than normal mortals.

You might see articles that are no more recent than a few years' old (and of course, PC technology has changed drastically during that time). Or you might notice that articles and help tips refer to hardware and software that's out of date (unless you're using an older PC setup).

Some of the best online technical help sites share these qualities:

- An active message base where most questions get some type of response within 48 hours

- A message base seems to have a lot of return traffic, meaning that people are happy with the level of help offered

- Friendly, easy-to-understand presentation of information (or at least a glossary to help you understand terms they may toss at you)

- Easy navigation

- Easy-to-locate help features

- Useful content (articles, tutorials, help files) that is updated regularly

- Working links within the site and a collection of links to other good technical information sites

- Respect for visitors' privacy and lack of Internet extras like wildly annoying pop–up ads or cookies

- A way to contact the site's staff or designer if you experience problems or spot an error

With that said, please understand that you're likely to run into a number of really good web sites with no glitz or glamour that just present how-to articles based on the writer's own experience. Some of these, like Jon Hildrum's site (`www.hildrum.com`), offer good articles for users still using Windows 95 and 98 that are very helpful to newer users unfamiliar with formatting and reinstalling.

A Glimpse of Online Support Sites

Some of my favorite all-around support sites for consumers are listed here, but you'll find far more once you go online and do a web search. For example, CNET's ZDNet Communities has a large message base for posting questions; they just don't happen to make my list of favorites because I find the level of help offered there hit-or-miss; some of it is very good, but more often, it's unexceptional.

Sadly, many technical help sites go online with wonderfully useful material only to disappear, get purchased by a larger concern, or fall into disrepair because they haven't been well maintained. This makes it hard to recommend good sites that will definitely be in business if you read this six months to a year after I have compiled the list.

But the flip side is that new sites go up all the time, and you can find them using web search engines and by word-of-mouth referrals from your friends, co-workers, and fellow onliners. Visit them when you find them and learn what you can, just in case they aren't there later.

TIP *When you find a good site, check its Links page to find other technical sites they recommend.*

My Favorite Online Help or Information Sites

Here are a few of my favorite online help and information sites:

Expert Zone (`http://www.microsoft.com/windowsxp/expertzone/default.asp`)   Discussed later in this chapter, Expert Zone is an excellent site for posting questions and getting answers on Windows XP.

ExtremeTech (www.extremetech.com)   While they can sometimes get a bit too technical for newer folks, ExtremeTech is one of the best (and newest) all-purpose support sites on the Internet and includes some articles with step-by-step instructions for resolving problems. It's a great site to bookmark and return to when you're looking for specific details or help. It boasts a good message base for posting questions or reading replies and a strong user community.

HowStuffWorks (www.howstuffworks.com)   HowStuffWorks isn't a help site, but some of its articles on PC components like CD recorders, DVD players, and PC video can really help you understand how they work.

Microsoft Knowledge Base (http://search.support.microsoft.com)   Fun reading, it isn't, but I use the Microsoft Knowledge Base frequently to check for details and solutions to problems with all Microsoft products and to look up information about error messages and recommended updates.

PC911 (www.pcnineoneone.com)   A tech friend regularly recommends PC911 to his clients for its wide range of how-to articles written in plain English. On my first visit, I learned something in their message boards that I'd missed in the news about hard drive warranties dropping to as low as a one-year term.

The PC Guide (www.pcguide.com)   While PC Guide isn't updated as frequently as it once was, it still serves as an excellent component-by-component tour of your PC hardware, especially if you're using a Pentium II or earlier PC.

PC Mechanic (www.pcmech.com)   PC Mechanic (see Figure 15.4) is a good site with a particularly strong set of tutorials for building your own PC. You can use these tutorials to get a better handle on your PC hardware. Register with this site, and you can click the Forums option to join the forums to ask questions.

PC Pitstop (www.pcpitstop.com)   Discussed in earlier chapters, this is a good all-around info site, with tools for simple virus checking and other online utilities.

Tech Support Guy Forums (http://forums.techguy.org)   While I'm new to this site, several friends have recommended it for the decent level of help offered in its active message boards.

Figure 15.4 *PC Mechanic offers a mix of how-to tutorials and reviews.*

Windows XP-Only Online Support Options

One feature I particularly admire about Windows XP is that it has finally integrated into Windows Help and Support the support tools that you usually had to know about on your own.

This section identifies these XP-based support options, including ways to get information before you ask for help using the Remote Assistance option to bring someone else in to help you fix your dysfunctional PC. This section also gives you a quick look at the Expert Zone newsgroups that Microsoft makes available for XP users.

Help and Support's System Data Information

Three good sources for collecting information about your system before requesting technical support are found in the Help and Support Center. (This is true to some degree for Windows Millennium, although it's not as detailed or helpful as XP.) These sources are

- My Computer Information

- Advanced System Information

- The System Configuration utility

Let's look at each, since you should be aware of them for troubleshooting purposes and they may save you from calling in the cavalry.

My Computer Information

Choosing this option gives you a profile of the hardware and software installed to your PC. Particularly useful for troubleshooting is the View Status menu selection, the results of which are shown in Figure 15.5.

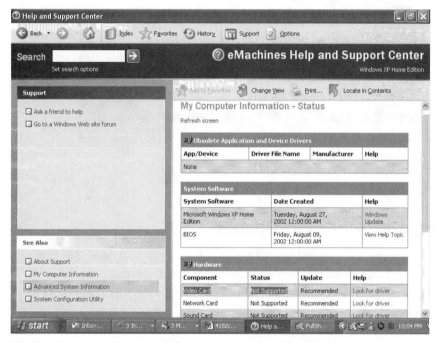

Figure 15.5 *My Computer Information provides information about the hardware and software on your PC.*

To use My Computer Information, take the following steps:

1. Choose Start ➢ Help and Support.

2. Choose Get Support or Find Information in Windows XP Newsgroups.

3. From the left-hand pane under See Also, click My Computer Information.

4. A list appears in the right-hand pane. Click each option to get more information.

Advanced System Information

The information found in Advanced System Information offers the meat-and-potatoes details you need to provide when you go online or call for support. To use this feature, follow these steps:

1. Choose Start ➤ Help and Support.

2. Choose Get Support or Find Information in Windows XP Newsgroups.

3. From the left-hand pane under See Also, click Advanced System Information.

4. Click any of the options listed in the right-hand pane to get more detailed information about your PC configuration.

As you can see in Figure 15.6, the Advanced System Information's Error Log window tells me something I didn't notice before: my CD-RW drive is having a problem that started the very day I pressed the new PC (with the drive) into service. Time to call the manufacturer and complain!

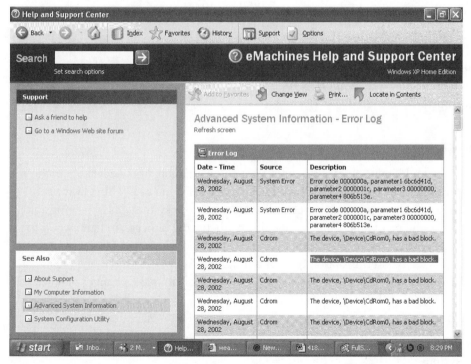

Figure 15.6 *Advanced System Information's View the Error Log option gives you an indication of any problems on your PC.*

System Configuration Utility

The System Configuration utility, discussed in Chapter 7, "Restarting a Problem PC," is used for troubleshooting a cranky PC boot or startup. This utility is also called `MSconfig.exe`.

Requesting Support from Microsoft Online

You can use tools in Windows XP to request a support session from Microsoft. This may or may not be free, depending on how you purchased your copy of XP and whether you've previously contacted Microsoft for support (you get two free calls with XP). When not free, you typically pay a per-incident fee.

One of the bonuses of this option is that Windows automatically checks your system for necessary information and submits it as part of the support request, without extra steps on your part. You may be asked later by Microsoft technicians to check other areas of your PC.

To submit such a request, connect to the Internet and take these steps:

1. Choose Start ➤ Help and Support.

2. Click Get Support or Find Information in Windows XP Newsgroups.

3. Click Get Help from Microsoft.

NOTE *If you don't see this option under Help and Support, your copy of Windows XP may not be eligible for free support, which means you need to call Microsoft directly or use other options.*

Using Remote Assistance

Do you ever wish you could invite an expert—or at least someone more knowledgeable than yourself—into your PC, so to speak, so they could see exactly what you see? Think how useful that could be when you have problems, or even a disaster, with your system. It's like being able to get a troubled car to the mechanic while it's actually misbehaving rather than later, when the mechanic can't imagine what you're talking about.

Professional folks have had this option for some time. PC Anywhere is just one of several commercial packages for letting someone access your PC remotely to make changes or software-based repairs as you would at the system's keyboard.

Windows XP brings this capability to you in the form of two features:

*   Remote Desktop, an option you can install to work on your Windows XP PC from another system

- Remote Assistance, the feature discussed in this section that allows you to invite some-one into your PC to help identify and resolve problems

There are some minimum requirements for using Remote Assistance. It only works if both you and the party you're asking for help use Windows XP. Other requirements are

- You need to know each other, at least in terms of being able to supply each other with contact information for Windows Messenger or e-mail.

- Windows Messenger (or a MAPI-compliant e-mail software such as Microsoft Outlook or Outlook Express) must be installed.

- You must be online at the same time.

- You must be sure you're not using firewalls or other types of Internet protection soft-ware that may not permit the type of direct point-to-point connection Remote Assis-tance uses.

TIP *The Windows Update site (*`http://windowsupdate.microsoft.com`*) includes a fix for helping users who have problems using Remote Assistance with a personal firewall enabled.*

What happens is this: Either through Windows Messenger or e-mail, you send an invitation via Remote Assistance to the person you want to help you. The other party accepts that invita-tion by opening the invitation and clicking Yes. At this point, the other person is connected to your desktop, seeing it pretty much as you do.

Whether the other person has permission to actually do anything (either to repair or modify your PC settings) depends on how you've configured this remote access to work, which I'll talk about next.

Configuring Remote Assistance

To check or modify your Remote Assistance configuration settings, take these steps:

1. Choose Control Panel ➤ System and click the Remote tab.

2. Verify that Allow Remote Assistance Invitations to be Sent From This Computer is checked if you want to permit Windows XP to send an invitation for someone to connect to help you.

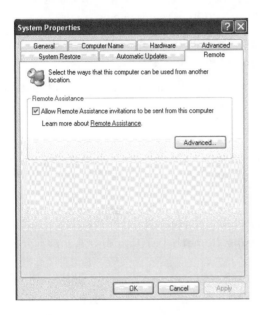

3. Click Advanced.

4. Verify under Remote Control that Allow This Computer to Be Controlled Remotely is checked if you want the assisting party to be able to make changes to your system. If you don't want to give them this level of access, make sure that option is unchecked. Click OK until you exit.

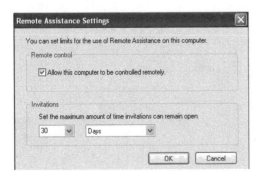

To Send a Remote Assistance Invitation

As you just learned, you need to invite the party to help you, which typically involves sending them an e-mail with the invitation attached. They open the e-mail, click Yes, and connect to you. (Remember to provide them with a password if required for access.)

To send an invitation to someone you know, take these steps:

1. Choose Start ➤ Help and Support.

2. Click Invite a Friend to Connect to Your Computer with Remote Assistance.

3. In the right-hand pane, click Invite Someone to Help You.

4. Below the Windows Messenger option, go to Or Use E-mail and enter the e-mail address of the person you want to ask for help.

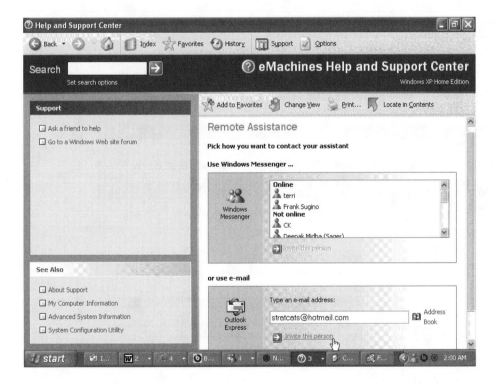

5. Click Invite This Person.

6. On the next screen, make sure your name appears under From as you want it to read. If it doesn't, click the box, delete what's there, and type what you want. Enter a personal message for this invitation, then click Continue.

7. From the E-mail an Invitation screen, click to set the number of hours before your invitation will expire, meaning, the person can no longer accept and be connected to your PC.

8. From the same screen, if you want to require a password for your helper to access your machine (recommended), click to check Require the Recipient to Use a Password. Then type a password and re-type it to verify it.

WARNING *Remember to provide the password to the person you're asking to help or they won't be able to access your PC.*

9. Click Send Invitation.

You may receive a warning from your e-mail program asking if you really want this program to issue an e-mail. If so, click Send.

You should receive a message telling you the invitation was successfully sent. From this same screen, click View Invitation Status. A window appears (see Figure 15.7) that allows you to check to see if the person you asked has accepted or declined your request. From this status window, you can opt to resend the invitation (if time has passed without a response) or click Delete to kill the invitation altogether.

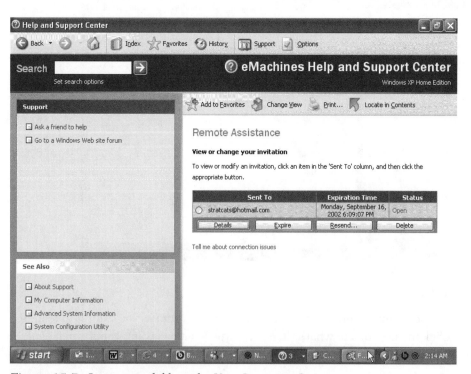

Figure 15.7 *Options available under View Invitation Status*

When the helping party accepts the invitation and successfully connects to your PC, a Remote Assistance window appears asking you if you want to share control of your system with the other party. Once the session is initiated, you and your helper see your desktop slightly differently.

Your helper sees a large window with a slim, left-hand pane where the two of you can chat by typing back and forth. On your helper's right, he or she sees your desktop much as you see it and is able to use it in the same way. You see a similar window, but your taskbar looks different and includes an option to Take Control Back From the Expert.

To end a Remote Assistance session, click Disconnect on your Remote Assistance taskbar.

NOTE *If you're running Windows XP but would like to use something like Remote Assistance, get a copy of PC Anywhere or similar software. However, you and your helper must both have the same software installed and configured. Note that none of this software is apt to help if you can't boot your system.*

A Cautionary Tale: Choose Your Helper Wisely

Forgive my candor here, but I have to say this: Just because someone claims to know more about PCs and Windows than you does *not* mean they are knowledgeable or that they won't (accidentally or intentionally) make a bad situation worse.

Unfortunately, one of the best PC technicians I've ever run into is also someone who, when he gets irritated, deliberately instructs people through steps designed to hurt their systems. One of the worst technicians I've met—and she insists she's Microsoft-certified—still tells people they have to repartition their hard drives to install a new video driver (something I've never found necessary in almost two decades) just because she doesn't seem to know better.

And the scary part is both of these people are frequently found in Internet help chat rooms offering "assistance" to those in need.

But you're apt to know people close to you who think they're PC experts. The road to many PC junkyards is paved with good intentions coupled with really poor help. So choose your assistance carefully, especially in a situation like Remote Assistance where you give them direct power over your PC. You might be better off asking them for recommendations, writing them down, and then checking out that advice (and its possible negative effects) before following them.

Remember to check Help under Remote Assistance for tips on using it, since Remote Assistance should be disabled when you're not actively using it, and you should use it in conjunction with Windows Update to make sure all security patches are current.

Asking for Help in the Expert Zone

The Expert Zone is an area hosted by Microsoft and monitored regularly by a group of super users known as *Microsoft MVPs* and *Associate Experts*. These experts provide online help on various topics and try to answer questions posted in the Expert Zone newsgroups.

Don't mistake this support for Microsoft product support because it's not; few of the folks posting there actually work for Microsoft. They are, however, chosen to help there because they're especially knowledgeable about PCs and Microsoft products. More times than not, they seem to offer significant help to users. And the price is right: free with your Windows XP package, where Expert Zone resides as an online link in Help and Support.

To read newsgroups and post questions in the Expert Zone, follow these steps:

1. Choose Start ➤ Help and Support.

2. Under Ask for assistance, select Get Support or Find Information in Windows XP Newsgroups.

3. Under Support, click Go to a Windows Web Site Forum.

4. From the right-hand pane, click Go to Windows Newsgroups.

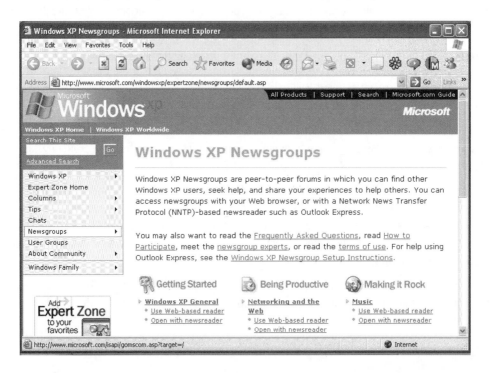

5. Your web browser opens to the Windows XP Newsgroups home page. In the right-hand pane, look for the topic category that matches the problem for which you want help.

6. Under the Windows XP General category, click Use Web-Based Reader.

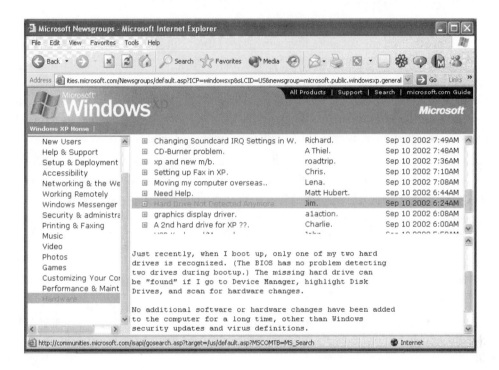

NOTE *You can also choose Open with Newsreader, which opens Outlook Express for those using Internet Explorer as a web browser. Newsreader access is often preferred by users with advanced experience using newsgroups or who have very slow Internet access (since web-based postings can take a long time to load). Web-based readers are preferred by users who are newer to this type of help system.*

7. When the web-based newsgroup opens, the major topic categories appear at the left and the main roster of message folders (groups of messages on a given subtopic) for the chosen topic appear at the right. Look for a folder title that appears to match the problem you have.

TIP *Use the Search button to search the message base for a particular word or group of words.*

8. If you find a post that matches your problem, click the message to preview it in the lower pane to see if there is information in this message post that may help you. (Or, click the + sign, if present, to expand the list of messages.) Click Reply to send a comment to the person posting, as others can reply to a post of yours.

9. Click New Post to create your own message for posting to this area. Fill in your name, your e-mail address, the subject of your message (short but descriptive), and then prepare your message. When done, click Send. Click OK.

WARNING *While some users who answer your question may reply to you via e-mail, don't forget to check back in the newsgroups later for other responses. Add the site to your Favorites list so you can find your way back quickly.*

A Cautionary Tale: Don't Make Them Drag the Info from You

All too often, people go looking online for help, and when they find a place where they feel they can find it, they'll post something like, "My computer is broken. How do I fix it?"

That's all they say, too, which means they don't need a good technician, they need a great technician who is also a psychic. After all, how could anyone make a diagnosis let alone offer a suggestion based on so little information?

Nobody—not the person seeking help or another person trying to offer it—wants to get into a situation where it takes 10 or more posts to get the necessary information presented in such a way that a knowledgeable person can offer suggestions for resolving it.

Whether you go looking for help online in newsgroups/message boards, chats, e-mail, through Remote Assistance, or by calling Customer Service or a local technician, be prepared to state your situation clearly.

The more detailed information you can supply, the more likely you'll get the help you need. Try the suggestions under "Before You Ask" earlier in this chapter, as well as the suggestions in Chapter 18.

The next chapter, "Starting from Scratch the Smart Way," comes after this chapter for a reason: You shouldn't have to start fresh very often. Before you do, explore other options like those found through online support before you consider formatting your disk and reinstalling everything all over again.

But now it's time to consider what you have to do if the only way left seems to be to start fresh.

CHAPTER 16

Starting from Scratch the Smart Way

Now you've reached the point that I often cautioned you to avoid doing prematurely in previous chapters: the time when you decide to wipe the electronic slate clean, so to speak, and start fresh.

Why have I asked you to wait? Because starting from scratch destroys the files already stored on your hard drive. You're wiping everything out so you can completely redo your file system and the Windows installation. You're obliterating your documents, sound files, updated drivers, unique configurations, and Windows customization.

This is *very* significant.

However, sometimes starting from scratch is necessary. This chapter explains in what situations a fresh start may help and takes you through the steps for doing it intelligently and with your best chance for success. You'll also learn why it's smart to stop after you've installed Windows to evaluate your system for performance and stability before installing any applications.

This chapter also covers taking your workplace from your old PC to a new one, offering shopping tips and explaining why you can probably skip that extra warranty.

When to Start from Scratch

There are many good reasons to format your hard drive and reinstall your operating system, your applications, and all those files you've stored elsewhere. Yet starting fresh isn't a magic bullet. There are many problems it won't cure, including

- Problematic or failing hardware (A formatting won't fix a dying hard drive or an overheated CPU.)

- Situations that arise when you reinstall an application or utility that isn't compatible with your version of Windows, your file system (the FAT), or some other component on your system

The Right Situations for Starting from Scratch

There are many good reasons for starting your system with a refreshed hard drive, operating system, and file system:

- You've had numerous problems with your PC and have already systematically ruled out

  - outdated drivers or the wrong type of driver

  - too little memory or the wrong type of memory

  - insufficient disk space

- hardware conflicts

- overheating or power instability

- Windows instability

- You obtain a used PC and want to rid yourself and the PC of the previous owner's junk.

- You have an older system on which your original hard drive has not been reformatted since you first got the PC three or more years ago. This is especially true of older systems, where many operating system and application upgrades have been installed.

- You have a large hard drive that you want to partition to better organize your system and to reduce the amount of time it takes to perform maintenance on a large physical drive. (Partitioning a hard drive divides it into two or more logical drives.)

- You've watched system performance deteriorate over a period of time and the improvements you experience following disk maintenance seem to be less and less dramatic.

- You can no longer use troubleshooting modes such as Safe Mode and Windows XP Recovery Console to successfully load Windows.

- Using the System Restore feature fails to apply a decent working restore point.

- You're a serious download- or install-aholic (or beta tester) and you install and remove programs frequently. You may find it beneficial to reformat the hard drive and start fresh after six months to a year of such practices. This will remove all the extra files and Registry entries that the uninstall utilities for those defunct programs didn't take with them.

- You've experienced file corruption after a virus. Check your drive partition(s) and reformat the affected hard drive if necessary. (The section "Starting Fresh but Stopping Between Steps" discusses this in detail.)

NOTE *Someone asked me the other day if he needed to replace his hard drive because it had been infected with a confirmed virus. This made me realize I've heard that question many times before. It made me wonder if there's a misconception about viruses. A computer virus isn't like a human virus that sometimes leaves its imprint on your genetic code; so long as the PC virus has been properly removed, there is no need to replace the hard drive. Thankfully, viruses that actually damage physical hardware are still seen more in users' overactive imaginations than in day-to-day reality.*

The Wrong Situations for Starting from Scratch

Sadly, there are plenty of erroneous reasons to wipe your hard drive clean and start fresh. Many of them boil down to bad or lazy advice. This kind of advice is offered too quickly when you ask how to fix a problem, and the person, rather than considering a long, detailed process, shoots back with, "Why not format and start all over again?" After all, formatting won't fix a noisy drive or one with persistent errors. It won't cure basic incompatibilities between your PC configuration and your version of Windows, and it won't do a thing to combat overheating, power issues, or operating the PC in a less-than-ideal working environment.

Don't format and start over if

- Your problems are limited to one application or only occur when one program is running. Instead, try to remove (by uninstalling under Add or Remove Programs in Control Panel) the program first to see if this resolves the instability.

- You haven't yet done disk maintenance to improve your PC's performance.

- You haven't tried other measures, including those described in Chapter 9, "Stabilizing Your Operating System," to try to resolve your problems.

- A piece of hardware won't work. Getting the right device driver might work, but reinstalling the operating system probably won't.

- You're in a panic and don't know what else to do.

- You don't have what you need to reinstall your system. (See the section "What You Need to Start Fresh" later in this chapter.)

A Cautionary Tale: Don't Be Hit by Formatter's Remorse

You've no doubt heard of or experienced buyer's remorse. It feels terrible, but you know you can return the item you bought if the remorse gets too acute.

Formatter's remorse is much worse because you can't get back the data you lose by formatting (or normal repartitioning that requires a format), at least not without extreme and often expensive measures such as hiring a data recovery specialist.

Remember how I told you in the last chapter to pick your assistance carefully? In my experience, far too many people suggest you format and start fresh for situations that a) don't require it and b) won't be resolved by it. Such people mean well, but they may be too technically incompetent to even remind you to back up your files before you format.

Continued on next page

A Cautionary Tale: Don't Be Hit by Formatter's Remorse *(Continued)*

During my years helping folks with PC problems, many people came to me each week because they panicked and reformatted (or used those recovery disks that come with new PCs), only to discover later that everything they had created, downloaded, or otherwise saved to their hard drive was lost.

I've heard tragic tales about critical financial or legal papers, one-of-a-kind digital photographs, master's and doctoral degree theses, medical patient records, critical tax records, original plays and novels, and many other precious files disappearing in a moment of blind panic.

If you have software, settings, and files that exist only on your hard drive that you cannot lose, don't reformat or repartition without backing up those files.

Never format in a panic and don't take—or give—a recommendation to format lightly because it won't be a question of *if* you'll lose the files stored on your hard drive; you will.

Before You Start Fresh

Both the act of formatting and the act of partitioning (at least without using third-party software such as PowerQuest's PartitionMagic) a hard disk erases all data on that drive.

With a brand-new hard drive, both formatting and partitioning are required but it matters less because a new hard drive is essentially blank; no data has been written to it yet. With an existing hard drive, all your data will disappear, so you need to store your files to another medium (Zip disk, recordable CD or DVD, or a floppy drive) from which you can retrieve them later.

Backing up your files is not your only concern, although it's an important one. You also need to be aware whether or not your hard drive is using drive-overlay software (discussed shortly). And make sure you have everything you need before you start to format your hard drive.

Backing Up Critical Files

Even if you've been performing regular backups and/or drive images, take a moment to back up anything that may not have been placed in storage since the last time you copied your files.

If you haven't been following those strong recommendations to do so, now is the time to back up all your important files. If your system has reached the point where you feel you need to format, you may be better off backing up using a utility like Windows Backup instead of creating a drive image. This is because you may not want to take problems currently residing on your system into the newly refreshed system by restoring a drive image of your previous "mess."

Wait! Are You Using a Drive-Overlay Program?

Drive-overlay programs are the same as the "BIOS helper" software I've told you about, where special drive software acts as an intermediary between a (usually older) BIOS and a large-capacity hard drive. Drive-overlay programs allow the BIOS to detect and work with the full size of that large drive. Otherwise, older systems may only see 8GB or 16GB of a 20GB, 40GB, 60GB, or 120GB hard drive, which leaves you with a lot of unclaimed and unusable disk space.

Examples of drive-overlay programs are EZ-BIOS and EZ-Drive. These programs may have come to you via the disk management utilities packed with new hard drives to help you use the new drive even if your BIOS is outdated. Or, you may have purchased them separately.

Your drive documentation may tell you that the overlay program is working, or you'll be notified on the screen when your PC first boots. If you're using overlay software, you can't use the straight refreshing methods given here. Instead, visit the manufacturer's web site and locate and follow the exact directions for reformatting and/or repartitioning a drive that uses that overlay software. Of course, if you can update your BIOS to a recent enough version that you don't need to use the overlay software, you're better off removing the overlay software (per the software's instructions) and using the `format` and `fdisk` commands as described in this chapter.

These drive-overlay programs are great because they bridge the gap between older PCs and large new drives. However, the level of inconvenience they offer when you have a problem with the drive (because the overlay often prevents you from working directly with the drive) can be high. It's like trying to perform delicate surgery through impenetrable rubber.

What You Need to Start Fresh

Make sure you have what you need to start fresh. Most, if not all, of these things should be in your PC Recovery Resource Kit as outlined in Chapter 4. These include (but aren't necessarily limited to)

- Boot disk(s)

- Windows install CD

- Updated drivers for your devices

- Master disks or copies of all your installed software

- Product keys/install codes for all appropriate software (including Windows)

- Copies of backups or drive images

- Your PC journal (Enter the fact that you're reformatting in your journal and jot down notes about anything special you need to remember about the process.)

Now Is a Good Time to Clean Up

Problems with loose power, data cable connections, or dust insinuating itself between these delicate connections are not uncommon with hard drives. Whenever I'm freshening a hard drive, I do some cleanup and tightening up:

1. I follow the usual precautions for shutting down and turning off the PC, disconnecting power, removing the cover, and grounding myself.

2. Once the system has cooled for several minutes, I make sure the screws holding the hard drive I'm about to reformat are in place. I carefully put my fingers on either side of the drive to make certain it's firmly seated, and I eyeball it to be sure it's not cocked at a strange angle.

3. I make sure the connection from the power supply is firmly seated in the back of the hard drive.

4. I make sure the data cable is firmly seated into the back of the hard drive, as illustrated in Figure 16.1. Pin 1 with the red-coded line of the data cable faces the power connector.

Photo courtesy of Emily Sherrill Weadock

Figure 16.1 *The ribbon cable connection to the hard drive must be firmly connected.*

5. If there is an unusual amount of dust around the drive, I use a can of compressed air (utilizing its focus wand, the plastic tube you insert into the nozzle) to remove dust from around the connections.

6. I double-check the connections one more time, making certain dust didn't get blown somewhere it shouldn't be.

7. I replace the cover, reconnect power, and then start the formatting process.

Redoing Your Hard Drive from Scratch

Preparing a hard drive to accept an operating system is one of the most important hardware operations you can do. It can also be one of the easiest, although it's very detail-oriented.

This section discusses repartitioning and whether it's something you need to do as part of refreshing your system. Partitioning must be done with a new hard drive that has not been prepped for use yet. This section also explains how to format your hard drive. Special instructions for those of you using Windows XP are included.

Then I'll explain how to install the operating system and the rest of the software and data you had before you started this process. The end result will be a system that performs much better from an operating system and disk speed perspective.

Starting Fresh: Basic Procedures and the Usefulness of Evaluation

When I talk about starting fresh, it means a process in which you take all of these steps in sequence:

1. After backing up needed files, reformat the hard drive.

2. Install the operating system.

3. Update hardware drivers as needed.

4. Install your applications and/or restore backups or drive images.

If all you're doing is refreshing a system, these are the only steps required. If you're replacing an existing hard drive with a new one, partition that new drive and format it, and complete the rest of the steps.

Experience has taught me to modify this procedure a little for maximum results (and fewer nasty surprises). I find this method particularly helpful when troubleshooting situations where all other steps to make the system perform better have failed.

Starting Fresh but Stopping Between Steps

If you're using the reformatting process as a means of troubleshooting a problem with your PC that has resisted all other attempts to rectify it, you've got a different situation. You should use my modification of the preceding steps (described in this section), but stop between each major step past step 2 to evaluate the system's performance. In evaluating, take these steps:

- Check the video display by opening up windows, which also tests the responsiveness of the system once you make a selection.

- Open a document or file and print it.

- Check in Device Manager for conflicts or devices that should be listed but are not.

Here's how the sequence of events changes slightly to accommodate the evaluation:

1. Back up any critical files.

2. Reformat the main hard drive (or the hard drive containing Windows).

3. Reinstall the operating system.

4. Evaluate the system's behavior once the operating system is successfully installed.

5. Update hardware drivers as needed (many may have changed since your version of Windows was published).

6. Re-evaluate the system again for good behavior once the drivers have been updated.

7. Reinstall your software or restore a good backup/drive image.

8. Evaluate one last time.

A great example of when to start fresh by reformatting and reinstalling everything is when you've exhausted all your other options for what may be causing

- Poor system performance

- Blue screen of death and other errors/warnings

- System freezes and crashes

- Garbage appearing in your folders (usually caused by file corruption)

Once you've completely refreshed a hard drive and reinstalled a fresh copy of Windows (and before you reinstall all your applications), the system will seem amazingly fast and clean compared to your previous setup (depending, of course, on how bad your previous situation was).

If your PC is not behaving well by the time you reach step 6 and before you perform step 7, you've probably got a serious hardware incompatibility or impending failure. Bad hardware shoots to the top of the suspect list at this point because the process of starting fresh can't fix problems like a corrupted Windows installation, misbehaving programs, an obese Registry with ancient entries, and accumulated crud.

While other issues could still be a problem (for example, running too recent a version of Windows on too old a PC), it's time to investigate hardware. You can do this through memory checking and other methods, including the barebones approach discussed in Chapter 10, "Understanding and Troubleshooting Hardware Failures." Or, you can have your system checked by a professional as described in Chapter 18, "Knowing When to Call Professionals."

TIP *What if your system purrs along until you complete step 7? Since you install your applications in this step, it's likely that something about one or more of these applications is causing some instability or incompatibility. Evaluate your system after installing each application.*

Repartitioning the Hard Drive

Partitioning the hard drive, or in the case of an already partitioned and formatted drive, repartitioning, is not normally part of the fresh start process, formatting the hard drive is. Be aware that while you can format without partitioning, you cannot partition without formatting because partitioning structures the drive but formatting prepares the drive for the operating system or files to be installed.

You can use partitioning to prep a new drive but you must use partitioning to create a primary DOS partition. This section includes the basic steps for partitioning a main hard drive from a Windows Startup disk. But don't repartition unless you have a distinct need to reorganize.

For all other Windows versions (Windows 95, 98, 98 Second Edition, or Millennium), you'll need a Windows startup disk for that version. Then take these steps:

NOTE *Remember, both (re)partitioning and (re)formatting will destroy all data on the drive.*

1. Insert the startup disk into the floppy drive.

2. Shut down and restart your system.

3. From Windows 95, a command prompt appears. Type **fdisk** and press Enter. From other Windows versions, a Start menu appears. Click Start Computer Without CD-ROM Support. When the command prompt appears, type **fdisk** and press Enter.

4. You'll be asked whether you want to enable large disk support. Type **Y** and then Enter.

5. From the FDisk Options menu, choose 1, Create DOS Partition or Logical DOS Drive. Press Enter.

6. Assuming you want to use the FAT32 file system, you're asked Do You Want to Use the Maximum Available Size for Primary DOS partition. Type **Y** and then press Enter.

7. Press Esc twice until you quit `FDisk` and return to the command prompt.

Once you partition or repartition your drive, you must format it. This process is described in the next section.

Reformatting the Hard Drive

Since all versions of Windows before Windows XP use similar methods for formatting a hard drive, the instructions for using Windows XP are found in the next section. This section describes the process for reformatting a hard drive for Windows 95, Windows 98, Windows 98 Second Edition, and Windows Millennium.

For all Windows versions, you'll need the Windows startup disk. Then take these steps:

1. Insert the startup disk into the floppy drive.

2. Shut down and restart your system.

3. From Windows 95, a command prompt appears. Type **format c: /s** and press Enter. From other Windows versions, a Start Menu appears. Click Start Computer Without CD-ROM Support. When the command prompt appears, type **format c: /s** and press Enter.

WARNING *If you're formatting a drive other than your C: drive, substitute the command* **format [drive-letter:]**

4. The message "Warning, all data on non-removable disk drive [*drive letter*] will be lost! Proceed with format?" appears. Type **Y** and press Enter.

5. When formatting is complete, enter a name for the drive and press Enter.

Congratulations! You have a freshly formatted hard drive and you're ready to receive your operating system, described in "Reinstalling the Rest."

TIP *What if the drive won't allow you to refresh it (it just sits there or stalls when you try to reformat) or appears dead? See Chapter 17, "Resurrecting a Dead Hard Drive," for help.*

Repartitioning and Reformatting with Windows XP

Windows XP offers you two ways to partition and format a hard drive:

- Use the `fdisk` and `format` commands (or usually, just the `format` command) already discussed.

- Use Windows XP Setup right from the install CD. (You may find this easier than using the Startup disk.)

If all you want to do is format your C drive, use the first method. If you want to repartition and reformat your existing drive, or you're prepping a new hard drive, use the second method.

WARNING *Your PC must be able to boot from the CD/DVD drive for the second method to work. You can enable this option under BIOS Setup by adding the drive letter for your CD/DVD drive to the list of bootable drives.*

The steps for using Windows XP Setup are as follows:

1. Place the Windows XP install CD into your CD/DVD drive.

2. Shut down and restart your PC.

3. When the PC restarts, it should boot from the CD. (Make sure you don't have a floppy disk inserted in the floppy drive or it may be mistaken for a boot disk.) From the Welcome to Setup screen, press Enter.

4. When prompted, press the F8 key to accept the Microsoft Windows licensing agreement; if you don't accept, you can't run Setup.

5. Setup detects your previous Windows installation and offers to repair it. Press Esc to opt out of this repair.

6. Setup then lists known physical hard drives and partitions on your PC. Select the C drive that you want partition.

7. Since the C drive should have at least one existing partition, this partition must be removed so a fresh partition can be created. Follow the on-screen instructions: type **D** to delete the existing partition, then type **L**, and then type **C**, which creates the new partition.

8. At this point, choose the size of the partition. Press Enter if you want to use the entire drive as a single partition or enter the size (in megabytes) of the new partition you want (for example, 10240MB, which equals 10GB). If you don't use the entire disk as a single partition, repeat steps 5 and 6 to create additional partitions.

9. Select the partition on which you want to install Windows XP (usually, the primary DOS partition on your C drive). Press Enter.

10. Choose from these Format options:

    • Format the partition using the NTFS File System (Quick).

    • Format the partition using the FAT File System (Quick).

    • Format the partition using the NTFS File System.

    • Format the partition using the FAT File System.

    • Leave the current file system intact (no changes).

NOTE *Notice that Windows XP has both a Format and a Quick Format option. The difference between the two is the Format option scans the disk for bad sectors (not a bad idea with a used hard drive) as part of the formatting process while the Quick Format option does not. However, you can run CHKDSK after the formatting is complete, and Windows is installed on a drive if you used Quick Format on the disk.*

11. Choose the format option you want and press Enter to start the formatting process.

12. When formatting is complete, follow the on-screen instructions to continue Setup to install Windows XP.

WARNING *Don't see FAT listed as a format option? Your partition must be no greater than 32GB in size to format for FAT. Otherwise, the NTFS format must be used.*

If you followed along, you should now have a repartitioned and reformatted hard drive with Windows XP successfully installed.

TIP *Problems running Setup? If you have a second Internet-ready PC available, visit the Microsoft Knowledge Base (*http://search.support.microsoft.com*) to look up Setup errors and research work-arounds.*

Replacing a Hard Drive

Sometimes you may choose to replace your existing hard drive as part of starting fresh, probably because you need more disk space. The first step is to properly install the brand-new hard drive into your PC, following the drive's instructions. Make sure the drive is detected by the BIOS by going into BIOS Setup.

Then if the new drive is going to be used as your primary drive, it needs to be partitioned and formatted, and then an operating system needs to be installed on it. Once this has been accomplished, you can

- Reinstall your applications to the new drive and copy back any data you stored elsewhere.

- Use a drive image of your previous setup to create an environment (with your applications, customized settings, and saved data) like your former one.

- Restore a backup.

You can also use drive copy software (such as PowerQuest's Drive Copy) to transfer the contents of your former hard drive to your new one. If you go that route, be sure to read its documentation before starting.

Reinstalling the Rest

Although I took a side trip to talk about a replacement hard drive, let's get back to the hard drive you formatted using the `format` command from your Startup disk.

With the drive formatted, it's ready to re-commence its work life. It's time to reinstall the operating system and its settings and reinstall your applications.

Reinstalling the Operating System

Pre-Windows XP versions of Windows require a Windows Startup disk with CD-ROM support. This means your disk has drivers installed to support your CD-ROM drive to run your Windows install CD, which you took care of in Chapter 4 (right?).

Since installing the operating system is the next step after formatting the hard drive, let's assume you still have your Startup disk inserted into your floppy drive with your PC sitting at the command prompt. Take these steps to reinstall Windows:

1. Push the reset button on your PC or press Ctrl+Alt+Del twice to restart the system with the Startup disk still in place.

2. Insert your Windows install CD (full version) into your CD-ROM drive.

3. From Windows 95, at the command prompt, type **CD-drive-letter:\Setup**, where **CD-drive-letter** is the letter of your CD-ROM drive (usually D). Press Enter.

   For Windows 98, 98 Second Edition, and Millennium, from the Start menu, select Start Computer With CD-ROM Support. When the command prompt appears, type **CD-drive-letter:\Setup**, where **CD-drive-letter** is the letter of your CD-ROM drive. Press Enter.

The Windows Setup wizard launches and steps you through your operating system installation. Be sure to have your Windows product key handy since you'll need it during the setup process.

Once the operating system has been installed, there are several different options for reinstalling your applications:

- Restore a drive image taken when your system was in good shape to reset this default Windows installation with your custom settings and set your applications up again.

- Restore a backup following the same basic guidelines, assuming you performed a full backup of the drive.

- Install your important applications and then copy back the data you stored offline on a removable medium.

Let's talk about each of these options in more detail.

Drive Image

Let's assume you want to restore a good drive image to your newly reformatted PC. A drive image effectively copies back all of your material from before, including your custom Windows settings and data stored at the time the drive image was created.

The example in this section is based on PowerQuest's Drive Image, the software I use most often. Prior to this procedure and after Windows is installed, install PowerQuest's Drive Image software.

You can restore a complete image or you can search through an image using ImageExplorer to restore individual files from the massive .pqi (the file format for the drive image) file stored on a CD or on another drive.

To restore a complete drive image, take these steps:

1. Choose Start ➢ Programs ➢ PowerQuest Drive Image ➢ Drive Image.

2. Select Restore Image.

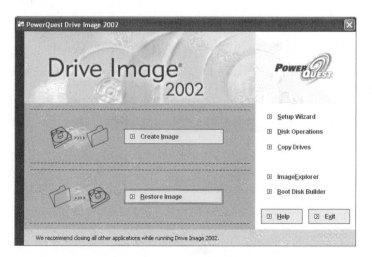

3. From the Restore Image window, click Select Image File, which opens a right-pane Explorer-type window.

4. If the image you want to restore immediately appears in the right-hand pane, proceed to step 5. If not, click Browse and locate and select the desired drive image. Click Open.

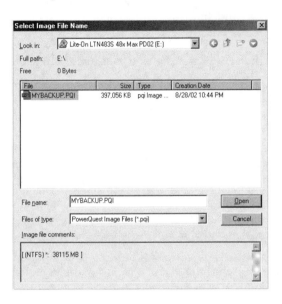

5. From the left-hand pane, click Select Destination. By default, Restore to Original Location is checked. If appropriate, click OK. If not, click to uncheck this and specify the location where the drive image should be restored to.

6. When prompted, click Finish.

To restore individual files, take these steps:

1. Choose Start ➤ Programs ➤ PowerQuest Drive Image ➤ ImageExplorer.

2. Locate and double-click the drive image you want to restore using either the Locate or My Recent Images Pane.

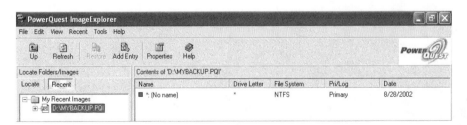

3. Click the desired partition (if more than one is present) that you want to restore.

4. Select the files or folders you want to restore.

5. Go to File ➤ Restore.

6. Click To This Destination to specify where to restore these files, from which you can indicate a particular location or choose Restore to Original Path to restore these files to their former location.

7. Click Restore.

8. When you are notified the restoration process is complete, click OK and then Close.

Restoring Backups

Since the process of restoring backups varies among versions of Windows, let's look at the utility most people use: Restore for Windows 98/98 Second Edition and Windows XP Professional.

For Windows 98, take these steps to restore your backup:

1. Choose Start ➤ Programs ➤ Accessories ➤ System Tools ➤ Backup.

2. From the Welcome to Microsoft Backup window, click Restore Backed Up Files. Click OK.

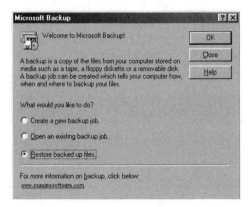

3. From the Restore Wizard window, under Restore From File, click to select the backup file you want to restore or use the Folder icon to locate the desired backup file.

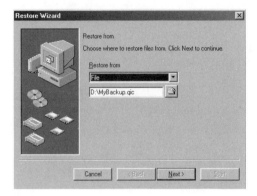

4. From the Select Backup Sets window, click to check what backup set you want to restore. Click OK. A Logging Process window appears and tells you a temporary catalog is being created.

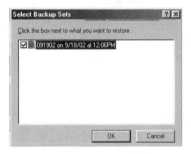

5. Next, select the folders you want to restore as part of the backup. Be sure all the folders you want are checked. Click OK.

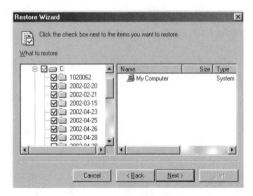

6. Under Where to Restore, select Original Location. Click Next.

7. Under How to Restore (since you're restoring the operating system), click Always Replace the File on my Computer. Click Start, which opens a progress window.

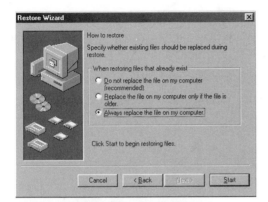

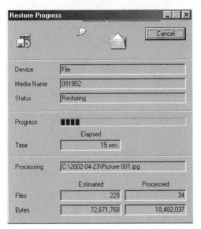

For Windows XP Professional, take the following steps:

1. Choose Start ➤ Programs ➤ Accessories ➤ System Tools ➤ Backup.

2. From the Backup or Restore Wizard window, click Advanced Mode.

3. Select the Restore and Manage Media tab.

4. Under File, select the backup file you want to restore.

5. Next, select the folders you want to restore as part of the backup. Be sure all the folders you want are checked.

6. To restore the entire operating system (including its previous settings), click to select System State.

7. Under Restore To, click to select Original Location (usually set by default).

8. Click Options.

9. Under Method to Use for Backup File Replacement (since you're restoring the operating system), click Always Replace the File on My Computer. Click OK.

10. Click Start Restore. When a warning message appears telling you that continuing will replace your current system state with another, click OK.

11. When the Confirm Restore prompt appears, click OK.

12. Once you're notified that the restore process is complete, click Close. You may be prompted to restart your PC. If so, click Yes.

Reinstalling Your Applications

If you aren't using drive images or backups to restore your PC to a previous environment, go ahead and reinstall the applications and programs formerly installed on your PC.

Be sure you have your product keys or serial numbers for each application as part of the installation process. And remember that it's wise to stop after installing each application to make sure it opens and runs properly before reinstalling the next application. In this manner, you can catch a problem when it crops up, rather than after you've installed 20 more applications.

Once you've reinstalled your applications, use Windows Explorer (Start ➤ Programs ➤ Accessories ➤ Windows Explorer) to locate and copy back the individual data files you may have stored on other hard drives or on removable media.

Time to Give Up and Buy a New PC?

After going through this process to start fresh, are you still having significant problems that make you feel like it's time to chuck the old PC and buy a new one?

Before you read on through my "Tips for Smart PC Buying," consider calling in a professional (the topic of Chapter 18). If you think the hard drive itself is the issue, see Chapter 17. It's always possible that the issues causing your problems can be corrected for a fraction of the cost of a new PC.

Tips for Smart PC Buying

If you're anything like me, you may find that the time you really must replace an old PC with a new one is often just about the worst time to do so.

Let me share my top 10 tips for smart PC purchasing:

1. Never make a purchase without comparing prices and features, or you'll pay too much.

2. Never shop in a panic.

3. Try to compare prices among multiple systems in more than one store or online vendor.

4. Don't buy less than you need thinking you'll upgrade later. Often you won't upgrade, or you'll pay more to add something than you would have if you'd bought it as part of a package originally.

5. Determine whether the PC has many integrated components (video, network, sound, and/or modem) and whether you can upgrade with add-in components later if needed.

6. Make sure that the PC you're buying runs the version of Windows you want to use.

7. Don't buy a PC with less than a 20GB hard drive or you'll exceed your disk capacity too quickly.

8. If you're buying a PC in a store or receiving one through the mail, don't accept one packed in a damaged box because it may indicate that the box (and the delicate system inside) was mistreated.

9. Determine the vendor's return policy before you buy. You shouldn't have to pay restocking fees or go through a lot of hassle to return defective equipment.

10. Finally, but importantly, make sure to price power protection (a good surge protector and/or a UPS) for the new system. It may be cheaper to purchase power protection separately than to buy it with the new PC.

There are two more issues that can be important:

- The need to buy "up"

- Whether or not you should purchase additional protection or an extended warranty

Buy "Up"

Don't just buy a PC for what you need right now; buy it for what you feel may be your maximum needs a year from now. For example, even if you're not currently planning on having a home or small office network, it doesn't hurt to buy a PC with a network adapter installed or integrated into the motherboard just in case your needs change over the next year.

IEEE 1394 ports for high-speed external drives and digital video connections still aren't found on all new PCs. If that's important to you or you expect it to be important in the next year, order a PC with IEEE 1394 ports or plan to buy a 1394 adapter (you install this to an available PCI slot on your motherboard) later.

If you're buying a budget machine with the idea that you can upgrade the frequently integrated components such as video, modem, sound, and network at a later time, make sure the system you buy allows that kind of expansion room. For example, the last budget system I purchased thinking, "I don't like that video setup but it's OK because I have a spare AGP card" brought with it a nasty surprise. One of the budget features of the system included a motherboard *without* an AGP video port, so I couldn't use my existing AGP video adapter in it. The manufacturer's specs did not make this clear, although I could have found out by checking the motherboard information before I purchased it. Live and learn.

Adding Protection at Purchase

Just like when you buy a new big-screen television or a fancy stereo system, you're often asked when you purchase a new PC if you want to purchase an extended service agreement to provide support and repairs past the 90-day to one-year warranties offered by the manufacturer.

While you need to evaluate this for yourself and your particular situation, my inclination is to refuse extended warranties (with the possible exception of Dell, which has a long history of offering decent after-sales support).

If you're the type of person who frequently calls for customer service or technical assistance, it's possible you'll benefit from the extra period of coverage to support your system depending on its cost. However, it's my understanding that most people who are going to use support services usually do so within the first 90 days of owning a new PC. If you haven't called during that period, how likely is it that you'll call one year and 90 days later? It's possible the time will run out on the warranty without you making use of the extra price you paid for it.

A Cautionary Tale: The "Fun" Doesn't Always Stop Here

Remember how I told you that I totaled one of my systems in recreating disasters for this book?

Just to prove my point about the time you have to buy a new PC usually not being the best time to do so, let me tell you a sad story. Today, just three weeks after receiving my new system, as I was beginning to write the last pages of this book, my new PC simply shut itself down. There were no error messages, no warnings.

Continued on next page

A Cautionary Tale: The "Fun" Doesn't Always Stop Here *(Continued)*

When I tried to restart it, the system began to beep wildly, and not in one of the recognized beep codes mentioned in Chapter 6, "Transforming Yourself into a Smart Troubleshooter: Detecting, Analyzing, and Diagnosing." I turned it off and went through the usual precautions so I could check under the cover. I tried to start the system a third time, and noticed a terrible smell (if you've ever fried a motherboard, you know this smell).

I also noticed the CPU fan wasn't turning.

On a three-week-old pristine system that I haven't had the time to customize yet, this shouldn't happen. It was running with a full roster of power protection and had not been subjected to any unusual situations, so I ruled out overheating and other issues.

I called eMachines, the manufacturer, and the helpful technician agreed with my diagnosis: fried motherboard. Once the motherboard is dead, any connections supplied with power by the motherboard will no longer receive power, even if the power supply is working. That's why the CPU fan wouldn't turn and the monitor had no display.

What killed it, I'll never know. It may have been damaged in transit but managed to work for three weeks, or the motherboard may have been defective to start.

The point is, sadly, that your problems don't always end with the purchase of a new system, no matter how well you protect it from harm. But by protecting it from harm, I could rule out whether I contributed to its swift demise.

I'm told I'll get a replacement motherboard…in three weeks. <Insert big sigh here.> Unfortunately, this system *was* my replacement.

Panic and inconvenience have been mentioned often in this book, as they should be when the subject is disaster recovery. Yet panic and inconvenience can combine themselves rapidly and forcefully when you hit that miserable phenomenon known as a dead or dying hard drive. This is the subject of the next chapter.

CHAPTER 17

Resurrecting a Dead Hard Drive

Somewhere, at some time (and it will be a bad time, trust me), a hard drive will fail on you. Statistically speaking, this is one of those hard computer lessons almost all of us experience at one time or another.

Why? Are the drives poorly made? Probably not, although hard drives today cost a fraction of what they used to cost; that price reduction must have some effect on production and quality control. Instead, I think the problems have more to do with the use and abuse these workhorses receive.

Did you know the platters inside your hard disk turn at the rate of 5400, 7200, 10,000, or even 15,000 revolutions per minute? Can you imagine the wearing effects of that speed? What about the amount of heat that's produced in that tight little casing with that speed of operation?

A hard drive is critical to a successful system boot. And since we left the dark days of DOS, the hard drive is necessary to store and support the ever-bloating operating systems; they used to fit on a floppy disk but now they challenge a 2GB hard drive. You use hard drives as temporary workspace, as if they were computer memory, to move chunks of large files on and off your Windows desktop. You make them unhappy when you shut down your PC before data is properly written to them. You repeatedly restart your PCs, expecting the hard drives to work the first time and every time. Few other pieces of PC equipment have such demands placed on them, and only a few are as important to your PC's operation.

Sure, some drive manufacturers have told you that you can expect storage on the recent hard drives to last up to 35 years. But you're not likely to still have those drives, after all. You'll probably throw away the hard drive with your PC when you replace it every 2–3 years. This means you'll probably retire your hard drives long before they die.

Yet some hard drives will die on you in service. And even if you've been scrupulous about backing up your files, invariably, you'll need something on that failed drive that you'll try almost anything to retrieve—at least until you hear the price tag of professional data-recovery services.

This chapter is devoted to last-ditch efforts to resurrect what appears to be a dead drive, even if just to pull off any irreplaceable files.

With that said, however, you won't always—maybe not even frequently—be successful in your recovery efforts. Users without the money to pay for professional recovery, usually consumers and small business people, may find that their lost data will stay lost. The easiest way to prevent the loss from occurring in the first place is to scrupulously copy your files to a second source (almost anything other than your primary hard drive) regularly, before such a disaster strikes.

Symptoms of a Dead or Dying Drive

Hard drives often report errors that signify a problem with the drive (or with reading or writing to it). But they can also offer some scary visible and auditory signs that tip you off to a hardware issue as opposed to something like a virus.

Some of the warning signs and symptoms of a dead or dying drive include

- Horrific or loud noises that involve brr-ing or buzzing, clicking, grinding, or scraping sounds

- Loud vibration (although this can also be caused by a drive that is not securely mounted in its drive bay)

- No drive light (If instead, the drive light remains on all the time, this is usually a sign of a reversed drive cable, which can fry the drive.)

- Smoke, sparks, or a strange odor coming from drive

- Drive not being detected by the BIOS (indicative of a dead drive if the drive was previously detected by the BIOS), which you can see (or rather, *not* see) by going into BIOS Setup

- All other drives respond with the PC turned on except for the suspect drive

- A drive that shows garbage, corruption, or confusion after an event like a serious power surge

- Repeated drive errors

- It takes two or three PC restarts to get the hard drive to respond when starting up the PC

- Water-marking (like dried water spots) on the exterior drive shell (This may indicate it's been subjected to water, or the computer was operated while very cold and condensation formed.)

When Dead Isn't Really Dead

Let's start on a hopeful note by looking at the types of problems that can make it seem to you and to your system that a hard drive is having a problem that might lead you to think it's dead or dying. Most of these problems can be resolved without replacing the drive, especially if you don't do anything to exacerbate the damage.

NOTE *Remember as you troubleshoot that you can use the techniques described in Chapter 7, "Restarting a Problem PC," to get into your system if you can't boot up normally.*

Here are some of the issues you should examine as possible causes:

Hardware conflicts   Your hard drive is not listed in Device Manager, but your hard drive controller (the interface between your drive and the PC) is. If another device is using the same IRQ as the hard drive controller, you're going to have a problem that behaves much like a dead hard drive, even though the drive is fine. I'll discuss this later under the "Troubleshooting Errors and Warnings" section.

Corrupted or damaged drive-overlay software   If there are problems with your drive-overlay software, you'll probably see a message to this effect on the screen. This topic is discussed in more detail in the section "Are You Using Drive-Overlay Software?"

Corrupted or missing master boot record (MBR)   A corrupted or missing MBR can usually be fixed by recreating the MBR. To do this in Windows 95/98/Me, reboot with a boot disk and type the following command at the command prompt: `fdisk /mbr`. In Windows XP, use the Recovery Console and the `fixmbr` command. However, don't use either method if you're using drive-overlay software.

File system or BIOS corruption from a computer virus or catastrophic event
Check your system regularly for viruses using anti-virus software that's updated for the most recently released viruses. For file system corruption, completely reformatting the hard drive may help. For BIOS corruption, you may need to apply a fresh BIOS update or contact the BIOS manufacturer for assistance.

Driver corruption   Special drivers called *bus-mastering drivers* that work with your hard drive are installed as part of your PC setup. If these drivers become outdated and/or corrupted, it's possible that the results could mimic a dead or dysfunctional drive. The best measure for this is proactive; use Windows Update to alert you to critical updates for this type of driver as well as for other drivers.

Drive diagnostics and/or drive-management software comes packed with a hard drive or can be downloaded from the manufacturer's web site. Such diagnostics are designed for that particular drive. Look to see whether the problems you're having are serious enough to replace the drive. Also check out the "Troubleshooting Errors and Warnings" section later in this chapter.

Practices That Put Your Drive at Risk

Let's assume that you've still got a hard drive you can repair and use. Once you've stabilized your PC and completed a backup or drive image with everything working well, be aware of practices that place your hard drive at risk:

- Failure to shut down your PC properly, or forcing the PC to perform excessive reboots

- Failure to watch conditions that can contribute to excessive heat within the PC case, particularly in the area of the drive bays

- Failure to use proper power protection such as a good-quality surge suppressor or, better yet, a UPS

- Failure to observe proper precautions when working with drive connections that can lead to reversed cables, shorting of the drive (if not the motherboard) by plugging in the drive with the PC turned on, and other disasters

- Not regularly scanning your system for viruses using anti-virus software

- Operating the PC in a dirty environment where ash and dust can be pulled inside the PC case and into the drive (Drives are extremely sensitive to contaminants.)

- Operating the PC in extremes of temperature and moisture

- Using a large magnetic device in close proximity to the drive

- Poor mounting of the drive (A drive angled in an odd position or that vibrates excessively can seriously increase wear on internal components.)

NOTE *Most experts agree that the leading cause of hard drive failure is prolonged overheating. This situation is exacerbated by the large capacity of new drives, which means they have to fit a lot more data into the same size physical drive. Many experts recommend buying a drive-cooling fan (such as those discussed in Chapter 11, "Avoiding Power and Overheating Problems") to reduce heat-related wear.*

Immediate Safety Concerns

Let's be clear on one point before going further: If you smell smoke (whether it's coming from the drive or another part of the PC), see sparks or fire, or hear a terrible noise coming from the vicinity of your hard drive, shut the PC off and disconnect it from power immediately.

Similarly, if a disaster of some type produces water that is coming close to the PC, kill power and disconnect the PC from its power source as soon as possible.

Should you find your PC in a situation where the hard drive is visibly damaged, don't try to plug the drive back in, even into a different machine. A drive with serious physical injury is not one you can try to work with yourself. If you want to salvage data from it, seek professional assistance (discussed later in this chapter).

Continued on next page

Immediate Safety Concerns *(Continued)*

Finally, please don't assume that you can just open up the drive casing and try to repair it yourself, even if friends and associates tell you it's possible. Ask them to show you a drive they've fixed that way in good operation. There aren't many.

When you send a drive to be repaired or recovered, workers open them in sterile, clean environments and exercise grave care; this isn't the same as taking a hard drive out to the garage workbench. The least amount of damage you can do there is to contaminate the platter surfaces with debris that makes the drive harder or impossible to recover.

First Response

There are many types of hard drive failure or damage that will be exacerbated by your efforts to make the drive work again. Seemingly "little" steps like trying again and again to restart a PC with a damaged drive can actually contribute to the problems.

For example, if you have a damaged drive head and you repeatedly try to access that drive, that bad head may destroy more of the stored data on the drive each time you do so.

Such efforts may distance you from the ability to recover the unsaved data from the drive; the damage to the drive may increase because of your attempts to recover data, making it tougher for special software or drive-recovery specialists to pull your data successfully from that drive.

For this reason, it's vitally important that you neither panic nor try to bully your way through such a problem. It's also important that you make a decision early on whether to

- Scrap the drive and eat the data loss.

- Try all the measures you can to pull off data yourself.

- Immediately pack the drive into a plastic bag (if the drive is wet, don't dry it yourself first) before sending it off to data-recovery specialists.

Why? First, data recovery in such situations is time-consuming and expensive in terms of buying special software. Consumer versions of this software are priced between $50 and $100, but the cost goes up with the software's level of sophistication; more features or more recovery potential equals a higher price tag.

Second, once you turn to this software, especially if you make multiple attempts to extract data from the drive, you may inadvertently further damage the drive. This can drastically reduce the likelihood that a drive-recovery specialist will be able to recover more data from your drive later. Plan to use the software *or* a specialist rather than calling in a specialist *after* the software fails.

If you need more time to consider your decision, leave the PC off or leave the suspect hard drive completely disconnected from it (remove the power connection and data cable).

However, if you have already booted the PC and the drive seems to be working during that session, copy important files off the hard drive however you can. This should be your first priority because you can't assume that the drive will still be functioning in 20 minutes or in an hour or tomorrow. I'll go over some emergency backup measures in a moment.

A Cautionary Tale:
Why a Good Swift Kick or Slap Probably Isn't Going to Help

I keep running into people who believe that the cure for a bad noise in the drive or a drive error is to slap their drive (this really scares me because no one ever mentions the issue of power or grounding oneself) or kick their PC case to "help the disks spin."

While this worked for the starter mechanism on my ancient college-era Toyota, it won't help a hard drive work better. At best, this might help you work off your frustration. You're probably going to hurt at least the drive, if not yourself and the rest of the PC.

Emergency Backup Schemes

What if you're in a situation where you feel a drive failure could happen at any moment, but you simply don't have a means of backing up the drive? I saw this recently with a system that had become too unstable to get through something as disk intensive as a backup; the system died each time someone tried to record files to a CD-R.

In a situation where you have a small number of files you desperately need to save off the hard drive, copy them to a floppy disk or a Zip disk. If you have access to a file compression utility like WinZip or FreeZip, archive up to 1MB of files and send them to yourself in an e-mail; don't retrieve that e-mail until you come out on the other end of your drive problem. Most web-based e-mail sites allow for file attachments.

If the PC with the failing drive is on a network, move as many important files to a drive on another system where you have access (the drive or folders on the other PC gives you share-level access to save files to them).

Online Backup Services

Online backup services provide you with an account and special software or a browser-based interface for uploading files to their storage servers for an annual fee. The goal of these services isn't to upload the entire contents of your hard drive but to store strategic files that you can't afford to lose or that you want stored in a second location accessible through the Internet. Many business travelers subscribe to such services so that if something happens to their laptop while they're on a trip, they can always log onto the backup service from a borrowed PC or laptop from virtually anywhere and grab the files they need. The following sites provide online backup storage:

@Backup (`www.@backup.com`)   You download and install their software, which provides an easy-to-use interface for uploading files to their storage servers. Pricing here starts at an annual service fee of $49.95 for 50MB or $995 for 2GB. At the time this book was being prepared for release, @Backup was offering a 30-day free trial with annual signup.

Virtual Backup (`www.virtualbackup.com`)   Virtual Backup offers a Simple Plan that allows you to store up to 50MB of files at an annual rate of $39.95 or 100MB for $79.95 a year. Like @Backup, they offer a 30-day free trial.

A Quick E-mail Trick

Here's a quick trick I learned when I was rushing to secure a really important document for work on a drive that sounded like it would grind itself to death at any moment.

If your word processor or other application has a Send To feature on the File menu (Microsoft Word is one program that has it) and you currently have access to the Internet, send a copy of the file to yourself through e-mail directly from the application.

Let's pretend I'm furiously trying to finish this chapter on a PC where the drive appears to be having problems. Naturally, I don't want to take the chance of losing the work, so I would take these steps:

1. Save the most recent version of the file. If that's not possible, proceed to step 2.

2. In Word, I choose File ➤ Send to ➤ Mail Recipient (you can also choose Mail Recipient as Attachment, if preferred).

3. When my e-mail software opens, I address the file to myself and click Send. (If you used the Mail Recipient as Attachment option in step 2, you'll have to specify the name and location of the file you want to send.)

4. Later, once the hard drive crisis is corrected or from another PC, I retrieve my e-mail and my attached file.

Once your important data is saved in a retrievable format, it's time to start checking the source of the hard drive problem.

Check This First

If the drive is not responding at all, do a quick check of the entire PC, followed by a look at your physical setup. If you can get the drive going, you can perform other checks (using Windows' disk-checking tools, for example) more easily.

In this process, try not to assume, since you might miss other clues. Here's a case in point: Someone asked me to come by the other afternoon because he didn't think his hard drive was working, but he couldn't get the system working with a startup disk either.

With the case open, I carefully connected power, turned the system on, and listened to the power supply roar to life. But that was all that engaged—there was no video, no sound of the drives engaging, and no fans turning except for the power supply fan. A bad hard drive doesn't generally kill power and won't render you without a display. No, his motherboard was dead. The power supply was feeding power to it, but nothing connected to the motherboard, including the CPU and fans, was getting any juice. Even if they were, a fried motherboard wouldn't let them work.

A test for this can be done easily, assuming you're reasonably sure your PC components work. Under most conditions, you should be able to boot using a boot or startup disk. If you can't and you know you're working with a good boot/startup disk (because it will boot another PC, for example), suspect something other than your hard drive.

Visible Signs

When you have a hard drive that does not appear to respond at all when you turn on the PC, first establish that everything else on the system is working. Can you hear the power supply? Do you see some kind of display? If the entire PC is off (meaning, not even the power supply comes on), you have a power issue. And as I said a moment ago, a dead drive won't keep you from having a display.

Once you've established that the rest of the PC responds as much as it can, look for a drive light. If there is no drive light, the drive is not getting power from the power supply or can't get power because the drive is dead.

Also, be aware that the drive startup power is coming from the 12-volt section of the power supply. It's very possible that the 5-volt section is running and the 12-volt section is not. On power up, if the keyboard is scanned (the keyboard LEDs flash) and you do not hear any of the drives start up, you probably have a power supply failure, not a hard drive failure. The keyboard uses only the 5-volt section of the power supply.

Physical Setup

Next check your PC's physical setup, including all of its connections (from the data ribbon cable to the motherboard and to another drive or from the power supply to the drive) and its jumpers. This is especially important if the problem you're experiencing is with a new drive. But this step should be done even if the drive formerly worked fine and you haven't been inside the case recently.

Before you check your PC's physical setup, remember to

1. Turn off the PC.

2. Disconnect the PC's power.

3. Remove the cover and don your anti-static wrist strap.

WARNING *If the drive is brand new, did you partition and format it or use the drive's Setup software to prepare it for use? If it's a booting hard drive, did you install an operating system? A new drive won't do much without your help.*

Physical Connections

There are two primary physical connections with an IDE/ATA internally mounted hard drive: the connector running from the power supply to connect to the back of the drive and the data ribbon cable connecting the drive to the motherboard (or to another drive or both).

Power Supply Connector   One of the hardest connections to establish in a PC is the plastic connector from the power supply that plugs into the back of the hard drive. This is keyed and must be seated firmly.

However, if you could see a drive light before you checked the physical setup, this is probably properly attached.

TIP *Have another free power connector available? Remove the current connector and try the other one, just in case it's a bad connector.*

Data Ribbon Cable   The data ribbon cable must be inserted firmly into the connection at the back of the hard drive, with the colored (usually blue or red) edge of the cable lined up to pin 1 on the drive's data connection.

If at all possible, temporarily replace your current data ribbon cable with another that is known to work. This rules out a bad ribbon cable as the source of your problem.

Jumpers

Be sure the jumpers on your hard drive are set for the way you're using the drive. The section "Installing an IDE Hard Drive" has more information on jumper settings.

When BIOS Doesn't See the Drive

Your hard drive is SMARTer than you think, at least in terms of the Self-Monitoring, Analysis, and Reporting Technology (SMART) built into it.

Hard drives now contain detailed information about themselves (type of drive, ID number) contained in programmed chips on the drives, which helps both BIOS and Windows know what type of drive they're working with. This information makes it easier for the drive to be detected by the BIOS, to be seen as part of the essential hardware inventory when the PC is started. For those of us who remember a time when adding a new hard drive meant an hour or two of complicated debugging commands, this stored drive information makes life much easier.

But damage to the recorded information, as you might see with a power surge, extreme overheating, or when you forget to disconnect the PC's power before you plug in a new drive, can make it impossible for the BIOS to read these identifying details. BIOS may not even realize a drive is connected at all.

The BIOS may not recognize a new drive when the drive capacity is larger than your BIOS version is designed to support. Some Pentium II and III systems, for example, may have problems when you add a 20GB or larger hard drive simply because their BIOS hasn't been updated since these systems were first built in 1997–1999. To resolve this problem, do one of the following:

- Obtain and apply a BIOS update (described in Chapter 8, "When Upgrades Go Wrong").

- Use drive/BIOS overlay software (discussed in Chapter 16, "Starting from Scratch the Hard Way").

Another problem with new drives is improper cable connections and improper jumper settings can keep the BIOS from detecting the hard drive. However, once a drive has been installed and detected, the BIOS should see the drive each and every time your PC starts. If it doesn't (and outside of some of the disaster conditions such as smoke or a terrible sound from the drive), you should

1. Restart your PC.

2. As the PC restarts, follow the on-screen directions to enter BIOS Setup (as in, "Press <this key> to Enter Setup").

3. Locate your drive listings (usually on the general information screen).

4. Click Auto Detect (if available) to see if this picks up the drive.

Also check your manufacturer's web site for other suggestions for getting the BIOS to recognize the drive. Some web sites have specific settings for the drive that may help get it recognized again if the actual hardware on the drive itself isn't damaged.

Then you must rule out a loose data ribbon cable or dust interposed between the drive and the ribbon cable interface, or a loose power cable. If no power is getting to the drive, the power light on the drive should remain dark.

If the drive still can't be detected by the BIOS, contact the drive manufacturer, or your PC manufacturer if you got your current hard drive with a new PC and the PC is still under warranty.

Using ScanDisk/CHKDSK

ScanDisk and CHKDSK are Windows utilities for disk checking that have been discussed in earlier chapters. Use them whenever you need to examine a hard drive for problems, following these steps:

- For ScanDisk (the Thorough option) for Windows 95, 98, Millennium, choose Start ➤ Programs ➤ Accessories ➤ System Tools or switch Windows to a command prompt and type **scandisk <drive-letter>:**

- CHKDSK for Windows XP can be run from the Command Console or from the Recovery Console by typing **chkdsk <drive-letter>:** or **chkdsk <drive-letter>: /f** to do a check and repair.

If you have problems running ScanDisk (the scan continuously restarts because the drive contents have changed), restart your system with nothing running on the desktop except Scan-Disk, or run it from the command prompt rather than from Windows itself.

Manufacturer-Supplied Disk Tools and Diagnostics

If you installed drive-management software when you installed your problematic hard drive or you have a disk from the manufacturer containing a diagnostics tool, run this software to see what it reports. If you have to call the manufacturer for support on the drive, you may be asked to provide the results from the diagnostics testing. The "Troubleshooting Errors and Warnings" section discusses these tools in more detail.

Checking Related Issues

If ScanDisk or CHKDSK fails to report a problem or if you still haven't reached the point where you can run them, consider some of the issues described in this section.

TIP *This is another situation when having a spare Internet-ready PC can be a true blessing. Use the second system to check the drive manufacturer's web site to see if the specific problems or error messages you're seeing are covered there. If so, follow the site's recommendations for correcting them.*

What Did You Do Last?

Stop and think: What did you do during the last session the drive responded normally? For example, did you

- Modify drive settings in the BIOS Setup?

- Install drive software or utilities? (A common culprit is a utility written for a different version of Windows or one using a different file system.)

- Try unsuccessfully to repartition or reformat your drive?

If available, check the troubleshooting section of any documentation that exists for anything you did install. You might be able to glean from it what went wrong.

In addition, try to reverse whatever you did to see if this rectifies your current problem.

Did It Suffer a Disaster?

Do you know if the hard drive suffered some type of physical disaster? Was the PC on when you lost power in a storm or experienced a power surge (especially if the PC wasn't protected by a surge suppressor or UPS)? If so, it's more likely, but not certain, that there has been actual hardware-level damage. The same is true if you tried to connect the drive with the PC turned on.

That damage can be there even if it's not immediately visible. For example, even if a PC itself does not get touched by a fire, the sheer heat of a fire (not to mention the smoke and water damage) can damage components like a hard drive. This can be true even when the heat doesn't melt or soften the plastic pieces in and around the PC.

Are You Using Drive-Overlay Software?

Discussed in Chapter 16, drive-overlay software is often packed with new hard drives to allow PCs with slightly older BIOSes to work with that hard drive and recognize its full capacity.

When drive-overlay software is preventing a hard drive from performing, you'll typically see an on-screen message telling you to insert the recovery or boot disk for that overlay software. This disk is likely one you created when you installed the drive and configured the drive-overlay software.

If your current situation involves error messages that reference that drive-overlay software, check the software's documentation and/or the manufacturer's web site for troubleshooting notes (another good use for a spare Internet-ready PC). You need to resolve the drive-overlay issue before you determine whether the hard drive itself is having a problem.

Have You Scanned for Viruses?

If you're seeing a drive light for the hard drive but it's not responding or it's giving you an error message, use a floppy disk-based virus scanner.

Viruses can do a number of nasty disk-based tricks, including overwriting the master boot record (MBR) needed to boot the hard drive (the fix for that is discussed in Chapter 7), deleting core operating system files, and scrambling drive partitions.

How Is Your PC Power Supply?

While this is a long shot, it's possible that your PC power supply is failing and needs replacement or is underpowered so it doesn't have enough juice to supply to this drive along with the other components that require power.

A few of the ways I've seen my power supplies fail was to watch one or two devices (usually drives) that formerly were powered up fine suddenly receive no power while everything else operated normally. It took changing out the power supply (usually as a last-ditch effort because I couldn't figure out what else could be responsible) each time before I got power back to everything that needed it.

Troubleshooting Errors and Warnings

Problem hard drives often announce their displeasure in the form of on-screen errors and warnings or through error codes you find when running your manufacturer's drive diagnostic utility. Let's look at the major drive-related error messages and learn how to use them to figure out what's wrong.

> **NOTE** *For troubleshooting purposes, turn off Power Management in Windows or in your BIOS, as first discussed in Chapter 6, "Transforming Yourself into a Smart Troubleshooter."*

Responding to On-Screen Errors and Warnings

Hard drive error messages and warnings usually appear when you first try to start the PC and after a brief wait (while the system tries in vain to access the drive), an error appears on the screen before Windows would load normally. Sometimes such messages appear as you work in Windows itself and usually, when you're trying to read from or write to the affected drive.

Errors Indicating a Problem with the Data or Drive

The following messages often indicate either physical damage to the drive or corruption of the data or file system on the drive:

    Data Error Reading Drive <drive-letter>

    Error Reading Drive <drive-letter>

    I/O Error

    Seek Error/Sector Not Found

    Serious Disk Error Writing Drive <drive-letter>

With these errors, try to check the disk for errors if you can keep the PC working. For this, use ScanDisk or CHKDSK. If either ScanDisk or CHKDSK reports errors they can't fix or mentions possible physical damage to the drive, immediately make your best attempt to back up the data on the drive. Then contact your hard drive manufacturer, try data-recovery software, or consult a data-recovery specialist. In any event, replacement of the hard drive will probably be necessary.

You should be aware that it's possible to see some or most of these errors and warnings without actual damage to the drive or its data. Certain temporary or easily fixed situations like a loose or failing data cable or short-term overheating can generate errors. For example, if I'm operating a hot-running PC in a very warm room without good PC cooling practices, I might see a seek or reading drive error message. If I'm smart, I'll shut down my PC properly and let it cool down before I attempt to do more work; this temporary problem could turn to drive or data damage if I don't. Of course, if I'm very smart, I'll consider buying a drive-cooling fan as discussed in Chapter 11.

Overclocking, a practice where you modify BIOS settings past their recommended operating levels to achieve better speed and performance, can produce these errors, too. Errors can be the direct result of excessive settings and the overheating that accompanies pushing hardware to its limits. If you overclock and then begin to see drive errors, consider this a distinct possibility and reverse the changes you made to see if the errors stop.

NOTE *You may hear the term* head crash *referred to in relation to hard drive failures. A* head crash *is a specific type of hardware failure where the read/write heads of the drive, normally positioned carefully to move over but not touch the drive's platters, instead come into contact with the surface, damaging the platter and the data it contains. The result may leave you temporarily able to open files (or not), but you'll notice a great deal of noise coming from the drive (clicking, grinding, or strain). This is something you cannot repair.*

Working with a Drive Stuck in MS-DOS Compatibility Mode

In pre-Windows XP versions (95/98/Me), you'll sometimes see hard drives running in what is called *MS-DOS Compatibility Mode*. This means that the drives have failed to clear the Windows' startup evaluation for whether such drives can load and run properly.

Unfortunately, you won't always see an on-screen error message about this, and you may not even discover it until you go looking. Instead, what you may notice is a deadly slow system, particularly with any operation that involves the hard drive.

However, when you choose Start ➢ Settings ➢ Control Panel ➢ System ➢ Performance tab, you'll find the message

```
Compatibility Mode Paging reduces overall system performance
```

This problem may occur due to

- Failure of the hard drive's on-board controller. This requires drive replacement because today's hard disk controllers are typically built into IDE/ATA hard drives.

- A virus. Use anti-virus software to perform a full scan.

- A hardware conflict between the hard drive controller and another piece of hardware, for example, both devices trying to use the same IRQ. Check Device Manager for a yellow exclamation mark (!) indicating a conflict, find what else it's conflicting with, and rearrange them based on information described in Chapter 6.

- Something (you or software) has disabled the hard drive controller in Device Manager, where it appears as a red x. Click the x, try to enable the controller again, and investigate what you may have installed that caused this problem.

NOTE *I've seen Compatibility Mode crop up frequently with older laptops where you have to swap in and out different drives such as a CD-ROM and floppy drive. In this case, shutting the laptop down and restarting it often makes Compatibility Mode disappear.*

Manufacturer-Specific Error Codes

In addition to the kinds of error messages your BIOS at bootup and Windows during your session produce related to hard drive problems, you may find that your drive manufacturer has a list of error codes their drives might report. Such messages are either generated by or only seen within the drive-management software that comes with some hard drives.

For example, Western Digital hard drives typically come with Data Lifeguard software that can report various errors, many of which mean "replace the drive if you get this error." There is even an online version of the Data Lifeguard software to test your drive through your Internet connection and browser while connected to their site (`http://support.wdc.com/dlg/onlinedlg.asp`).

Many hard drive manufacturers do not accept a hard drive for a return or repair without first running their diagnostics. Call the manufacturer first and ask for a return authorization. At this point, they usually ask for the error code. If they ask for the error code, they expect you to run the diagnostics. If you send in a drive without the error code, they'll simply return the drive to you without testing.

Drive-Checking and Data-Recovery Software

Before you purchase a software package off the shelf at your local computer store to try to rescue your drive, know what to look for. There are six important issues to understand with regard to drive-checking and/or data-recovery software:

It must work from a floppy.   If you buy a hard drive repair or recovery program that principally works from the hard drive itself (meaning, you have to install and run it from the problem hard drive), you may be stuck up the proverbial creek if you can't access the hard drive enough to run the software. You need to get software that will run in emergency mode from a floppy disk. Make sure to add this disk to your PC Recovery Resource Kit (discussed in Chapter 4).

You must be able to undo the changes it makes.   Some of the best drive-checking and data-recovery software includes a feature that allows you to undo changes it may make as part of the recovery process. This is useful because you may discover later that the changes may not have corrected a problem and you need a way to undo them. Check the documentation carefully before using it to make sure you can reverse the changes.

It must support your version of Windows and your file system.   Make sure the software you choose is compatible with your version of Windows and that it supports your file system type. Your file system type is probably FAT32, although some drives use FAT16 or the NTFS format available in Windows NT and XP.

It shouldn't write to the problem drive.   You have a problem if you use software that works by writing "recovered" files back to the drive you're trying to salvage. Most good utilities only read from the problem drive; they write any recovery files to another drive or media type such as a floppy.

Use the software as directed.   You generally can't pick and choose what functions the software performs because there are set procedures it must follow to do its work. Read the documentation and follow the instructions carefully.

Make sure you understand what it can and can't fix.   The type of drive-recovery software you can either download as shareware or purchase off the shelf in your local computer store isn't designed to salvage files off a physically damaged drive. For that, you need a drive-recovery service that uses sophisticated electronics and special tools to retrieve data, and their success rate can differ from drive condition to drive condition.

WARNING *If after reading the documentation and the web site supporting the product, you still can't figure out how to use the software, don't use it. This is not a good area in which to guess.*

Types of Recovery Software

Let me first tell you about one of the most talked-about pieces of software of this type. Often considered the premier hard drive diagnostic and recovery utility, Gibson Research's venerable SpinRite (www.grc.com) is still going strong. Although I haven't used it recently (I mostly use Windows XP; SpinRite's last version, 5.0, only states support for Windows 95/98/Me), SpinRite saved my sanity, my drives, and lots of my data many times over the past few years. In one of its first versions, it fixed a hard drive for me when the manufacturer insisted it was a lost cause. That drive lasted another few years before I retired it without experiencing another serious problem. Several years ago, when I compared SpinRite against other products of this type, SpinRite did the best job, by far.

Why SpinRite works so well would take a book of its own to document, but let me summarize by saying it approaches the drive from a more basic organizational level than most disk utilities (some of which seem to focus on more surface issues), and it seems more aggressive in its efforts to repair and recover data. For $89, you can purchase a copy and download SpinRite directly from the web site; it's still the utility I recommend most often.

Even better known is Norton Disk Doctor, available as part of Symantec's Norton Utilities. Like SpinRite, Disk Doctor used to be one of my top-recommended PC utilities because of its comprehensive disk diagnostics and special tools. Many people I know and admire still use

Norton Disk Doctor, although I myself don't always have the latest version handy. Disk Doctor doesn't seem quite as robust as SpinRite and wasn't always as informative as some of the manufacturer-supplied diagnostics.

Let's look at some other products:

GetDataBack by Runtime Software (www.runtime.org); $69   With versions for both FAT and NTFS and that support Windows 95/98, GetBackData (see Figure 17.1) takes you through a five-step drive-recovery process and offers useful information about the drive's characteristics. You can download a copy-disabled demo to give it a look before you opt to buy.

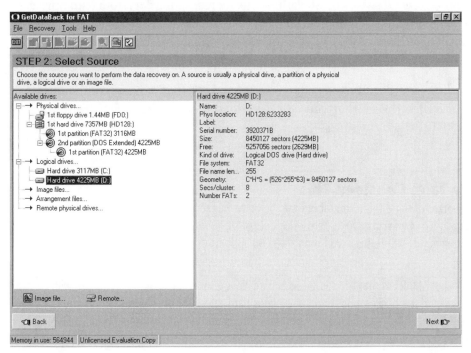

Figure 17.1 *Step 2 in data recovery in GetBackData: Selecting a drive to salvage*

Hard Drive Mechanic Deluxe/Gold by Higher Ground Software, Inc. (www .highergroundsoftware.com); $69.97 retail   Hard Drive Mechanic works with a Windows boot disk (Hard Drive Mechanic Gold supports Windows 95/98/NT/Me/2000/XP) and includes both diagnostics and IDE/SMART utilities designed to get to the root of a problem and repair it. The Rescue Disc option lets you create a set of master disks from which you can undo any change or repair made by the program. A free demo is available for downloading from their web site.

Media Tools III by ACR Data Recovery Services (`www.data-recovery-software.com`)
The unregistered version of Media Tools III that you can download from their web site offers some important information about drive health, but it can't perform any repairs.

R-Studio by R-Tools Technology, Inc. (`www.r-tt.com/RStudio.shtml`); $49.95   R-Studio can do remote data recovery over a network (as well as on local drives) and supports all recent versions of Windows plus both FAT and NTFS file systems. Their downloadable demo restricts you to saving files under 64KB.

Stellar Phoenix by Stellar Information Systems Ltd (`www.stellarinfo.com/data-recovery.htm`)   A friend swears by Stellar Phoenix for recovering data from hard drive corruption, but the only pricing available is listed in Indian rupees. It's possible to order a copy from the U.S., but you'll have to guess what the conversion rate is. Versions for both NTFS and FAT are available for purchase online.

NOTE *When I discuss data-recovery services later, note that several companies offer do-it-yourself software that you can download (usually for a registration price) and use to recover the data yourself.*

A Cautionary Tale: Consider This

When a former co-worker of mine found out about this book, he suggested I mention Active SMART (`www.ariolic.com/activesmart/`), a hard drive analysis tool he credits with saving three weeks' worth of intricate designs just before his seven-month-old 60GB hard drive (which replaced another disastrous drive) failed.

Active SMART (recall that SMART is the technology your hard drive uses to help the system work with it) is a diagnostic utility that sits in the background, monitoring your hard drives for problems that indicate the drive is under stress or may fail. It can be configured to alert you through an e-mail or through your network if it detects a situation that needs your attention.

My workmate said he installed a free demo version of it on the advice of someone else, and upon running it for the first time, it reported a few problems related to the way his primary drive was behaving. This fellow knew he hadn't been backing up because he had been too busy. Nervous, he was smart enough to do a full backup of his sensitive data "just in case."

Two mornings later, he turned on his PC to a full drive failure. Those warnings that got him to do a backup prevented him from missing an important client deadline.

He tells me it's $25 (for the registration of Active SMART), very well spent considering what you risk losing.

Of course, if he had been backing up his data all along…

Data-Recovery and Drive-Recovery Services

Data-recovery services or drive-recovery services (although it's usually not the drive you get back) are usually performed by companies that specialize in this kind of work. You ship your drive to them, and they try to extract the data from it and ship it back to you, usually on CD or DVD or tape cartridge, along with the drive.

Data recovery in such situations is a clinical process. Many companies perform it in a clean room because controlling dust particles is important in this kind of work. These companies use advanced hardware and software tools, and they often create their own software as part of the work. If you know anything about forensic science, where technicians pore over minute particles looking for evidence, understand that data recovery is considered something of a forensic science itself.

A good data-recovery technician is part hardware guru, part archaeologist, and part detective, and likely possesses a great deal of patience along with some special training.

Some local repair shops or PC technicians may offer data recovery as one of their services, but I'd think carefully before going this route. There are many single-person PC repair shops that do a remarkable job, but don't take your hard drive to anyone other than a qualified data-recovery specialist. Personally and professionally, I'd take my chances with data-recovery software before I'd trust it to an unqualified person. In fact, several technicians who advertise these services rely on products like SpinRite or Norton Disk Doctor.

Serious data recovery isn't a routine procedure, and not everyone can do it with the same level of precision and success. Since you now know that every time you access a damaged drive, you reduce your chance of recovering data from it, you really want to have the right people do it from the start.

In larger metropolitan areas, you may be able to locate data-recovery specialists in your telephone yellow pages. However, you can also find a number of them online with web sites that describe their services.

Some of the Services Available

Let me give you some examples of online data-recovery services so that you can get more information before you contact them or get a free online cost estimate. But before I list them, here's a tip: Many of these web sites offer invaluable information about drive errors, types of drive damage, and data recovery. They can be worth a visit to learn more even if you don't decide to go the professional recovery route.

Disaster Recovery Group (www.disasterrecoverygroup.com); 1-909-509-7754 or e-mail at sales@disasterrecoverygroup.com   The Disaster Recovery Group offers an online quote tool and a free drive evaluation before they begin work.

DriveSavers Data Recovery (www.drivesavers.com); 1-800-440-1904 or e-mail at recovery@drivesavers.com   Claiming a 90% success rate and a great story about recovering information from Sean Connery's computer, DriveSavers (see Figure 17.2) offers a complete line of professional data recovery services and a great informational site as well. Check out the pictures of hard drives that look as if they've been driven over by a Hummer or dropped from a plane flying at 35,000 feet.

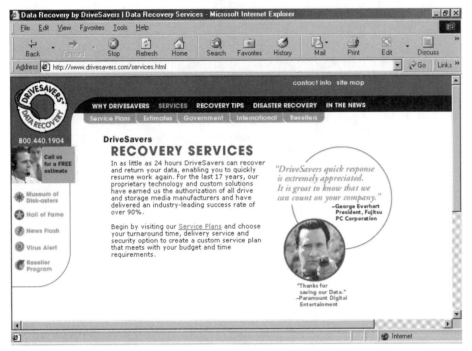

Figure 17.2 *Drivesavers.com is one of the recovery specialists offering a free estimate.*

Ontrack (www.ontrack.com); 1-800-872-2599   You've probably encountered Ontrack's name before, since they write drive installation and management software for many hard drive manufacturers. But many consumers don't realize they also offer data-recovery software (including Ontrack EasyRecovery) and a complete roster of professional data-recovery services. Their web site offers a wizard-driven recovery assessment program that analyzes the recovery job needed and gives you an online service quote. They can also attempt to recover your data remotely through a high-speed Internet connection without your needing to physically ship the drive to them.

Total Recall (`www.recallusa.com`); 1-800-743-0594   Total Recall boasts 15 years of experience, an online recovery quote system, and some software solutions for letting you try to recover the data yourself.

NOTE *You can find more data-recovery specialists by using a web search engine and searching on "drive recovery services" or "data recovery services."*

The Cost of Data-Recovery Services

The costs of professional data-recovery services vary widely and change based on a number of factors, including the overall condition of the drive you send them, how much data needs to be recovered, and how much work they have to put into the job. As you might expect, this can be labor-intensive work that's usually performed by highly trained people.

Some groups offer basic recovery services beginning at around $250; you should normally expect to pay between $400 and several thousand dollars.

Check the recommendations in the next section for more information.

What to Determine

Because you're a single individual or a small businessperson, you may find it easier if you limit your search for drive-recovery services to those who can

- Give you an estimate in writing up front (e-mail is fine).

- Don't charge you for data that can't be recovered, although you'll still have to pay a basic charge for their effort.

If you do decide to contract with an individual or company, make sure you determine up front

- the firm's level of experience and their success rate

- all anticipated costs, including any special fees

- what your charge will be if nothing can be recovered

- when you can expect to get back the recovered files (if any) and in what format

- their privacy policy (You don't want your private records being seen by anyone else.)

A Cautionary Tale: Don't Assume You Have Protection

Let me relate a short but scary story from someone who used to work for a "discount" investigative agency that was situated next to a large PC sales and repair store that specialized in upgrading computers with better components like larger and faster hard drives.

One day, one of the co-owners of the investigative agency happened to be standing out in the alley having a cigarette when he noticed how many hard drives were getting tossed into the dumpster. Business hadn't been great at the agency lately, and all that discarded data gave him an idea for generating some new accounts.

The investigator approached the owner of the PC shop, asking him if he was willing go in together on an innovative proposition: the owner or one of his technicians would pull information like e-mails and private documents from the discarded drives and pass them to the detective, who would sell this private data to others. The investigator figured he could make a small mint selling incriminating information to other parties in divorce cases, for example, and he'd be helped along by having the upgraded PC customer's name.

Thankfully, the PC shop owner was horrified at the idea and refused. When he later found the investigator in the dumpster, diving in to retrieve some of those drives himself, the police were called. Local authorities were none too amused.

Still, there are firms that do drive forensics for the express purpose of uncovering deleted, confidential material for divorcing spouses and employers trying to make a case against someone.

The moral of this story: Watch what you put in a dumpster and watch who you do business with.

Steps for Installing a New IDE Hard Drive

I'd feel remiss if I didn't explain the process of removing a damaged hard drive and installing a replacement *just in case*. For this, you'll need the following:

- The replacement hard drive
- A screwdriver (This is usually a Phillips screwdriver, but check your existing hard drive installation to see what's required.)
- A working data ribbon cable
- A boot or Startup disk with CD-ROM support and a full (not upgrade) version of your operating system (For those of you using Windows XP, you need the Windows XP install CD.)

- Installation documentation for your new drive
- Drive-management software for the new drive (if included)

TIP *Keep your new hard drive in its anti-static bag prior to its actual installation.*

Before you start the actual installation, check your new drive to be sure it's the exact one you thought you purchased; check the serial number and capacity, both of which should be listed on the metal identifying plate on the drive itself. If the new drive shows any signs of damage (denting, watermarks, and so on), contact the place where you purchased it for a replacement.

It's also important to jumper the drive for the way you want to use it. *Jumpers*, first mentioned in Chapter 2, "How Your Hardware, Operating System, and Applications Work Together," are two parallel rows of pins that are jumpered using a squarish-shaped piece of plastic called a *shunt* that is pressed over the two pins on two separate rows of pins, creating a bridge or jumper to configure the drive for its proper use.

How you jumper a drive depends on how it will be used and corresponds to markings on the back of the drive (where the two rows of pins are located, along with the ribbon cable and power connection), as you can see in Figure 17.3.

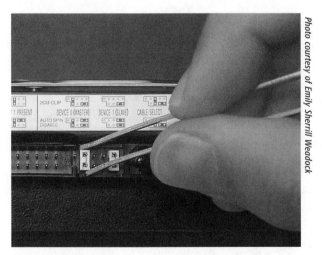

Photo courtesy of Emily Sherrill Weadock

Figure 17.3 *How a hard drive is jumpered*

These markings typically designate Master, Slave, Single, or Cable Select:

- Jumpered as Master (M)—The M setting is used when the hard drive will be the first of two IDE drives attached to a single IDE channel on the motherboard, with the Master drive being the only one of the two directly connected to the IDE channel on the motherboard. Note that some drives require no jumper on the M setting when there is just one drive attached to the cable. This was done so that PC builders did not have to set a jumper if the PC had only one drive. If you add another drive to that cable, the Master will have to be jumpered.

- Jumpered as Slave (S)—The S setting is used when the hard drive will be the second of two IDE drives attached to a single IDE channel (cable) on the motherboard. The second drive is connected directly to the first (master) drive, which in turn is plugged into the IDE channel.

- Jumpered as Single—Use this when a drive is the only one connected by ribbon cable to the IDE channel controller on the motherboard.

- Jumpered as Cable Select—Often this is how a new drive is jumpered to start, but use this only if drive instructions specify you should do so for your situation.

There's a wealth of helpful information about your hard drive on your drive manufacturer's web site. For example, I easily located a jumper diagram when visiting the Support section at Western Digital's site (www.wdc.com), as shown in Figure 17.4.

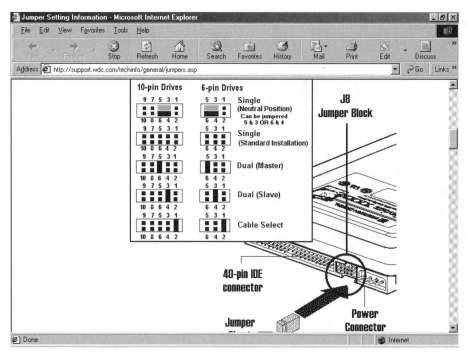

Figure 17.4 *A jumper diagram for a Western Digital Caviar drive from Western Digital's web site*

Once the drive is properly checked and the correct jumper set for the way you intend to use the drive, you can proceed with the hard drive installation by following these steps:

1. Shut down the PC, disconnect power, and remove the cover.

2. Don your anti-static wrist strap.

3. Locate the hard drive in its drive bay that you intend to replace, note its current orientation (how and where it sits), and find its corresponding screws (on either side of the drive frame within in the case) that mount it into place. Remove these screws (usually four) and set them aside.

4. At the back of the drive, note the exact installation of the data ribbon cable where the blue or red wire is located because you want to duplicate it later when you install the new drive. Then carefully remove both the data ribbon cable and the power supply connector from the drive.

5. Carefully slide the old drive out of its bay and set it aside.

TIP *If you have lingering questions about how the new hard drive should be jumpered and you're installing the new drive as a replacement for the old one and not changing anything else, check the jumper setting on the old drive. While the exact jumpers may vary, see whether it's set for Master, Slave, Single, or Cable Select and duplicate those settings.*

6. Remove the new drive from its anti-static bag and slide it into the recently vacated drive bay.

7. Using the screws you removed to take out the old drive, screw the new drive (through the drive bay) into place. Be sure the mounting is level (not wildly tilted) and secure (doesn't wobble).

8. Attach the drive ribbon cable to the back of the drive (see Figure 17.5) so that the color-coded edge of the ribbon cable is oriented to pin 1 on the hard drive. Pin 1 is almost always to the right side of the drive as you look at it from the rear perspective. Be sure the seating is firm. If the drive is the master or the first of two drives using the same ribbon cable to attach to the same IDE channel controller on the motherboard, make sure the cable connection to the second drive is secure as well.

Photo courtesy of Emily Sherrill Weadock

Figure 17.5 *Attaching the data ribbon cable to the back of the drive*

9. Insert the power supply connector into the power connection (it is keyed) at the back of the hard drive. Again, make sure this is firmly seated; this is one of the tougher connections to get right the first time.

10. At this point, you can replace the PC cover (or do what I do and leave it off until I know the drive is seen and working). Then, reconnect power to the PC.

What you do next depends on your particular situation. Assuming your drive is brand new and hasn't been partitioned and formatted yet, do that using the instructions found in Chapter 16 for partitioning and formatting with one caveat: The drive-management software that came with your new drive (or the drive software you downloaded from the manufacturer's web site) may take care of this when you run its Setup utility. Some software does it all except for installing the operating system, while other programs need you to partition, then format, and once that's done, you can run Setup to configure the drive the rest of the way. Read your drive documentation or check the manufacturer's web site for more information related to your specific drive.

The drive Setup software checks your BIOS to make sure it works with the capacity of the new drive and, if not, applies something like drive-overlay software so that it can. As I've mentioned before, drive-overlay software can get messy later if you have a problem with the drive or your system, so I avoid using it by first seeing if a drive can be recognized by the BIOS on its own and, if not, trying to obtain the right BIOS upgrade.

If you plan for the new hard drive to be your primary hard drive, the operating system must be installed after formatting (Chapter 16 provides instructions for that). Once this is accomplished, install your applications, restore a previously stored drive image or backup, or use a program like DriveCopy to copy the contents of an existing hard drive to the replacement drive.

If the drive was previously partitioned and formatted for use on another PC and simply transferred to this system, it's possible that the drive will be detected and made available to you just like it was always there. For example, while I was writing this morning, I stopped to take a moment to remove a second hard drive from one PC and install it as a second hard drive in another PC. Under Windows XP, the drive was ready and available the instant I turned the PC on after the physical installation.

It's hard to believe, but we're about to move into the last topic of this book, "Knowing When to Call Professionals," in which you'll learn about warranties and tips for best success when contacting the pros for assistance.

CHAPTER 18

Knowing When to Call the Professionals

Sometimes, regardless of your best efforts and how many different times you've reread the instructions or troubleshooting recommendations, you just have to call for help.

In this last chapter, I'm going to explain why product warranties can be important and the limitations you face in exercising them. I'll also answer that time-honored question, "When do I take a problem product back to the store, and when do I go to the manufacturer to repair it?"

Just as critical, I'll describe what information you need to have on hand before you call for assistance and how you can increase your chances of success when you do call. You'll be amazed at how politeness, organization, and limiting your distractions can get you the results you want.

And finally, I'll discuss insurance reimbursement for nasty disasters. You should consider this *before* disaster hits because you might not be covered as well as you think, or you might not be covered at all.

Understanding Product Warranties

A warranty is a statement of good faith by the manufacturer or distributor of a product that what they sell you is free of known defects or problems and will operate as they say it will. Most warranties are designed to do two things: protect the company from unreasonable demands if they are sued by an unhappy customer and offer the customer a plan of recourse if he or she finds the product doesn't work or won't work properly.

The term *warranty* is essentially the same as what is also known as a guarantee; in fact, both names have the same old North French root word.

"Read one warranty and you've read them all," an associate of mine likes to say. But I don't think that's terribly accurate. While almost all product warranties suffer from an overabundance of legalese, there can be quite a bit of difference between what they offer and how they phrase them. Just the difference between hardware and software warranties can be appreciable, since few software companies offer repair or replacement of equipment potentially damaged by hardware, and few hardware companies take responsibility for software issues possibly arising from the use of their devices.

> **TIP** *When I purchase an important new piece of PC hardware or consumer electronics, I look carefully at the stated coverage period of the warranty. Then I record this information in my date-reminder software so that it alerts me when I'm near the end of my coverage. But, of course, as we all know, nothing ever breaks down until the day after the warranty ends.*

A Cautionary Tale: Keep a Copy

I know it's a pain but try to save your warranty in a place where you can find it again later.

Several years ago, I bought an expensive PC power supply via mail order from a firm no longer in business that arrived in horrendous condition. The box wasn't damaged but the unit looked like it had been on the Titanic and was salvaged in time to make it aboard the Hindenburg, only to somehow come back again to ride along with that Mars probe that disappeared into the atmosphere of the red planet.

Because the power supply arrived so damaged, I assumed I could return it and get another unit in good condition. It actually took three phone calls, four e-mails, and a snail mail letter to the corporate office to get them to take the unit for a return.

What did they replace my expensive new power supply with? A used one of far lesser value. When I complained, they pointed me to a copy of their product warranty on their web site that stated, "Unless special exception is granted, all damaged units will be replaced with reconditioned units."

Huh?

First of all, I wasn't exercising my warranty because I had never gotten the first unit in a condition in which I could try to use it. Strictly speaking, this doesn't fall under the warranty but under regular sales.

More importantly, the warranty they pointed me to was something new. When I had purchased my first unit three weeks before, I received a *different* warranty, with no such provision about replacing a new unit with a reconditioned one. Only the fact that I had made a copy of that original warranty made me successful in arguing with the company that they had to replace a new bad unit with a new good unit.

While you can take such matters to the Better Business Bureau or other consumer organizations, the most effective approach is making a strong case to the company.

Remember, if you don't want to store all that paper, you can always use a scanner to scan your product warranties and keep them on your computer (with a copy in backup, of course). That's what I do now, and it works well for me, especially since I always forget to file my actual paperwork.

Types of Warranties

There are many different types of warranties. An *implied warranty* is one that is unwritten and based on common law. It stipulates that a customer receive fair value for the money he or she spends. An *express warranty* is one that is documented and usually included with a product. An express warranty spells out the terms and conditions under which the manufacturer will act in good faith to correct a problem you may encounter with the device or service.

NOTE *Most warranties are written based on state laws that conform to a set of uniform guidelines for product merchantability.*

According to FindLaw's web site (`www.findlaw.com`), whenever a product costs $10 or more to purchase, a company is required to provide either a full or limited warranty for it.

Most warranties included with PC products are ones called limited warranties. While a *full warranty* offers certain commitments to the customer without restrictions, a *limited warranty* places limits on such conditions. Federal law prohibits companies from knowingly offering a warranty that may be perceived as deceptive, for example, claiming the customer will get a new replacement unit when the company only ships refurbished units if a defective one is returned.

Before looking at a sample limited warranty, let's talk about extended warranties, which were briefly touched upon in Chapter 16, "Starting from Scratch the Hard Way." *Extended warranties* are offered to extend or enhance the services offered under a normal limited product warranty. For example, you can pay extra and get three years of warranty coverage rather than a single year, or you can pay extra so that all parts and labor are covered rather than just those specified under the warranty.

I always recommend people gauge their likelihood of actually pursuing their warranty against the cost of an extended warranty. Many people buy extended warranties as insurance policies against future problems, and then they forget they are covered or never exercise them at all.

What a Product Warranty Means

Decoding a product warranty can take a few reads and may be easier to understand if you have experience with consumer or contract law to make sense of all the nuances of language.

In a moment, I'll show you a sample warranty and help you understand what the manufacturer is telling you about their obligations and yours regarding a defective or damaged product.

However, there are some important points you should look for in such warranties, including

- The time period the warranty covers. There may be more than one time period; for example, you might have a year's warranty on repair but only 90 days on any needed replacement parts.

- The terms of recovery or what you can expect from the manufacturer in terms of repair, replacement, or refund.

- Special limitations that may spell out conditions under which you may operate the product that will remove the warranty coverage.

- Your responsibilities, which usually include proper notification to the manufacturer of the problem and obtaining a return-to-manufacturer authorization (RMA) number or form before you return the product for repair, replacement, or refund.

- Your liability, meaning what you may have to pay (for parts, labor, or both) to replace a component if the problem found with the product isn't one the manufacturer feels it is responsible for.

A Sample Limited Warranty

Let's look at a sample warranty, this one carved from similar wording appearing in five different product warranties and paraphrased here (names have been excluded to protect the guilty):

> [Our company's] complete obligation under this warranty is limited to the repair or replacement of a part deemed to be defective by our company or its authorized service agents. No third-party evaluations are accepted of defective parts. Only at our sole and individual discretion will a refund of purchase price be tendered under any circumstances.
>
> The customer assumes all liability for the proper use of this product and its appropriate maintenance, and only at [our company's] option, upon full proof of proper purchase by the customer is repair, replacement, or refund made available to the customer. Such cases must be preceded by appropriate notification to [our company] within the time limits set forth by this warranty. Only if the customer is approved for further consideration should the customer send the product back, at customer's cost for proper shipping and insurance of said package, to the address provided to said customer, within ninety (90) days of the purchase date.
>
> If third-party software accompanies the distribution of this product, [our company] cannot be held liable for any problems it may cause for the user of that product and its software. Please see any accompanying literature and end-user license that may be included with that so-called third-party software, and contact that company for assistance.

Believe it or not, this is one of the easier-to-read warranties, devoid of the conditions that can make your head begin to pound as you try to understand the meaning behind the words.

In this case, the company is telling you that its only obligation to you, the customer, is to repair or replace a defective part and then *only* if the company deems that the part is defective. You and/or your PC technician deciding it's defective may not be good enough.

This warranty specifies that you must return the product at your cost (including any insurance you choose to place on the package you send) to allow the company to make this determination, and this must be done within 90 days of the day you purchased the product. Then, if they rule in your favor, you might get a replacement. This warranty makes refunds sound tough to obtain.

NOTE *To be completely fair, in reality, most companies honor their warranties regardless of how many caveats their product disclaimers offer.*

But notice that you're left on your own with any third-party software the manufacturer chooses to include with the product they sell to you. If you have problems with it, you're shuttled back to the software's publisher, even though you got it as part of your product package.

Returning a Product Under Warranty

Store return policies vary widely and can change frequently, depending on what other stores in your area are doing or as laws in your area change to provide better (or sadly, sometimes worse) protection for consumers.

Always check the return policy for the particular store from which you buy PC equipment. Most stores will refuse to accept a return if

- You don't show full proof of purchase.

- You return it incomplete, without returning major or valuable components of the product.

- You bring it back in an outrageous condition or showing damage only you could have caused.

- The item is marked "clearance" or "all sales final," and the reason you're returning it isn't because it is defective.

Some stores may charge a restocking fee, which may be a flat rate like $15 or $20, or a percentage of the product's purchase price (between 5 percent and 15 percent). However, regardless of store policy, you should be able to return a defective product without a restocking fee. If the store tries to assess one anyway, ask politely to speak to a manager.

Most stores establish a specific time period for returns. In my experience, this is often no more than 30 days from the day you purchased it and took it from the store or from the day they shipped it to you. Some stores and mail order outlets can be very strict about this, so that even if it took a week or two for your product to arrive at your home or office after it shipped, the clock on returns starts ticking the moment it shipped.

Once you exceed that time period, you'll need to contact the manufacturer, who may only accept it for return, repair, or refund if you have a condition or problem with the device covered by your warranty.

WARNING *Always try to install and use your new PC hardware as soon as possible after purchase to protect your ability to return it if it's defective or missing critical components.*

Unhappy Realities of Warranty Exercising

Don't think of a warranty as a quick fix for defective or malfunctioning hardware, because it's not. Some companies are very good and will actually ship a replacement to you before you send back the damaged device. Other companies can make you wait weeks and weeks.

Remember the brand-new PC with the dead motherboard I told you about in Chapter 16? It's been dead for two weeks, and I have yet to get my RMA so I can return the PC to the company to replace the motherboard. They've estimated it will take them two weeks to get it back to me repaired.

They've taken so long that I can no longer return it to the place I purchased it, and every day for the past week, I've listened to the manufacturer and the shipper (the company who is supposed to pick up and deliver it) blame each other for the missing RMA. It's taken so long now that I'm investigating other remedies, including a letter from my lawyer (but only because she's a friend with an ominous-looking letterhead) to simply get someone to take responsibility so I can get this repaired. Needless to say, I won't be buying a PC from this company again in my lifetime.

Understanding When a Warranty Has Been Voided

There are many things you can do to a product that will void its warranty and absolve the manufacturer of any obligation to help you in the event of a problem.

Depending on the type of product and its features, you may invalidate your warranty if

- You open a device that is clearly labeled "Do Not Open." Monitors often bear this warning, as do some hard drive cases.

- You operate the product in a manner specifically contradicted in the instructions. For example, the warranty may specify that the device must be plugged into a grounded outlet but you use an ungrounded outlet or you operate a device near moisture.

- You modify the device in some way that changes its operation, like overclocking a video adapter or motherboard.

- You destroyed the product through your own actions, even if accidentally. Someone I knew once tried to return a new hard drive he managed to run over with his car; he was quite upset when the store wouldn't take it back.

Issues Concerning Disasters and Product Warranties

Under normal circumstances, your warranty won't cover damage caused by a disaster, whether it's a natural one or a nasty event wrought by you or someone with access to your PC.

One exception to this is often protection devices such as surge protectors and uninterruptible power supplies (UPSs). Since these products are meant to act as mediators or protectors against the damage that may occur to your PC setup, some manufacturers offer exceptions to help cover the cost of equipment attached to the device if it fails to deliver the promised protection. For example, let's say that you bought a home/office-capacity UPS from American Power Conversion (APC) that offers something APC calls its Equipment Protection Policy, and your UPS takes a hit from lightning. If the lightning's effects push through the protective hardware of that UPS to damage your PC, you may be eligible to collect up to $25,000 (U.S.) in repair or replacement costs for that damage under this policy.

Some restrictions may apply, of course. Often, you need to have registered the product at the time of purchase (although some manufacturers accept proof of purchase in lieu of formal registration) in order to exercise a manufacturer's policy. Read your power protection device's included literature for details.

> **WARNING** *Don't expect to just call up and say, "Send me a check because my PC is damaged." Most companies offering such policies stipulate you must return the defective device for evaluation; usually they require proof of the damage that was incurred.*

Knowing the Technical Support Options

This section describes the professional technical support options available to you, along with some information you need to know about them. Up to 70 percent of the technical support people seek is done via telephone, but the advice offered for getting the best out of your support time applies across the board, regardless of how you find your help.

Types of Support Services

The documentation accompanying your new PC or PC hardware should spell out the support options available to you, which can include

- Telephone support. The manufacturer should provide the number to call to get help for your product; this may be a toll-free number but isn't always. You may have to pay a per-incident fee, typically through a credit card or by calling a special number that automatically bills your phone account for the service. Read the conditions carefully.

- Web-based support. You may be directed to reach the company's support technicians by visiting the company's web site. From there, you leave an e-mail using a Contact Us feature in a Customer Support area or post a message in a message board or newsgroup (see Chapter 15, "Finding Help Online").

- Fax/e-mail support. These options allow you to communicate with the company via fax or through e-mail.

- On-site support. This is available only on a limited basis and on selected products; check your documentation carefully to see what restrictions or special charges may apply if a technician comes to your house. Most of the time, a company will do everything in its power to correct a problem before they send a technician out, so be prepared.

- Authorized service centers. This is usually available only for hardware (including whole PCs) under warranty, although such centers may also repair non-warranty items on other types and brands of devices.

Types of Support Professionals

In many cases, the first person to answer a support call may not be a PC technician or an expert in a particular product. You may find that the person on the other end of the line isn't even physically located at the manufacturer's company.

This varies from company to company. With very small companies, the person you speak to for technical support may also be the person who wrote the software or developed the idea for the product initially.

However, when you're calling a manufacturer for support, you don't have a lot of choices except to go through their prescribed support structure. And you rarely have any choice about who you speak to, but hopefully, the manufacturer has enough talented and experienced people to field their support calls.

What to Expect When You Call for Support

If you're calling a free (you pay only for the cost of the call, and not even that if the manufacturer offers a toll-free number) telephone support line, expect to wait on hold for several minutes. Sometimes, this can stretch to 20 minutes or more, depending on many factors, including the time of day you call and the traffic into the support line at that time.

If, instead, you're calling into a special support line where you're paying per-incident fee or paying by the number of minutes you spend on the line, you can expect a fairly short wait. Often, your call will be picked up almost immediately because you're paying for what are known as *premium services*.

Should your product's manufacturer offer on-site technical services, you're still going to have to troubleshoot over the phone before they'll send a technician out to your house. Be sure it's covered under your warranty, too, or you may be stuck paying a hefty price if it turns out the needed repair is not covered by that warranty.

If the warranty or product documentation doesn't clearly spell out your obligations in terms of cost for technical support, make this your first question when you call for support the first time.

Outsourced and Tiered Technical Support

Many companies, to economize and to broaden the number of calls they can handle, hire outside companies to provide technical support for their products. Sometimes, such hired folks concentrate just on one product or brand of products. At other companies, your product may be just one of many brands and products they support. This can create even more variety in the type of person who may be answering your call.

Many companies operate their technical support on a *tier system*. Tier 1 is the initial contact between a customer and a technical support person, where basic questions are asked and essential troubleshooting is performed. The goal is to have most problems resolved at Tier 1 without demanding the time and expertise of the more experienced support staff.

When a problem defies the best efforts of Tier 1 support, a customer may get bumped up to Tier 2 support. At Tier 2, more experienced technicians may know a product far better than the Tier 1 technicians. The thorniest problems go to Tier 3 support, where the most senior technicians (and sometimes others) become involved in trying to rectify the problem.

A Cautionary Tale:
"I Waited Forever on Hold, and Then They Rushed Me Off the Line"

I've listened to some incredibly bad canned music and prerecorded ads over the years waiting on hold for someone to pick up the support line at a software or hardware company. If you haven't yet, you probably will.

Part of the problem is that technical support folks are often given an impossible number of calls to field in one day. They find themselves harassed by supervisors if they take longer than a predefined period of time (as low as two–three minutes) on a single call. When they're under the gun to spend no more than two minutes with you, you may feel like you're pulling teeth to get them to explain a complicated set of steps.

By presenting yourself as highly motivated to fix the problem in just one call and by keeping your frustration in check, you may be able to get them to spend the extra time now so that you won't have to call again.

If they can't spend a great deal of time resolving your problem, ask if they can send you a set of instructions via e-mail (providing your problem doesn't prevent you from getting online to access it) or let you jot down a series of steps or suggestions so that you can try them later, when you're off the phone.

Here's a suggestion: If you find that a particular technical support representative was especially helpful, please ask him or her for the e-mail address of a supervisor. Then send a note letting the company know that this representative took the time to win your satisfaction. Getting this positive feedback keeps good representatives willing to go the extra distance to help because their bosses know they aren't wasting precious time.

How to Improve Your Chances of Success

The following list is gleaned from talking with hundreds of technical support representatives and users to learn what helps them most in making that first call or contact most effective.

Have Information Ready   Wherever possible, know what you're going to say before you call or write for assistance. Have a synopsis of your system and your current problem ready, along with any registration or product ID. When calling Microsoft for Windows help, for example, you'll need to provide the product key for your Windows install CD or the label listed on the certificate stuck to your PC case.

The synopsis of your system might look like this:

I'm using a Dell Optiplex with a Celeron 500MHz processor and 128 MBRAM (upgraded from 64MB). I've been having problems with the video since I installed a new game called March Hare Madness. Ever since installing it, my desktop looks different; all the letters and windows look bigger and not as clear.

Prepare to Write   Have a pen and a piece of paper handy (or your PC journal) on which to jot down notes and suggestions that may be offered to you. You may receive an incident or tracking number for your problem that you'll need if you have to call back again later.

Stay Calm   Don't get nervous, and don't lose your temper. Emotionalism doesn't help much and in fact, can hamper your ability to hear and process important information.

Call From a Good Location   If you're calling, use a telephone where you can sit at your PC; only use a wireless phone if it has very good reception from where you and your PC are located. Don't try to call from a different room from the PC where you must run back and forth. Also, don't call when you have distractions (kids, TV, other people vying for your attention) that may prevent you from giving your entire attention to the call.

If you're having a technician come into your home or office, try to limit the distractions as well.

TIP *Timing is important, too. Technical support lines are often busiest in the first two hours at the start of a workday, at lunchtime, in the last few hours of the workday, and during the early evening hours. Schedule a time to call that avoids these peak hours to reduce the time you wait on hold and to increase your chance of having the representative not be in a rush to get to the next caller.*

Make Your Presentation Clear and Succinct   If calling or talking with a technician at your home or office, speak slowly and clearly so that the other person doesn't miss important information and doesn't have to ask you to repeat what you said.

Try to limit how long you speak before you let the representative confirm your information and limit the amount of extraneous information you provide. The representative will ask you if he or she has questions you haven't yet answered.

I once found myself unable to stop a user from giving me a 20-minute monologue about all the PCs she's ever owned, the prices she paid for every component, and the names of her exotic birds before I was able to get an answer to a simple question so we could proceed. (And I'm pretty experienced at getting information quickly.) After we were done and her problem was fixed, she complained that *I* had taken so long even though I was able to show her how to fix the issue in less than seven minutes after she finally let me speak.

NOTE *Technical support representatives say that you can help them understand you better if you don't eat, apologize, use a speaker phone or a cordless phone stretched to its geographical limits, or have conversations with kids and others while you're on the line with them.*

Ask for Follow-up   If you get suggestions for fixing your problem that you must perform after you're off the phone with customer support or after the technician leaves, ask the person if there's a way you can reach him or her again. Sometimes, a representative has a badge number or can provide an incident number that can help you be back in touch for follow-up discussion. Obviously, if you're able to talk to the original person who helped you, you won't have to explain the entire problem again because they're already familiar with it.

When to Ask for Escalation   All too often, people get frustrated when they don't feel like they're being helped and do one of two things: hang up or angrily demand to speak with a supervisor.

Rather than hang up, ask the person you're speaking with what other support options are available. For example, some hardware companies can recommend a qualified service professional in your area who specifically deals with that brand of product.

As for requesting to speak to a supervisor, this is a good technique to use when you feel you're getting the run-around or you have a legitimate beef that only a supervisor can resolve like issues about warranty coverage, returns, and so on. However, this is a bad technique to use right off the bat before you've let a representative try to help you. You don't want to bring out the big guns to tackle an ant or you might be out of ammunition when you really need it.

Look Over Your Notes After the Call   Stop for a moment and review your notes after you finish your call. If you're like me, what you write in shorthand you may not be able to decipher easily later on. Make sure you can read what you wrote now while it's fresh in your mind. Also make sure you took everything down. If not, now is the time to record it.

As soon as you can, try the recommended suggestions so you can use your current incident or tracking number again if needed. Such numbers usually only sit in a manufacturer's computer for a few weeks to a few months before they are closed out.

A Cautionary Tale: The Blame Game

There is an old joke in the PC industry that goes like this: *A hardware tech support line always tells the customer, "It's a software problem" while the software support line always insists that, "No, it's a hardware problem." And when all else fails, just blame it on Microsoft or the operating system.*

You don't know how much I'd like to be able to tell you that is simply a joke and you won't run into this yourself. But you very well may, because support lines do engage in this kind of behavior.

This is especially unfortunate because there are times when there is a legitimate issue where problems with hardware are indeed caused by software or the operating system, and vice versa, leaving many users scratching their heads.

The best way to avoid this is to keep your drivers and software updated and use only hardware and software that are compatible with your version of Windows, as you've read about in previous chapters of this book.

However, if you still find yourself caught between one company telling you it's the second company's problem and the second company making the same charges against the first, ask, "OK, how can I rule out whether your product or the other product is causing the problem?" Often, there may be a single procedure or a short series of tests that can give you this answer. Do your part by following through with such tests or suggested repairs to see if you can get more information or resolve the problem.

Using a PC Repair Shop or a Private Service Technician

Although not available in all areas, you may be able to find a PC repair shop or PC service technician in your area that can help you with disasters both large and small. However, there are a few things to be aware of when taking your PC in for repair or having a third-party technician come out to work on it.

First, the expertise offered by independent shops or individuals runs the gamut from people who know little more about PC hardware and repair than you do to incredibly talented and experienced professionals who can save you a bundle while fixing your machine quickly.

Most shops and technicians fall somewhere between those two extremes. Unfortunately, it may be difficult to determine this until after they've resolved a few issues for you. Wherever possible, ask friends and/or work associates if they use a local shop and if so, which one. If you notice one name keeps coming up, that may be the shop to try first.

> **NOTE** *Some computer and consumer electronics stores have a repair department, and some allow you to bring in equipment for repair even if you didn't purchase the hardware at that particular store.*

Second, but no less importantly, check your PC or other product warranty to be sure you aren't invalidating your warranty if you have someone other than a certified technician work on it. Many companies require that you only take their products to an authorized service center or a) your repair won't be covered by warranty, if applicable, or b) the rest of your warranty is voided.

Next, ask for a written estimate when you take a system in for repair. Recall from Chapter 2, "How Your Hardware, Operating System, and Applications Work Together," that there are many situations in which repairing certain hardware components can match and even exceed the price of a new device or PC. This is especially true with laptops, where a simple drive replacement or fixing a damaged laptop display can run several hundred dollars.

> **TIP** *Let the shop know that you want a limit placed on repair/replacement costs, and that they need to contact you before they apply a fix that may exceed that limit. Wherever possible, get this in writing, even if the shop simply writes it on the receipt they give you when you drop off the product for repair. This offers you some protection if they give you an initial verbal estimate of $50 and then suddenly present you with a $500 final bill when the work is complete.*

Ask some questions before you agree to let a repair shop work on your system:

- How long has the shop or individual been in operation? Longer is usually better, because it implies more experience and a lack of consumer-related issues that might force them to close.

- Is the shop or technical service a certified or authorized repair site for any manufacturers and, if so, which ones?

- How long does the shop or technician estimate it will be before your system is repaired or you know what else needs to be done to fix it?

- Can you try the system yourself, in the shop, before you take it home to be sure it works as well as they say it does?

- Can you get your damaged parts back after replacement?

NOTE *This last point is important because there's one story you hear about disreputable repair shops of all types: They tell a customer that a part has been replaced as part of the repair, but they never actually replace it. Of course, this works best if you know the make, manufacturer, and appearance or condition of the part they are replacing before the "replacement" is made. That way, you can tell if you have the same dirty power supply (for example) you thought they replaced.*

Does My PC Repair Technician Need to be Certified?

If you're asking this question, you're probably aware that various areas of the PC industry (usually related to technical service and repair) offer certification for professionals. Becoming certified involves studying for and passing a certification exam that tests key concepts and procedures. Two examples of certifications are A+ certification and Microsoft Certified System Engineer (MCSE).

Certification can be valuable because it implies that whoever holds it has mastered a certain level of competency in their respective area (hardware, operating systems, networking, and certain applications). Many corporations and recruiting companies demand this certification in order to hire people to staff busy IT departments.

But from my personal and professional experience, I've run into many talented technicians without certification and I've encountered a host of certified people whose skills are lacking. So while I think being certified can be valuable for someone trying to be hired, I'm not certain it always tells you, as a consumer, much about the type of person performing your PC repairs. In addition, because most people get certified in a particular area (say, networking), it doesn't always mean they know how to fix a problematic Windows installation or a failing motherboard.

Insurance Reimbursement for PC Damage

Is your PC specifically covered in the event of a disaster? You might assume it is if it's located in your home or office. Yet that's not always the case. Review your current insurance policies carefully now, before you experience a disaster.

The rule of thumb with homeowner's insurance is that it doesn't cover the specific value of a PC beyond the similar values attached to other appliances in your home such as a refrigerator or a television.

Renter's insurance is usually limited to a set amount of money; you might get $5,000 for the complete contents of an apartment or small office space rather than what it may actually cost you to replace all the individual items, including your PC equipment.

Comprehensive office insurance coverage may go a lot farther than homeowner's or renter's insurance in helping you recover your actual losses with regard to your computer setup.

If you think you want or need specific coverage for a PC and the value of the data in it, contact your insurance agent to add this coverage. Some plans start as low as about $50 a year for a basic desktop setup (higher for a laptop because of theft and damage potential), and cover a full range of disasters, including flood, fire, theft, and vandalism.

To Sum Up

Congratulations! If you've made it to this page, you've taken serious steps toward empowering yourself as a PC user and protecting your investment and your data in the event of a disaster, either natural or man-made:

- Become familiar with your PC setup (inside and out) before disaster strikes.

- Back up your files regularly.

- Use power protection.

- Keep your PC Recovery Resource Kit, including your PC journal, both updated and handy.

- Avoid unnecessary risks.

With such smart planning and protection in place, you're ready for almost anything life—or human fingers—brings your way.

INDEX

Note to the Reader: Throughout this index **boldfaced** page numbers indicate primary discussions of a topic. *Italicized* page numbers indicate illustrations.

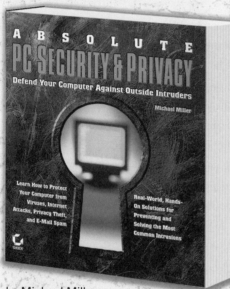